THE STORY OF MANKIND

A Picturesque Tale of Progress

By Olive Beaupré Miller

Assisted by Harry Neal Baum

EXPLORATIONS

PART I

THE BOOK HOUSE FOR CHILDREN
TANGLEY OAKS EDUCATIONAL CENTER
LAKE BLUFF, ILLINOIS

PRINTED IN U.S.A.

CONTENTS

This summary and those in the other seven volumes, if read consecutively, give an interesting picture of the whole sweep of history during the period covered in the eight volumes, with the meaning of events conveyed clearly and the *significance they have for us, brought down to the world of today.*

LIST OF MAPS

THE PICTURE ON THE COVER *is from a Maya relief sculptured on a temple at Yax'chilan, Southern Mexico, some time during the third century A.D.; and is representative of the wonderful civilization which flourished in America about the time of the barbarian invasions of Europe and the break-up of the ancient Roman Empire.*

The figure on the right is a noble, as is shown by his stone-bladed spear, his elaborate feather headdress, and also by the weird mask which hangs at his back. He wears the skin of a jaguar, a further indication of nobility, and the tail of the beast hangs behind him. The common man kneeling in homage before him wears the usual costume, a band wound several times around the waist with the ends hanging in front and behind. Both men are adorned with ear plugs and armlets, they have prominent noses of a Semitic cast and flattened, receding foreheads, artificially formed by binding and considered a mark of beauty.

In the background are the involved intricate glyphs of Maya numerals and written language.

I
Marco Polo Explores the East
(1271–1295)

The Lure of the East

An eager youth of fifteen stood in the cool dark shadows that streaked a sunny arcade on the quay of the city of Venice, gazing longingly out across the blue Adriatic. Mid a gallant medley of war-galleys and high-built merchant ships, a vessel from the distant East was drawing into port. Soon it was unloading, disgorging its cargo of spices, precious jewels, and silk, while the click and clatter of stevedores and sun-bronzed foreign sailors filled the clear morning air. In the nostrils of young Marco Polo was all the breath of the sea; in his eyes was the vision of strange unknown places and ports.

"To sail away like those sailors, how splendid that would be!" A true son of his birthplace was this eager young Venetian! Adventure was his life, as it was the very soul of glittering, gorgeous Venice, whither the colorful, picturesque East came to meet the more sober West. Marco walked back through the square, past the delicate white cathedral,

rubbing shoulders, meantime, with Arabs from the desert; tall, fur-clad Muscovites from Russia and the frozen North; gay Spaniards in pointed beards; black-faced Moors from Africa; sleek, well-groomed Greeks; Irish mercenaries; Jews, and kilted Scots! Bazaars and stores were everywhere; the gorgeous shops of the silk-merchants; the rainbow assortments of the glassworkers; and the booths with their precious stones, their handsome polished ivories, and slender jewel-hilted swords.

Hither to the Rialto, the center of trade and commerce, young Marco had been coming from his very earliest days; and many a time had he sat, a mere little slip of a lad, and listened open-mouthed while some picturesque old sailor with salt in his tangled beard, and the glint of the sea in his eyes, spun a tale of hardship, danger, and romance.

Of all this Marco thought, as he walked along the narrow little footpaths of the city toward the Polo mansion where, since the death of his mother, he had lived with a cousin. When he was but six years old, his father and his uncle Maffeo had gone to Constantinople, whence they had set out to trade in those wild lands beyond the far Black Sea.

Constantinople, bustling with trade, meeting place of East and West. (de Bry's *America*, 1590.)

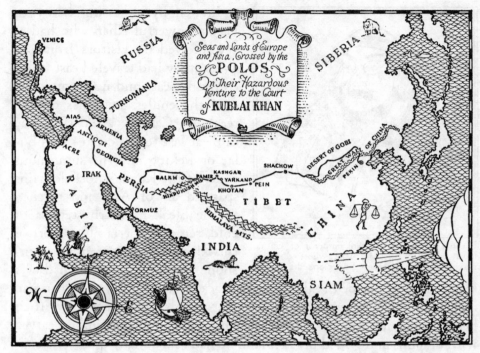

In all the nine years since then no one had heard a word of them. Were they alive or dead, imprisoned or still exploring?

Great was the lad's surprise, as he entered the living hall, to find there two black-bearded strangers clad in outlandish garments.

"Here are your father and uncle," his cousin calmly announced.

Deep was the thrill of that moment! Father and son embraced; then what alluring tales Nicolo and Maffeo told of those flat green plains where the Volga poured its waters through far-away Eastern Russia. They had lived for a year with Barka, chief of the Western Tartars, those swarthy, snub-nosed horsemen from the wind-blown Gobi Desert who in the last half-century had over-run most of Asia and terrified the world. They had spent three years in Bok-ha'ra mixing with the throngs of picturesque Orientals in the public square of the city, bargaining, buying and selling, or listening in eager silence to the men of the silk caravans as they told strange tales of China and the fabulous, golden East.

Ku'blai Khan, the Mongol emperor of China, most powerful ruler in Asia, whose domains reached Europe. (Chinese Encyclopaedia, Paris.)

Invited by a passing envoy to visit a powerful Khan who had as yet received no visitors from the West, they had traveled east in his company, east and north and east over the endless stretches of far-reaching Central Asia till they came at last to the city of Cambulac or Peking and the sumptuous court of the Khan, whose domains spanned all of Asia and reached to the bleak northern steppes of cold, remote Siberia. The court of this Khan was so gorgeous it far outshone anything the West had ever seen! Clad in a robe of silk, heavily brocaded with gold, the Khan had received his guests seated in an ivory throne on a platform above their heads, appearing strange and unreal in his weird, exotic chamber, carved with dragons and gilded beasts. And he had asked many questions concerning the Christian religion and government in the West.

Loading the Polos with gifts, he had then sent them home, bidding them bring him some oil from the lamp in the Holy Sepulchre and to request the Pope to send him a hundred men of learning, acquainted with the Seven Arts and the doctrines of the Church. But when the Polos reached Italy, they learned that Pope Clement IV had but recently died, and they had come to Venice, to await the election of a new Pope to whom they could deliver their message from the Great Khan.

Such was the tale of adventure told by the Polos to Marco. Marco was spell-bound with interest. All the thrill of the East, vivid, pulsating, alluring, seemed to enfold the boy and fill the very room. Seeing him carried away, Nicolo asked the youth if he wished to go along when the two men returned to China. Marco's eyes shone with eagerness. To explore this unknown land, to see all those wonderful sights! Nicolo smiled and embraced him and said that he might go.

Marco Sets Out for China

Two years passed while Marco Polo restlessly awaited the chance to go on the promised journey. But a new Pope had not been chosen, and from whom else could Nicolo get the hundred learned men to teach the Tartars Christianity and the knowledge acquired in the West? At last, as the months went by, and the cardinals still chose no one, the Polos decided to return and report the matter to the Khan. In the year 1271, father, son and uncle finally sailed from Venice in a deep-laden merchant ship, young Marco looking forward to the great adventure ahead with all the impatient longing of his strenuous seventeen years. At Acre, the Papal legate, a church official endowed with all the powers of the Pope, gave them letters to the Khan, elaborately sealed and beribboned, and aided them in securing oil from the Holy Sepulchre.

The three Polos leaving Venice for the mysterious, unknown East. A medieval drawing from one of the earliest manuscripts of *The Travels of Marco Polo* (1338) showing Venice in the background; and in the foreground, some of the strange beasts the travelers saw. (MS. Bodleian Library, Oxford.)

They had set out on the long trail that led east across Lesser Armenia, when news arrived that their friend, the Papal legate at Acre, had been elected Pope. Returning to this city, they now received papal letters to be delivered to the Khan. Moreover, the new-made Pope ordered two worthy friars, men of letters and science, as well as profound theologians, to accompany them to China and instruct the Khan and the Tartars in all they wished to know.

Rejoicing at this good fortune, the Polos thanked the Pope, and once more sailed away; but at Ai'as they heard rumors that savage, loot-mad armies come from Babylonia, had invaded Lesser Armenia and were ravaging the land, burning all the villages, slaughtering the men, and carrying women and children off into slavery. They passed through a land denuded, stripped of its harvest by the foe; they cautiously skirted villages ruined and still smoking; and now and then they came on a mutilated corpse. The friars grew every day more and more terrified, and anxiously urged the Polos to return to the safety of the cities; but the merchants stoutly refused. In spite of evil reports, they took their slow way eastward. At length they fell in with a Templar, journeying back to Aias with a little troop of warriors, and the friars, overcome by their fears, turned over to the Polos the letters and gifts which the Pope was sending out to the Khan, and begging the protection of the Templar, they forthwith deserted the caravan and departed for the coast.

Nicolo, Maffeo, and Marco, greatly disappointed, continued their journey without them, passing through Turkomania, southeast through Greater Armenia, Georgia, Irak, and Persia. Most of the country was mountainous and swept by fierce cold winds that blew gustily morning and night, but there was plenty of water and pasturage for the beasts composing their caravan.

Two men of Persia, originally Nordics of the same race as Northern Europeans. They have aquiline features, and dark or red hair. (Fresco, Bazaklik, Turkestan.)

The Polo caravan, with camels for baggage, and horses for riding. (Catalan map, Bib. Nat. Paris.)

Sometimes the travelers camped in a well-protected hollow far from any habitation; often they spent the night in a tiny squalid village or a larger city with walls. At length, however, they left this high and windy country and entered the low hot lands of Mesopotamia or Irak. Here the heat was stifling; the blazing disk of the sun beat steadily hour after hour, parching the throat and lungs, and enormous clouds of dust enveloped man and beast, so the travelers had to swathe their heads in many folds of linen to protect them from the dust.

After following the sun-baked and sand-blown caravan-route through scorching desert-places for many weary days, how grateful to their eyes were the valleys of stately date palms and green pistachio trees which greeted them in Persia! Amid the shade of the leaves, turtle-doves and pheasants flitted; and here, for the first time, Marco saw the broad-tailed Persian sheep equal to asses in size; and the white humped oxen of the country, sturdy, sleek and beautiful, carrying burdens with ease, and kneeling down like camels to receive their heavy loads. Certain of the villages here were surrounded by very high walls, and Marco was told that the peasants built their villages thus to protect themselves from raids of the wicked Ka-rau'nas bandits, who harried great stretches of land, raiding terrified villages under cover of desert-dust-storms, butchering old men savagely and selling the young as slaves.

Shortly after leaving this country of mud-walled villages, the travelers journeyed across a beautiful, well-watered plain, and so came at last to Or'muz whence they had been planning to proceed by ship to China.

Hiring lodgings, they rested, and found themselves drawn once more into crooked streets, dirty smelling markets, shadowy shops and bazaars, where all the treasures of India lay spread out on display. But after they viewed the wretched ships lying in the harbor they gave up all thought of reaching China by way of the sea. Assembling a caravan, they crossed the desert of Ker-man' to make further progress by land.

The desert passage was difficult, tiring to man and beast. For three days the only water they found was tainted with salt and green scum. Not until the fourth day, when throats were parched and cracking, and strength was rapidly failing, did their bleared and blood-shot eyes behold the welcome sight of a river of fresh, cool water. Halting by this gurgling stream, they renewed their health and strength.

North and eastward they went, past Balkh, the "mother of cities," now sadly sunk in decay; they plunged into perilous passes, and wound through mountainous land where there were numerous lions, but neither dwellings nor people. They passed a great hill of salt, and entered a vine-clad country where the people wore skins for clothing and where Marco, eager for change, hunted porcupines with the natives.

With parched throats and sun-scorched eyes, the Polos plod wearily across the desert of Kerman, traveling three whole days without water through hot, barren sands under a blazing tropic sun.

In the Himalayas, narrow mountain trails, bordered by steep precipices, were toilsome and dangerous.

Then they pushed on to the lofty, majestic peaks of the Hindu Kush Mountains, famed for their mines of silver, rubies and lapis lazuli, and standing out against the sky, snow-capped and glistening white. Life among the mountains was brisk and invigorating; but unfortunately, young Marco was now taken seriously ill. For days, severely stricken with fever, he tossed about on his bed. A whole year passed before their caravans again gathered that they might set out once more on the long trail eastward to China.

Mountain after mountain was climbed with tortuous, grinding effort, for they were now in the heart of the great Him-a'la-ya Range, and after days of struggle, they came to the Plain of Pa-mir' so high among the clouds, it was called "the Roof of the World."

Having passed the bleak, birdless Pamir, the travelers journeyed northeast, still through a lonely wilderness of mountains and desolate valleys. More than a month was spent in this uninhabited region, till they came to the city of Kash'gar surrounded by gardens and vineyards. blooming fields of cotton and beautiful country homes.

Men of Khotan in the jade country visited by the Polos. Above, a horseman, whose features show a mixture of Chinese and Indian blood. Below, a rider on a swift, high-spirited camel. (Panel, Dandan, Uiliq.)

They passed through Yar-kand' to Kho-tan', a prosperous city of melons, fruits, and glowing farmland, lying in the country of jade. At Pe-in, they began to sense the approach of the Go'bi Desert, and the people told of cities buried in the sands beyond. For five days, the caravan trudged through the outskirts of the desert, then resting a week they took a month's provisions and set out across the sands.

Never would Marco forget those nerve-wracking days in the Gobi Desert! The caravan crawled along beneath a dull red sun which became a malignant thing, searing and burning all. The fiery hot sands tortured and mocked the thirsty travelers, changing before their eyes to cool life-giving water, which receded as they advanced, receded, ever receded until it vanished from sight. Heavenly visions of verdure, shaded by pleasant trees, tore their souls in an agony of longing and desire; but always there was in reality nothing at all but sand, hills and valleys and plains of rippling sand, sand, sand! At night, beneath a leering moon, the desert goblins harried the tortured caravan with strange sights of ghosts weirdly dancing, or dead men marching past in silent cavalcades; and in the unearthly lull, they heard their own names called by enticing spirit voices! But he who followed these calls was trapped and lost in the sand!

When merciful sleep crept near, shattering sounds of drums rolled up, beating, beating, beating, till the nerves were torn with pain. There were days when not one single breath stirred the burning heat which lay like a fiery weight crushing the souls of men; then all at once a wind, a hot and flaming wind suddenly rushed upon them, suffocating man and beast and licking the sun-baked sands, till all the earth seemed to reel.

With intense relief did the weary, sun-blistered travelers find themselves at last at the beautiful city of Shachow on an oasis in the sands, with the goblins of the desert a nightmare of the past. Here the Polos rested and recovered from their ordeal before they continued farther; and here, for the first time, Marco noted that the life of the people was touched by the ancient civilization of China. At last the Polos were come into lands that were ruled directly by the mighty Kublai Khan.

The Land of Kublai Khan

Steadily the caravan plodded eastward and northward. They explored the great bend of the Yellow River; they crossed and recrossed the Great Wall of China; they passed through lands rich in silver, districts where skilled workers wove cloths containing gold tissue and gray-white mother-of-pearl; and at last they were met by an escort of nobles and ambassadors sent by the Great Khan himself. Messengers had kept the Khan informed of the caravan's progress since they entered his territory, and he had dispatched to meet them a royal guard of honor.

Cavalcade of Chinese nobles and soldiers in gorgeous uniforms and trappings. (Chinese painting.)

Nicolo, Maffeo, and Marco thus splendidly escorted, were led at length to Shandu, the summer palace of the Khan. Entering a park enclosed by a very high wall that was many miles in length, they found themselves in a hunting preserve of fountains, rivers, and meadows filled with all sorts of wild beasts. A magnificent palace of marble stood within the park, but the Great Khan was not there. He was at his Royal Pavilion deep in a wooded grove. As the little band approached, they saw that this pavilion was lightly built of bamboo, gilded and beautifully finished. It had gilded and lacquered columns, carved in the form of dragons whose heads and outspread claws supported the graceful roof. This building was held in place by two hundred cords of silk and could be taken down and put together again wherever the Khan might wish. And here at last, the Polos entered the presence of the Great Khan!

Enclosed in an extensive park, was the Khan's Royal Pavilion guarded by fierce Mongol warriors.

Journey's end. The Polo brothers and Marco at last stand before the mighty Mongol, Kublai Khan.

The travelers now found themselves in an airy, beautiful room of gilded and lacquered bamboo, ornamented with carvings very strange in design and rich in vivid color. Before them, on a high platform in an elaborate chair of state, sat Kublai Khan himself, gorgeous in flaming robes of brilliant red and gold, and flashing at every movement with priceless, gleaming jewels. The escort drew back against the walls, and alone the three Polos advanced to the open space before the ruler. Nicolo and Maffeo presented the letters from the Pope bestowing the crystal vases and other splendid presents entrusted to their care. They also made a great show of displaying the vial of oil from the Holy Sepulchre.

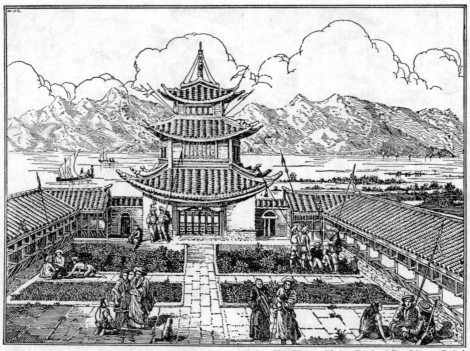

A dainty Chinese garden on the borders of an inland lake. (Sir Henry Yule, *Book of Ser Marco Polo*.)

The Great Khan asked many questions concerning matters in Europe. Then suddenly raising his head, he spied young Marco standing behind his father and uncle. "Who is this youth?" he enquired.

"This is my son, Great Lord, and your most loyal man," Nicolo replied in his most formal manner.

The Khan was pleased with the answer. Gravely nodding his head, he accepted the young man's service, as Marco bowed in homage.

That night, there was a great banquet held in the Royal Pavilion in honor of the guests from the West. Kublai Khan sat apart and partook of the evening meal seated upon a platform twelve feet above the floor.

And so Marco Polo of Venice became the loyal man of Kublai Khan in China, entering on a career which was to take him up and down throughout the broad lands of his master and give him an intimate knowledge of the mysteries and wealth of this golden, luxurious East.

II
Genghis Khan Conquers Asia
(1162–1227)
The Mongols in the Gobi Desert

Gold, jewels, palaces and slaves, untold wealth and luxury, had Kublai Khan when Marco Polo became his loyal man. Millions of people gave him unquestioned obedience, and lived or died at a nod of his head; his vast lands stretched for thousands of miles straight across Asia from the Sea of Pitchy Darkness, as the vast Pacific was called, to the treacherous waters of the Caspian. The multitude of his armies shook the earth, and even distant peoples sent him tribute. No one man had ever before controlled such enormous numbers of subjects, such endless stretches of land; no one man after him ever had such immeasurable authority. Kublai Khan was the most powerful ruler in the history of the world. But all this wealth of gold, men, and lands had not been won by Kublai Khan himself; nor had such wide dominion been built up slowly through the centuries. Kublai Khan inherited the lands won by his conquering grandfather, Genghis Khan, who rose from the depths of poverty to rule more than half of Asia; and this vast empire was created in swift, masterful strokes in less than fifty years!

Mongol warriors in lacquered leather armor. It was with such warriors that Genghis Khan was to launch a wave of conquest and devastation over all Central Asia. (MS. of Jami at Tawarekh 1310.)

Te-mu'jin's earliest days were spent in a felt *yurt*, or tent, the movable home of all the Mongol tribes of the grass lands of Northern Asia. Each family also carried with them a traveling chest on wheels.

In the year 1162, the year of the Swine in the Calendar of the Twelve Beasts, a man-child was born in the northern part of the wind-swept Gobi Desert, one of the least-known corners of Central Asia. Within the tiny fist of the little man-child a clot of blood was tightly clenched; and taking this for a sign of future greatness, his father named the babe after an enemy he had just slain, Te-mu'jin, the Finest Steel.

Temujin—the youthful Genghis Khan—was a Mongol of that fierce wandering people called Tartars by the Europeans; round-headed, black-eyed tribesmen of the Alpine race, akin to the Turks but quite distinct and different from the Chinese. A felt tent, called a *yurt*, was the home of the baby Temujin, and in summer this tent was one of an *ordu*, or moving city of yurts which followed the flocks and herds in the constant search for grazing lands. "The Mongols," said a Western traveler who visited them in their homeland, "set up the dwelling wherein they sleep on a round frame of withes interlaced and drawn together at the top into a little round hoop, out of which rises a neck like a chimney. This frame they cover with white felt. Oftentimes they cover the felt with chalk, white clay or powdered bone to make it whiter; and sometimes they use black felt. The felt around the neck on the top they adorn with a variety of beautiful designs; and before the door they hang a felt embroidered in colors with figures of different vines and trees and birds."

These yurts were often very large, sometimes having a width of thirty feet, but so light were they, that they could be lifted to a platform on wheels, and so moved from place to place. This same traveler, Friar Rubrick, tells of seeing twenty-two oxen in one team, drawing a house upon a cart, eleven abreast across the width of the cart, and eleven more before them. The axle, he said, was of huge bigness, like the mast of a ship, and one man stood in the doorway driving the cart.

Thus the moving city of tents traveled over the treeless plains, accompanied by its huge and well-kept flocks and herds. Most frequently the women or girls drove the tent-wagons while the men hunted or fought. One girl would lead twenty or thirty carts at once, as the country was very flat, and they tied the carts, with their oxen, one behind the other. There sat a girl in the first cart driving the oxen, while all the rest followed at the same pace. When they came to any bad place they untied the carts and guided them over one at a time. So the moving tent-villages traveled along as slowly as sheep or oxen walk.

Temujin's people, the desert-dwelling Mongols, built their houses of a light framework of interlaced withes bent in the form of a dome and covered with felt. When the desire for change moved them, these *yurts* could be placed on carts which were often twenty feet wide drawn by twenty-two oxen.

When they took their dwellings down, the Mongols turned the doors to the south. Then they placed the carts laden with chests on either side, within half a stone's throw of the house, so that the house stood between two rows of carts, as if between two walls. One rich Mongol might have one or two hundred such carts with chests. A chieftain of the first order could boast perhaps twenty-six wives, each of whom had one large house in addition to other little ones which were set up behind the great one, for the serving girls to dwell in; and to every one of the large houses belonged some two hundred carts!

Temujin's father, Ye-su-kai', was chief of the Yakka, or Great Mongol nomads, but chief's son though he was, Temujin like all the other children of the Gobi, was born to hardship and struggle. As soon as he was weaned to mare's milk, he had to fight for himself, even for warmth and food in the *yurt* in which he lived. His father and his warrior-friends in their great animal skins took most of the room around the fire and the best of the meat in the big boiling pot, and when the women had had their share, there was little left for the children.

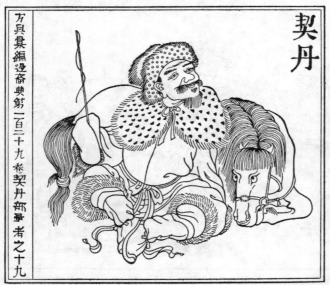

A hard and forbidding land was the Gobi Desert, home of the warlike Mongols. "Here are no towns or cities," wrote another Western friar, "but everywhere sandy barrens, not a hundredth part of the whole being fertile. The land is nearly destitute of trees, although furnishing pasturage for cattle.

A Mongol chieftain seeks rest and shelter behind his horse from the shrill, biting winds of the desert. (Chinese painting from Pien-i-teen.)

The climate is intemperate; in the midst of summer there are great thunders and lightnings by which many people are slain, and at the same time there are great falls of snow. Such tempests of cold winds blow, that sometimes people can hardly sit on horseback. In one of these we had to throw ourselves to the ground and could not see because of dust."

In this harsh, barren land, the wandering Mongols lived. Their herds gave them meat and milk and provided skins for their clothing. From the hair of their beasts they made felt for their tents, their clothes and ropes, while the hide made leather armor, saddles, and harnesses, and the bone furnished arrowtips. But constant struggle

Mongol warrior in typical dress with his constant desert-companion, his horse. (Chinese painting from Pien-i-teen.)

brought them only the barest existence. In winter the cold on this plain was so bitterly intense that feet swathed in heavy bedding were often frozen from exposure. The Mongols greased faces and bodies to keep out cold, yet often they froze to death. In the biting winter months, when the hunters brought in no game, and the mares gave no fresh milk, they had to be content with a handful of dried, sour curds, or a little boiled millet as food for an entire day.

Hard and severe was desert life, early forcing Temujin and other children to active self-preservation. By clinging to the wool of sheep they learned to ride, and they even hunted rats and dogs for food.

Driven by hunger, Te-mu'jin and the other children organized hunts of their own, stalking dogs and rats with clubs or with blunt arrows. Before the boys could walk, they had learned to ride on sheep, clinging to the wool. For years they lived out with the horse-herds, clad in wool and leather. Their food was of mutton stew left in the pot after the warriors had satisfied their hunger. The horse-herds were in their charge, and often they rode out into the plains after lost animals or searched for new pasture lands. They learned to keep in the saddle for days, to go without cooked food or even with no food at all, and many a night was spent in the snow without a fire.

But great as was the toil of the nomad youths, watching through the night for raiders, their play was little less trying. Their horse races were twenty mile stretches out into the prairie and back, and their wrestling matches were bone-breaking affairs. In the evening beside the glowing dung-fire they listened to the chants of minstrels, old men who rode from one *yurt* to another, and droned to a one-stringed fiddle, long tales of Yakka heroes. From them Temujin learned of Kabal Khan, his ancestor, who had once pulled the emperor of Cathay by the beard! He learned of To'ghrul Khan of the powerful Ka-rait' tribe who was his father's sworn brother. He learned of many a bitter feud to be settled, many an insult to be avenged when he grew older; for the Mongols were divided into many different clans ever fighting with one another, and fierce quarrels were kept alive for generations, being handed down from father to son and breaking out most unexpectedly.

It was a healthy, vigorous life. Temujin grew tall and straight. He learned to hold his own with the other boys of the tribe; no one could match him on horseback; and he was a skillful bowman, as well as an excellent wrestler. He spoke very little, and then only after meditation, and though he had an ungovernable temper, he had also a wonderful gift of making fast friends.

He was only thirteen years old when he suddenly fell in love. He and his father once passed the night in the tent of a certain warrior when the boy's attention was attracted by the little girl of the tent, and he asked his father, Ye-su-kai', if he might have her for his wife.

"She is young," the father objected.

"When she is older," Temujin replied, "she will do well enough."

Yesukai considered the girl, whose name was Bour'tai. She was certainly a beauty though she was but nine years old.

"She is small," her father observed, secretly delighted by the interest his visitors showed, "but still you might look at her." Of Temujin he approved. "Thy son has a clear face, and bright eyes."

Next day the bargain was struck, and Yesukai rode off, leaving Temujin to make the acquaintance of his gray-eyed promised bride.

The Mongols mated early, and when only thirteen, Temujin chooses his wife, a child of nine, meeting the girl for the first time when chancing to spend the night in her father's felt tent on the plains.

A few days later a Mongol galloped up with word that Ye-su-kai' was dying and asking for his son. The chief had passed a night in the tent of some enemies and undoubtedly had been poisoned. Leaping into the saddle, Temujin rode as fast as his horse could carry him to the tent village of the clan, but found his father dead.

Thus, Temujin became chieftain or Khan of the Yakka Mongols and took his seat on the white horse-skin of leadership when he was but thirteen years old. His father's standard of nine yak-tails snapped in the wind before his *yurt* door, but where was his clan? Where were the forty thousand tents that had been wont to follow that standard? A handful only remained faithful to the son of Yesukai. Afraid to trust themselves and their families to the protection of so young a boy, the rest had all departed to seek security elsewhere. The fertile valleys to the north among the Mongolian steppes, tempered by mountain ranges and watered by rivers, must be held against all invaders for the great herds of the clan on which life itself depended. Could a mere boy do this? "The deep water is gone," said many. "The strong stone is broken. What have we to do with children?" And they sought an older chieftain, refusing to pay the boy the Mongol tribute of four beasts, an ox, a horse, a yak, and a sheep. To make matters worse, Tar-gou-tai', a rival chieftain of the tribe of Taid'juts, now declared that he was the new overlord of the tribes of Gobi in place of Yesukai.

A desert Mongol rests his horse after a mad gallop. (Chinese painting.)

Targoutai descended upon the Mongol encampments determined to slay the youthful Khan and forever rid himself of a possible rival, but Temujin fled to the hills. He might have sought the aid of Toghrul, his father's blood-brother, but he was too proud to do so. "To go as a beggar with empty hands," he told himself, "is to arouse scorn, not fellowship." He would wait; later he would go to Toghrul as an ally and an equal, not as a weakling seeking protection.

For several years Temujin lived as a fugitive, hunted like any animal by his foes. Once when hunger drove him to desperation, he was captured by the Taidjuts and placed in a Chinese *kang*, a wooden

Captive Mongol khan with head and left arm fastened in wooden *kang* to hinder movement and prevent escape. (From a Chinese painting.)

yoke resting on the shoulders and holding the wrists at both ends. So he remained helpless until he was left with a single guard. Then, in the darkness of night, he struck his guard with the end of the *kang* and knocked the man senseless. Rushing forth to freedom, he leaped into a nearby river and sank down among the rushes entirely under water excepting for his head.

Angry Taidjuts were soon in hot pursuit, but as they searched the bank of the stream, Temujin noticed that one warrior spied him, hesitated, and then went on without betraying his hiding place. Temujin was saved for the time, but in the *kang* he was almost as helpless as before. Leaving the river, therefore, he stealthily followed the searchers back to the camp of his enemies and crept to the tent of the warrior who had seen him and kept his secret.

Escaping from pursuing Taidjuts, Temujin is set free from his burdensome *kang* by a friendly enemy.

At sight of the dripping boy, the man, more frightened than Temujin, split off the yoke, burned the pieces and hid the boy in a cart of wool. When the Taidjuts came to search the tent, one thrust his spear into the cart, wounding Temujin in the leg. But the boy was not discovered, and riding a borrowed horse, he made off to the hills.

Daily Temujin learned more and more how to keep out of ambush and to break through the lines of his enemies. He was hunted constantly and his cunning grew with the years; only a body of exceeding strength and a wolf's instinct for scenting danger kept the youth alive. Once he was left for dead in the snow, wounded by an arrow in the throat, but two comrades sucked the blood from his wound and melted snow in a pot to wash and dress his hurts.

In those dark days, Temujin learned cunning against treachery, and boundless patience and courage. He thought much of what he would do when he again headed the Mongols and was master of the desert; and even amid such dangers he was never entirely alone. One brother and one half-brother were always faithful to him. From time to time other youths joined him, and as he proved his skill in protecting the herds from attack, and even in leading skirmishes against his powerful foes, the scattered warriors of his father's tribe began to come back to him, finding in him a wise leader in whose strength and word they could trust far more than in many of the older, hot-headed tribal chieftains.

But the thoughts of youth will turn to other things than warfare; and at seventeen, Temujin bethought him with longing of Bourtai, the little gray-eyed girl he had seen four years before. So, with some hundred youths, fully armed and bedecked in sheepskins, leather jackets and breeches, and hideously painted breast-plates, their faces greased against cold, their water-sacks dangling well-filled from the cruppers of their high saddles, Temujin galloped off to the tent-village of Bourtai's father.

Then followed a feast of boiled sheep and horse-meat. The guests drank flagons of mare's milk and rice-wine to the clapping of hands, and danced clumsily in their deer-skin boots to the squeak of the one-stringed fiddles. On the third day of feasting, Bourtai in her long white felt dress, her braids of hair heavy with silver coins and tiny statues, her head-dress a cone of birch-bark covered with treasured silk and supported over each ear by the whorls of braided hair, was pursued through the tents by Temujin to be carried off, according to Mongol custom.

The wedding of Bourtai and Temujin was an occasion of feasting, dancing and merrymaking. Kinsmen and tribesmen came for miles to join the festivities which lasted for three days and nights and ended with a wild chase and capture of the bride, who was carried to the tent of Temujin.

A great destiny awaited the little thirteen-year-old bride; Empress of one of the world's greatest conquerors, she was to become the mother of four sons whose domains were to exceed Alexander's and Napoleon's put together! In later days Temujin married other women, but none of his wives was ever as dear to him as staunch gray-eyed Bourtai, the bride of his youth.

Steadily Temujin grew in strength and power until there came a day when he felt that he could visit Toghrul, his father's blood-brother. Bearing gifts, he now came, as he had wished to come, as a real chieftain and equal. Soon after this visit, the struggle of the tribes in the Gobi Desert blazed up anew. The Mer-kits' came down from their northern plain in the frozen white world where men traveled in sledges drawn by dogs and reindeer. They came at night, unexpectedly, casting blazing torches into the village of tents. But Temujin escaped, sought the aid of Toghrûl, and defeated the invaders in battle.

And now the young Khan of the Mongols began a struggle for supreme control over all the desert tribes. He had dreamed of this when he had lain hidden from his enemies in the depths of some thicket, scarcely daring to breathe. He had worked unceasingly to this end, gathering more and more men to his standard, and giving freely of the booty of battle that he might bind his men to him. The old men told him that never would the proud clansmen, his enemies, bow to his will. "Different hearts and minds," they said, "cannot be in one body." But Temujin refused to believe this; he was determined to form one great confederacy of clans, to unite the scattered units into one overwhelming power.

Wars with the nomad tribes passed and repassed across the steppes of Asia. Mounted hordes, screaming with rage, closed in under flights of arrows, wielded their short sabers, pulled their foes from the saddle with lariats and hooks on the end of lances, and fought hand to hand in bloody combat. Fierce were the struggles of Tartars and Mongols, Mer-kits' and Ka-raits', Nai'mans and U'gurs that swept from the Great Wall of China to the mountains of Central Asia, and countless were the victims of the wild blood-lust that seized upon these savage fighters.

There was no end to the tribal warfare of the Gobi, to the wolf-like struggle of the great clans, the harrying and the hunting-down. Though the Mongols were still one of the weaker desert-tribes, a hundred thousand tents now followed the yak-tail standard of the Khan. His cunning protected them, his fierce courage emboldened his warriors. Now more than thirty years of age, he was in the fullness of his strength, and his sons rode by his side, fighting or looking for wives, as he himself had done when he traveled the plains with Yesukai.

But the time had come for Temujin to win even greater power. The Mongols were strong enough to be a valuable ally for any of the great desert tribes and since Toghrul of the Karaits was the greatest chief of the Gobi with many followers and rich pasture lands, Temujin went to him and made him this proposal. "Without thy assistance, O my father," he said, "I cannot survive unmolested. Thou, too, canst not live on in peace without my firm friendship. Thy false brothers and cousins would invade thy land and divide thy pastures between them. Our one way to survive is through a friendship nothing can shatter."

Warfare in the Gobi was a constant struggle of merciless enemy clans each striving for mastery, and the strength of a chieftain was measured by followers, rather than by wealth. (Chinese painting.)

Vivid Chinese painting of a Mongol horseman, breathing the freedom and action of desert life.

Toghrul agreed, and accordingly, Karait and Mongol together overcame the Tartars, a third great nomad tribe, and broke their power in
the desert. But Temujin was now so strong that fear and envy of him
awoke in the hearts of his foes and they decided to destroy him before
he became more powerful. Persuading the aging Toghrul to add his
strength to theirs, they sought in a mighty battle to wipe out the Mongols forever; and this abrupt switch from friendship to enmity on the
part of the old chief Toghrul, gave the added strength necessary to
inflict a terrible defeat on the forces of Temujin. He managed to save
his herds, his tents, and a few fighting Mongols, but he had to live
in retirement all the following year. When he had recovered his
strength so far as to gather together his few remaining allies, he advanced unexpectedly and fell upon the Karaits in a surprise attack. In
a bloody, hand-to-hand struggle lasting all day long, he utterly routed
the foe. Toghrul and his son both wounded, fled in rout from the
field, while Temujin, riding victorious into the captured camp, gave
over to his men the saddles covered with soft, red leather, the tempered sabers, the silver plates, and all the wealth of the Karaits.

Quickly following the Karaits, who were fleeing in a body, Temujin surrounded them with his warriors and offered them their lives. "Men fighting as ye have done to save your lord, are heroes," he told them. "Be ye among mine, and serve me!" And the Karaits accepted this offer and straightway joined his forces, pushing forward with him to the Karait capital, a rude city of mud huts called Ka′ra-ko′rum, the Black Sands. Karakorum was easily taken and this city of the sands, Temujin made his capital. Using every effort to keep the Karaits friendly, he launched his hordes into further conquests without a moment's delay.

In the three years following the battle that destroyed the power of the Karaits and made the Mongols masters of the Gobi, Temujin thrust his veteran horsemen far into the valleys of the western Turks, the Naimans and the Ugurs. All these nomad tribesmen had been enemies of the Karaits and they might have banded together to destroy the conquering Mongols. But Temujin gave them no time to plan or act together. From the long white mountains of the north, down the length of the Great Wall, and far to the south of the desert, his Mongols swept in sudden, overwhelming raids that left the enemy powerless. All the men of a chieftain's family were hunted down and put to death; fighting men were divided among tribes who had proved their loyalty; women were taken as wives or made slaves, and Mongol mothers adopted wandering children of the foe. Thus were rival leaders destroyed and conquered tribes added to the forces of the new master who was welding together the power of the Gobi.

U′gur prince in flowered robe. The Ugurs were Turks, neighbors subdued by the Mongols. (Fresco from Bazaklik.)

Ugur princess. Such haughty ladies as this had to bow to Mongol Genghis. (Fresco, Bazaklik, Eastern Turkestan.)

Temujin had accomplished the very thing his elders told him could not be done; he had not counted the cost in bloodshed and destruction; but he had at least united all the warring tribes of restless, northern Asia. For the first time in several centuries, the Turko-Mongol people had one single master. In the year 1206, Temujin called together a council of all the chieftains who now paid him tribute. From the Great Wall of China on the east, to the borders of Persia on the west, and from the Land of Darkness on the north, to the Roof of the World on the south, the summons to the council went forth. When all were assembled in the Khan's great tent in the rude mud city of Ka'ra-ko'rum, Temujin addressed them. He said that now the desert peoples were one, it was only fitting that they should have one leader under whom all lesser chieftains should rule. One of their number must have power over all the others; the united nomads must have an Emperor!

Forthwith, the council of chieftains elected Temujin, and then they decided that a new title must be given him to show his exalted position to all the world. A soothsayer stepped forward from the throng and announced this name; henceforth their leader was to be called *Genghis Khan*, the Greatest of Rulers, the Emperor of All Men!

Genghis Khan

Gen'ghis Khan', Emperor of All Men, standing beneath the standard of the nine yak-tails, spoke to the chieftains. "These men who will share with me the good and bad of the future, whose loyalty will be like the clear rock crystal,—I wish them all to be called Mongols," he said. "Above everything that breathes on earth, I wish them to be raised to power."

The Khan was now a man of forty, and at the height of his powers. Under his standard were gathered the wildest and most unruly spirits of Asia. For the moment tribal feuds were forgotten. Tired by recent victories, all were held in check by the awe of Genghis Khan. But the new Emperor knew very well that it would be difficult to hold his unruly subjects, and keep them so occupied that they would not rebel against him. Therefore, he made for them a code of laws called the *Yassa*. This Yassa, a combination of his own will and the best of the tribal customs, was to be the only law throughout the whole of his Empire, and in certain odd corners of Asia, remains to this very day the only law of the land. It aimed at three things, obedience to the Khan, a binding together of the clans, and merciless punishment of wrong-doing.

Theft and adultery were to be punished by death; disobedience of children, younger brothers and wives, the failure of the rich to aid the poor, deeds of violence among one's own people, were very strongly condemned. Unpardonable sins were to flinch in battle, to retreat before the standard was carried back, and to abandon comrades on the field. Every man was free to worship his own god in his own way provided he obeyed the Yassa; but the Yassa must settle all disputes. It enforced the absolute will of the Khan. Whoever disobeyed the Yassa, disappeared, as the Khan himself said, "like a stone dropped into the water."

A camel, a beast used by the Mongols, but less often than their hardy horses. (Persian miniature.)

A Mongol Khan. A modern conception showing Asiatic cruelty and barbaric splendor. (*Encyclopaedia Britannica*.)

"The Mongols are the most obedient people in the world to their lords, reverencing them and never lying to them," wrote a visitor some years later. "They hardly ever quarrel among themselves. As for theft it is unknown; their dwellings in which they keep their goods are never locked or barred. If a man lose a horse they search for it until they bring it to him or the officer who has charge of lost things. They are courteous to one another and share their food in time of famine. But to other men they are disdainful and deceitful, and they think nothing of slaying other people."

In addition to giving the Yassa, Genghis Khan organized the horde of tribesmen who followed his banner. He would have no haphazard gathering of tribes; instead, his army had a permanent organization in units of ten to ten thousand, each under its own commander. This army was made up entirely of horsemen, every man having at least one horse, and often several remounts. The heavy shock troops had their horses well protected from arrows by thick, lacquered leather armor. Many of the men also wore leather armor, although some were protected by iron breastplates. Kits were small and useful leather sacks, holding nose-bags for the ponies, a cooking pot for the rider, and a rope for hauling siege engines. Itwas an army that could go anywhere.

Orders were given in the day by moving standards up and down and sidewise, or by arm-signals of the officers; at night by colored lights and the roll of drums. Into each and every unit was instilled Genghis Khan's own grimness of purpose,—not to hang back when an enemy was in sight, not to abandon a wounded comrade, not to fail to rescue one who had been taken prisoner.

With this horde of war-loving tribesmen, peace at home could only be secured by war abroad. All the Mongols were eager for conquest, and Genghis Khan himself was above all things a warrior. Playing the Emperor in the mud-and-reed city of Karakorum was all very well, but he longed to be off at the head of his 100,000 tents, his tens of thousands of fighting men; he longed for the joy of battle, for the fierce feel of hand-to-hand combat. His was no desire for wealth of gold or cities; his was no urge to convert the heathen to his religion; with the instinct of a savage, the most primitive urge of the jungle, he loved fighting for its own sake alone. "The greatest happiness in all the world," he once said, "is to crush your enemies, to see them fall at your feet, and to take their horses and goods!"

Now east and southeast of the Mongol territory lay the land of China, or Cathay. Between it and the rest of the world, stretched a wonderful wall built in the third century B.C. by a Chinese emperor, to protect himself and his empire from the troublesome Huns. It was twenty feet high and the top formed a roadway fifteen feet wide.

Emperor Kien Lung of the ancient, highly civilized kingdom of Cathay. (Chinese painting.)

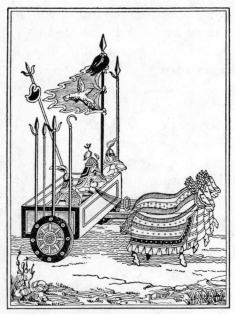

Gilded and lacquered two-wheeled war chariot of the Chinese army; brilliant, but clumsy and cumbersome in battle. (Chinese drawing.)

Behind this wall lived a people with an ancient civilization reaching back to the time when Egypt and Babylonia were the greatest nations in the world. Here was a vast country of mountain ranges, beautiful valleys, crowded seaports, and great walled cities wherein lay quiet gardens and lovely pleasure lakes. Here dwelt an enormous population: peasants who tilled the soil, priests who prayed to the tablets of the dead, mandarins who wore finest silks and rode in gorgeous chariots attended by numerous slaves, poets who wrote of moon-gleams falling across a lake, painters who sketched a snow-capped mountain on a bit of silk, brave and skillful soldiers, ancient astrologers and wisemen.

The land of China was at this time divided into two empires. In the north was the Empire of the Golden dynasty, the Chin; in the south was the Empire of the Sung dynasty; and the two were enemies. The Great Wall lay along the boundary of the Chin Empire, yet it was against this that Genghis Khan first led his desert hordes. The Chin Emperor demanded tribute of Genghis Khan, saying that the desert tribes had always paid him tribute; but Genghis Khan paid tribute to no man! His anger was kindled against the proud Emperor, and he sent an envoy with this message to the Golden Khan: "Our dominion is now so well ordered that we can visit China. We will go with an army that is like a roaring ocean. It matters not whether we encounter friendship or hostility. If the Golden Khan chooses to be our friend, we will allow him to govern under us; if he chooses war, it will last until one of us is victor, one defeated."

Sending before him the fiery Chepe No-yon', most daring of all his commanders, Genghis Khan marched a thousand miles across the desert with the horde. A gate in the Great Wall was opened by Chinese sympathizers, and to meet the Mongols, the Chinese emperor foolishly divided his forces. These were badly defeated by the Mongols, fighting in silence and shooting arrows with deadly swiftness. Only the fact that Genghis Khan himself was badly wounded forced a retreat of the horde. Back to the Gobi went Genghis; but only for the winter season; in the spring with troops refreshed, he descended on China again.

The Chinese no longer dared to take the field against the Mongols; they were quite secure in their cities, they thought. But the well-nigh impregnable walled-cities, able to withstand any siege, fell before Mongol cunning. One favorite trick was a mock retreat, leaving baggage, carts, and supplies before a city's gates. The inhabitants, thinking they had seen the last of their foes, would rush out and plunder; whereupon the Mongols, galloping back in a single night, would massacre every living thing, and level the city to the ground. Fear and confusion spread before the "northern devils," and in 1214 the Imperial City, Yen King, or Peking, fell before the savage nomads from the Gobi. The Chin emperor fled southward into the domain of his old enemy, the Sung, and all of Northern China was left to the mercy of the Mongol. Genghis Khan was at last undisputed Lord of the Golden Empire.

Archery practice, more of a sport to the Chinese than actual training for war. (Chinese drawing.)

Genghis Khan, the merciless conqueror of powerful empires. (A Chinese ink portrait. Peking.)

But once Northern China was conquered, Genghis lost interest in it entirely. His fierce, unbridled spirit coveted not the learning of scholars; the luxury of palaces irked him; nor was he lulled by the sound of temple bells. The lure of the desert was too strong for him to be happy elsewhere.

Before leaving, however, he divided the old Chin Empire into provinces, and over each he set a prince of the Li-ao-Tung' people, who had once been lords of the land, but whom the Chin dynasty had subdued. The Liao-Tung welcomed the Mongols as deliverers, and were only too glad to act as vice-regents for the Khan. They undertook to send great stores of tribute every year to Ka'ra-ko'rum, and to govern Cathay faithfully in his name. Over them all, as governor-in-chief, Genghis appointed one of his generals, Mu-hu'li, bestowing on him a banner with the nine yak tails.

Moreover, since the Sung Empire was still unconquered, Genghis Khan left Muhuli a portion of the Mongol horde, bidding him finish the task so well begun. Then with the rest of the horde, together with thousands of new recruits and wagon upon wagon-load of spoil, he returned to his barren city of Karakorum.

Never was such a strange desert-city! From the face of the level, treeless plain, rose mud-and-thatched dwellings mid the black felt domes of tents, with no thought of order, and surrounding the city instead of a wall were rows of ox-drawn tent-carts. Scattered here and there, were vast stables for the Khan's horse-herds, granaries for storage against famine, and caravansaries for countless envoys and merchants.

The great Lord of Lords himself held court in a silk-lined pavilion of white felt, seated on a low bench. About him sat his nobles in long wadded coats with hanging girdles and uptilted white felt hats.

The Emperor's own household had grown; daughters of royal Turkish families, princesses of China, and the most beautiful maids of the desert-clans, had he taken to wife. But always he loved Bourtai of the gray eyes, and chose for his close companions the four sons she had borne him. When they were young men, he entrusted them with the highest offices of the Empire. Juji, the first born, he made Master of the Hunt; Ja-ga-tai was Master of Law and Punishment; O-go-tai, the gentle, was Master of Counsel, and Tuli, the youngest, became Chief of the Army. By this time, too, there were grandsons, and dearest of all was little Kublai, son of Tuli. "Mark well the words of Kublai," Genghis would say. "They are full of wisdom." As dear as his favorite sons and equally free to come and go in the Khan's sacred pavilion, were the Tar-Khans, his great generals. Many of them were comrades of his fugitive days in the desert, others had aided him in moments of crisis, and in his eyes they were all privileged and could do no wrong.

Court of the lordly Genghis Khan, Emperor of All Men, now luxurious with the spoils of Northern China. From the grotesque drawings of the arm of the Emperor, it is perfectly apparent that a conquered foe is kissing his master's hand in submission. (Miniature in Bibliotheque Nationale, Paris.)

The Conquest of Western Asia

Persian painting of a Disputation of Doctors, showing the refined, cultured civilization soon to feel the sword of the Mongol. (Bodleian Library.)

For three years Genghis Khan remained at Ka'ra-ko'rum, organizing his army, enforcing the Yassa, receiving the tribute which poured in from Cathay and the desert tribes, building up the strength of both men and horses against further campaigns. For now that he had looked on lands different from the Gobi, a great curiosity stirred within him to know more of the outer world.

A great mountain barrier, the Himalayas, lay to the west of the Mongol domains, shutting out the rest of the world. Seventeen centuries before, the Persian kings had come with their mailed cavalry as far as the Indus and Sam'ar-kand', and here, two centuries later, the great Alexander had been halted. Genghis Khan was curious to know something about the people in that "Far Country" beyond the great divide, whose caravans brought the finely tempered steel blades and the best chain mail, white cloth and red leather, ambergris and ivory, turquoise and rubies; and from the merchants he learned that his nearest neighbors to the west were the Kha-res'mi-an Turks ruled by the courageous and crafty A-la'ed-Din' Mohammed, Shah of Kha-resm', known as "The Warrior," and "The Second Alexander." He, too, had conquered a wide domain reaching from Northern India to the steppes above the Caspian Sea, including modern Kho'-ra-san' and Persia, and centering in the great cities of Bok-ha'ra, Sam'ar-kand', Her-at', and Nish'a-pur'.

To this Shah the Khan sent envoys and a message: "I send thee greeting. I know thy power and the great extent of thine empire, and I look upon thee as a most cherished son. On thy part, thou must know that I have conquered China and many Turkish nations. My country is an encampment of warriors, a mine of silver, and I have no need of other lands. To me it seems that we have an equal interest in encouraging trade between our subjects."

Mohammed Shah agreed to this suggestion of peaceful trade and so for a time all went well. From merchants, spies and envoys, Genghis Khan learned about the gardens of Asia,—fertile valleys, rich with game, grazing lands where snow never fell, walled cities filled with riches; but he was content with his power in the Gobi and with peaceful trade with his neighbor, the lordly Shah of the Kha-res'mi-an Turks.

Hunting scene in the kingdom of the Kha-res'mi-an Turks. Following the Mongol custom, a large circle of countryside is surrounded and the game driven to a center. (Contemporary Persian painting.)

Mongol warriors in quilted coats and padded helmets gather in camp. (Japanese painting, 1293.)

It chanced, however, that a Mongol caravan of several hundred merchants was seized by one of Mohammed's governors because there were spies with the traders, and the Shah at once commanded that all should be put to death. Genghis Khan sent an embassy demanding satisfaction for this act, but the Shah, like the Chinese Emperor, was altogether ignorant of the strength and fury of the Mongols. He killed the chief of the envoys and sent the others back with the insult of beards burned off.

"There cannot be two suns in heaven," said Genghis in his rage, "nor two Khans on the earth." And he straightway prepared for war. The slaying of a Mongol envoy could not go unpunished; tradition demanded revenge. Now further conquest and the invasion of foreign lands meant that he must leave a large, newly-knit empire behind him. To insure peace at home, therefore, he summoned to Karakorum from every conquered province or subject-tribe, all those men of ambition whom he distrusted, and who might cause trouble in his absence.

When the last one had ridden in and reported his arrival, they were all ordered to join his army. He would take them with him where they could do no harm!

On a mild day in the autumn of 1218, the mighty Khan rode out from Karakorum on his swift-footed, white charger to review his men in the pastures of Irtish where the horse-herds had been fattening. There he saw a quarter-million warriors, perfectly attuned to his will. He gave the command and the multitudes moved; the conquest of Western Asia was at last begun!

The vast horde of Mongol warriors moved slowly at first, driving herds of cattle with it for provisions. First went parties of merchants to serve as spies, then marched the scattered scout patrols, and behind came the divisions of the armies with the herds, spreading over fifty miles so that the horses could graze.

The way lay over the Himalayas, the icy Roof of the World. Bleak mid-winter found the horde passing through high mountain ranges, barren, desolate, and offering no food. All their cattle were slaughtered.

Well protected from biting winds, the Mongol horde crosses the Himalayas. (French miniature.)

They hunted in vain for game, and the shaggy ponies got along as best they could on a little barley and the dead grass they dug up from under the snow with their hoofs. Even the sand dunes of the wastes were snow-covered, and withered, gray tamarisk danced under the wind-gusts like the ghosts of old men. In that terrible march men and beasts suffered hardships that would have killed a Western army. All day long they struggled against biting winds, and blinding blizzards. At night the men, wrapped in their sheep-skin coats, slept in the drifting snow. When their scanty supplies of dried milk and millet were finished, they opened the veins of their horses, drank of the hot blood and closed up the veins. The weaklings died; the rest kept on for nearly a thousand miles. At last, lean, stripped of everything save weapons, the horde came down the slopes when the grass began to show green. Below they could see the first frontier of Islam on the river Syr now swollen by spring freshets.

Mohammed Shah was waiting with his huge, perfectly disciplined army. In wonderful suits of chain-mail and silk turbans studded with gems, their broad scimitars a-flash in the sun, their proud, pure-bred steeds a-tremble with excitement, their lances streaming with pennon and banneret, the haughty Turks called Allah to witness the coming defeat of the barbarians. "Hitherto," they said, "the Mongols have fought only with Unbelievers; now the banners of Islam are arrayed against them." And when they first caught sight of the vast horde, clad in disreputable sheep-skin coats, and mounted on shaggy, unkempt ponies, the Turks laughed loud and long.

But they little knew their enemy! It was one thing to catch sight of the Mongols, and quite another thing to draw them into battle. Genghis Khan had split up his army, and scattered his warriors over five hundred miles of enemy territory. Putting their rations consisting of strips of dried meat under their saddles, the men from the Gobi Desert galloped a hundred miles a day, changed to fresh horses when their mounts grew tired, and harried the land here, there, and everywhere, Pity was unknown to them. They burned and pillaged far and wide, massacred whole villages, and were off before the Shah's troops could come to the rescue. Wherever the Shah mustered his troops, there was not a Mongol to be seen; but ten, twenty, or a hundred miles away, they were at their work of destruction!

Out-maneuvered, tricked and teased by the genius of Genghis Khan, the Shah lost his head. Like the Chin emperor of China, he betook him to his walled cities, taking refuge first in Bokhara. But news came that Genghis Khan and his terrible general, Chepe Noyon, were marching on Bokhara, determined to take the Shah. In a panic, Mohammed fled, accompanied only by his favorite nobles, his elephants and camels, his household troops, his family and such of his treasures as he could hastily gather together and carry on his flight.

Meanwhile Genghis Khan appeared before the beautiful city of Bokhara, with its parks and gardens surrounded by a wall thirty miles long. It was defended by twenty thousand Turkish warriors, and by as many inhabitants; and was guarded by iron gates and massive towers too strong to be taken by the Mongols while they had no siege engines to use. Nevertheless, Genghis Khan marched his host around the walls so that the defenders might witness the strength of the attackers, and scouring the countryside, he seized great masses of captives whom he forced to build movable towers to make the assault of the city. Facing foes of such frightful appearance, the people of Bokhara were too disorganized by the flight of Mohammed Shah to make any real resistance. Indeed, the Turks of the garrison fled secretly by night, while the Mongols, learning of their plans, allowed them to pass through their lines only to follow them quietly and take them unawares next day, driving them into the river, and cutting them down almost to a man!

With the garrison gone, the Mongols shot flaming arrows into Bokhara until the governor opened the massive gates and came out to surrender the keys of the stronghold and beg for mercy. Then Genghis Khan rode in on his prancing charger, looking curiously about. Bokhara was the first of the large cities of Islam to fall into his hands and there were many strange sights to be seen. Drawing rein before an imposing building, the chief mosque of the city, he asked if it were the dwelling of the Shah, but was told it was the house of Allah. At once he rode his horse up the steps and summoning the sheiks to hold his steed, he hurled the reader's giant Koran beneath the feet of the horses.

"Who is this man?" one of the captives asked, beholding the warrior in gleaming helmet and black lacquered armor.

"Hush!" whispered another. "The wrath of God stands near us."

Addressing the people, who had expected to see fire descend from heaven to blast this ungainly figure in strange armor, Genghis Khan now said: "I have come to this place, only to tell you that you must find provender for my army. Open the doors of your storehouses."

Genghis stayed only two hours in Bokhara; then he hastened on to seek the Shah in Samarkand. Behind him, a pall of smoke rose over the city; flames swept through the dry structures of wood and baked clay until the domed academies of Bokhara vanished. The captives were driven toward Samarkand, but unable to keep up with the mounted Mongols, many stumbled and were slain in hundreds by the wayside.

In vain had Mohammed hoped that his strong walled cities would hold the Mongols in check. Flourishing Samarkand fell after a brief struggle of only four days, and was sacked, burned and abandoned to the mercy of the wild animals; noble Khiva was soon taken; parts of Afghanistan, Persia and Caucasia were quickly overrun and conquered.

Turks and Persians on left and Mongols on right battle with savage fury for the wealthy cities of Central Asia. (MS. Bodleian Library.)

Some of the cities opened their gates without a struggle; then, if the idea appealed to the Mongols, the townspeople were permitted to live, though always the garrisons were massacred; otherwise all were slain without mercy. Haughty Herat rebelled, and experienced a terrible revenge that started with a roll of drums and a clash of cymbals. The Mongols never

Clad in jointed, lacquered-leather armor, the fierce, hardy, desert-devils of Genghis Khan emerge unexpectedly from mountain passes, and fall upon the civilized cities of Central Asia. (MS. 1396.)

withheld their hands nor drew back until the strength of the defenders was exhausted. Every living being was slaughtered; buildings were plundered and pulled down at leisure and the site of the ruins was forbidden to all men, becoming a mere tangle of weeds and a haunt of beasts.

In this terrible fashion, the Khan drove home the lesson that those who resisted would be exterminated. He forbade mercy in his officers without his own special order, believing that a conquered enemy was never really subdued but always hated his new master. Establishing his camp in the mountains where there was grazing for his horses, he tricked or stormed into subjection all the historic cities of mid-Asia. For two years the grim struggle went on, a hundred thousand men of the horde gaining the mastery of twenty kingdoms while multitudes, beset with all the warlike fanaticism of Mohammedans, exhausted themselves in vain against the military genius of Genghis Khan.

Desperate now, Mohammed cried: "Is there no place on earth where I can be free from the Mongols?" Fleeing through the mountains toward the Caspian Sea, he entered a boat to sail to an island of refuge, but even as he stepped into the skiff, his pursuers were at his heels shooting at him with arrows. Mohammed reached the island, but weakened by hardships, he died, leaving his shattered kingdom to Jel-al′-ud-din′, his son. So hunted-down and poverty ridden had the great potentate become that his only shroud for burial was the shirt of one of his followers.

And now struck by the advantages of the Caspian region, the two Mongol generals who had pursued the unfortunate Shah, sent a courier to Genghis Khan asking permission to explore and conquer farther west. The Khan gave his consent, and under the daring Chepe Noyon and the famous Su-ba-tai, the tireless Mongol hordes swarmed through the gorges of the Caucasus and the lofty mountains of Georgia to the shores of the Black Sea. Tricking the hastily-gathered armies of the Russian granddukes in the steppes, they annihilated those forces, even wandering down into the Crimea and storming a Genoese trade citadel. And though Chepe Noyon died, Subotai's curiosity still remained unappeased; he was about to cross the Dnieper River into Europe, when Genghis, having reports concerning him by courier, ordered him back to Central Asia, some two thousand miles away.

Meanwhile, Genghis Khan, determined that no capable enemy should be left behind his back, had hunted down Jelal-uddin, son of Mohammed Shah. The young prince had defeated a Mongol division and retired in safety to India, and furious at this defeat, the Khan pursued without rest, casting away his helmet at the siege of the city of Bamian where one of his grandsons was slain and leading the attack, bareheaded advancing through a breach in the wall. The Mongols finally caught up with the prince on the bank of the Indus River, outflanked and defeated his army. Casting off his armor and taking his standard in his hand, the young man mounted a fresh horse and leaping a thirty-foot bank, he plunged boldly into the river, while Genghis, riding up, spoke ungrudged words of praise in admiration of his courage and leadership.

The conqueror, nevertheless, sent men in pursuit of the prince who escaped by his daring deed, only to be forsaken by all his own followers and killed by a Kurd in Armenia.

The battle of the Indus was the last stand of the Kharesmian cavalry. From Tibet to the Caspian Sea resistance had ceased, and the survivors of the people of Islam had become the slaves of the conquerors. Genghis even dreamed of extending his conquests south into India, but the oppressive heat and the impure water sickened his men, accustomed to the clean, sharp air of the high, central plateaus of Asia. Thus India was saved, and the Khan reluctantly withdrew to Samarkand. On the banks of the Syr River he set up his tent village, whither in the spring of 1222 A.D., he summoned to a great council meeting all the leaders of the hordes. North, south, east, and west, the summons went by mounted messengers along a mighty system of roads which linked every part of the Mongol Empire. This connecting system of continuous cross-continental roads was Genghis Khan's own idea; in order to keep in touch with governors of all the provinces as well as wandering generals, he had developed the horse-post called the *Yam*.

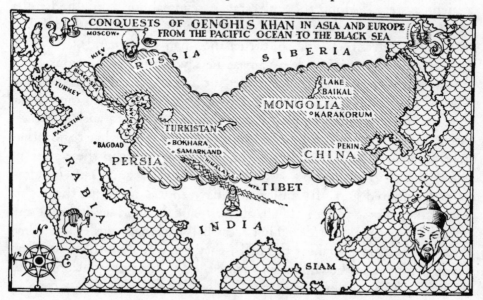

A rider of the *Yam*, the post system reaching in all directions, and uniting the Mongol Empire.

For untold generations, the Gobi clansmen had been accustomed to pass news from village to village by mounted messengers. When a man galloped up to one village with a summons of war or a bit of gossip, another saddled a horse and galloped off to tell the people at the next village. Genghis Khan merely organized and improved this ancient system. Along the old caravan roads about a hundred miles apart, were stations where relays of horses were kept with a handful of men to look after them and to further the Khan's commands.

Marco Polo described the Yam as he saw it two generations later: "At some of these stations there are 400 horses, at others 200. Even when the messengers pass through a roadless tract where no inn stands, the stations are still to be found, and they are provided with all necessaries so that the Emperor's messengers coming from what region they may, find everything ready for them. There are men in these stations who, when there is a call for great haste, travel a good two hundred or two hundred and fifty miles in a day, and as much in the night. They take a horse ready-saddled, all fresh and in wind, and mount and go as hard as they can ride. They wear bells on their girdles and when those at the next post hear the bells, they get ready another horse and a man equipped in the same way, and he is off to the third station. Thus the dispatch speeds on always at full gallop."

But the Yam was used by others besides the Khan's messengers. Merchants, travelers, wandering priests, ambassadors from other nations, bands of prisoners and slaves, all passed up and down the post roads. Chinese, wrapped in quilted coats, trotted up to the stations in two-wheeled curtained carts to prepare a precious cup of tea over the dung fire. Up from Samarkand came endless lines of camels, laden with woven stuffs, ivory, gold ornaments and pearl-sewn veils. Thin-faced Jews led strings of pack-donkeys; sallow, square-chinned Armenians rode by with curious glances at the silent Mongol guards sitting at the *yurt* doors. Shivering captives stumbled past on the long road to the desert capital. Yellow-hatted lamas swinging their prayer-wheels, their eyes fixed on remote snow summits; black-hats, from the barren slopes of Tibet; slant-eyed Buddhist pilgrims, bound to spend their years in seeking the paths once followed by their Holy One; barefoot ascetics, and long-haired fakirs, all these and many more passed up and down the roads. The post was indeed the very backbone of the great Khan's government, and the Mongol governor of each town or camp made the *Yassa* the law of the land. The successors of Genghis Khan kept up the system of the Yam, and this in later days did more than anything else to bring to the people of Europe a knowledge of China and the East.

The *Yam* roads uniting a far-flung empire gave safe passage to all the various peoples of Asia.

To the court of Genghis Khan came officers from China accompanying beautifully painted tent-carts.

Summoned by the riders of the Yam, the Mongol leaders gathered, but not in half-ruined Samarkand; for Genghis Khan with the true nomad's distrust of cities, had chosen instead, a meadow, seven leagues in circuit, on the bank of the river Syr. There the tent-carts were set up on three sides of the Khan's great white pavilion, a tent so large that within it two thousand men could find shelter, and here Genghis Khan awaited the coming of his generals.

One by one they came riding in from the four quarters of Asia, each bringing gifts to prove his own prowess and delight the eyes of his master. Muhuli was dead, but other officers came from China, driving beautifully painted tent-carts, drawn by matched yokes of oxen and gay with captured banners. Officers from the slopes of Tibet had covered wagons gilded and lacquered, drawn by lines of silky long-haired yaks.

Mongol generals from Tibet brought lacquered covered wagons drawn by ponderous, long-haired yaks.

From Khorasan came fierce Tuli, Master of War, with long strings of greatly prized white camels.

Tuli, Master of War, coming up from Khorasan, brought with him strings of white camels. Jagatai, descending from the snows of the ranges, drove in a hundred thousand horses. From the Gobi came young Kublai, now nine years old, and quite a man in the eyes of himself and his fond grandfather. Subotai rode in from Poland and with him, Juji, the Master of the Hunt, bringing one hundred thousand Kip-chak' horses. And all these Mongol officers wore cloth-of-gold and silver, covered with sable coats and wraps of silver-gray wolf skin, while the horses wore jingling chain-mail, their harness bright with silver-work and all afire with jewels. Never was seen such a gathering! The eyes of the old Khan shone as he gazed upon his people come to do him honor, and his old heart swelled with pride; for had he not made a nation, an all-embracing empire from a raw, undisciplined desert tribe?

Jagatai, descending from the snows of the ranges, drove in a hundred thousand hardy, desert horses.

Genghis holds court with Bourtai. His favorite sons, Jagati, Ogotai, Juji, and Tuli, paying homage. Ogotai succeeded Genghis, and was followed by his son, Kuyuk, and Tuli's sons, Mangu and Kublai.

Seated on a golden throne, which had once graced the palace of Mohammed Shah in Samarkand, Genghis Khan received his generals, with Bourtai, his favorite wife, seated a step below him. Conspicuous under his throne, was a square of rough, gray felt, to show that the Mongols were a desert people, and before the Khan was the table laden with fruit and mare's milk which always stood in his tent. And now for the first time, the Mongol lords learned how widespread were their conquests, as each recounted his story and listened to those of his fellows. The Khan himself showed his people how powerful they had become and what a heritage was theirs. Then he urged them to obey the Yassa, and always to stand by each other, while he commended to them those four favorite sons who were to be his heirs. Ogotai he had chosen as his successor rather than either of his elder brothers, for Juji was fierce and sullen, Jagatai was rash and quick-tempered, but Ogotai was wise and gentle. He would know how to bring together in harmony the widely scattered empire, how to use tact as well as force. "Do not allow quarrels to come between you," he cautioned his sons and generals. "Be faithful and unfailing to Ogotai."

The generals, Batu and Su-bo-tai, who conquered Russia; Hu-la-gu', the grandson who subdued Persia; and little Kublai, son of Tuli, some day to be the great Kublai Khan of China, also greet their lord.

When the audiences were over, there was feasting for a month in the city of tents by the Syr. Then generals were sent to those districts which were not entirely subdued, but the Khan returned to Karakorum for he felt that his end was near and he wished to close his eyes in death in the land that had given him birth. In Karakorum he rested, enjoying once more for a season, the companionship of Bourtai, and regaining a measure of health in his native desert air; but he felt that his task was unfinished while in southern China the Sung Dynasty still survived; so, in spite of his age, he set out on his last campaign with Subotai and Tuli by his side and the vast horde at his back.

With his old skill and vigor he defeated and cut to pieces an army made up of hill-robbers, fugitives from Cathay, Turks, Tibetans, all whose lands he had laid waste, who now thought to have their revenge. Then, in the depths of winter, he led his horde over the Yellow River into the Land of the Sung. But his strength was failing fast. Sending for Tuli and his chief officers, he gave them his last commands as he lay wrapped in his sable robes before the fire in his tent. War against the Sungs must be continued, and his conquests divided as he had arranged.

A few days later in the year 1227, the year of the Mouse in the Cycle of the Twelve Beasts, Genghis Khan died, leaving to his sons the greatest empire ever conquered by one man, and the most destructive army in the world.

They carried him back to the desert he had loved, and as the sad procession wound its way through the soft air of early spring, the hardened veterans of long warfare mourned aloud:

> "Aforetime thou didst swoop like a falcon; now
>   a rumbling car bears thee onward,
>   O my Khan!
> "Hast thou in truth left thy wife and
>   children, and the council of thy people,
>   O my Khan?
> "Wheeling in pride like an eagle
>   once thou didst lead us; but now thou
>   hast stumbled and fallen,
>   O my Khan!"

Lest the news of his death should reach Ka'ra-ko'rum before them, the warriors escorting the body slew every man, woman, and child whom they met, and so they brought Genghis Khan back to the tent of Bourtai. They buried him, not in Karakorum, but in the valley where he had lived as a child. There under a great tree he lies, but no man knows the place of his grave.

Savage as the wildest barbarian, intent on conquest by force, ruthless, and without mercy, seizing all of Asia from the Pacific Ocean east to the Caspian Sea, and from the Arctic regions south to the confines of India, Genghis yet had qualities of organization and leadership that made him truly great. The power of the Yassa promoted peace and order; the system of the Yam encouraged trade and kept every part of the empire in touch with every other part. Tolerant toward all religious beliefs, Genghis permitted no one creed to predominate above another, and he exempted from taxation all doctors, priests and savants. Justice, tolerance and discipline were taught and practised at his court. Great though his sons and grandsons were, not one was as great as he.

III

Mongol Conquests in Russia and the West

(1235–1547)

The Invasion of Europe

Two years were spent in mourning. Over the barren wastes of the sun-baked Gobi Desert, and throughout all the lands of the Great Khan's conquests, the laws of the Yassa were respected, and the spirit of the master still held undisputed sway. Nowhere was there rebellion against the mastery of the Mongol; nor did the sons and generals strive with one another; the enormous Empire of Genghis Khan, built upon blood and conquest, still remained whole and intact.

On his deathbed, Genghis named O-go-tai, his third son, as his successor; and when the time of mourning was ended, the great Mongol leaders and generals came from all parts of Asia to hold a council meeting and follow out the wishes of the Khan. But Ogotai refused the honor his father had done him. "It is not fitting," he declared, "that I should be honored above my uncles, nor above my elder brother." Astonished, the Mongol leaders passed forty days in uncertainty while they argued about the matter. Then they waited on Ogotai and spoke to him angrily thus: "What doest thou? The Khan himself hath chosen thee for his successor!"

Ogotai, the new Mongol Khan. (Peking Museum.)

65

Rebuked on hearing these words, Ogotai felt obliged to mount the gold throne of his father. Cha-ta-gai, the elder brother, threw himself down and did homage before the new Khan's throne, and all the officers and nobles likewise knelt in obedience. Thereafter, followed days of mighty feasting and drinking; and thus did Ogotai become the great Kha Khan of the mighty Mongol Empire.

Genghis had left a multitude of savage, war-thirsty riders to be divided among his three sons, Ogotai, Chatagai, and Tuli. Action was life to the horde; and to satisfy these men and keep them from killing each other, new battles must be found. For a few years they were occupied with a series of minor wars to make complete the subjugation of partly conquered lands. Jelal'-ud-din', last of the house of the great Mohammed Shah, was defeated and put to death; Armenia and the regions west of the Caspian Sea were subdued and devastated; and Subotai and Tuli subjugated the Chin Empire. In the year 1235, a council was again called to select new lands for invasion.

Ogotai with his wife on an elaborate throne, surrounded by courtiers, receives ambassadors from lands bordering Mongol conquests. In accordance with Mongol custom a table of refreshments is placed before his throne for the use of tired travelers. (Persian miniature.)

Subject envoys bringing homage and the gift of a beautiful vase to the Khan of the Kip-chaks', those frightful barbaric nomads of the steppes who sorely harassed Southern Russia. (Miniature.)

That fierce old general, Subotai, had on this occasion a very great deal to say concerning the lands to which he wished to go for further conquests. Never had he forgotten the rich pasture-lands that lay off to the west in Russia. Over these he and Chepe Noyon had galloped with their horde in search of Mohammed Shah. Slashing through mountain gorges, they had come out on the northern slopes of the lofty Caucasian Range to find an army of highlanders and men from the flat steppes below, waiting there to meet them. There were Alans, Circassians, and those frightful Turkish Kipchaks who wore two barbaric pigtails on their otherwise shaven heads. The mountain folk were defeated, and the Mongols, rushing forth like a band of loosened demons, drove the astonished Kipchaks through the salt steppes northward into Russia. For a century these Kipchaks had been harassing the Russian princes; but now they sent fleet-footed messengers to their foes imploring aid. "The Mongols have seized our country," they said: "tomorrow they will seize yours!"

The Russians rallied to their aid and advanced to the river Kalka. There Subotai and Chepe Noyon watched them mass their troops, noting their sluggish movements and how the Russian princes quarreled among themselves, even in the face of an enemy of whom they felt so much dread. The Mongols attacked at last with incredible speed and fury. For two days the battle raged; great were the Russian losses. The Prince of Kiev, shut up in an armed camp on the shore, held out longer than the others; but he, too, in time surrendered. Promised the opportunity to buy his life and freedom, he found himself, when actually fast in the power of the Mongols, placed with other Russians under a movable floor whereon the Mongols were feasting. As the victors ate and drank to celebrate their victory, their vanquished foes were crushed to death by the weight of the men above them.

Suddenly disappearing, Subotai and Chepe Noyon then vanished off to the south. But of all the countries seen by Subotai in his adventures, he best remembered that where, across wide pasture-lands, the bulb-like domes of churches rose above the white walls of little Russian villages! To this rich Land of Promise he wished again to return, and when he described it in council, Batu, the grandson of Genghis, took fire at his description and declared that he, too, would go there. Korea, China, and Persia interested other generals, and it was agreed to send armies into all these regions, but Subotai and Batu, equipping a powerful horde, turned their faces toward Russia. So magnificent in gold-embroidered cloth was Batu, grandson of Genghis, that he was called Batu the Splendid, and so gorgeous was his great felt tent with its roof of gold, that his army was called the Golden Horde. Of such luxurious vanities, Subotai, the old warrior, would have naught. Skilled, relentless, fierce, he led the way into Russia.

The Beginnings of Russia

In Eastern Europe and Western Asia, the vast, silent, mysterious, treeless steppes of Russia, with their long grass waving in the wind, stretched forth in endless monotony, broken only by undulating hills, regions of small salt lakes and little river valleys wooded with oak and pine. In the great white North were the frozen marsh tundras, covered with reindeer moss, lichens and stunted shrubs. Farther south were virgin forests where little white birches and aspens gleamed amid tall dark pines, larches, and silver firs. In this region, dense thickets of trees often rose from a carpet of thickly interlaced grasses which concealed deep treacherous bogs impassable save in winter; but of all the varied features forming the landscape in Russia, none was so distinctive, so truly Russian as the steppes.

Rising in Central Russia, three great rivers wound their way through forest, swamp, and steppe, forming highways for trade and commerce. The Volga, wide and powerful, flowed to the Caspian Sea, the Dnieper to the Black Sea, and the Western Dvina to the Baltic. Now in very ancient times, there came to live in the marshes and thickets of the Upper Dnieper, a sociable, good-natured people, the brown-haired, grey-eyed Slavs. They lived in small family groups, governed by a council of elders, and in time formed trading-posts with Kiev on the steep, right bank of the stream as their most important settlement. Second only to Kiev was Nov'go-rod or New Town in the snow-laden, wind-swept forests on the Vol'kov River to the north. Between these two primitive settlements, the Slavs plied back and forth in dug-outs made of a single tree. Spreading out over a widely-linked system of water-ways, they were a friendly people, not yet united into a nation.

Some lived in huts in the woods, others in little villages on islands in lake or river, or along the banks of a stream. Their houses were made of logs with the staircase on the outside, leading to a roofed porch which was often elaborately carved and painted in vivid colors. The principal beam of the roof had each end roughly hewn in the semblance of a horse's head, and to protect the house from the Evil Eye, an actual horse's skull often glowed white on the roof. When the village was on an island, the little wooden houses were all built up on stakes to isolate them from the ground. Seeing such little houses with four legs like a beast, old grannies would tell the children tales of the witch, Baba Yaga, whose house went about on hen's legs and walked from place to place! Down by the water-side were skiffs and fishing nets and everywhere about were skins brought in by hunters, lying spread out to dry, foxes, bears, and wolves, the smooth, tan fur of the beaver, the soft rich brown of sable, and little white ermine skins.

Early Slavic village upon a river-island in Russia. The Slavs belonged to the brown-haired, round-headed, grey-eyed Alpine race. (See Vol. V, p. 117, Vol. VI, p. 24.) From the custom of raising their log houses on stakes, there arose folk tales of the witch, Baba Yaga, whose house walked about on hen's legs. The Russian folk tale in *My Book House*, Vol. VII, p. 112, describes the witch and her queer house.

Primitive Slavs in Russia greet the return of spring. The ancient song on this page is still sung by the Yakuts in Siberia. (*The Joy of Art in Russia* by N. Roerich, *Art and Archaeology*, March, 1922.)

In such a village as this, each spring saw merry-making to hail the victory of the Sun over winter's cold and snow. Having tramped around in the forest and enjoyed with laughter and gaiety the first grass and tender blossoms, the people came back to the village wearing wreaths of new green on their heads. Quick and alert, they danced to the piping of wood-and-horn-pipes. The men wore heavy coats reaching half-way to the knees, made of felt or leather and heavily trimmed with fur; little caps, like stocking caps, waved jauntily on their heads, and their trousers were tucked in half-boots of red or other gay color. Furs and needle-work adorned the garments of the crowd, and the younger generation wore ornaments of amber, stone beads, and talismans' teeth. Forming into rings they danced and sang with joy, while bonfires clove the dusk and their figures were silhouetted against the living gold. One could hear their blending voices far beyond lake and forest:

> Hail, thou juicy-green hill!
> The spring warmth is reveling!
> The silver birch is unfolding!
> The smooth fir is brighter!
> The grass is green in the glen!
> This is the time for games, the time for merrymaking!

Thus lived the Slavic people in the great eastern plains of Europe, almost shut out from civilization by the wild tribes who hemmed them in. On the north, in the fens and marshes around the frozen Baltic, lived the vigorous, slant-eyed Finns, a short, hardy Turkish people akin to the Huns and Bulgars; and associated with the Finns were the tall, red-haired Estonians and the short, bullet-headed Lapps, herding great droves of reindeer. On the south, the Slavs fought for existence against nomadic Kipchaks and Khazars who dwelt on the plains, living in tent wagons, breeding cattle, fighting, and migrating slowly from their homes in the barren stretches north of China to Russia's rich pasture-lands and her regions of sweeping plains. And far off there to the east, Finn and Tartar met and melted into the vast, unprofitable stretches of the arid Gobi Desert.

Having little contact with Europe, surrounded by these wild tribes, the Slavs dwelt quite alone, sufficient unto themselves. Scattered all over the land with no great numbers able to gather at one spot to resist an invading horde, they quietly melted away and hid in thicket and swamp whenever raiders appeared, their sturdy self-reliance keeping up a determined resistance. Leaders of enemy bands, marching into the land, were often most unexpectedly pierced by swift, silent arrows shot by hidden marksmen from some place that seemed deserted. Unable to guard against such attacks, they were forced by their unseen but stubborn Slavic foes to withdraw in defeat to the steppes.

Стрѣлецъ (Изборникъ Святослава)

A Slav sharpshooter with bow and arrow alert for defense against all invaders, one of the earliest drawings of the Slavs in Russia. (From the Sviatoslav Collection.) For the national epic of Finland see the *Kalevala* in *My Book House*, X, 151.

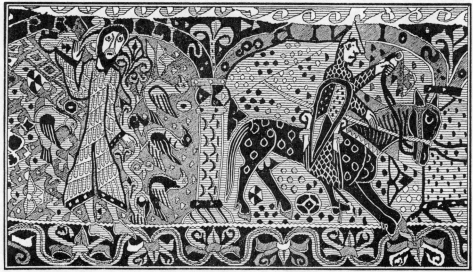

Bearded farmer and Viking warrior. Such were Russia's Va-ran'gi-an invaders. (Norse tapestry 1180.)

But now in the days when King Alfred was fighting against the Norsemen to keep them out of England, certain boisterous Vikings made their way up from the Baltic by way of the rivers of Russia into the very heart of the country owned by the Slavs. Tall and lusty for battle, these flaxen-haired Va-ran'gi-ans grounded their dragon-ships at each little Slavic village along the water-ways and swaggering between the log huts, overawed the short, shy Slavs with their enormous bodies, blustering manners and mighty weapons. Clad in helmet and mail, with long sword and battle ax, they came first merely as traders, eager to exchange their wares for honey, wax, furs, and slaves. But should villagers prove to be treacherous or refuse to make trades with their goods, these wild Viking adventurers were always eager for combat; and often, when the trading was done, they engaged in bloody battle for the joy of conflict alone.

Gradually, however, the Slavs grew accustomed to seeing these strangers, and gathered together articles to exchange with them when they came. And the Vikings found much to their liking in this land of forest and stream; they visited it often for hunting, and soon established settlements along the river Volhov and the shores of La'do-ga Lake.

Viking dragon-ships, carved, painted in vivid colors, and manned by lusty, mailed warriors, gather in their favorite bay of Northern Russia, called after them, the Varangian Sea. A painting by N. Roerich, one of the greatest modern Russian artists who best expresses the spirit of Early Russia.

Some portaged their serpent-ships across the narrow water-sheds into the Dnieper River and gleefully sailed away to distant Constantinople; others roamed afield, finally settling down and building strong, permanent forts in the forest-covered marshes and lowlands about Novgorod.

But the neighborhood of Novgorod was far from a peaceful place; for both the Slavs and the Finns had made their settlements there and were always at war with each other. The brave, hardy Finnish colonists, who had recently entered the region, were determined to remain and constantly made raids on the little Slavic settlements; the Slavs returned their attacks stubbornly and fiercely, equally determined to drive them from the land. And as long as neither people bothered the Viking settlers, the Northmen took no interest in their constant squabbles and fights. In the year 862, however, the Slavs invited the Vikings who lived near Novgorod under Rurik, their red-haired leader, to put an end to their feuds and become the rulers of the land. Rurik and his Varangians were loath to accept this offer, "for dread of the beast-like manners of the men of Novgorod;" but changing their minds in time, they put down all the raiding and subjugated the Slavs. Thereafter, the land of the Slavs was called after Rurik, Russia.

Other Viking adventurers possessed themselves of Kiev; but Oleg, Rurik's successor, advancing to the southward, took Kiev from his fellow-countrymen and transferred his court to that place. Now under Varangian rule, the Slavs spread in every direction, and checked the nomad hordes who threatened them from the steppes. Thanks to this Viking leadership, an infant Russian nation began to take form at last.

Thus when Russia emerged into the full light of history, Kiev in her shimmering birchwoods, was already the acknowledged political and intellectual center of the land, a place where life was gayer than in Novgorod and the North. Through Kiev went the road to the south that led off to distant Byzantium and the bright light of civilization. Through Kiev also went the highways to Italy, India, Persia and other glamorous places beloved by the Lord of the Sun. Within the walls of Kiev and on the hills round about, lived rich patrician families of powerful merchant-warriors. Orchards and blooming gardens surrounded the wood-built town, and to its markets huntsmen brought

Brilliant and barbaric was the half-civilized Russia of Viking times.

the costly furs for which Russia was known to the world. In the farm-yards ducks, pigeons, geese, and swans fattened as food for the rich, while woodsmen gathered honey from the hollow trees, that there might be wherewithal to make the golden mead on which the Great Ones feasted. And while the peasants worked, prince and boyar made war, hunted the boar or rode to the chase. Generous, brave, and hospitable, all loved gay music and dancing, feasting and good cheer.

Slowly Russia began to take on a smattering of civilization. The dress of the people changed. Men continued to wear wide trousers and boots or leather leggings, but instead of the old long-sleeved, double-breasted coats of felt, they began to wear linen shirts and dark, sleeveless, woolen coats, lined with colored quilting, open down the front, and held by a girdle at the waist. Queen Olga, the lovely and witty wife of Oleg's successor at Kiev, went away on a journey to gay Constantinople and came back home a Christian. Her son, a broad-chested fellow, with the usual long mustaches, and the nobleman's tuft of hair on the crown of his shaven head, was more like the Slavs than the Vikings both in his habits and dress. Even his name, Svy'-a-to-slav', was not Nordic but Slavic; the vigorous Varangians had ceased to be strange people come from a foreign land; they had melted both in their customs and language into the Russian Slavs.

The early Slavs dressed much like the Scythians, the men at extreme left, in long-sleeved, double-breasted coats of felt and wide trousers tucked into half-boots. Later, however, although clinging to their baggy trousers, they began to wear linen shirts and sleeveless, woolen coats lined with quilting, open down the front and held by a girdle at the waist, as in the family group at right. Following Viking custom, the Slavs also took to wearing caps of spiral wire and head bands, leg bands, fibulae, and other ornaments of golden bronze, and they had a primitive delight in striking designs of gay embroidery.

Nevertheless, a few old Germanic customs survived, including the very troublesome one of splitting up the land by division among all the sons whenever a ruler died; and this old custom caused Russia a period of great disorder when King Svy'a-to-slav' died. Vlad'-i-mir, the youngest son, was driven by his brother from his inheritance of Novgorod, and sought refuge in Scandinavia. But returning with a band of Vikings he quickly reconquered his city, and then marched in force on Kiev

Svy'a-to-slav' and family. The first Russian ruler more Slav than Viking. Note long moustaches, fur caps and boots. (Russian MS., 1073.)

where his brother now ruled supreme, sending messengers on the way to Ragvald, Prince of Po'lotsk, begging the hand of his daughter, the Princess Ragnilda, in marriage. And when the haughty princess refused his offer with scorn, he stopped to attack Polotsk and took the disdainful princess, whether she willed or no. Then, resuming his march to Kiev, he seized the proud capital-city, slew his brother by treachery, and immediately was proclaimed by all the boyars and nobles who divided the land among them, Prince of a reunited once more peaceful Russia.

Pagan Russia. Primitive Slavs in animal skins dance before enormous, carved, and colored wooden statues of their nature gods, honored long before they entered Russia. (Painting by N. Roerich.)

Vladimir was a heathen when he came to the throne of Russia, and he was at first determined to have naught to do with Christianity. Before his palace, he placed impressive figures of the old Slavic gods— Sva-rog', the father of the gods; Ve-les', the god of the cattle that roamed the pasture-lands; Stri-bog', the god of the winds blowing the grass of the steppes; and, most important of all, Perun, the god of thunder, having a huge head of silver and long mustaches of gold, him to whom men prayed in the dim-lit aisles of the forest, under giant oaks. Then, to celebrate his triumph over his brothers and kinsmen, Vladimir held a great feast and savagely sacrificed a thousand lives to his gods.

In those days, there were seers and wise-men among the Russians, but there was no caste of priests nor regular public worship. Every head of a household sacrificed for his family, while all the good folk impartially met for the picturesque festivals, sang their songs to the gods, and danced their old folk-dances in honor of spring and the sun, the hunt, and the fruitful fields awakened from winter's sleep. When a warrior chanced to meet death, men said that his soul had gone in the wake of migrating birds, to that beautiful land of Rai where birds passed the winter-time; and to make him happy there, they buried in his funeral mound his best domestic implements, weapons and musical instruments, his favorite horse and dog, and that one among his wives who professed to love him most. For year upon year without end, their story-tellers told in public and private gatherings quaint old tales of the nymphs who dwelt in forest and field, the sprites who shone in the frost, or glittered in the ice, and the lovely white maid of the snow.

Frost and Wood Spirits, a painting by N. Roerich. The Russian Slavs peopled forest and field with elves and sprites, and loved to tell of the Snow Maiden who appeared only during winter, pined away in spring and fled north in summer. See *My Book House*, "The Little Snow Maiden," Vol. IV, p. 119.

But now in spite of the orgy of savage paganism with which he began his reign, Vladimir soon grew convinced that in order to bring unity to his kingdom, his people needed a definite creed, and a certain set form of worship, in which everyone could join. He, therefore, began to question travelers arriving in Kiev about the different religions then in vogue in the world; but as each traveler said his religion was the best to be found, Vladimir, still at a loss, called together his boyars and elders and asked their advice in the matter.

"If you are anxious to find out the truth, O Prince," the boyars and elders said, "you have men whom you can send out to see how all these serve their God."

Now this speech pleased the Prince, and he selected good and clever men to the number of ten, and sent them out to investigate the religions of the world. The Jews, it was decided, thought too much of their sins; Islam had too little gladness; the Roman Church had no beauty, and furthermore the Pope was above all emperors and kings. But when the shy, uncouth, grey-bearded Russian elders, in their long coats and fur-brimmed hats, came to beautiful Constantinople, they were dazzled by its glory and fairly lost their heads. The Emperor Basil II received them with a great banquet and sent them to the

Grey-bearded boyars like those sent by Vladimir to investigate various religions. (From N. Roerich.)

Patriarch saying: "Some Russians have come to find out about our faith; so have the church and clergy in order and yourself don the holy garments, that they may see the glory of God!"

Having heard this, the Patriarch called together the clergy to celebrate the day according to the custom, and he had the censers lighted and arranged the singing and the choir. The Emperor went with the Russians to church and they were placed in a prominent place where they could see the beauty of Sancta Sophia,

Vladimir, Grand Duke of Kiev, with moustache and beard. (A coin.) Needing a religion to unify Russia, Vladimir demanded Christianity and a Greek wife of royal blood at the point of the sword!

hear the singing and watch the service. Then they were surprised and marveled. And the Emperors Basil and Constantine, two brothers who were ruling together, sent them away with gifts.

They came back to their country, and their Prince called together his boyars and old men. Said Vladimir: "The men we have sent away have come back. Let us hear what has happened!" And he said: "Speak before the druzhina!" And they spoke: "We came to Germany, and we saw many ceremonies in their temples, but of beauty we saw none. We went to Greece, and they took us where they worship their God, and we do not know whether we were in heaven or upon earth, for there is not upon earth such sight or beauty. We were perplexed, but this much we know that there God lives among men, and their service is better than in any other land." And the boyars answered and said: "If the Greek religion were bad, your grandmother Olga, who was the wisest of all *men*, would not have accepted it."

So Vladimir decided to accept Christianity from the Greek Church of the East, not from the Roman Church of the West. But with true Russian pride he made up his mind not to humble himself by requesting baptism into the Church. He would get it the Russian way. By force of arms and threats, he would make the Byzantine Emperors beg him to be baptized.

Crown given Vladimir by the Byzantine Emperor when he married the unfortunate Princess Anna in 988 A.D. Used by all Tsars from the time of Ivan the Terrible.

Accordingly, he went with his warriors and laid siege to the city of Kor-sun', which belonged to Constantinople, and having taken the city, he entered it with his druzhina and sent this word to the Emperors Basil and Constantine: "I have taken your famous city. I hear you have a sister who is still a maiden. If you will not give her to me for a wife, I shall do unto Constantinople as I have done to this city!"

Aghast at the very thought of wedding their sister to such a barbarian, the Emperors still dared not refuse this request with that savage army of Slavs all ready to descend upon them. So they answered Vladimir as he had hoped they would, asking him to be baptized. "If you will receive the baptism," they wrote, "you shall get our sister Anna as your wife and you will receive the kingdom of heaven also."

Thus having forced from the Emperors an invitation to be baptized, Vladimir agreed to do so. Then the Emperors requested that he should be baptized before they sent their sister to him.

But Vladimir answered defiantly, "First send your sister to me, then will I receive the baptism."

So the Emperors had to send Anna to him though the poor maid wept at thought of wedding this barbarian, who already had eight hundred wives. "It is as if I were going into captivity," she sobbed. "It were better if I died here."

But her brothers said to her: "Perchance God will through you turn the Russian land to Christianity, and free Greece from a dire war!" And they persuaded her with difficulty. She boarded a boat, kissed her relatives with tears, and went across the sea to Korsun.

Then Vladimir was baptized in the Church of St. Basil in Korsun, and afterward he led Anna to the betrothal. As a marriage price, he gave Korsun back to her brothers, then he returned with her to Kiev.

Upon his return, he ordered the idols to be cast down, and some to be cut to pieces, and others to be consumed by fire; but Perun he had tied to the tail of a horse, and dragged down the hill over the Bo-ri-chev' to the brook. And he placed twelve men to strike him with rods, not as if the wood had any feeling, but as a scorn to the devil who had through him seduced people, that he might receive his due punishment from men. As Perun was dragged along the brook to the Dnieper, the unbelievers wept over him, for they had not yet received the holy baptism, and he was cast into the Dnieper. Vladimir stood by, and said: "Should the water carry him to the banks, push him off, until he has passed the rapids, when you may leave him!" They did as they were told. And when he had passed the rapids, the wind carried him on a sandbank, which is called after him to this day "Perun's bank."

Having decided to accept Greek Christianity, Vladimir ordered the great image of Perun, god of thunder, to be flogged, dragged by tails of horses, and thrown into the Dnieper. Then he ordered his people wholesale into the river to be baptised, and Russia was considered properly Christianized!

After that Vladimir proclaimed throughout the whole city: "Whosoever will not appear tomorrow at the river, whether he be rich or poor, or a beggar, or a workingman, will be in my disfavor." Hearing this, people came gladly and with joy, and said: "If this were not good, the Prince and boyars would not have accepted it." Next morning Vladimir went out with the priests of the Empress and of Korsun to the Dnieper, and there came together people without number. They went into the water, and stood there up to their necks, and some up to their breasts. The younger stood nearer the shore, and some held the little ones, but the grown people waded into the water. And the priests stood there and said the prayers; and there was a joy in heaven and upon earth at the sight of so many saved souls, but the devil groaned, and said: "Woe to me! I am driven away from here. I shall no longer reign in these lands!"

Then the people having been baptized, all went to their homes, and Vladimir ordered churches to be built and to place them there where

Vladimir is now called *Saint Vladimir* because of his adoption of Christianity. (Ancient banner.)

formerly stood the idols. He built the Church of St. Basil on the hill where stood the idol Perun. And he put away all his wives save Anna. Ragnilda, the proud beauty whom he had taken by force from her father, the Prince of Polotsk, retired into a nunnery. Bohemians, Czechs, Bulgarians, all his eight hundred wives, he gave in marriage to his vassals and boyars. And he began to locate churches and priests over the towns, and to lead people to baptism in all towns and villages. He sent out men to take the children of noblemen, and to put them out for book instruction; but the mothers of those children wept for them as they were not yet firm in their faith, and they wept for them as for the dead.

Up and down the water road of Kiev, Christianity was willingly received, and the priests and monks who traveled along the river made many converts in the land. But in the far corners of Russia in the forests and the swamp-lands cut off from the

Byzantine portrait. (10th cent.) Crown and costume resemble those of the Princess Anna who wed Vladimir. This history is from the 12th century *Chronicle of Nestor*.

rest of the world, heathenism still lingered, the old heathen songs were still sung, the old heathen dances danced, and the old heathen folk-tales told. Here, as in other lands, the early Christian priests were compelled to adapt new ideas to the old firmly rooted beliefs and merge the pagan festivals into holidays of the church. Thus Perun became Elijah with his chariot of fire, and Veles became St. Blaise who is still the patron of cattle. The anathemas of the church against the old pagan rites could not wholly stamp them out; Christianity and paganism continued side by side. Moreover, the rich fancy of an imaginative people adorned with various trimmings all such Bible tales as they now told and retold.

Jesus, standing on the cross, raises Adam from the mouth of
Hell, represented by the enormous yawning jaws of a beast
with a huge eye. (Russian icon, Stroganoff School.) The legend
of Jesus' descent into Hell and other stories not found in the
Bible are typically Russian, and arose from the fact that the
peasants could not read and had no actual Bibles accessible.
They, therefore, mingled the Biblical stories told them by the
priests with the most fantastic of their ancient legends, and
the entirely imaginary Descent into Hell was favored far
beyond scenes of the Resurrection and almost superseded
them. Such tales became the basis of the Russian peasant's
religion. Native Russian art reached its full flowering in icon
painting; but though these flat pictures were meant to offer
nothing lifelike and realistic enough to tempt people, as
sculptured figures did, into false worship and idolatry, the
Russians soon attributed miraculous powers to their icons.
Later ages often covered parts of these sacred pictures with
beautifully engraved metal covers to protect them and adorn
them. See the charming Lady of Vladimir, Vol. VI, p. 19.

Being unable to read,
so they never got the
actual words of the Bible,
they mingled Bible
stories with legends.
And that has been their
Christianity down to the
twentieth century, for
not until then were these
Russian peasants, always
ground down by their
rulers and the upper
classes, ever permitted
to learn to read.

But with the Princess
Anna many new ideas
beside Christianity came
from Constantinople to
Russia. She brought
with her Greek artists,
and Kiev soon blossomed
magnificently with the
red, blue and gold of
colored mosaics, flat
figures of parallel lines,
and the light airy domes
of Byzantine art. Long,
straight, Byzantine robes
became all the rage in
Russia. Trousers and
short quilted coats, once

so characteristically Russian, were given away to servants, while the
women traded off everything that had belonged to their grandmothers,
and eagerly dressed themselves in the latest Byzantine modes.

At Vladimir's death, in 1015, he was canonized as a saint, and the songs of the peasant-folk praised him as Fair Sun Vladimir, and Knight of the Sunrise Red. He became a national hero, the great King Arthur of Russia. Yar-o-slav', his son, likewise proved to be a wise far-seeing ruler. He drew up the first *Russkaya Prayda* or code of laws; he extended his territory by adding a third of Finland and conquering Galicia; and he made his capital city of Kiev the glittering jewel of all Russia, gorgeous with colored doorways, gleaming tones of enamels, and wonders of metal-work. He had his white stone wall with its golden gates around Kiev, his white-walled temples and towers, shining as white as cheese, and his splendid Sancta Sophia, gay inside with frescoes of pirouetting dancers and hunters pursuing wild beasts. Thanks to his zeal in building, the ancient Scandinavian and Slavic structures in Kiev were everywhere beaded with pearls of the finest Byzantine art, and clusters of bubble-shaped domes began to prick the sky in graceful forms of fairy-like beauty.

Icons, like those so commonly used in Constantinople, now became popular in Russia. Russian Orthodox Christians seized with enthusiasm on these flat pictures of Jesus, Our Lady, or the Saints. Some were masterpieces, painted with religious ecstasy by true artists, elated by the eternal spiritual beauty they were to embody; others were commonplace pictures, and soon there was scarcely a home without its painted image, before which candles were lit and the prayers of the family said.

Yar-o-slav', the Lawgiver, a typical Russian with long hair and beard, in characteristic fur cap. (Fresco, Church of Spassov'Nereditsa, 1199.)

"Sacred Lake," a Russian monastery built in remote regions. (N. Roerich.) For life in Kiev at this period see the ancient Russian epic, *The Word of Igor's Armament* in *My Book House*, Vol. X, p. 119.

Perched high on the cliffs overhanging the Dnieper near Kiev, began the Monastery of the Caves, where amid cavernous passages cut through the friable stone, monks in their stern ascetic attempt to triumph over earthly things, had themselves half buried, eating at decreasing intervals until the time of their death. This monastery became an object of pilgrimage, the first center of the Church in Russia.

Thus Kiev became the home of a powerful court, and the center of a great trade, with a Grand Duke as overlord, but it never became the capital of a strongly united state. On the death of Yaroslav, quarrels broke out anew. "In those days the warriors rarely walked behind the plough," cried the old bard who sang *The Word of Igor's Armament*, the oldest of Russian epics, "but they went forth to the battle."

As the leadership of Kiev passed from one prince to another and all failed to make of Russia a real united power, a scourge from the steppes appeared. The bronze-skinned Kipchaks or Cumans, a powerful Turkish tribe who had wandered over from Asia, now gazed enviously toward the fair white walls of Kiev. Laden were the monasteries of Kiev with gold and silver chalices, with costly jeweled crucifixes, and rich, religious vestments; the bodies of the slant-eyed Kipchaks swayed buoyantly in their saddles as they thought of the plunder ahead. Mercilessly, they harried the lands of the Lower Dnieper; often they trapped Russian armies, surrounded them on all sides, and destroyed the southern trade. In vain did a grandson of Yaroslav call on the princes of Kiev to combine against the enemy.

"Sadness spread over the Russian land and a heavy gloom, yet the princes still fostered discord among themselves, while the pagans victoriously overran the land!"

Steadily Kiev declined in greatness and in glory, till at length in 1169, a certain northern prince, named Andrew Bo'go-ly'u-bov, disgusted with quarreling princes who permitted the Kipchaks to ravage, stormed and destroyed the gay and magnificent Mother of Russian cities, and moved the Russian capital to Vladimir on the Volga.

Andrew Bo'go-ly'u-bov, Prince of Suzdal, and his boyars lead their mounted warriors against the capital city of Kiev. (Icon, Novgorod.)

A log church of the tenth century, purely Russian in design, a jumble of unusual forms with rectangular additions and odd-shaped towers to make a magnificent structure.

Russia now fell apart, and in place of one distinct center of leadership, three began to appear. In the north was the republic of Novgorod; on the Volga, the principality of Vlad'-i-mir-Suz-dal'; in the west, the duchy of Galicia. Novgorod, left to itself during the time that Kiev had been supreme in the land, had wrested from Yaroslav a charter of self-government, and the merchants of Novgorod, journeying far and wide into the cold, gray Baltic, had made trade the life of the city, exchanging ermines and sables, tallow, hides, hemp, cloth, and wines with the rich Germanic cities of the Hanseatic League.

A city so rich, so proud, and independent as Novgorod, soon developed an art and architecture of its own, losing Byzantine influence more quickly than did Kiev. In this land of forests, churches were built of wood, and as the peasant-carpenters, building in untaught freedom, sought to make more magnificent structures, they jumbled all sorts of shapes into a rambling mass, octagonal central towers, rectangular additions, tall conical spires, and lastly instead of the low flat dome of the Byzantines, an onion-shaped dome pricking upward to shed the snow down its sides. Thus Russia found herself with a characteristic architecture, and the Russian onion-shaped dome.

Moreover, in the peat bogs and forests of Vladimir-Suzdal, where lay the new Russian capital, new impulse was given to art. The Cathedral of the Assumption at Vladimir, built in a combination of Byzantine and Lombard style, showed all the Germanic love for grotesque decoration, monstrous gargoyles and griffins fighting with marvelous beasts. True, the Russian churchmen did not approve of these figures, but the Slavs in their childishness, liked them, and they began to appear on every important building now rising up in the land. Fabulous monsters enmeshed with interlacing bands appeared not only in carvings but in the illuminated manuscripts made in the Russian monasteries, and became in time characteristic of a national Russian art.

Cathedral of St. Di-mi'tri in Vladimir, built about 1194, a striking edifice of white sandstone with helmet-shaped dome. Grotesque decoration appears carved on the upper walls. See Vol. VI, p. 28.

Russian sledges traveled over wide snow-clad steppes in a land almost unknown to Europe. Shut in by forests, swamps, and savage Turkish tribes, Russia knew nothing of Western Europe. Her only access westward was through Poland, and since Poland was Roman Catholic and Russia, Greek Catholic, the two countries feared each other. Poland would let in no knowledge from the West to stir the dormant consciousness of Russia and wake this great sleeping giant just at her back door.

But as Russia began to grow more race-conscious and truly Russian, she also began to grow more withdrawn into herself, more exclusive of foreigners and shut off from the world. The Greek Catholic clergy inculcated in their followers undying hatred of those who had their Christianity from Rome, and to guard against Roman Catholicism, they inflicted severe punishment upon Russians who crossed the frontier.

Sufficient to herself alone, with no schools, no knowledge, no science to offset the superstitions of her primitive, fanciful peasants, she was to sleep for centuries generally unprogressive. Her peasants tilled the soil under the same old conditions, a good-natured, kindly people, little changed by Christianity and knowing nothing whatever of what went on in the world. Indeed, the Russians were better acquainted with Tartars, Turks and other peoples of the East than with the Germans or French. To them Western Europe scarcely existed at all. Shut in by forests, swamps, and swarming savage tribes, Russia had only Poland through which she might reach Europe.

But though Poland, too, was Slavic, the duke, who in ancient times had gathered the Poles together and made them into a nation, had saved Polish independence from the incursion of German neighbors by accepting Christianity, together with a Christian bride, from the Roman Church of the West. Thus, the Poles were Roman Christians, while their Russian cousins were so strictly Orthodox Greek. As Poland grew in power, she heartily feared that great Russia that covered so vast an expanse there at her own back door. Russia was fast asleep, a great, sprawling, ignorant giant, and Poland wished no knowledge to come from Western Europe to wake that huge Colossus and stir him to sudden consciousness of his own tremendous power. Wrapped in complete seclusion, Russia remained asleep.

A marriage in Russia with the ceremony of the Greek Catholic Church, the religion of this vast land. (After Racinet.) Russia faced east toward Byzantium and Asia, rather than west toward Europe.

The Ravaging of Russia

It was in the year 1236 that the Golden Horde started westward toward Russia and Europe. Moving slowly at first, driving huge herds before them, followed by thousands of tent-wagons, the great mass of Mongol invaders passed from the highlands of Asia into the Siberian steppes.

In the wide pasture-lands, between the Ural Mountains and the Volga River, they came upon the nomad Kipchaks; and these savage, warlike tribes, remembering the coming of the Mongols fifteen years before and the fate that lay in store for them if they could not check their advance, battled fiercely for their homes; but one and all they were broken before the onrush of the Mongols. Wherever the Golden Horde passed, no living thing was left; there was only a trail of corpses.

Interior scene from Racinet. Simple, kindly, emotionally religious, barbaric in their fondness for brilliant color and decoration, the Russians had developed a distinct civilization suited to their nature.

Realizing, at last, the uselessness of resistance, many of the Kipchak tribes joined with the Mongol invaders, determined to profit at least by the conquests of their foes. Thus, everywhere victorious, the horde pushed on to the northward into Greater Bulgaria. Here, however, the open steppes gave place to wide stretches of forest, and it became difficult for horsemen to keep together.

Bulgarian noble and wife in beautifully embroidered robes. (Wall painting, Church of Boiana, Sofia, 1259.) The Bulgarians were a Finnish-Turkish people who settled in the Balkans and intermarried with the ancient Slavs and the Byzantines. See Vol. VI, pp. 11-12.

The Bulgarians told Su-bo-tai that farther north the trees grew thicker still until there was no open country. A few fishermen and hunters, they said, were the only inhabitants of that land other than great packs of wolves and ferocious roaming bears; and the only means of getting from place to place was on the rivers that threaded their way through the still depths of the forest. Clearly, this was no land for a swift-riding Mongol horde; and Subotai and Batu turned west into Russia.

All Russia, prince as well as peasant, was aghast at the enormous army of inhuman horsemen that burst suddenly down upon them. It seemed as though a whole people were moving from one part of the world to another. But despite their tremendous numbers, the success of the Mongol armies was due to military knowledge rather than to

THE LANDS OF RUSSIA BEFORE THE MONGOL CONQUEST, A.D. 1250

mass attack. Subotai and his generals knew in advance the politics and internal feuds of Russia; they knew all about the character of the land they were invading; what booty and supplies they would find; and the full strength of the forces that would be sent to oppose them.

Ravishing with fire and sword, the invading host rode northward, leaving Kiev unharmed and aiming to strike at Vladimir. Behind them, as far as the Volga, there stretched stark desolation, blackened crops, and leveled villages, heaped with the bodies of the slain. Ri-a-zan' was the first town which attempted to bar their progress.

Subotai surrounded the city and rode forth to survey its defences. Then he set part of the horde to constructing siege engines and catapults, and the rest to building a wall completely around the town. "There must be no escape for the conquered, once the city is taken," he said and when all preparations were made, he ordered his men to attack with scaling ladders and battering rams. The Russians resisted stoutly. Again and again the Mongols found themselves driven back, but they came on in ever-fresh numbers while the ranks of the defenders grew ever more weary and thin. Moreover, the Mongols shot flaming arrows and great stones over the walls, so that many houses collapsed and many more took fire. Confusion spread through the city. The defenders wavered at last and the Mongols, in one grand rush, burst through breaches in the weakened walls. Riazan was taken! The first Russian city had fallen!

There followed a scene of fire, looting, and wanton slaughter such as only the Mongols could order. Men, women, and children died amid horrid tortures. The Golden Horde was mad with the lust of slaying and burning, nor could any of the conquered escape because of the wall which the Mongols had built surrounding their own walls.

Aroused by this frightful destruction, Yuri II, Grand Prince of Vladimir, hastened north to raise a new army. But the Golden Horde reached the capital before he could return and erected overnight that hideous wooden wall which proclaimed that in Vladimir, too, not one was to escape. At daybreak, the battle began; by mid-day the city was taken. The Russians fought stubbornly to kill all the Mongols they could before they themselves were slain, but the horde crushed all before it and Vladimir soon burned in one vast conflagration.

Yuri's princess with her relatives, many of the people, the clergy, and the bishop took refuge in Vladimir Cathedral. The smoke of the city's burning and shouts of the on-coming Mongols pierced the cathedral walls and foretold the coming of the savages. Soon they forced the door, seized the gold and silver church vessels, and cut down everyone who did not hide in the galleries. Then they brought brushwood and timber, and set the cathedral afire. Smoke rose up in columns. The roar of the burning building and the cruel shouts of the conquerors mingled with the wails, the shrieks, and prayers of the dying.

The horrors of Riazan were repeated in Vladimir. Young women, and strong laborers were led away as captives; but the sick, the weak, and the aged were slaughtered on the spot. Ruins alone remained; not a groan or a cry was heard, for Vladimir's people were dead.

And now these savage invaders set out to find Grand Prince Yuri, and as they passed up the Volga, every town was destroyed. They came upon Yuri in the marsh country and in a massacre slew him.

Swiftly then they swooped down on one Russian city after another. All suffered the horrors of conquest until there remained in the north, only Novgorod, the greatest of Russian cities. The Mongols advanced on her confidently. But long, weary stretches of bog and the tangled forests of Northern Russia wearied their horses and hampered their movements. At last they were forced to turn back, and Novgorod was saved.

Loaded down with countless treasures, urging on long lines of captives, the Horde now moved swiftly southeastward to the pasturelands of the black-earth region of Southern Russia. Batu then established himself on the banks of the Volga River where he built the city of Sa-rai' to be his residence and capital. For three long years all Russia had been laid waste by the Mongols. And now just across the Dnieper, Batu saw with covetous eyes the beauty and wealth of Kiev.

View from a boyar's palace in Novgorod, towers of the city showing through the window. (N. Roerich.)

Across the frozen Dnieper, the Mongol horde advanced relentlessly upon the beautiful city of Kiev.

As soon as the Dnieper was frozen, he gave his orders and struck. Clouds of savage riders in gold and black lacquered leather, clattered across the ice. From the walls of Kiev, the people saw column after column of horsemen approaching; they heard the shriek of wheels, the neighing of countless horses, and the querulous grunts of the camels. Watching the Mongols enclose them with the customary, fateful wall, they waited for the attack, knowing that no help could save them.

Soon after, heavy battering-rams pounded the walls day and night; but so bravely did the Russians fight that for days they held back the foe. The end, however, was certain. Over the crumbling walls the Mongols poured into Kiev. From houses and public buildings the Russians hurled weapons upon them; men, women and children strove at least to die fighting. The harder they fought, however, the more destructive grew the Mongols. All buildings were looted and burned. Of the people of Kiev, scarcely one survived the slaughter; and of the queen-city, herself, nothing save ruins remained.

The whole of Russia was now subdued. There were no more treasures there, to overflow the great carved chests in the tent-wagons of the Mongols; but off to the west were still lands that had not bowed the head to the all-conquering Golden Horde. Moreover, Batu learned that the kings of those western lands were mustering great armies against him. He would advance and strike before his foes could unite.

European Conquests

Dividing his forces, Batu sent half under Kaidu and Baidur into Poland, while he with Subotai marched over the Carpathian Mountains into the plains of Hungary. Near the city of Cra'cow, his general, met the army of Bo-le-slav' IV, King of Poland; but though the Poles fought bravely, they were defeated with great loss. Those who escaped, took refuge in forests and swamps; and the Mongol horde rode on, burning the deserted Cracow and laying waste the land.

Henry the Pious, Duke of Silesia, another Slavic country, summoned the knights of Western Europe to stay the advance of the savages; but the knights of Western Europe were too busy fighting each other; only a few hundred Teutonic Knights of Germany, with cumbersome mail and great, heavy broadswords, answered Duke Henry's call.

Kings, clergy, and nobles of Poland at the time of the Mongol invasion. (Racinet.) Staunch adherents of the Roman Catholic Church, the Poles disdained their fellow-Slavs in Russia who were Greek Catholics, and acted as a barrier state to close communication and keep out Western knowledge.

The Mongols far out-numbered the forces of the Silesians, but Henry scorning shelter behind the city walls, faced them in the open, beside the river Keiss. Again and again Henry charged, he and his chosen knights everywhere fighting like madmen, slashing with their great

Mongol under the feet of Duke Henry II of Silesia who died resisting the slaying, devastating Horde. (Tomb at Breslau.)

broadswords, wrecking havoc in Mongol ranks. But for every Mongol that fell, a dozen came up from behind. There was no end to their numbers. Moreover, wherever the battle chanced to rage most furiously, there rose the nine white yak-tails, the terrible Mongol standard, and around it, the choking fumes of some foul-smelling incense which the standard bearers burned. Gasping, unable to breathe, the Silesians were forced to fall back. To their horrified senses, the standard seemed a hideous head framed in waving masses of hair. They were not fighting men! They were fighting the devil himself!

Many, unnerved by fear, turned in a panic and fled. The rest fought blindly and fell. The Teutonic Knights died to a man! The Silesian leaders went down till only Duke Henry was left. Trying to flee from the field, Henry was borne down at last and slain by the sheer weight of numbers. Then the Mongols cut off his head, and, sticking it on a spear, they bore it back in triumph to present to Kaidu and Baidur. Going over the blood-soaked ground, the men of the horde cut an ear from each of their dead foemen, and filling nine large sacks with these grim trophies of victory, they sent them to Batu Khan.

Kaidu and Baidur then swept on through Silesia, and before Duke Henry's head, borne transfixed on its spear, the people of Silesia fled to the shelter of caves or the dim recesses of forests, leaving behind them only the burned remnants of houses and crops. The Mongols, finding nothing further to plunder, turned southward into Bohemia.

King Wen'ces-laus, leader against the Mongols, and patron saint of Bohemia, now Czecho-Slovakia. (A 14th century statue at Prague.)

Now Wen'ces-laus, King of Bohemia, had had a longer time than either Bo-le-slav' or Duke Henry in which to marshal his forces, and he awaited the Mongols with a large and well disciplined army, larger even than the Mongol horde. If he could have forced his enemies into a pitched battle he might have overwhelmed them. But the wary Mongol generals had no intention of fighting with a superior force. They split into several divisions, and overran Bohemia, ravaging the land, swooping down on unprotected villages, burning the monasteries, slaughtering every inhabitant, and making off on their swift little desert ponies before the slow foot-men of Wenceslaus could arrive.

Affairs were going thus when a messenger came from Batu bidding the Mongol generals make all speed to rejoin the Golden Horde. Tricking King Wenceslaus into marching northward, the Mongols marched off to the south. In Hungary, they found that Batu, having sent insulting messages to Bela, the king of the land, had met with powerful resistance. Preparing to defend his country at his chief city, Pesth, on the Danube, Bela had gathered together a hundred thousand warriors, Hungarians, Magyars, Croats, French Templars and German knights.

What was now to be done? The Hungarians were too strong to be attacked openly. The Mongols must use their old tricks,—pretend flight and tempt the Hungarians to leave their protecting walls. Slowly, at a hand pace, the Mongols retreated from Pesth. The baggage they left behind, lured their foe from the walls, and sight of the retiring Mongols, always just out of reach, led the Hungarians on. Warily creeping eastward, hunter and hunted proceeded till they came to the plain of Mohi beside the river Theiss. A stone bridge spanned the river, and the Mongols hastening their steps, crossed to the farther bank before the darkness fell. Ostentatiously, they made camp, while their adversaries, not daring to attempt a crossing by night, camped on the other side. When everything was quiet, Batu sent Subotai to re-cross the river secretly by a ford farther up the stream, and at dawn he set up at the bridge-head seven great catapults and gave the order to charge. Back over the narrow bridge raced the Mongol horde with thundering hoofs and whistling arrows. A thousand bold Hungarians, guarding the end of the bridge, were swept away like chaff. The play of the great catapults prevented other troops from coming, and in a very few minutes the bulk of the Mongol army was in the Hungarian camp.

Too weak to attack Pesth, the Mongols feign retreat to draw the Hungarians from behind its walls.

Attack on a Hungarian city in the seventeenth century. The city itself was undoubtedly much the same at the time of the Mongol attack. (Engraved gun stock, Magyar Museum, Budapest.)

Bela and his knights fought like heroes. Hour after hour, they fought. But at midday, Subotai came swiftly up from behind and made an attack from the rear. Finding themselves surrounded, the Hungarians fought valiantly on till they could endure no more. Then fleeing, panic-stricken through a breach in the Mongol ranks, they raced out over the country pursued by their swifter foes.

Advancing again on Pesth, Batu and the Golden Horde now found no defenders there, and they burned the city to the ground. King Bela escaped from the battle, thanks to the swiftness of his horse, and after wandering miserably about his ruined country, he came at last to Moravia and the monastery where Boleslav of Poland had found a refuge, and there, he, too, remained.

Western Europe, so long unprepared and heedless of its danger, now lived in the hideous shadow of this terrifying race from the East, who moved with the swiftness of a storm, turned fertile countries to deserts, and populous cities to tombs. Frederick II of Germany, roused to the point of wishing to unite with his Christian enemies against the invading Mongols, offered a truce to his foe, Pope Gregory IX, with whom he was waging a war for supremacy of the West. But Gregory refused, and Frederick as vainly sought aid from Henry III of England.

"If the Tartars should penetrate into Germany," he said, "and meet no opposition, the rest of the world will feel the suddenly coming tempest. They confidently hope to destroy the rest of the human race!"

Batu pushed over the Danube, ravaging and slaying. The slow-moving King of Bohemia again tried to block his path, but Batu avoided him easily. West, ever west, rode the Mongols, seeking new nations to spoil. But now the land grew mountainous. The space-loving Mongols felt stifled, cut off among narrow valleys and limited mountain-pastures. Barred by the lofty Alps, they turned south to the Adriatic, sacking every city save Ra-gu'sa along the Dalmatian Coast.

What Batu might have done next, cannot even be guessed, but just at this time, word came that Ogotai Khan was dead. Batu and the royal princes must return to Asia to choose a new Khan at once. In one last orgy of cruelty, Batu gathered together all his Hungarian captives and slew them, both male and female. Then, laden with the rich spoils of twenty once-prosperous nations, back through prostrate Hungary, through desolate, ravished Russia, staggered the Golden Horde.

Ku-yuk', the son of Ogotai, was chosen the new Khan and crowned with elaborate ceremony according to Mongol custom. As he came forth from his tent to the sound of martial music, all the people bowed before him, rhythmically inclining staffs having fluffs of red wool at their tops. Then journeying three or four miles, the crowd assembled again on a plain between sacred mountains. While the multitude faced the south, a certain number making continual prayers and kneeling on their knees went farther and farther southward. Then all returned to a tent lined inside with rich brocade and supported by wooden pillars covered with plates of gold. There they placed Kuyuk on his throne.

Staunch Hungarian horsemen defend their lands from invaders. (Engraved gun stock, Budapest.)

Russian dukes are forced to submit to the Mongol Khans, and are allowed to govern for their masters.

Immediately after this ceremony, Batu returned to Russia, the country he liked best. For the lands of Western Europe, the Mongols had no liking; they were too cramped and narrow to suit a nomad people; Poland, Hungary, and Bohemia, were therefore spared further destruction; and Sa-rai', on the Volga River, in the midst of the wide-stretching steppes, became Batu's capital city, with Russia as his domain. Here the Mongol ruled in splendor. "This Batu," reported a friar who visited his court, "carries himself very stately and magnificently, having porters and all officers after the manner of the Emperor, and sits in a lofty seat together with one of his wives. The rest, namely, his brothers and sons, and other great personages, sit underneath him in the center upon a bench, and others sit down upon the ground behind him. He is most cruel in fight and exceedingly crafty in war."

Such was the imperious manner of the Mongol Khans who held Russia in bondage for the next three hundred years. Slowly the real Russia, the Russia of the Slavs, retreated to the swamplands surrounding Moscow, which stood on a hill above the river Moskwa. Here Prince Yuri Long Arm had set up a country estate in the depths of primeval pinewoods. On the hill called the Kremlin he had built a stout oaken wall to enclose both the wooden lodge where he feasted his friends and the little wooden settlement around the old church of St. Savior of the Pines. Constantly more and more Russians came flocking to this fortress, and in time the Metropolitan of Vladimir, the highest dignitary of the Russian Church, moved to the Kremlin, thus making Moscow the center of Russian Christianity. So the Kremlin grew ever more splendid until it was no longer a simple wooden fortress but a city with churches and palaces, a fairy town of white buildings, gilded turrets and onionshaped domes enclosed within a white wall.

And as Moscow grew, her rulers kept gaining more land and more power. Though they served the Mongols as tax collectors, they finally grew so powerful that they made themselves hereditary grand dukes. Then in 1547 Grand Duke Ivan IV did what his forebears had never dared to do. Heretofore, the title Czar had been used only by the Mongol Khans, but Ivan had himself crowned as Czar of all Russia, thus becoming the first Russian Czar, and so weakening the waning power of the Mongols that they began to withdraw from Russia.

Ivan the Terrible this Czar was called. For, though he was well-educated and a great admirer of Western culture, he had within him a strong strain of cruelty amounting almost to madness at times,

Moscow, rising around the fortress of the Kremlin, became the new center of conquered Slavic Russia.

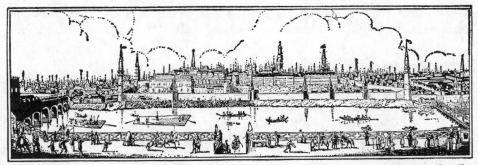

Ancient engraving of the Kremlin, Moscow, with its many bulbous-domed spires and turreted walls.

so he not only killed the son he loved in a fit of fury, but also slew thousands of the people of Novgorod whom he suspected of plotting rebellion against him. Yet he succeeded in uniting Russia and holding it together. Moreover, he started Russia's advance to the east by his conquests in Siberia, an eastward march which was to continue through the centuries until Russia reached the Pacific, finally owning far more land in Asia than in Europe and becoming in truth a huge colossus overpowering in size. Ivan also tried to spread out to the west and to import skilled workmen from Germany to teach his people the trades and crafts of Western Europe, but in both these attempts he was balked by his neighbors, the King of Poland and the Emperor Charles V of Germany, who had no wish to see Russia advance any further in their direction.

Like the Mongol Khans, Ivan was an absolute ruler, an autocrat whose will was law. Batu had held that since he had conquered Russia the land belonged to him alone and all the Khans after him had held as firmly to that idea. All lands, all property were theirs, solely theirs. There was no private ownership of anything in Russia. If Russians were permitted to remain on the land and work it, that did not make the farms their own, nor were they permitted to call themselves free men. Every Russian could be called upon at any time for any kind of service the Khan required; and each year, in return for the privilege of working the land, one-tenth of the harvest and one-tenth of every kind of increase must be given to the master.

Three centuries of absolute obedience to the Mongol master formed a habit of thought slow to change in the Russian people. No man, woman, or child had any rights of his own; all must submit to the state, whether represented in the person of Khan or Czar. The horse or ox with which the poor peasant plowed his meager land could be taken instantly from the furrow by any officer or messenger of the Khan; it belonged not to the peasant but to the Khan or Czar.

Through generation after generation, the good-natured, slow-thinking Slav, with almost no contact with Europe grew ever more accustomed to the ancient law of the Mongol, which the Russian Czars took over, the law of unquestioning obedience, with no rights for individuals, and the head of the government an absolute autocratic master.

Typically Russian in architecture was the famous old Pak-rov-sky' Cathedral in the Red Square beside the Kremlin. (Old engraving.)

IV

The Mongol Conquest of Persia

(1252–1355 A.D.)

Travelers to the Mongols

Returning now to the days when Batu was ruling Russia, we find all the kings of Western Europe fearing lest this savage Mongol should invade their lands again. So in 1245 Pope Innocent IV, spurred by this haunting dread, dispatched to Batu on the Volga two gray-frocked Franciscan friars with letters urging the Mongols to accept the teachings of Jesus and to acknowledge the authority of Rome.

Great were the hardships suffered by these two dauntless friars, the fat and venerable Friar John and Monk Benedict, his companion. Arrived at the golden court of Sa-rai' on the Volga, they were sent forthwith to present their letters to the great Kha Khan. Suffering from cold and with his body tightly bandaged to withstand the racking weariness of constant riding on horseback, Friar John was at times so ill he could scarcely sit his horse; often he made his bed on a bare white mound of snow. And when he reached Ka'-ra-ko'rum, the only result of his journey was to receive from the Kha Khan Ku-yuk' a lordly message to the Pope: "We the Oceanic Khan of the entire great people of the earth: our order. This is an order sent to the Great Pope. If you act according to your own words, you, who are the Great Pope, with the Kings, will come in person to render homage, and we will then have you learn our orders."

Upon his return Friar John was made an archbishop, but the hardships of his long journey to the Mongol capital had so weakened him, that he soon died.

The seal of Kuyuk Khan, which speaks of the Mongol lord as "the Oceanic Khan of the entire great people of the earth."

Miniature showing how the Persians would have pictured Sar-tach', Batu, or other Khans. (Brit. Mus.)

In the year 1253, King Louis IX of France, known as St. Louis for his piety, sent another Christian traveler to the camps of the Mongol hordes. St. Louis had heard that Sar-tach', son of Batu the Splendid, had become a Christian, and he was convinced that if Sartach was taught his full duty to the Pope, Western Europe would suffer no more from invasions by Mongol savages. Accordingly, he entrusted William of Rubrick, a burly, Franciscan friar, with the delicate task of instructing Sartach in his Christian duties and converting his pagan horde.

Friar William set out from France to ride on this dangerous mission, half convinced before he started, that he would be tortured to death. For two months, he and his comrade, Friar Bartholomew of Cremona, journeyed through Southern Russia, seeing not a single city but only the tombs of the Kipchaks. Coming at last upon Sartach in a moving city of tents, William went before him in the splendid garments of the Catholic Church, chanting *Salva Regina* and accompanied by a man waving a fragrant censer. He found the Mongols, however, interested, not in his doctrines but in the rich embroidery which adorned his robes, making him stand to one side that they might the better observe him.

Sartach would decide nothing; he sent William to Batu, his father; and Batu, sitting with one of his wives high up on a golden seat at the top of a flight of three steps, would likewise make no decision. Ordering that William be provided with a sheep-skin gown and felt foot-socks, boots, and a hood of skin, Batu sent him off in charge of a wealthy Mongol to Man-gu, the new Kha Khan in Karakorum.

"Of hunger and thirst, cold and weariness, there was no end," said the friar; but arriving at the desert city, he saw a house with a cross close to the tents of Mangu, and, supposing he had at last found a Christian Church, Friar William greatly rejoiced. To his keen disappointment, however, though he found in this building an altar bedecked with cloth of gold and images of the Savior, the Virgin, St. John and two angels, he learned that it was a church of that Nestorian Sect which was so despised at Rome, because it held that Mary was not the mother of God but simply a human being. This, in William's opinion, was no Christian Church at all. And to add to his disappointment, when he entered the huge palace-hall, past the silver tree which spouted wine and mare's milk, he found that the great Kha Khan would not let him remain to convert the Mongols to his faith. Returning to France, he reported to Louis hopelessly: "It seems useless to me that another religious man like myself be sent or friar-preacher go to the land of the Mongols."

Man-gu, the new Khan, grandson of Genghis, with his wives and a son. (From a Persian miniature.)

The Attack Upon Persia

Mongol unity was breaking. Jealousy and discontent stirred among the nobles, and rival claims between the descendants of Jagatai and Ogotai, sons of Genghis, were threatening sudden rebellion. The wise and wrinkled graybeards among the Kha Khan's counselors advised a new war of conquest.

War, then, it must be; and the summons went forth for the assembling of a mighty army of conquest. Discord was forgotten, and the wild

Peaceful camp scene in the ancient land of Persia, showing women milking and spinning beside their tents. (Miniature, British Museum.)

Mongol spirits soared at the thought of more lands to ravage, more men to trample and overcome. Mangu's brother, Hu-la-gu', was given command of the host, with instructions to march westward and destroy that sinister secret order known as the Assassins, whose shadow lay like a vulture over the Mohammedan world. Then he was to take Bagdad, overthrow the Caliph, and any princes living off beyond Persia. Little difference who was destroyed so long as the Mongol devils were fighting.

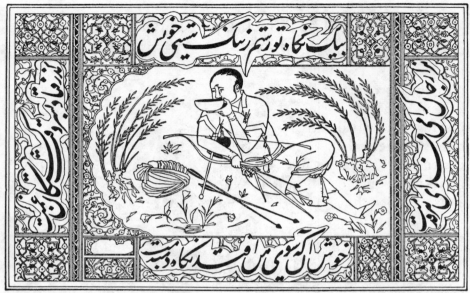

Hulagu, commander of the Mongol horde, takes his ease in Ki-an-i-gul'. (Persian MS. Brit. Mus.)

It was in February, 1254, that Hulagu's vast horde was launched against Western Asia. Over snowy ranges and larch-clad hills, over dreary deserts, broad rivers, and fertile valleys marched the Mongols until they came to the beautiful land of Ki-an-i-gul', the Mine of Roses, near Samarkand. Here they rested; and for forty days and nights, Hulagu feasted in a magnificent, silken tent. From here he sent lordly messages to the princes of Western Asia. "We have come," he said, "to destroy the heretics. If you come in person with your troops, you shall be rewarded. If you hesitate, I will, with the help of God, after I have destroyed this people, return and treat you the same way."

Knowing well that they could not withstand the fierce onslaught of the wiry Mongol horsemen, numbers of lesser chiefs and lordlings obeyed this haughty command. Many appeared before Hulagu with their armed warriors, bearing gifts, the richest their treasure-houses could produce. Two rulers, however, treated the Mongol's message with silent contempt. These were the Grand Prior of the Assassins, and the Caliph of Bagdad, spiritual head of all Mohammedans.

Bagdad, Glittering City of Caliphs

Great had grown the power of the Mohammedans. Fired by a fanatical zeal to win the world to Islam, the Arabs had conquered Syria, Palestine, Egypt, Africa, Persia and part of Spain in the century after Mohammed. At first Damascus was the capital of this enormous Mohammedan Empire, but when A'bu-Ab-bas' overthrew the Om-mi'ad Caliphs and founded the Ab-bas'side line a new capital was established. On the banks of the Tigris River, on the site of a summer park of the Sassanian kings of Persia, there arose golden Bagdad, gorgeous and magnificent. Caliph Man-sur', brother and successor of Abu-Abbas, laid the

first brick with his own hand, declaring in ringing tones: "In the name of the Lord! Praise belongeth unto Him and the earth is His: He causeth such of his servants as He pleaseth to inherit the same. Success attend the pious! Now, with the blessing of the Lord, build on!"

A perfect circle, four miles in circumference, was Mansur's beautiful city and it was surrounded by three walls. In the very center stood the Caliph's Palace of the Green Dome; nearby was the Great Mosque, and within the surrounding area were the treasury and government buildings where the Caliph received ambassadors, governors, dervishes, poets and philosophers.

Vivid color, intricate ornamentation, and flowering gardens, made Bagdad beautiful and gorgeous. (Brit. Mus.)

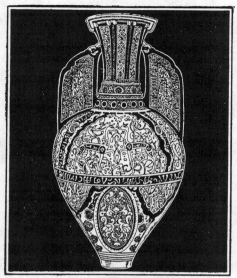

Exquisite pottery vase of blue and gold lustre, with an intricate Arabian design of formal flowers and geometric figures. (Alhambra, Spain.)

Every department of government had its office here; and here, too, were the palaces of the ladies of the harem. No one save the Caliph was permitted to ride on horseback within these sacred precincts in the very center of the city.

Beyond the inner wall was the bazaar-and-merchant-quarter. The Koran, "the Book to be Read," praised handwork as pleasing to God, and many were the Arabs who prided themselves on skillful craftsmanship. Within this quarter, were makers of enamel and drawn glass, creators of marvelous jewelry, of gold and silver vases, pottery makers and weavers, whose craft was most important, since cloth of glowing color was always in great demand for the rich, voluminous robes worn by Orientals, and the dwellings of the wealthy were hung with brocades and tapestries embroidered in figures of gold.

Equally prized with the textiles were the rich oriental carpets, the knotting of which had started among the wandering herdsmen who drove their flocks through the wilderness and slept on the bare ground at night. Loving the carpet of blossoms that covered the plains each spring, these humble people had wished to preserve the color and joy of that season;

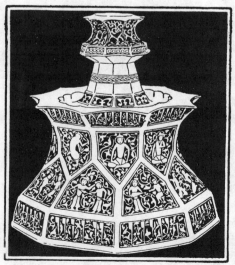

Arabic candlestick with silver inlay. (Tehran.)

and so they adorned with figures of flowers, knotted in bright-colored thread, the miserable mats which carpeted their dingy black camel-hair tents. Feeling the very same longing that moved the heart of the nomad, a Sassanian king of Persia, the mighty Chos-roes' I, in his great White Palace at Ctes'i-phon, ordered woven a *winter* carpet to make him forget in the flowerless time the absence of his garden. During the cold winter months, he gave gay garden parties on this rich Oriental carpet whose patterns showed beds of spring blossoms, foliage, murmuring brooks, and winding paths like a garden. The art of making fine carpets thus had royal approval and gradually improved; new designs were invented and new colors added until often there were from ten to twenty different hues, and during the Bagdad Caliphate, Persian carpets became true miracles of craftsmanship.

Trade routes from the corners of the world crossed at Bagdad. From the Scandinavian countries came amber, furs, and wax to be exchanged for the precious wares of the East. Long caravans of camels, laden with gold and silver, spices, silk, and rhubarb, and wearing embroidered halters with strings of blue beads round their necks to ward off evil, came swaying into town, having threaded the long, dusty road from China.

Persian painting showing an early rug with geometric figures instead of floral designs. (Vever Collection.)

Over the barrier ranges of the snow-clad Him-a'la-yas, from India and
the isles of the distant Indian Ocean were borne rich loads of cinnamon,
pearls, and precious stones. From Africa came slaves, ivory, and gold-
dust. And all this stream of trade flowed into the laps of the caliphs
till they lived in a golden haze of luxury and splendor, fabulously
wealthy, while Bagdad, their city of gardens, rose as gorgeous and brilliant as dreams from the *Arabian Nights*. Sumptuous palaces of fretted
gold and colored stucco or faience, mosques with gilded domes and
slender minarets, and long lines of arcaded buildings sprang up as if by
enchantment. Gardens of flowers appeared with fountains, secret pa-
vilions and charming hidden retreats; and the costly houses of nobles,
artificially heated in winter, were cooled in the summer months by
snow from the mountain-
tops, brought down by
relays of slaves.

Surrounded by the luxury of wealth, the Caliph holds
daily audience in his palace garden. (Persian miniature.)

Best known of the Bagdad
caliphs, Ha-roun'al Ra-schid',
or Aaron the Upright, fa-
mous scholar and poet, was the
prince glorified of legend in
the opulent, glamorous tales of
that great collection of Arabian literature called *A Thousand and One Nights*. He lived
in a glittering palace and to
his court came all the learned
men of the Empire—poets,
musicians, judges, grammari-
ans, and scribes. Story-tellers
said that he loved to disguise
himself and wander among
his people on the streets
of Bagdad at night. Here
he had strange adventures,

rewarding most unexpectedly many an honest citizen who had done some worthy deed. So great and powerful was he that he knew himself the equal of Byzantine and Frank, and from "Bagdad's shrines of fretted gold, with high-walled gardens, green and old," he sent gifts to Charlemagne, rare perfumes, spices and silks, ivory chess-men and books, and that beast so strange to the Franks, a royal elephant.

Bagdad was the capital of a wonderful civilization, rich in knowledge and learning, in enterprise and ability. The quick, alert mind of the Arab, emerging from the long sleep of centuries in the desert, seized the ancient learning of the Persians and as the sun-bronzed tribesmen intermingled and married with the fair-haired, blue-eyed Persians whose culture and civilization stretched so far into the past, their own capacities blossomed, and they carried on the learning of this conquered land. Great universities rose throughout the Arabic world, when Europe, still grossly ignorant, had but a few monastic schools. In Persia and Spain, literature began. Arabic scholars studied astronomy and geography, and contributed algebra to mathematics. From India, they brought Arabic notation, while European school boys were still obliged to struggle with clumsy Roman numerals. In agriculture, they took particular delight, developing with patience and years of devoted care, the vegetables, fruits, and gorgeous flowers which graced their lovely gardens.

Court scene at the height of Arabic power. The men below the throne are playing chess. (Persian miniature.)

خوش آن كره كه كره آرویجی   كه باش دجه یوسف زنهب كی

كمره جا بهمن كما كردند   بقد راب رودرجا كرانه

محت آمدر سعادلمن مری   سوی آب جوان زنر دیی

بنارتی چا ان خر سیا   فرواد بخت دلواكب بیا

An incident from the Old Testament of the Jews;
Persian painting of Joseph being drawn up from the pit.
The Koran, the Mohammedans' Book of Books, contained many Old Testament stories, because Mohammed
took his religious ideas from the teachings of Moses,
Zoroaster, and Jesus, hoping that all religions would
join his new faith. See Vol. V, Chapter IV, pp. 124, 128.

"He who plants," runs an Arabic saying, "he who sows, he who makes the earth bring forth food suited to man and beast performs an oblation of which account will be kept in heaven." The Arabs first brought into Europe the jasmine, double-rose and camellia. From India they introduced rice, sugar cane and oranges; from Egypt, papyrus and cassia; and it was from them that Europe learned to grow oranges, hemp, apricots, lemons, asparagus, artichokes, and kidney beans.

In art, the Arabs possessed an innate feeling for grace and delicacy of line. The Koran forbade the representation of the human figure, and although this law was not always strictly obeyed in Persia, where Zo'ro-as'tri-an-ism and ancient Persian fire-worship more stubbornly resisted Mohammedan belief and kept a greater degree of mental independence than in other lands conquered by Arabs, no caliph dared flaunt in public the works of sculptors and painters, portraying men or beasts, much as he might admire them. But adapting the art of Byzantium, Persia, and India, the Arabs formed beautiful buildings with domes and graceful pinnacles, ceilings of drooping stalactites, colored horse-shoe arches, geometric scrolls, and verses of the Koran in decorative script.

Moreover, these vigorous tribesmen were great explorers and travelers; and had visited India and China both overland and by water through the Red Sea and Persian Gulf, long before Europe had any knowledge whatever of these distant lands. They were master seamen before the time of Mohammed, and by 300 A.D. had established a trading post at Canton in far off China. Their ships furrowed paths over unknown seas to lands of whose existence Europe had not even dreamed.

From these daring journeys rose the famous stories of Sinbad the Sailor, told by the lovely Sche-he'ra-za'de in *A Thousand and One Nights*. True romances of adventure in the ninth and tenth centuries, the Sinbad stories sprang from the thrill of seeing strange lands and unknown beasts and birds which the fancy of explorers transformed and magnified. Like the hero of the four-thousand-year-old *Story of the Shipwrecked Sailor* from another adventurous period, the Twelfth Dynasty in ancient Egypt, Sinbad encountered marvelous beasts in a setting of actual scenery and incidents of travel met by real explorers in their many journeys to lands with customs so different from their own.

Camels fighting, a familiar occurrence to these adventurous travelers and traders. (Tehran.) See *My Book House*, Vol. VIII, p. 109 for another story from the collection, *A Thousand and One Nights*.

A Story of Sinbad the Sailor

It occurred to my mind one day to travel again to the lands of other people, and I felt a longing for the occupation of traffic and the pleasure of seeing the countries and islands of the world. So I embarked my bales upon a ship and we traveled and traded until destiny conveyed us to a beautiful island, abounding with trees, with birds warbling, and pure rivers; but there was not in it an inhabitant, nor a blower of fire.

I landed upon the island and slumber overcame me; and when I awoke I found the vessel gone. I climbed a lofty tree, and looking with a scrutinizing eye, there appeared to me on the island, a white object, indistinctly seen in the distance, of enormous size; so I descended from the tree and went toward it; and lo, it was a huge white dome, of great height and large circumference. I drew near to it, and walked round it; but perceived no door to it; and I found that I had not strength nor activity to climb it, on account of its exceeding smoothness.

The close of the day, and the setting of the sun had now drawn near; and, behold the sun was hidden, and the sky became dark. I raised my head and saw a bird, of enormous size, bulky body, and wide wings,

Arabic boat like that which carried Sinbad to adventure in foreign lands. (Persian drawing, 1306.)

flying in the air; and this it was that concealed the body of the sun. At this my wonder increased, and I remembered a story which travelers had told me long before, that there is, in certain of the islands, a bird of enormous size, called the roc, that feedeth its young with elephants. I was convinced, therefore, that the dome was one of the eggs of the roc. While I was in this state, lo, that bird alighted

Persian drawing of that imaginary bird, the roc.

upon the dome, and brooded over it with its wings, stretching out its legs upon the ground, and completely covering that huge, white dome.

Thereupon, I arose and unwound my turban from my head, and tied myself by it to one of the feet of that bird; and when the dawn came, the bird rose from the egg, and drew me up into the sky. I ascended and soared up so high that I imagined it had reached the highest region of the sky; and after that, it descended gradually until it alighted upon the earth. I hastily untied the band from its foot, and walked away.

I found myself in a large, wide, deep valley, surrounded by mountains so high that no one had the power to ascend them. And I beheld its ground to be composed of diamonds. All that valley was likewise occupied by serpents and venomous snakes, everyone of them like a palm-tree. As I walked about the valley, lo, a great slaughtered animal fell before me, and I found no one. And I remembered a story that I had heard long before from certain merchants that the men who import diamonds from this valley know a stratagem by means of which to obtain them. They take a sheep, and slaughter it, and skin it, and cut up its flesh, which they throw down to the bottom of the valley; so, descending fresh and moist, some of these stones stick to it. Then the merchants leave it until midday, and birds of the large kind of vulture descend to that meat and, taking it in their talons, fly up to the top of the mountain: whereupon the merchants scare them away from the meat.

I then selected a great number of these stones, and put them into my pocket. And while I was doing thus, lo, there fell another great slaughtered animal. So I bound myself to it with my turban; and, behold, a vulture seized it with its talons, and flew with me attached to it until it had ascended to the summit of the mountain. Thereupon a great cry arose from behind that vulture; whereat the bird flew away in fear.

And, lo, the merchant who had cried out at the vulture, advanced to the slaughtered animal and saw me standing there. Then I gave to him an abundance of diamonds and he was delighted and prayed for me, and he and the other merchants who had come to this place for the diamonds made me welcome, and we journeyed over that great moun-

Arabic adventurers observe a ferocious lion crouched among the trees, while another strange animal, probably a crocodile, rends the water. (Persian miniature.)

tain, until we arrived at a garden in a great and beautiful island. In this island is a kind of wild beast called the rhinoceros, which pastureth there like oxen and buffaloes in our country. It is a huge beast, with a single horn, thick, in the middle of its head, a cubit in length.

For the diamonds in my pocket, the merchants of our party gave me in exchange goods and commodities; and we made our way, selling and buying until we arrived at the city of Bas'ra. We remained there a few days, and then I came to the city of Bagdad, the Abode of Peace, and entered my house, bringing with me a quantity of diamonds and goods in abundance.

A Decaying Empire

From the clear and accurate description of the rhinoceros given in this story and from other vivid descriptions of foreign animals and places, it is known the Arabs visited and explored, not only India and China, but also the islands of Borneo and the Malay Peninsula, the coast of Zanzibar in East Africa, the beautiful island of Madagascar, Sumatra, the Clove Islands and Ceylon.

But the golden age of the caliphs of Bagdad did not long endure. For seventeen years, Ha-roun' al Ra-schid' was served by four Persian princes of the noble House of Bar'-me-cides, and his Empire prospered.

Giraffe, that strange, mute animal of Africa, brought to grace the garden of a wealthy Persian. (Miniature.)

But jealous enemies filled the magnificent Caliph with the poison of distrust, and one day, a few hours after he had loaded his Persian minister with presents, Haroun had him beheaded. The Caliph himself died a few years later, and at once the great Mohammedan Empire was torn by strife and revolt.

Egypt was the first to break away. Certain Mohammedans had always believed that the descendants of Ali, son-in-law of Mohammed, were the true and lawful caliphs. These Mohammedans, called Fat'i-mites, from Fat'i-ma, Mohammed's daughter and Ali's wife, now rebelled and captured Cairo, and soon ruled all Egypt. Soon after, the Persians regained control of Eastern Persia and Trans'ox-ia'na, and established an independent kingdom in Khorasan. Then the Turks appeared.

A reckless, rough-riding Turk with slanting eyes and typical, Eastern turban. (Persian miniature.)

A dark-haired, round-headed people belonging to the Alpine race, the Turks were first heard of north of China. Moving westward, they settled around Lake Bai-kal' in the region later inhabited by the Mongols; indeed, Turks and Mongols are only different tribes of the same general race. Moving farther west, one branch of Turks finally settled in Turkestan near the Caspian Sea.

A number of these Turks, captured in border warfare, had become slaves of the Mohammedans, and accepted the religion of Mohammed, and a certain Caliph of Bagdad, fearing Persian disloyalty, formed a bodyguard of Turkish slaves and mercenaries, separated completely from Arab and Persian soldiers and commanded by an officer with the title of sultan or prince. Dressed in splendid uniforms, this Turkish bodyguard galloped recklessly through the streets of Bagdad, knocking down everyone who chanced to get in their way. The answer to their insolence was a howl of rage in the capital, so the Caliph, fearing a riot, removed his favorite troop to a safe place called Sa-mar'ra, several days' journey from Bagdad. Here he built a palace with barracks for two hundred and fifty thousand soldiers and stables for a hundred and sixty thousand horses. Certain parts of the city were given to the officers, and their elaborate dwellings rivaled the very palace of the Caliph.

From this time on, the Turkish bodyguard assumed more and more control over the weakening caliphs who finally became little more than figureheads. Like the Praetorian Guard of the ancient Roman Empire, the Turks soon set up caliphs and murdered them as they chose.

They let the caliphs keep up the old glittering court with a pretense of power, but even here in Persia, the last remnant of the old Arab Empire, the Turkish Sultan of the bodyguard was the real ruler of the land.

The eager, aggressive Turks strove mightily for power. A certain Turkish soldier who had begun life as a slave, made himself the master of a part of Eastern Persia where he and his parcel of Turks ruled the native population from their capital city of Ghaz'ni, and this kingdom so expanded that soon it was controlling the whole of Central Asia, while the impotent Caliph in Bagdad, anxious to secure the favor of such powerful conquerors, bestowed on them the princely title of Sultan.

Most famous of these sultans was Mahmud the Victorious. Time and time again, he led his troops into India sweeping all before him, but he was a raider only, seeking its fabulous treasures of gold and jewels and he had no desire to remain in this hot, humid land and the permanent conquest of India by a Mohammedan was left for his successors.

Turkish cavalry strike recklessly at the elephants and solid masses of India. (Persian painting.)

Sultan Mahmud returned to his beautiful city of Ghazni, with its fragrant fairy gardens and glistening marble palaces, and here he set up a court famed for its pomp and magnificence. His palace became the meeting place of painters, astronomers, musicians, poets and craftsmen.

To the court of Mahmud, came the greatest of all Persian poets, A'bul Ka-sim' Man-sur', called Firdu'si or "Paradise," from the exquisite beauty of his verse. Mahmud ordered him to write a history of the kings of Persia, promising that for every thousand couplets, he should receive a thousand pieces of gold. For thirty years Firdusi studied and labored on an epic poem, called the *Shah Namah* or Book of Kings, recounting the history of the kings of Persia down to the death of the last Sassanian king of the land who was overthrown by the Arabs. When at last the work was completed, an exquisitely written copy was sent to the Sultan, but Mahmud received it coldly. Instead of the gold, he sent the aged poet 60,000 small coins, and this so enraged the old man that he gave the paltry sum to his bath attendants. Later, Sultan Mahmud, realizing his error, sent him the pieces of gold, but Firdusi had died just before the messengers arrived. Nevertheless, with the drama, the music, and rhythm of the Book of Kings, Persian literature had flowered most beautifully.

Scene from Firdusi's *Shah Namah* or Book of Kings, showing the great Persian hero, Rustem, fighting his valiant son, Sohrab, neither knowing the identity of his opponent. The Persians love to tell how Rustem was nurtured by a giant bird, how he won his famed horse, Rakush, how he delivered his country from the Deevs, dark demons who dealt in sorcery, and other tales of daring and steadfast courage. The episode of his fight with his son Sohrab has even become a part of the lasting literature of England. See *My Book House*, Vol. X, p. 228, for *A Story of Rustem, Hero of Persia*, from Firdusi's *Shah Namah*.

Now on one of the occasions when Mahmud was absent from Persia on an expedition to India, a large body of those wild Turks who still lived to the north in the steppe-lands of Turkestan, came across the river territory. Returning again to Ghazni, Mahmud saw with distrust this horde of his wild warrior kinsmen swarming into Persia, so he transferred one of the tribes to the farthest corner of the land, the mountainous Khorasan.

Warriors, brave and daring, were both Turk and Persian. (Miniature.)

There they grew so powerful that in time they came down again and overthrew the kingdom of Ghazni. Under their leader, Tughul Bey, grandson of the fierce old Seljuk, from whom this tribe of Turks took their name, they became the most powerful nation in western Asia. Overwhelming were they in their keen love of battle, in unflinching fatalism and reckless daring and with so fierce an enthusiasm for the religion of Mohammed that they set out determined to convert the world by force, driving the Christians from Jerusalem, attacking the Byzantine Empire with such bloodthirsty zeal, that the frightened Emperor Alexius called on Pope Urban for help, thus starting the Crusades.

Persian drawing to illuminate the verse quoted. From the earliest illustrated book of Omar Khayyam's poems.

But before the days of the Seljuks, when beautiful Khorasan was at the height of its power, a second Persian poet, some hundred years after the rise of Firdusi, graced the Persian tongue with another undying work, a song of peace and content in marked contrast to the history of the barbarous Turk in his land. Benevolent, easy-going, intelligent, Omar Khay-yam' was a poet in spite of himself and not by direct intent. Not for him was the serious study of delicately turned phrase and elaborate metaphor; he was interested in life, the joy and thrill of living! He loved the vine and the flesh pots, the joys of song and boon companionship, the gayety of crowded taverns, the magic of scented gardens with his beloved at his side. Many a late afternoon, with a book of verse, a jug of wine and his beloved, he reclined at ease in his garden as dusk was turning to night. The fragrance of rose bush and oleander drifted faintly in the still air, blossoms dropped soft and glowing from flowering vine and tree; the silver tinkle of fountains came gently to his ear; and overhead, the nightingale poured out its notes of ecstasy. Then, as the nightingale ceased, and Omar's beloved sang softly in the dusk, utter contentment filled his heart, and he sang of his happiness in one of Persia's great songs.

A Book of Verses underneath the Bough,
A Jug of Wine, a Loaf of Bread—and Thou
Beside me singing in the Wilderness—
Oh, Wilderness were Paradise enow!

The Assassins

Utterly different from Omar Khayyam, yet in his early days a friend and schoolmate of the poet, was that brilliant Persian with a winning tongue, Has'san-ben-Sab'bah, the mystic, unorthodox, teaching strange mysteries opposed to the faith of Mohammed. Forced to flee from Cairo because of the things he taught, Hassan, soured and embittered, gathered together a band of headstrong, wild young dare-devils, impatient of restraint, rash and scornful of death. With these he seized the fortress of A'la-mut or the Eagle's Nest, high on a steep rock in the rugged mountains near the Caspian, and there, perched above the earth, he founded a secret order that soon became the terror of all the Mohammedan world; for Hassan, drunk with power, forgot his mysticism and built up a stronghold impregnable and an order whose members would murder anyone in the land.

Near the rock of the Eagle's Nest in a beautiful smiling valley, enclosed between two lofty mountains, Hassan built a secret garden, where fountains flowed streams of wine, honey, milk, and pure water. Here were gorgeous palaces, ornamented with gold, with paintings and silken hangings; and within these palaces dwelt the loveliest of damsels, accomplished in the arts of singing, playing, and dancing, and ready to entertain any happy man who might appear among them.

Men eating the drug hash-hish, as did the Assassins in the luxurious paradise-gardens within Alamut. (Miniature.)

Beautiful damsels and all the joys of the
Mohammedan Paradise were given to Hassan's
Devoted Ones in his garden. (Persian miniature.)

But no member of Hassan's band ever entered this garden save those whom the leader had chosen for some most dangerous mission. These were first drugged with hash-hish, and when they were sunk in deep sleep, they were carried into the garden. When they awoke and found themselves in this truly heavenly spot, surrounded by charming damsels, they believed in very truth that they were in Paradise. And here they remained, surrounded by every joy, till Hassan had them drugged and removed again in their sleep.

Having tasted the pleasures of Paradise and believing that death would only bring a return of these joys, they became their leader's Devoted Ones, risking their lives with eagerness and readily persuaded to murder any of the tyrants whom the brotherhood was sworn to destroy. Clothed in white robes, with blood-red girdles and sandals, each carrying a pair of long curved knives, they were usually sent on their missions in little groups of three. Often they killed their victim at the hour of public prayer. The first leaped on him to stab him, and if he failed, the second and third tried. At other times, they carried out the death orders disguised as camel men, or water carriers; and they were called Assassins from the hash-hish with which Hassan drugged them.

Men referred in a whisper to Hassan in his Eagle's Nest as the Old Man of the Mountains, and princes, kings and caliphs, Christian and Arabic, feared his terrible power. Many tried to destroy him, but the Eagle's Nest was too strong. Once a powerful teacher dared to curse him in public. Lo! a white-robed Assassin knelt on the chest of the preacher in the seclusion of his study, and a long knife threateningly pricked the soft skin of his stomach. The Devoted One then vanished, but the preacher no longer cursed. "They have arguments that cannot be refuted," he told his students.

The secret order of the Assassins grew and prospered enormously. Other castles, fortresses, and strongholds were secured in wild and mountainous districts difficult of approach. Hardly one of these but could have been defended by a mere handful of men; and when Hassan died, he left in Persia and Syria, a strange, mysterious kingdom ruling by terror alone. His successor was known as the Grand Prior, and throughout the length and breadth of the eastern Mediterranean lands and Asia, his followers were commonly called "the heretics."

It was these heretics whom the Mongols had set out to destroy, and since their Grand Prior had heeded not the summons Hulagu sent him, the Mongol leader marched his savage horde first into Ku-hi-stan', the chief province of the Assassins. One by one the Assassin strongholds

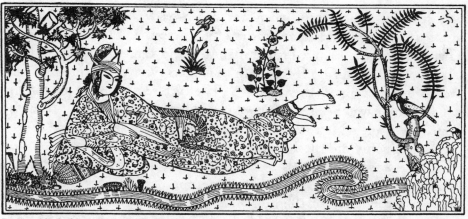

Persian ideal of beautiful womanhood. Such were the maids in the gardens of Alamut. (Water color.)

Raised to opposite heights in baskets, the Mongols attack the famous fortress of Alamut. (Miniature.)

fell. Some they took by storm and some they starved into submission.

Bravely the Assassin chieftains held out as long as possible. Those who were able sent relief to those hard pressed; brave men made their way through the Mongol lines bearing precious supplies of rice or henna, which the besieged used, not for dyeing their nails or beards, but as a preventative against sickness. It was all wasted effort. One after another the towns and castles fell, and their people were slaughtered.

Again and again, Hulagu sent to the Prior, bidding him surrender and come in person to the Mongol camp if he would save his country, but the Assassin sent first his brother and then his son instead. At last the Mongol lost patience and laid siege to the city where the leader was staying. Then, at last, the Grand Prior lost heart, and came to prostrate himself before Hulagu who forced him to ride to every uncaptured fortress and to order them all to surrender. The bitterest moment of his life came when he watched the Mongol horde begin to tear down, stone by stone, the Eagle's Nest, the original home of his order.

So thoroughly did the Mongols finish their work of destruction that of all the Assassin fortresses scarcely a trace remains. Nor did the Assassins fare better. Those who were not destroyed were enslaved. Every living relative of the humbled Grand Prior was butchered, and the Prior himself was murdered as he traveled alone in his ruined land.

The Conquest of Bagdad

Having thus completely destroyed the terrific power of the Assassins, Hulagu advanced on Bagdad. The Caliph was a weak and worthless man, whose name, Mos-ta-sim', meant "He who clings to God for protection." But though he was given over to luxury and was controlled by his Turkish bodyguard, his name was still spoken with reverence throughout the Mohammedan world. And Bagdad, City of the Caliphs, was still a place of holiness. Unthinkable that it should ever be spoiled by the hands of infidels. Yet to the sacred Caliph of the sacred city of Bagdad, Hulagu, from his camp, now sent a summons to submit:

"Strike not the point of an awl with thy fist, mistake not the sun for the glowing wick of a flameless taper. Level the walls of Bagdad at once, fill its moats; leave the government to thy son for a season and come to us. If we march against Bagdad thou wilt not escape us, even should'st thou hide!"

The Caliph answered as if to a forward child. "Knowest thou not that from the west to the east all who worship God and hold the true faith are my servitors and obey my commands? Walk in peace and return to thy eastern home in Khorasan!"

A decrepit old woman halts the magnificent Mohammedan Caliph, to present a petition. (Persian miniature.)

The Mongol envoys who went back with this vainglorious message, returned also with their clothes half ripped from their backs, and told their general how the people of Bagdad had spat in their faces with scorn. Hulagu's anger was roused at this insult. "The Caliph is as crooked as a bow," he declared in a rage to his officers, "but by the help of God I will chastise him till he is as straight as an arrow!"

As he advanced, the country people fled in terror before him, abandoning their houses and fields and taking only what money and valuables they could hastily snatch up. Their one thought was to reach safety behind the walls of Bagdad. For miles around the city, the dusty roads were alive with hurrying, frightened people, glancing back over their shoulders to see if the Mongols were yet in sight. Men, women, and children stumbled along as fast as their weary feet would carry them. More fortunate ones sped by on camels or little donkeys, scattering the pedestrians. Day and night streams of fugitives poured through the gates of Bagdad, increasing the confusion and terror within.

In a time, unbelievably short, the Mongol horsemen appeared, and twenty-four hours later, they had surrounded the city with ditch and rampart to prevent the doomed inhabitants from making their escape.

Bound, stripped of his clothes, a prisoner of war is led to execution by his captors. (Miniature.)

PERSIA, THE CONQUEST OF HULAGU & THE EMPIRE OF THE ILKHANS.

For six days they battered the walls. Then Hulagu made an attack, and for the first time the Turks, barbarous, wild and warlike, learned what it meant to fight at close range with those still more terrible warriors, the wild and barbarous Mongols. Another attack like that and the devilish, blood-thirsty savages would force their way into the city!

At this point, Mostasim realized that he must forfeit his dignity and kneel to this ignorant Mongol if he would save himself and perhaps his threatened city. With his three sons and a guard of three thousand proud grandees, he went in state to the Mongol camp. Prostrating himself before Hulagu, he begged him to accept the gifts which he offered.

When the Mongol had sufficiently enjoyed the sight of the Caliph of Bagdad, thus prostrate at his feet, he raised him up and spoke kindly, declaring to him that Bagdad did not stand in danger. But he was curious, he said, to know how many subjects the Caliph had in the city. Let Mostasim, therefore, command that his people come outside the gates into the open spaces, that they might be numbered before him.

The attack on Bagdad, 1258 A.D. Mongol horsemen surround the walls, while a catapult throws stones upon the city. (Persian MS.)

Messengers went accordingly, bidding the people of the town to come out without fear. A hundred thousand inhabitants, so say the Persian chroniclers, believing the word of their Caliph, left the protection of their walls; and the Mongols ruthlessly slew them, every single one.

Then for seven days and nights the Mongols sacked golden Bagdad. They stripped every building of its treasures, from the humblest shop on the Date Market to the noblest palace of the Caliph. Only the church of the Nestorian Christians, and one or two large mosques were saved from the wholesale destruction. Of the eight hundred thousand inhabitants, all died save the Christians, the teachers from the colleges, and such skilled craftsmen as Hulagu chose to spare for his own use. Nor did any die more horribly than the unfortunate Caliph who was tied in a sack and trampled to death by horses.

The Empire of the Ilkhans

A wave of horror ran throughout Islam. Bagdad fallen! The Caliph slain! Allah have mercy, have mercy! Yet all things came from Allah. What man could resist fate? Man could only submit!

As a sad result of this hopeless spirit of submission to fate, the Mongols met little resistance as they marched into Syria. But submission did not save the lives of the Syrians. Hulagu left such a trail of death that the hearts of those in front turned to water before him. They had no courage to fight, no courage to remain. All they could do was to flee, to sell their houses and lands, buy swift-footed camels or horses, and get them down into Egypt. In Aleppo and Damascus the most beautiful houses sold for a handful of silver, while the price of camels rose to many handfuls of gold. Those who remained to brave the fury of the Mongols grew rich for the time, yet this availed them little. Hulagu came all too soon, razed Aleppo to the ground and slew or enslaved its people. Damascus he spared, as he passed, but he took what he would of its treasures and set up a Mongol governor to receive a huge yearly tribute.

The Sultan of Egypt began to collect an army against him. But just at that time word came that the Kha Khan was dead, and that Hulagu was needed in Karakorum to help choose a successor. Further conquests were thus abandoned, but when his younger brother, Kublai, made himself the new Kha Khan, Hulagu went back to Asia Minor and established the Empire of the Il-khans'. Syria he could not hold, but from Bagdad to Nish-a-pur', Hulagu was undisputed lord, and in the ancient land of Persia his descendants ruled on his throne after him for fully a hundred years.

Like the people pictured on this Persian vase, many frightened Syrians fled their homes on horseback before the advancing Mongols. (1300.)

V

The Mongols in China

(1280–1368)

Ancient China

Kublai had been fighting the Chinese north of the Yang'tze or Great River, when he received his summons to the council at Ka'ra-ko'rum. As he sped back toward the capital, disturbing reports were brought him; the Mongols of the desert favored their ruler, A-rik-bu'ga, who was his brother, to fill the vacant post, and Arikbuga's election was certain. In the swift, masterful way inherited from his grandfather, Kublai halted his troops at Kai Ping, and there had himself duly elected Kha Khan,—not by the Great Council, but by his own officers, resuming the march at once! Well had the mighty Genghis, shrewd judge of character, decided that Kublai was his favorite among all his promising grandsons!

At Karakorum sat the Mongol Khans and nobles who alone had the right to elect the ruler. Over many cups of fermented mare's milk, they had agreed that Arikbuga would be their choice, when suddenly Kublai appeared at the head of a mighty army declaring that he himself had already been chosen Kha Khan. At once the storm broke in fury; and again the sands of the Gobi drank the blood of men and horses; again the barren hills echoed to the wild shouts of men, lust-mad with slaughter.

Kublai emerged triumphant. Then partly because the desert Mongols were unfriendly to him, and partly because of his own love for the wealth and luxury of China, the new Kha Khan decided upon a step which no other Mongol leader had taken. Since the days of Genghis, all Great Khans had lived at Karakorum and had ruled their wide domains from there. But Kublai determined to build a new capital more suited to his magnificence; and this new capital was to arise in glittering, gorgeous splendor, not at some point in the bleak and barren home-land of the Gobi Desert, but in the age-old, foreign kingdom of China, where luxury and learning had existed from the days of a dim and misty past.

The history of this ancient nation went back through the centuries to some four thousand years before Christ. When Egypt was still divided and the Sumerians were still in Mesopotamia, the kingdom of China had its beginning near the far-off, eastern coast of Asia. Settling around the Hwang Ho or Yellow River, the migrating Chinese, come from lands unknown, began to drive out the Mi-a'-o tribes whom they found in the basin of the river, there to build their homes.

Hostile, primitive people surrounded the newcomers on all sides. In the north roamed and raided the unwashed, fur-clad, flesh-eating Ti, forefathers of the Huns, Turks and Mongols. The far west was the haunt of the desert-dwelling Jungs. On the eastern shore and the islands beyond, were the tall, long-haired I, or Tung Hu; and in the south swarmed the Man tribes, cropping their hair and tattooing their bodies so that they would be taken for the sons of dragons when in the water.

Chinese writers told a story of Chinese history which extended over many millions of years, and the earliest days were completely wrapped in legend and fable. Pan-ku, they said, was the first man, who fashioned the world out of chaos with his adze. He worked at this task for eighteen thousand years, and each day that he worked, he grew six feet in stature. He died only when his task was completed; then his head became mountains, his breath wind and clouds, and his voice thunder; his veins were changed into rivers, and his flesh into fields; his skin and hair became herbs and trees; and the insects on his body became people.

Shen Nung, the Divine Husbandman, who the Chinese believed taught them farming. (From a stone carving.) The Chinese belong to the Yellow branch of the three great groups of the races of man: the White, Yellow, and Black. They are called Mongoloids, and have yellow skin, straight, stiff, jet-black hair, brown eyes in an oblique eye slit, and prominent cheek bones.

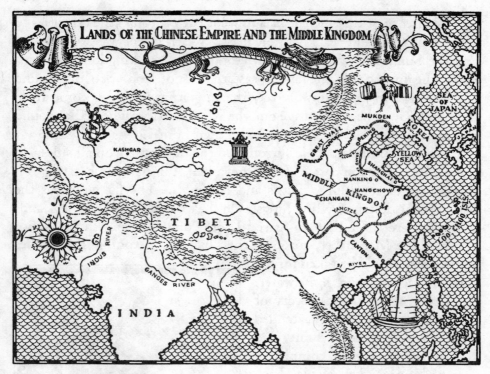

Strange beings ruled the people in those dim distant days,—beings with the faces of men and the bodies of dragons or serpents. Gradually order was established, and slowly the Chinese became more civilized. The first plough was made by bending a piece of wood. Silk worms were raised, and a beginning made in the weaving of silk. Picture messages were simplified into ideographs, straight crossed lines that stood for ideas as well as things, and thus Chinese writing was invented.

During these early days before their history really began, the Chinese had become a nation of farmers. The Miao tribes were pushed south to the Yangtze River, and the Chinese settled in little family groups of villages, each centering about a well. Their houses had only one room; in the center of the roof was an opening through which the smoke escaped, and the dark southwest corner, where the seed grain was stored and sleeping mats laid, was the home of Ao, the sacred household god.

The oldest man in the family told each member what to do. No one lived or worked for himself alone; he was always a part of the family and everything he did affected the family and not himself. Thus the family became the basis of Chinese life; and from the exalted position of the oldest man there arose ancestor worship. Ancestor worship simply meant that the family ties had not been broken, even though the oldest man had died. His spirit still lived to exercise authority and protect the family from harm; the ground where his body was buried was the abiding place of his spirit; and this spirit, represented by a tablet, was worshiped in every home. Ancestor-worship made it important that every man have a son to carry on this family worship.

The Chinese also worshiped a Supreme God, whom they called Shang Ti, "The Most High God" or "Heaven"; and this God was assisted by other gods or spirits of the Heavens, Earth, and Man. Moreover, there were spirits of mountains, rivers, and seas, the field, and the home; and there were temples and altars to all these gods. They were worshiped by burning sweet-smelling wood, by music and dancing; and in order to learn the will of Heaven, the Chinese studied cracks in the burned shell of a tortoise or the position taken by well-scattered milfoil.

The spirits of departed ancestors were represented by tablets on which their names were written, and these tablets were solemnly worshiped by all the family with offerings of food and incense.

Earliest rulers of China, mythological emperors with the bodies of men and the tails of dragons to show their descent from the gods. (Stone rubbing from a tomb, Shantung Province, about 150 A.D.)

The earliest kings of the Chinese were priest-kings. At first these kings had no capital, but moved from village to village as they were needed. The Emperor Yao who ruled until 2258 B.C. was a priest-king; he was called the "Son of Heaven" and was looked upon as a real father to his people, plowing in the sacred field and performing sacred rites to the Supreme God for all the Chinese, thus making certain that justice, peace and plenty reigned on earth. The people looked to him as they did to the sun or moon, and loved him as they did their own parents.

By the time of the Emperor Yao, the Chinese had gathered together into a great many different clans or tribes, each governed by its own local lord or noble. The early emperor-priests were chosen by the nobles for their wisdom and ability, and Yao and his successor, Shun, were looked upon as model rulers. When a certain Emperor Yü came to the throne in 2205 B.C., however, he established the first dynasty or family of rulers, giving it the name Hsi-a dynasty.

The Shang dynasty or family next governed China, beginning their reign in 1776 B.C., and after them came the Chous who controlled the kingdom for almost nine hundred years. This was far longer than any other ruling family ever governed China, and during this time the Chinese developed the beginning of that culture, that exquisite refinement of art which makes up Chinese civilization, and which has continued to rule the lives and thoughts of the Chinese to this very day.

At the beginning of the Chou dynasty, China was practically confined to the basin of the Yellow River and to the lands of the Hu-a'-i River flowing into it. But as the centuries passed, the boundaries were extended in all directions; a certain Ki-tsze migrated to Korea and conquered the land, giving it the name Cho-sen, "Land of the Morning Calm"; far to the south where the Mi-a'-o dwelt around the swiftly flowing Yangtze, the bordering lands were conquered; and north and west great stretches of territory were taken, until the original settlements of the Chinese became the central or "Middle Kingdom" of a wide-spread state.

Although most of the Chinese still loved the lands which they had farmed for generations, a few became merchants and craftsmen, and towns began to grow up. During the thousand and more years they had dwelt in the Middle Kingdom, the Chinese had passed from the polished Stone Age through the Bronze Age into a knowledge of iron and other metals. But bronze vessels were still greatly admired, and the finest bronzes of China with their decorations of dragons, birds, animals and people; and their complicated geometric and ribbon-pattern backgrounds were cast at this time, and even a little later.

The Chou emperors tried to direct and control the life and work of every person in their kingdom. So the common people were grouped into classes in charge of a superintendent, and were little more than serfs whose lives were spent in serving their masters.

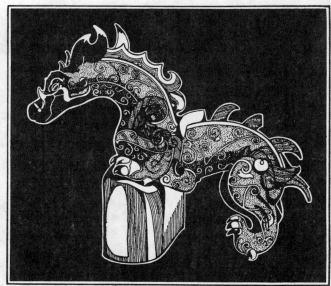

Bronze winged dragon. (3rd cent. B.C.). Dragons were believed to be heavenly creatures, and became symbols of the Emperor and China.

In sharp contrast to the labor and misery of the poor was the idleness and luxury of the rich. The homes of the poor were mere hovels,—but the palaces of the nobles were often built of brick with roofs of brightly colored tile. There was only one kind of building in China, and the most striking feature of this building was the roof, steeply pitched and broadly overhanging, with the corners curved upward. In some homes the partitions were richly carved; and fine wood formed beautiful paneling. The beams of the great halls were polished, or carved and decorated in colors, the floors were of tile covered with mats, and the furniture was lacquered. In the early days there were neither chairs nor tables; people sat on mats and food was placed on small trays beside them.

Buildings in China were usually made of wood with tile roofs, and were vivid in color and carving. The custom of upturned corners probably went back to the prehistoric days of cloth tents. A cloth spread over upright spears would sag just enough to form the upward curving corners of the Chinese roof. This roof did not rest upon the walls of the building, but upon special columns; walls were built after the roof, and simply filled in the space between roof and ground. Chinese buildings had only one story, although often temples and public buildings were erected with two or more roofs, each supported by its own columns. Instead of building upper stories, space was secured by adding more buildings, and the home of a wealthy man was simply a group of buildings facing a court.

A Chinese home, simply furnished, but with every article cunningly carved or decorated. (Vase painting.) The woman here wears a ceremonial costume, but usually it is the little girls and women who wear the trousers, and the boys and men who dress in skirts. Other customs are books that begin at the top of the last column on the last page and go backward until they end with the first column on the first page, and dinners that begin with fruit and sweets and end with soup and rice. See *My Book House* for folk tales of China and Korea showing other strange customs.

Knives and forks were not used in China. Instead, the people were remarkably skilled in the use of "chop sticks" held between the thumb and fingers of the right hand, which conveyed to the mouth food already cut into small pieces. There were many rules of etiquette, and to place the chopsticks across the top of the bowl meant that the guest wished to leave. The Chinese considered knives and forks barbaric. "We sit at table to eat," they said, "not to cut up carcasses." Cooking was already a fine art, and a banquet was not complete without the "five flavors," the sweet and sour, the salty and spicy, and the bitter.

When they were not dining, the rich passed their time with chess, archery, lute-playing, hunting or cockfights. Under the Chous they certainly lived grandly on the labors of the poor and this fact was to continue for the next three thousand years. Especially ground down were the patient, long-suffering, hard-working farmers. Often they suffered famine when crops were bad, sometimes they starved to death, but always they were uncomplaining, courteous and polite. Submissively they paid over to greedy masters and venal tax collectors, who kept a huge share of the taxes they collected, all too much of the produce from their small farms, for they were a peace-loving people, taking life as it came and having for many centuries no thoughts of revolt.

But the nobles were no such lovers of peace. In the days of the Chous they grew so powerful that they paid no heed to the Emperor. Instead, they acted as little independent rulers and made war upon one another in attempts to increase their lands. It was an "Age of Confusion" just like the feudal age in Europe when there was no strong central government to curb the ambition of the nobles. So destructive was this constant warfare that in 545 B.C. a certain minister of the State of Sung thought of the idea of a league to preserve peace. Fourteen states entered into an agreement to end war; five years later they again signed a covenant of peace; but within a few more years the plan was abandoned as hopeless, and the rival states were again tearing at each other's throats.

Battle on a bridge between the armies of powerful nobles, each struggling to secure more land and more influence for himself, regardless of the Emperor, in China's feudal age. The soldiers use bows and long iron swords, and often fight from high-wheeled chariots. (Stone rubbing from a tomb.)

Lao Tze and Taoism

In such an age of confusion and misery, when
famine and death stalked the land, earnest men
sought eagerly to bring peace and happiness
back to China. It was during this time, therefore, that two of China's great religions arose.
The first, Tao'ism, was the thought of a certain
La'o Tze' whose name meant, "the old philosopher." Born about the year 604 B.C., Lao Tze
lived for many years at the court of the dukes
of Chou as keeper of historical records; but realizing at length the corruption of the rulers, he
abruptly left the court. As he sought to pass
through the gate leading from the royal domain, the warden said to him: "You are about
to withdraw yourself out of sight; I pray you
to compose me a book before you go." And so
Lao Tze made a writing, called the *Classic of the Way*, in which he set
forth his views of the *tao* and virtue. Then passing on and out into the
lands beyond, he died in a place unknown, leaving only his book behind.

La'o Tze', who taught men the
Tao or *Way*, the serene, radiant, natural, unstudied road to
perfection. (*Classic of the Way*.)

Tao is the Way, radiant and serene, never to be shut up and wholly
defined by words, but ever flexible and limitless, inviting contemplation
through the very elusiveness and vagueness of its meaning. Now it is
the way to bring the soul into perfect harmony with the fundamental
law of the universe, as that is increasingly felt through experiences of
the spirit; now it is the way to virtue, unstudied and unselfconscious,
the way to ultimate reality in a life more rich and deep beyond this
worldly sight. It was the greatness of Lao Tze to define God by the one
word *Spontaneity*, that is, right action taking place through all that
lives by natural feeling, from internal impulse, not by outward con-
straint or force. Therefore the Way or Tao, is the way of unstudied
action, working in orderly fashion, naturally and unselfishly. It is
that Universal Spirit which breathes throughout nature and man.

A laughing La'o Tze' seated upon a buffalo to indicate his conquest over earthly desires. (Enamel statuette.) Lao Tze's conception of the spontaneous naturalness of good is in striking contrast to the self-consciousness and self-righteousness of Western thought in the matter of virtue. His conquest of the world's illusions is a matter for laughter and joy. (See page 171.)

"It is the way of the Tao," said Lao Tze, "not to act from any personal motive, to conduct affairs without feeling the trouble of them, to taste without being aware of the flavor, to account the great as the small and the small as the great, to return kindness for injury."

But great as were Lao Tze's thoughts, it was not he who spread them. It remained for a later student, Chu-ang' Tzu, to make Taoism one of the great religions of China. Realizing that man lives from within, in the world of thought and feeling, not from without in the world of objects Chuang Tzu said: "The true sage takes his refuge in Universal Spirit."

So taught Chuang Tzu; but from the most ancient times, the Chinese had believed in two souls or breaths in the universe. These were the *Yang*, representing light, warmth, and life, and the *Yin*, associated with darkness, cold, and death. The *Yang* was divided into an infinite number of good spirits called *shen*, and the *yin* into evil spirits called *kwei*. As the years passed, most of the common people forgot the teachings of the masters concerning one Universal Spirit, and came to think of the *Tao* or Way, as the mere material force of Nature, both good and evil, the working of the *shen* or gods, and the *kwei* or devils, in every aspect of life. The innate naturalness of good then departed from the faith, and Taoism sank to a religion of superstition and magic. Only a few poets, artists and thoughtful men retained the vision of true Taoism, still feeling the Universal Spirit pulsing through all that has life.

Confucius, Sage and Teacher of China
(551 B.C.–479 B.C.)

Con-fu'ci-us was the author of the second great religion of China, which was quite different from the Taoism of Lao Tze, for while Lao Tze sought to help men find the way to that spontaneous right action which is prompted by the heart and needs no compulsion from outward restraints and elaborate regulations, Confucius sought to save society by a return to the ways of the ancients and this meant not only emphasis on moral training but also the complete regulation of human conduct in accordance with the ceremonies, rituals and customs that had come down from the past.

His father belonged to a noble family related to the Shang dynasty, and was already over seventy years old when his son Confucius was born. The old man's first wife had borne him nine daughters and no son to attend the spirit of his ancestors; so deciding to marry again, he presented himself to a gentleman of the noble house of Yen, and secured his fair young daughter, Ching-tsai, as his second wife. He did not live long thereafter, and died when young Confucius was but three years old.

Hearing his grandfather sigh one day, Confucius said quickly: "Sir, have I done anything to grieve you?"

The grandfather asked who had taught him to speak so gravely and wisely.

"You, sir," answered Confucius, "for I have often heard you say that a child who behaves ill brings disgrace upon his ancestors."

Hearing which words of wisdom, the grandsire was awed and silent for very joy.

Even as a boy, Confucius was grave, formal, courteous to his elders like the small boy in this porcelain dish.

Grave and formal was Confucius always. From the beginning he loved knowledge, and at the age of fourteen he had learned all that his master could teach him. Thereafter he aided in the teaching of the other boys as he pursued further studies into the past. But he grew up a manly youth as well as a scholar, being regular in gymnastic exercises, a skillful charioteer, a huntsman, fond of the chase, and a lover of music and poetry. Indeed, he was in all ways an example of a great Chinese gentleman, stately-mannered, valiant, talented.

When he was twenty-four years old, Confucius lost his mother; and that due honor might be paid her, he retired from the position he held in the service of the Duke of Lu. Burying her at the original home of his ancestors, and removing his father's coffin that the two might lie in one grave, he remained for three years in the neighborhood of their tomb, fulfilling the ancient command:

> Three years the infant in its parents' arms.
> Three years the mourner at his parents' tomb.

Stately, reserved, and dignified, Confucius sought always to obey old customs in every detail and to mold his life according to the lives of the ancient emperors and wise men.

He did not return to public office when his days of mourning were ended. Instead, he became a teacher. One of the ministers of the old Duke of Lu who had been a great student of the Rites honored from of old, called his chief officer to him as he lay upon his deathbed, and said: "A knowledge of the inner rule of conduct is the stem of a man. Without it he has no means of standing firm. I have heard that there is a man named Kung, or Confucius, skilled in this. After my death tell Ho Kei to go and study the inner rule of conduct under this man."

Ho Kei with a son's obedience enrolled himself as a student of Confucius. Others of the family followed and the standing of these noble students brought Confucius such fame that within a very short time he had three thousand students, though none were bound to follow him but were always free to come or go. When the desire to move about and visit new scenes and places seized upon the Master, he and his students set out in any direction they chose and roamed the countryside.

And when Confucius sat down for a little rest and quiet near a cool green bamboo thicket, or beneath the shadow of a rock, he spoke those words of wisdom which were so carefully cherished in the hearts of the younger men.

As he journeyed with his students to a nearby province, he passed the mountains of Tai and there saw a woman weeping at a grave. Confucius stopped and asked the reason. "My husband's father," said the woman, "was killed here by a tiger, and my husband also, and now my son

Confucius, teacher of right conduct and respect for antiquity, followed by a student. (Temple at Chufu.)

has met the same fate." When asked why she continued to live in such a dangerous place, she replied: "Here there is no oppressive ruler." Confucius was deeply impressed, and turning to his students said: "Remember this, my children, an oppressive ruler is more feared than a tiger."

He became Minister of Crime of the province of Lu, and by close adherence to the principles of ancient rulers, he brought about such reforms that jewels could be left in the streets and remain untouched by thieves. The province prospered under his leadership and soon became so powerful that neighboring rulers feared it; but in time the Duke of Lu came to neglect affairs of state, leaving Confucius without support for the various reforms he intended.

Accordingly, Confucius sought out new states to reform, but although other rulers often asked his advice, none gave him office and power. None really wanted reform. Discouraged by what seemed failure, the wise old teacher died at the age of seventy-two and was buried at Chu-fu, where his grave is visited to this day by multitudes of pilgrims.

Confucius, a typical portrait accepted by the Chinese, although no actual portraits exist. (Stone rubbing, Museum, Sian.) The five volumes collected and edited by Confucius are known as the Five Classics, and throughout the history of the nation, from Confucius' day to the present, they have formed the basis of all Chinese education. Well-educated men can recite them completely from memory, and even the lowest laborers know many passages by heart. The Five Classics have moulded Chinese character and have given it a solidity and dignity which has checked the adoption of modern ideas, but which has kept the distinctive, Chinese civilization intact throughout the ages. The Five Classics are the *Shu Ching*, the Book of History; the *Shih Ching*, the Book of Ancient Poems; the *Yi Ching*, the Book of Divination; the *Li Chi*, the Book of Rites; and the *Chun Chiu*, the Spring and Autumn, a history of Lu.

Confucius taught his students to respect and honor the ideas and customs which had governed their land in the past, taking his material from four books which he compiled and edited from the writings of the ancients, a volume of history, one of poetry, one of divination, and one on etiquette or the rules of conduct. To these he added a history of his own called *Spring and Autumn*. His plan of education was to arouse an interest in the poets, then establish character by the study of manners and customs, and finish the student's course with music.

By such means, Confucius hoped to develop what he called "the superior man," one who sought not riches or fame, but was modest, reverent, sincere, and self-possessed. The great Sage and Teacher was interested in the welfare of all the people, and he taught a principle of conduct and relationship which was like the Golden Rule of the Christian religion.

As the years passed, the ideals of Confucius became the ideals of the Chinese nation, and his standard of what made a "superior man" became the object of every Chinese gentleman. Confucius was honored and exalted and his teachings were followed because he made simple and systematic, he practiced and taught, what had long been known and accepted in ancient China as the standard of perfection in man.

Character was to be improved because it brought harmony and right living upon earth, not because goodness in this life would bring a future beyond the grave. Confucius was an ethical teacher, like the ancient Greeks, concerned only with bringing a right attitude and a right adjustment to the actual conditions and complexities of life. Whether a man were a Taoist, or the follower of any other religious teacher, he could also be a Con-fu'cian-ist in his relation to society and government.

The influence of Confucius upon the Chinese people was enormous. In Confucius, the Chinese beheld the ideal man, the "superior man," the man of perfect virtue, whose portrait the great Sage and Teacher had drawn so often and so lovingly as the hope of China. "Confucius is, in the Empire of China, the one man by whom all possible personal excellence is exemplified, and by whom all possible lessons of social virtue and political wisdom are taught. After the lapse of more than two thousand years, the moral, the social, and the political life of about one-third of mankind continues to be under the full influence of his practical, matter-of-fact mind."

Confucianism has united the Chinese people in custom and thought, it has set its approval upon ancestor worship and has thus kept the family as the basis of Chinese civilization. But the constant care to do only those things that Confucius sanctioned, the unquestioning belief in the perfection of the past, made the Chinese resist all change and proved for centuries to be a serious bar to progress, so China at last faced all at once her adjustment to the modern world.

Image of Confucius in the Great Temple of the Sage at Chufu where certain Chinese worship him as a god. (From a photograph. The quotations on this page are from two authorities, Drs. James Legge and von der Gabelentz.)

The Growth of China

Both Lao Tze and Confucius had endeavored to show rulers and people how they might bring back peace and safety to a land torn and ravaged by war. But the rulers refused to heed their utterances; war continued to bring death, destruction, and misery, and so long did the fighting continue that, for the first time in the history of China, men abandoned farming and other pursuits to become professional soldiers who made their living by fighting.

During these bitter years of disorder, the northern and western frontiers were left unprotected; and seizing upon their opportunity, great numbers of Huns, Turks, Tartars, and Mongols swept across the borders to settle, intermarry, and form in Northern China a people of mixed blood, taller, stronger, and tougher than the purer Chinese in the more protected lands of the South. But gradually a new China was welded together out of much bloodshed and suffering, and in the year 249 B.C. the powerful State of Chin succeeded in uniting North and South.

Although the Chin dynasty ruled less than fifty years, one great leader did more for China than did countless emperors of the century-old dynasty of Chou. This Emperor called himself Chin Shih Hu-ang' Ti, or First Emperor of the Chin dynasty, and he came to the throne when he was only thirteen years old. Then it was that the land received the name by which it is known today. China simply means "the land of Chin," and it was given to the country because the power of Chin was so great.

One of the first tasks the Chin Emperor set himself was the building of the Great Wall. There had been ramparts and walls at various places along the northwestern frontier before this time, but Chin Shih now strengthened, rebuilt, and united them so that there arose a stupendous structure extending from the eastern edge of Turkestan to the sea. Up and down the steep mountain sides it traveled, with watchtowers rising at regular intervals. It was partly of stone, partly of brick, and in some places scarcely more than a rampart of earth. In its building, the Emperor used thousands of criminals with shaven heads and iron collars about their necks, and many were the stories of magic about the work.

But the Great Wall was only a part of the Emperor's plan of connecting the different parts of the Empire and defending its borders. Immense roads were built, avenues fifty feet wide; and these pierced mountains, leveled hills and bridged rivers with an engineering skill that far surpassed earlier achievements. Moreover, watchtowers, huge, lofty, strongly guarded, flashed vigilance and defiance throughout the Empire and across the borders. And to help the peasants to regain their prosperity, a great irrigation system was built in the valley of the Wei which added nearly seven hundred thousand acres to the farm land of the kingdom.

Then the Emperor took from the nobles the lands which they held and divided China into provinces governed by men whom he appointed, though this change was strongly opposed. The old students of Confucius said that such action was against the teachings of their master, and backed up their stand in defence of the ancient government with so many references to Confucius that the Chief Minister finally suggested the destruction of all these writings. To this the Emperor agreed, and the command went forth that all copies of the Book of History, the Book of Odes, and all histories of the states should be brought to the local authorities and burned. Moreover, all who talked about the teachings of these books and all who quoted the authority of the ancient writings were to be put to death with their relatives. Thirty days were allowed the people to bring in their books, and at the end of this time, those who still kept them were to be punished.

The early Emperors divided China into nine provinces and had, in their courtyards, nine sacred tripods representing these divisions. The tripods were lost, and the Emperor Shih Hu-ang' Ti, learning that they were in a certain river, ordered them recovered. As his servants were raising the first tripod, however, a dragon suddenly appeared, bit the rope in two, and the tripod fell into the stream, never to be seen again by mortals. (Stone rubbing from a temple.)

Officials of the Chin Emperor, Shih Hu-ang' Ti, burning the Confucian books because they were opposed to the reforms of their master. It was this Emperor who sought the "Isles of the Blessed" and the "Fountain of Youth," and stories about these wonders made their way to the West to inspire the voyages of Ponce de Leon and other Spanish explorers who sought in vain to find in America, in Florida and on the banks of the Mississippi, the cure for old age and the charm against death.

This was the famous "Burning of the Books." Thousands of copies of the works of Confucius all went up in smoke; but a few determined scholars hid the forbidden volumes in the walls of their homes. It was difficult to conceal such books, however, because printing had not yet been invented, and a book was simply a great number of narrow bamboo slabs, carved with ideographs and fastened together on swivel pins. Four hundred and sixty scholars were put to death for refusing to obey the Emperor's command, but almost all the forbidden books were saved and were brought out from hiding places during the next dynasty.

As Shih Huang Ti grew older, he became a prey to superstition. Stories were told him about fairy islands lying in the ocean where old age and death were unknown, and in 219 B.C., he sent a fleet to find the Isles of the Immortals. The commander returned, saying that he had met one of the immortals who had said that the gifts his vessel carried were too cheap. "You may see the Fountain of Youth, but you may not taste its waters." "What gifts do you desire," asked the commander. "Young men and maidens, and craftsmen of all sorts," was the reply. The Emperor, therefore, sent three thousand young men and women with the commander, but they never returned, and probably settled in Japan.

The Glorious House of Han

Shortly after the Great Emperor's death, the Han dynasty was established and this family ruled the Flowery Kingdom until 220 A.D. The reign of the Han was a glorious period for China. One great leader, Wu Ti, the Warrior Emperor, found that not even the Great Wall could protect his kingdom from the Huns. He, therefore, launched campaign after campaign against them, and so successful was he that he forced the Huns to move westward, a migration which finally resulted in the attack of Attila on the divided Roman Empire. During these wars a number of powerful generals arose and carried the fame of China to countries before unknown. Chang Chien "pierced the void" of Central Asia, made treaties with thirty-six small states, and brought back the Persian grapevine. For the first time in its history, China came into direct contact with the West, and actual trade with Rome probably began in the year 36 B.C. when Mark Antony was ruling in the Eastern Mediterranean.

A Chinese mandarin in official robes. By passing examinations any man might become a mandarin in this Empire dimly known to the West long before the days of Alexander the Great, and called *Seres* by the widely-traveled Greeks and Romans.

One of the first deeds of the Han Emperor was to visit the tomb of Confucius and there make an offering. His books were taken from their hiding places, and Confucianism now became a formal religion. The Emperor also decided upon a new plan for selecting his *mandarins*, or officers of his government. Examinations were held which required a knowledge of the Five Classics of Confucius and the Four Books. Anyone in the Empire regardless of his station could take these examinations, and knowledge rather than family position now made a man a government officer. Paper was invented and many books of history, biography, and poetry now began to appear in great numbers.

"The Three Religions" of China, a painting of the Yu-an' dynasty. Left, La'o Tze', teacher of Tao'ism, kindly and happy; center, Buddha, serious, stern, ascetic; right, Confucius, practical, matter-of-fact.

Together with the interest in learning came an interest in art, and the pottery of the Hans glowed with beauty and taste. Now there appeared a great deal of funeral pottery, imitations of household furniture, farm implements, and tiny buildings to be buried with the dead. More beautiful and artistic were the jars, vases, and censers used in life. Many of these were decorated with the same kind of designs used on the bronzes of earlier days; there were hunting scenes, tigers, dogs, birds, lions, and dragons.

One event of far-reaching importance during the reign of the Hans was the introduction of Bud'dhism, the third great religion of China. Buddha, a title meaning "the Enlightened" was the name given to Gau'-ta-ma, the son of an Indian rajah who lived about 550 B.C. Renouncing his wealth, his family, and his inheritance, Bud'dha left home at the age of twenty-nine, and after six years of struggle and meditation, he at last gained what he believed to be enlightenment. The rest of his life was spent in teaching what he had learned, and in establishing an Order of Monks and an Order of Nuns to carry on his teachings.

Buddha taught that men should follow the "Eightfold Path" of Right Understanding, Right Thought, Right Speech, Right Conduct, Right Living, Right Effort, Right Mindfulness and Right Rapture. This path was also the Middle Path, lying midway between sensuality and asceticism, and Buddha admonished his disciples to aim at purity in thought, word, and deed.

By meditation and the control of the mind, taught Buddha, a habit of thought could be reached in which man would cease to desire anything selfish, and he would have perfect peace and joy. It was a knowledge of life and living that Buddha taught, but after his death when the influence of his purity and simplicity was gone, the Order of Monks which he had established to spread his teachings, developed into a highly organized, wealthy, and powerful body. Then Buddha was transformed into a god to whom prayers could be made; he was regarded as the Savior of mankind, and a religion was established which recognized the value of prayer to images of the teacher.

Hsüan Tsang, a Chinese monk returning from India with rolls of Buddhist books. (Painting.)

The Chinese must have known about Buddhism for years; but it was not until 68 A.D. that a certain emperor, Ming Ti by name, sent ambassadors to India to learn more about it. Upon their return a temple was built, Buddhist books were translated into Chinese, and the new faith found some followers. Buddhism spread slowly, and Buddhist missionaries came and went for six hundred years before it became well established in China. Degenerate forms of Buddhism and Taoism then existed side by side with Confucianism, which to the Chinese masses had become mere ceremony and ancestor-worship.

Conflict and Culture

Battle of troops before a frontier fortress. (Chinese painting.)

Anarchy and disorder followed the fall of the Han emperors and it was four hundred years before the Tangs brought peace again to the land. Northern and Southern China divided and although the South remained Chinese, barbarian chieftains of foreign tribes of Turks, Huns, and Mongols controlled the North for nearly three centuries.

Meanwhile, Southern China, south of the Yangtze River, grew in strength and prosperity. Yang Ti, an emperor of the short-lived house of Sui was an active, energetic builder and warrior. He forced men to work on the Grand Canal which was to connect the Yellow and the Yangtze rivers, and when his supply of men ran out, he drove women to the task. He assembled a hundred scholars to produce an encyclopaedia which contained seventeen hundred chapters dealing with agriculture, geography, literature, medicine, divination, dogs, falconry, and games. Many campaigns were undertaken against the Turks, and other expeditions were sent against the Loo'choo Islands and Korea. Yang Ti even invaded Cambodia, and sent an embassy to Siam to establish trade.

The trade of Southern China developed steadily. All sea commerce was in the hands of the Arabs, and by 300 A.D. there was a large colony of Arabs and Indians at Canton, the most important port. Arabian mastery over the sea-trade in the Indian Ocean continued for twelve hundred years, but in the North, foreign trade was controlled by the Empire of the Turks.

Buddhism slowly became the most popular religion in China, and Buddhist monks greatly enriched Chinese art. They usually chose picturesque spots in the mountains for their monasteries, and surrounded them with groves and gardens made attractive with rockeries and winding brooks crossed by artistic bridges. Monastery walls were often adorned with beautiful paintings from the life of Buddha.

But the deep love of beauty, so characteristic of the Chinese, found its expression in other forms of art also. The demand for pottery had grown steadily and it had now become an important industry which attracted the genius of brilliant men. New kinds of pottery were developed. In addition to the glazed earthenware of the Hans, a seagreen was made, and also a blue porcelain. From Syria, the Chinese learned to manufacture glass jewels. Before this time the Chinese had always sat on mats, but now they took the idea of chairs from the Turks, and made themselves more comfortable.

Exquisitely proportioned vase with scene in delicate colors showing a seated woman. (18th cent.) In texture, color, and form, the Chinese developed their porcelain and pottery to wonderful heights of artistry.

Women have brought their children to the garden of a friend for the delightful ceremony of tea-drinking. (Enamel salver.)

It was during these days of prosperity also that tea-drinking became a social custom, and friends gathered at the homes of friends to sip the scalding hot liquid with loud noises to show their host how good it was. Within the wall surrounding every better-class Chinese home there was a tiny garden with a fish pool and lily-pond, a bridge, and a curly-roofed tea-house, and it was here that friends gathered in the late afternoon to visit and drink tea. The women had been brought from their homes in sedan chairs, cushioned and curtained boxes with doors and windows. The tops of these chairs were made with curved corners like Chinese roofs and the sides were of gilded wood.

Arrived at their friends' home for the tea-drinking, the women went first to the room of their hostess. Here were stools and tables of carved black wood, inlaid with pearl flowers. On the walls hung pictures embroidered on red satin, or painted on rice paper. There were vases and jars of red and gold, and blue and white. All around were singing birds in tiny wooden cages. And when tea was served in the garden, the tea trays were silver with gold birds on them, the cups were tiny, thin white thimbles without handles; and the ladies opened and shut their scented fans as they followed the ceremonial etiquette of tea-drinking.

Although Southern China was thus developing a luxurious civilization while Northern China remained rough and crude, the ideal of a united China remained in the minds of men, and the Tang emperors succeeded in establishing a strong ruling power which governed a re-united China until 907 A.D. Greatest of all Tang rulers was Tai Tsung who broke the power of the Turks and ruled over the largest empire governed by Chinese. His beautiful capital of Sian, or West-Peace, was one of the most civilized and enlightened cities in the world. Travelers, merchants, missionaries, and ambassadors from all

An important Chinese city, such as Sian, adorned with artistic buildings and crowded with wealthy people. (Porcelain plate.)

parts of Asia met in its caravanseries and jostled one another in its crowded streets. The King of Tibet was brought to friendship and with picturesque ceremonies was given a Chinese Princess in marriage. Gorgeous embassies came from Central India, from Cam-bo'di-a, rich in temples; from Korea, Japan; and even from the powerful Greek Emperor far away in Constantinople. So great was Chinese influence on Japan, that the new Japanese capital was named after the Chinese city, Kyo'to, "City of Western Peace," and Japanese dress followed Chinese fashions.

Now there was in the harem of the Emperor, a beautiful woman named Wu Chao who, upon the death of Tai Tsung, retired to a Buddhist convent when she was still only twenty-seven years old. But Kao Tsung, son of Tai Tsung, who was now emperor, visited the convent one day, and fascinated by the beauty of the young woman, he had her returned to court. Here the Lady Wu soon took the place of the real Queen. She had the Queen imprisoned, tortured, and put to death; and finally she became the ruler of China.

Court ladies, like those attending the Lady Wu, making their toilet before going to their mistress, a charming and intimate painting of Chinese life drawn by Ku K'ai-chih in the fourth century.

During a time when the Emperor was ill, Lady Wu acted for him and showed so much wisdom that the ministers were glad to have her advice and help. Steadily she took more and more power to herself, and when Kao Tsung assumed the title, Celestial Emperor, she called herself Celestial Empress. Together, Emperor and Empress ruled China as "The Two Holy Ones," and when Kao Tsung died, the Lady Wu refused to turn the throne over to their son, but herself acted as emperor, performing the sacrifices to Heaven reserved to the emperor alone. The Lady Emperor ruled with vigor and success; her generals completed the conquest of Korea, and defeated the Tibetans. Her title, "The Warrior Empress," was the reward of these victories.

Other rulers of the house of Tang gave more thought to the arts of peace than to those of war, and in the ninth century, toward the end of their reign, the first printed book appeared. Each step in the invention of printing had been slow and laborious and now, for the first time in the history of the world, the Chinese produced a printed book! This marvel of thought and inventive genius was the greatest gift of Chinese civilization and the greatest mechanical triumph of the Tangs.

Painting was encouraged, and Wu Tao Yu-an', the greatest of all Chinese painters, lived at this time. His landscapes had so much reality and marvelous beauty that they were beyond description. Nevertheless, it is said that a famous picture of his, entitled "The Western Paradise", was criticized adversely; and Wu, so the story reports, answered his critics and proved the wonderful fidelity of his work, by stepping calmly into the Paradise he had painted, and so disappeared forever.

The musicians, actors, poets, and painters who gathered at the palace, often met in the Pear Garden to give dramatic entertainments. Here, against the lovely background of white pear blossoms, the courtiers dressed in gorgeous costumes of scarlet, blue, and green, splashed with gold and jewels, went through a lively presentation of song and dance and acrobatic tumbling that delighted the Emperor and his favorites. Wearing carved wooden masks, the artists spoke and moved from posture to posture. The Emperor was so charmed by these entertainments that he at once established the Pear Garden, a court-school of music, dancing, ballet, and acting. This was the beginning of Chinese drama and the stage, and so popular did this new kind of entertainment become that the words "Pear Garden" were taken as the name of the theatrical profession, and the Emperor Tsung became the actors' patron saint.

Mei Lang Fang, celebrated modern Chinese actor, in the part of one of China's four greatest beauties. (From a photograph.) At one time female actors were forbidden to appear upon the Chinese stage, and there arose a class of female impersonators, called *tan*. Men attained an amazing ability to portray women, as graceful in poise and carriage as lovely little ivory statuettes, and even today are preferred to true female actors.

Chinese landscape painting on silk, delicate as mist and rainbow. (Freer Gallery, Washington, D. C.)

Painting reached marvelous heights under the Tangs. The most important forms of painting were frescoes, hanging scrolls, and long scrolls. Most of the frescoes have disappeared, and only the panels and scrolls remain. These were not framed. The Chinese never framed their pictures; nor were they kept on display. Instead, they formed a part of the family treasure and were shown only for a short time on special occasions. Afterward they were rolled up and put away.

Chinese paintings were made on silk with the same kind of brush used in writing. The Chinese word for landscape meant "mountains and rivers," and this was an exact description of the most marvelous landscape painting of the world. Before ever putting his hand to the brush, the artist devoted long hours to the study of his subject, until he felt the scene as a rare and noble mood of a harmonious and infinite nature. So attuned was he finally to this poetic mood, that quickly, spontaneously, and unerringly, he transferred his feelings to the silk.

But great as was the attainment of the artist, even greater was the triumph of the poet who then reached heights of feeling and expression which have never been surpassed. The poetry of these artists is universal, immortal; and today, the Chinese gentleman still turns for his greatest pleasure to the poetry written under the Tangs.

The Poetry of China

Dreamy, quiet, peaceful, the early poetry of China breathed forth simple joys or sighed with gentle regrets. All other nations in the world had, in their earliest days, sung stirring ballads of warfare and the bold deeds of warlike heroes; but the primitive poets of China sang of content and peace, of happiness in the home, the simple pleasures of farm-life and contact with the earth. Their songs were as placid and quiet as the streams of which they sang.

> Cold from its source the stream meanders
> Darkly down through the oleanders,
> All night long in dreams I lie,
> Ah me! Ah me! to awake and sigh,
> Sigh for the City of Chow.*

Such were the Odes collected by Confucius, some five hundred years before Christ. They soared to no great heights of joy and exaltation, and searched no dark depths of despair, breathing in sweet sing-song of the everyday things of life.

But a hundred years after Confucius, there came a deeper cry from the heart of a Chinese poet. Chu Yu-an', the loyal minister to a petty feudal prince, fell into disfavor at court and retreated high into the hills, into the depths of the forest.

> Lonely I stand
> On the lonelier hill-top,
> Cloudland beneath me
> And cloudland around me.
> Softly the wind bloweth,
> Softly the rain falls.
> Joy like a mist blots
> The thoughts of my home out.
> There none would honor me,
> Fallen from honors!

*This account of the poetry of China is based on *A Lute of Jade* by L. Cranmer-Byng. A note to "The Wisdom of the East Series," of which this book forms a part says: "The object of the editors is a very definite one. They desire above all things that, in their humble way, these books shall be the ambassadors of good will and understanding between the East and West, the old world of Thought and the new of Action. This series has a definite object. It is, by means of the best Oriental literature—its wisdom, philosophy, poetry, and ideals—to bring together West and East in a spirit of mutual sympathy, good will, and understanding." And this quotation best expresses the purpose and hope of this section on Chinese poetry.

Intense desire for peace has characterized the Chinese from the beginning. Cooperation, self-effacing politeness, deference, and humility have been their ideals of conduct, rather than individualism and aggressiveness. This love of peace has brought invasion and conquest; it has often caused them to cry peace, peace, when there was no peace; to submit when, from the Western standpoint, they should have rebelled; but it has also created a nation with a strong sense of mutual obligation and moral right; and produced a unity which has enabled their civilization to continue, so that it is to-day the oldest civilization still in existence.

Communing with the Spirit of Poetry.
(Painting by the Emperor Hui Tsung.)

Alone in his solitude, plucking azaleas or orchids, or sitting while thunders rolled shattering the valley of clouds, he communed face to face with the very Spirit of Poetry. Poetry must not baldly and flagrantly surfeit a man with overabundance of imagery, gushing forth unrepressed. The poet must cull no more than the perfume of sweet flowers and leave in the heart a dream-blossom delicately haunting the memory. So Chu Yuan in his poem on "Falling into Trouble" or Li Sao struck the note which was most beautifully to characterize all of Chinese poetry, that delicate fragrance of suggestion rather than bald description which lingers, distilling its perfume, long after the poem is read, a dream blossom haunting the heart.

Two hundred years after his time, the brilliant house of Han became great patrons of literature, sometimes even poets themselves, and under their patronage, new and vital forces began to develop. Buddhism came to China and in the light of its teachings, poets sang not only of that fresh and blooming green world their two eyes saw about them, but more of that ideal world unseen by the human senses, that inner world of thought, of fancy and of feeling, so much more intensely real than the outer world seen by the eyes. Confucius had given his country-men a set of rules for conduct, sensible and usable because he knew Chinese nature and of what it was capable; but he gathered little in his Classics to produce great poets of vision. No depths of heart or soul had forced him to look beneath the outward forms of things.

To Buddha, on the other hand, all that he saw about him was only a fleeting shadow, insubstantial as a mirage. Quiet as his sitting statues, he sought the source of reality beyond the world of sense in the depths of thought and spirit. Said a Chinese poet of a Buddhist priest:

> You were foreordained to find the source.
> Now tracing your way as in a dream
> There where the sea floats up the sky,
> You wane from the world in your fragile boat—
> The water and the moon are as calm as your faith;
> Fishes and dragons follow your chanting,
> And the eye still watches beyond the horizon
> The holy light of your single lantern.

In some peaceful mountain retreat beside a deep clear lake, with the moon for his pure-hearted friend, the Buddhist mused as in some court of silent dreams, to lose his worldly cares and find the flash of Truth Eternal.

> In the pure morning, near the old temple,
> Where early sunlight points the tree-tops,
> My path has wound through a sheltered hollow
> Of boughs and flowers, to a Buddhist retreat.
> Here birds are alive with mountain light,
> And the mind of man touches peace in a pool,
> And a thousand sounds are quieted
> By the breathing of a temple-bell.

But while the Buddhist grieved with sighs of infinite sorrow over the fleeting nature of all things material, looking on them as evil, sinful and a snare, the followers of Lao Tze, with his doctrines of Tao or the Way, the shimmering way to serenity, harmony and perfection, likewise regarded the outward world as shadowy illusion, but they saw all its wondrous beauties in tones of lyric joy as the symbols of things more glorious. Through the beauties seen by their eyes, the gold of leaves in autumn, a lone

Pottery statue of a Buddhist priest. The above poem, concerning such a Buddhist priest, is much more than the outward picture of a man passing upstream and beyond the horizon carrying a lantern. There is the implied picture of a serene, Buddhist philosopher seeking with calm faith the ultimate source of reality and harmony, and chanting as he goes, while those of lesser vision listen to his words and see the holy light of the truth he has perceived, after he has passed the horizon of their worldly understanding. (Statue now in the British Museum.)

Maidens at the Lotus Pool, a Chinese painting. The difference between the Buddhist and Taoist philosophers in their interpretation of the fleeting, unstable nature of things material, is best exemplified in their reaction to the sight of a beautiful maiden. The Buddhist thought sadly how soon her beauty faded, but the Taoist saw her with joy as the symbol of eternal youth. To the Buddhist material things were symbols of decay, of which men should beware; to the Taoist they were symbols of life, inspiring the soul to unite with joys beyond human sense, the greater, wholly limitless, universal joys of spirit. "The Buddhist regards the senses as windows looking out upon unreality and mirage; to the Taoist they are doors through which the freed soul rushes to mingle with the colours and tones and contours of the universe." *A Lute of Jade*. See also p. 149.

crane soaring in space, the glow of moon-swept skies, the souls of the Taoist poets were set free as the winds to rush forth from time and space and every limitation as though escaping from prison, to find all the glow and color of universal spirit; to escape from the little and personal into the boundless and free, the vast, the universal; to be one with the first bright dawn, the many-colored spring, the scented hearts of flowers.

> I feel the great world's spirit through me thrill
> And as a cloud I drift before the wind,
> Or with the random swallow take my will . . .
> Thus strong in faith I wait and long to be
> One with the pulsings of Eternity.

So sang the old Taoist poets while they and their Buddhist friends sought deeper harmonies than the outward appearance of things.

By the time the third century dawned, the Seven Sages of the Bamboo Grove formed a literary comradeship, the first guild of good fellowship among the poets of China. Gathering almost daily in a quiet secluded nook in the gardens of the Emperor, they sat together on the grass, beside the tall green stalks and delicately cut leaves of flickering bamboo clumps, or by a lotus-pool, talking in courtly phrases, discussing with equal facility court gossip, poetry, or the deepest truths of philosophy, eating, drinking, and praising the Lady Moon.

Between these Seven Sages and China's Golden Age, the dynasty of the Tangs, there was only Tao Chien with his exquisite Peach Blossom Fountain delicately breathing forth: "I want not wealth; I want not power—let me stroll through the bright hours as they pass in my garden among my flowers."

All the great masters of song—China's most brilliant poets—lived in the three hundred years from 618 to 906 when China was ruled by the Tangs. Seeking with utter simplicity the beauty that lies deep hidden, far beneath outward forms, surrendering themselves completely to the mood aroused by a thing, they mused long over a subject till its very spirit infused them, then labored with ceaseless patience to pour forth their fire and force in complete perfection of form, with energy so concentrated as to press a world of meaning into a few short lines, sending the reader's thought traveling on and on, long after the words have ended, and opening a door for him into beautiful halls of fancy where he may wander at will, impelled but never led.

Flocks of birds have flown high and away;
A solitary drift of cloud, too, has gone, wandering—

The words cease but the reader's thoughts travel on and on following the bird and the cloud. An echo is roused in his heart and he is made as responsible as was the original poet for feeling the mood and the spirit, making it his own and enjoying it for himself. It is this quality of suggesting only and awaking the reader to do the rest which makes Chinese poetry so different from the poetry of the West.

As in following the flight of birds, the reader of Chinese poetry finds his thoughts carried on and on unendingly.

Ming Huang and his favorite in the palace gardens where Li Po sang of the lady's grace and beauty. (Sung painting, Boston Museum.) Although most students declare that Li Po is the greatest poet of China, the Chinese call Tu Fu, God of Verse.

The Emperor Ming Huang, polo-player and sportsman, was the foremost patron of literature of the imperial line of Tang. On his embroidered lawns, where lovely maiden-faces, reflected in the lake, were only to be told from the lilies growing on the marge by the tinkle of roguish laughter, Tu Fu and Li Po, most famous of Chinese poets, struck their lutes by night to catch the firefly fancies that swarmed beneath the moon.

Tu Fu, breathing the very spirit of gentle gracious nature and seeking after simplicity as though it had been a pearl, sang of the Little Rain that fell on the thirsty furrows and refreshed a waiting earth.

> Last night cloud-shadows gloomed the path that winds to my abode
> And the torches of the river boats like angry meteors glowed;
> Today fresh colors break the soil and butterflies take wing
> Down broidered lawns all bright with pearls in the gardens of the King.

Li Po gave little glimpses, like delicate prints on silk, of the court in its paint and powder, and Chang-an, the beautiful capital with its palaces and towers. To his suite of rooms overlooking the gardens of the King, Ming Huang himself retired to enjoy the genius of the poet, write down the verses he sang and afterward put them to music; and when the Emperor lost his heart to Tai Chen, the lily of China, he summoned Li Po to her beautiful little pavilion in the park where jasmine, climbing the balcony, sweetly scented the air and peonies in bloom leaned down to the calm blue lake.

In all the clouds he sees her bright robes trail
And roses seem beholden to her face.
O'er scented balustrade the scented gale
Blows warm from spring and dewdrops form apace;
Her outline on the mountain he can trace;
Now leans she from the tower in moonlight pale.

So sang Li Po; and yet despite these lovely pictures of life in gay Chang-an, all things visible were to him as to other great Taoist poets, but as passing tenement-dwellers, forever coming and going, never stable in the universe; and human existence was nothing more than a dream of little joy unless one sought with the poets in sunset and in flower for that beauty beyond beauty, that glory beyond human sight.

Without the touch of verse divine
There is no outlet for the pent-up soul!

Mid fluctuations of time and sense, he loved to retire to the View-Tower and dream of the ancient poets, their beauty and fadeless fire.

I, too, have felt the wild-bird thrill of song behind the bars; But these have brushed the world aside and walked amid the stars.

Bold, impulsive, careless, moved by moments of great exaltation and alternate depression, Li Po was held in high honor till jealousy forced him from court and he was set free to wander like a strolling troubadour up and down the land, writing little poems of nature, deep and hauntingly beautiful;—blue mountains in the evening;

Li Po, with his three brothers, gathered at night in the beautiful palace gardens of Chang-an. The lanterns are quenched, for the invisible moon sheds sufficient light to paint the glory of the fragrant blossoming trees. (Painting at Kyoto, Japan.)

the frosty gleam of moonlight; the wind among the pines. Now he sang of the Yang Tsze gorges high in the colored dawn; flush of clouds in the morning sun and sail of a friend's little boat vanishing on the river in the misty month of flowers. Now he dreamed of mounting the wind, mounting a ladder of clouds, sailing for Heaven's Jade city, and the Great Purity beyond.

> Renouncing in ruddy youth the importance of hat and chariot
> You chose pine-trees and clouds; and now white-haired,
> Drunk with the moon, a sage of dreams,
> Flower-bewitched, you are deaf to the Emperor.

In Li Po was more of that vast, Universal World-Spirit than in any other Chinese poet.

Meanwhile heart-breaking misery had come to the Emperor Ming Huang. As he lost himself more and more in revelry with Tai Chen, passing the warm spring nights in the white hibiscus bower, rebellion broke out against him and the fish-skin war-drums roared. Fleeing with his sweetheart in a mighty cloud of dust, he was halted by his sullen soldiers and told he must surrender her to instant execution or they would desert him completely and leave him to his foes. Broken-hearted, he consented, burying his face in his hands, while she of the dark moth-eyebrows, lily pale, shone through tall avenues of spears to die. But after Tai Chen's death, life was wholly empty and vain. For years Ming Huang roamed in exile, the brightness of the foreign moon saddening his lonely heart, and he only returned at last to end his days in regrets, with dreams of a happiness lost and forever beyond recall.

> There is the pool, the flowers as of old,
> There the hibiscus at the gates of gold,
> And there the willows round the palace rise.
> In the hibiscus flower he sees her face,
> Her eyebrows in the willow he can trace,
> And silken pansies thrill him with her eyes.

Po Chü-i, most romantic and tender of Chinese poets, born a quarter of a century after this love-tragedy, sang its pathos in one of China's favorite poems, "The Never-Ending Wrong," which pulses with deep compassion, varying in rhythm with every changing mood.

And Ming Huang and Tai Chen became in Chinese legend types of ideal lovers whose rich warm human affection suggested and gave promise of the fullness of perfect love. Man, said the Taoist poets, attains not by himself, nor woman by herself; like one-winged birds they rise together and their love and union symbolize the world of love and beauty toward which mortals reach.

Clothing the Taoist ideals in the shimmering garments of verse, Ssu Kung Tu, most philosophical of the Tang poets, thus expressed the soul's outrush to find the center of the universe and blend with all things into one beyond the bounds of thought and dream.

> I revel in flowers without let,
> An atom at random in space;
> My soul dwells in regions ethereal
> And the world is my dreaming-place.
>
> As the tops of the ocean I tower,
> As the winds of the air spreading wide,
> I am 'stablished in might and dominion
>   and power,
> With the universe ranged at my side.

In the days of the Tangs in China, all gentlemen wrote poetry. The greatest use of leisure was to look around in quiet, enjoy the beauty of the world and the dreams it conjured up, and so make of the moment a bit of eternity. Such was the poetry of China in the days of its deepest feeling and its most perfect, outward expression.

Cultured Chinese enjoying the beauties of Winter. (Painting at Kyoto.) The proper use of leisure is something that the Western World has never understood. Even in his hours of freedom, the European and American is essentially materialistic, rushing madly from business to social event and strenuous physical activity, then back again, ever tense, ever hurried, ever moving. He knows little of the Easterner's delight in true leisure and its joys,—peace, tranquillity, vision, serenity, insight, repose and deep feelings richly savored.

Marco Polo in the Service of Kublai Khan

Confusion and disorder once more swept over China when the line
of the Tang emperors came to an end, and again the Empire divided
into two parts. The North suffered constantly from invasions by the
wolf-packs of Khi-tan' Tartars and other ferocious Mongol tribes, but
the South was left to itself, and here there was finally established the
cultured, wealthy, and civilized government of the Sung emperors.

Not for long, however, could Southern China remain free from the
savage nomads who had overrun the North, and when the wild, relentless hordes of Genghis Khan entered China, the fall of the Sungs was
simply a matter of time. Genghis himself did not complete this conquest, but when his grandson, Kublai, became Khan and moved the
capital of the Mongol Empire to the beautiful, exotic, new city he built
at Peking, a vigorous attack was launched upon the glorious civilization
of the South.

It was at this time that Nicolo and Maffeo Polo returned to China,
accompanied by Marco, then in the strength and vigor of young manhood. And when Nicolo presented his son to Kublai Khan saying,
"This is my son, Great Lord, and your most loyal man," the young
Venetian entered upon a career of service, in the most enlightened and
fascinating country of the world. He was enrolled among the attendants
of honor of the mighty Mongol, and was soon held in high esteem by
all the court.

Within a remarkably short time, Marco learned four different lan-
guages, and adopted the manners and dress of the Mongols. Finding
him so accomplished, Kublai Khan decided to send him on an important
mission; and the young man conducted himself with so much wisdom
and tact that the Khan was greatly pleased. Marco noticed that Kublai
greatly enjoyed hearing about strange manners and customs. He therefore took especial note of all that was new and different among the
people he visited; and related his interesting observations with such
spirit and understanding that Kublai was delighted, and decided, then
and there, to keep the young man and make good use of his cleverness.

After the conquest of the Sungs, Marco visited the ancient capital of Hang'chow many times, and never ceased to marvel at its luxuriant beauty and marvelous display of wealth. Its name, he said, meant "the Celestial City," and this it certainly merited; since it was, indeed, above all others in grandeur and beauty, as well as in its abundant delights which

A banquet outing on the beautiful lake at the luxurious palace of the vanquished Sung emperors at Hang'chow. (Painted bowl, Berlin.)

might assuredly lead an inhabitant to imagine himself truly in paradise.

Here were canals and spacious squares, an eastern Venice, so large that it was a hundred miles in circumference. Here was a lake of exquisite beauty, thirty miles round, and lined with the richest mansions and palaces, a lake dotted with park islands for marriages, festivals, and picnics. On the lake were pleasure boats and barges all furnished for feasts and poled from the roof which formed a level deck. The shores were lined with graceful drooping willows, wherein flitted and fluttered gorgeous, golden orioles.

Ashore were broad, paved streets faced by stores and houses. Everyone wore silk; it was so cheap and plentiful. And, said the observant Marco, the women of this city are so splendidly attired and abundantly perfumed, they are such dainty and angelic creatures that strangers seem to get bewitched and go back home babbling of the day when they may return to the "City of Heaven."

But Kublai Khan was not satisfied with the conquest of all China; he had learned of new lands beyond the borders of this great nation, and these he was determined to attach to his domains. Off the coast of Korea were the islands of Japan; but here, although two attacks were made, the armies of the mighty Kublai were beaten off with heavy losses. An expedition to the tropical, spice-growing island of Java was also unsuccessful. However, the armies sent south into the hot, luxuriant, forest-covered lands of Burma and Cambodia, conquered, in spite of hundreds of war elephants arrayed against them; and a tribute to satisfy the Khan's pride was exacted for many years.

Marco Polo was thrilled and excited by the fighting. The horses of the Mongols were so frightened by the Burmese war-elephants that they snorted, reared, and utterly refused to obey. The Mongols then dismounted, and shot arrow after arrow into the thick hides of the elephants until the infuriated beasts turned on their masters and crushed them. Later Marco visited the city of Mien, capital of Burma, on a mission for the Khan, and told of its many marvelous gold and silver towers.

The city of Mien, magnificent with statues, temples, and gold and silver towers. (After Yule.)

Of China itself, Marco had many interesting things to relate. Kublai quickly adopted Chinese customs, and even appointed Chinese officials to government offices. He sincerely tried to be a Chinese emperor, rather than a conquering Mongol war-lord, and, at his command, a large temple was built for the tablets and spirits of Genghis, Ogotai, and other Khans, in accordance with the ancient religion of ancestor worship. Under his direction the Grand Canal was completed. This was one of the most valuable works of the Yu-ans', as Kublai named Mongol rule, and joined the capital with the most fertile districts of China.

Shrine to the spirits of departed ancestors such as Kublai erected for the worship of Genghis Khan and other Mongol leaders. (Photograph.)

Marco noted that the Khan had ordered the merchants and business men to use a kind of money printed on special paper made from the bark of the mulberry tree and stamped with the royal seal. All persons in the kingdom were compelled to accept this money on pain of death, and this was the earliest report of the now common practice of using paper money. Through the invention of paper money, through taxes and tribute, Kublai had enormous wealth at his command, but he had need of it all; for his court was magnificent in luxurious display, his entertainments were lavish, and his rewards unstinted.

On September twenty-fifth, the Khan's birthday, there was a great celebration. Kublai was dressed in his best robes, embroidered with strips of beaten gold and was attended by the twelve thousand nobles in silk and gold, similarly, but not quite so richly dressed, each wearing a golden girdle. Some of these suits were so covered with jewels that Marco decided they must be worth ten thousand bezants. Each suit was a present from the Khan, and this, together with a pair of boots made of Russian leather embroidered with silver threads, was given to each noble three times a year. Other great feasts were on New Year's Day and the Feast of Herds.

Magnificent chariot of the kind used by Kublai in traveling about his empire. (Sung painting.)

Kublai was extremely fond of hunting, and Marco told that from the first of March until the middle of May the court was occupied in a great annual hunt organized on a gigantic scale. The Khan had two chief huntsmen called *chinuchi*, or keepers of the big dogs. Each of these chiefs had 10,000 men under him, one body dressed in red, the other in blue. When the Khan went out to hunt, one of these groups with five thousand dogs went toward the right, the other to the left, forming a great circle to enclose the game. Chetahs, lynxes, and even tigers were used in hunting wild boar, wild cattle, bears, wild asses and stags; and the Mongols succeeded in training the golden eagle to catch foxes, deer, and wild goats.

In the middle of May the court returned to the Khan's palace, at Peking for three days, before continuing to the summer palace at Shandu. But whether hunting or traveling, or in residence at his magnificent palace at Peking, Kublai Khan was still the ruler of the great Chinese Empire.

He encouraged Chinese literature, and it was during the Mongol dynasty that the novel and drama first became important. The Chinese classics were translated into the new Mongol language, and a history of the Mongols was compiled so that all might know of the deeds of their famous ancestors. In addition, the Khan caused Ja'mal-ad-Din, a Persian astronomer, to draw up a calendar; he founded an academy and schools, and even had his sons, the princes, taught by a Chinese scholar. The army was reorganized, a valuable system of roads was constructed, postroads were maintained, and trees were planted beside them. In every act of government and policy, Kublai Khan was Chinese rather than Mongol. The savage nomads of the desert had become civilized; though conquerors of China, China had conquered them by its superior civilization.

Chinese children studying and writing like the sons of Kublai Khan; at left, an older boy teaching his baby brother to walk. A charming scene from a roll of the Ming period. Mongol blood became even more common among the Northern Chinese as a result of constant intermarriage; and although all Chinese are today called Mongolians, this name is descriptive only of the people living in Northern China. Southern China is inhabited by Chinese of almost an entirely different race, quite unlike the Northerners in physical build as well as in thought, occupation and their distinct civilization.

Through all these years the three Polos remained at the court of the Khan, and during this time all were intrusted with many difficult missions. Marco, now a man in the prime of life and an especial favorite of the Khan, served three years as the governor of the Chinese city of Yang'chow. On several occasions he was sent into Southern China, and at another time he was dispatched as a special ambassador to the western territories of the Khan. Marco, therefore, had unusual opportunities for knowing China, and the things he learned were all faithfully reported. It was Marco who first told the Western World about coal. "In the province of Cathay," he said, "there is found a sort of black stone which they dig out of the mountains where it runs in veins. When lighted it burns like charcoal, and retains the fire much better than wood; insomuch that it may be preserved during the night."

From the time of Kublai Khan, there was a steady weakening of Mongol power. The desert hordes lost their strength when they lost their savage, ruthless, brutality; for within them was no other power, no civilizing force. What they were not by brute strength, they were not at all, and the days of their decline were relentlessly approaching.

Kwan-ti, the Chinese war god, dear to the hearts of the Mongols. (Carved soapstone.)

However, none could see this in the time of the great Kublai; his strength seemed to be irresistible, his power greater than Mongol power had ever risen, his wealth and magnificence beyond the description of mere words. In every department, in every activity, save one, Kublai Khan, as Marco said: "surpassed every sovereign that has heretofore been or that now is in the world." Only in some of his foreign wars in which ships were used to attack the neighboring islands in the Pacific was the great Khan unsuccessful; and of these, the most disastrous of all were his wars against Japan.

Japan and the Japanese

Kublai had been told that the island of Japan was fabulously wealthy, and Marco Polo repeated the tales related to his master. "Ci-pan'go, or Japan," said Polo, "is an island towards the east in the high seas, fifteen hundred miles from the continent; and a very good island it is. The entire roof of the sovereign's palace is covered with a thick plating of heavy, solid gold."

Fu'ji-ya'ma, the snow-capped, honored by the Japanese in poem and painting. (Photograph.) See *My Book House*, Vol. VI, p. 210, for folk tale.

But this report was purely imaginary. Japan was very poor in gold, and whatever wealth it possessed was the wealth of the character of its people. Compared to the Chinese, whose legendary history went back to 2852 B.C., the Japanese were newcomers; even their legendary history did not begin until twenty-two hundred years later. The Japanese were a mixed race. One important part was made up of Korean and Mongolian people, called Ya'ma-to, who entered the island from the west; of equal importance were the Malay, or mixed Pol'y-ne'sian and Mon'gol-oid people who came from the east. Both people had to fight the Ai'nu who were the earliest inhabitants, and from the mixture of these three races came the Japanese.

The Ai'nu, the inhabitants found in Japan by the invaders, were a hairy people, fierce and vigorous. Stubbornly they resisted every attempt at settlement; but gradually the invaders took possession of the island. Then they invented a divine origin for their conquest, and an age of gods.

"Of old," reports the ancient *Chronicle*, "Heaven and Earth were not separated. They formed a chaotic mass, the purer and transparent part of which rose up and formed Heaven, while the heavier and opaque settled downwards and became the Earth." After the appearance of a reed shoot that stretched between Heaven and Earth, I-za-na-gi, the Male, and I-za-na-mi, the Female, were created in "the Plain of High Heaven."

Jim'mu Ten'no, first emperor of Japan, descended from the Sun Goddess. A statue typifying the spirit of the Japanese.

These gods, standing upon the Floating Bridge of Heaven thrust a spear into the ocean beneath them. When the spear was withdrawn, the drops of water from it became solid and formed the island of O'no-go'ro.

Izanagi and Izanami dwelt upon this island as husband and wife. Then they brought forth "the Great Eight-Island Country" seas, mountains, rivers, herbs and trees. But someone must be created to rule over this country, so A'ma-te-ra'su, the Sun Goddess was born. The Sun Goddess married Tsu'ki, the Moon God, and from this union there descended in the course of time, the first emperor of Japan, Jim'mu Ten'no. Meanwhile, A'ma-te-ra'su and Tsu'ki quarreled and parted, each going separate ways, and like the Sun and the Moon in the heavens, never to meet again.

Now it happened that Susa-no-o, the Storm God, offended the Sun Goddess and was banished from Heaven to the islands created by the drops of water from the spear point. There he and his relatives established control over the earth people. For a long time the banished gods were permitted to live as they pleased, but at last the disorder and confusion upon the islands moved the Sun Goddess to send one of her descendants to conquer and rule the earth people. Jimmu Tenno, the first emperor of Japan, was the one chosen for the task, and with his three brothers, he descended from Heaven to take command of the people.

It was this ancient legend which made the Japanese believe throughout the centuries that their emperor was a god, a descendant of the Sun. Always he must be obeyed and his commands were no more to be questioned than those of the gods in Heaven.

The earliest rulers were chiefs of only one clan, or family. Gradually, however, the chief of the most powerful clan established his authority over other Ya'ma-to chieftains. Thus the land was united in time and the ruler became an emperor. But the capital of the country did not remain in one place. It changed to the residence of each new emperor.

Not until around 200 A. D. did the Japanese begin to reach out beyond their islands. Then, according to legend, a woman, the Empress Jingo Kogo, saw a vision of a land awaiting conquest in the west. Seeking to learn whether the gods wished her to go and conquer that land, she went to the seashore to bathe, praying as she dived in the water, "If I am to go may my hair be parted by the waves evenly on either side." And when she came up her hair was in truth evenly parted in the middle. So she set forth to Korea on the mainland, which had long ago been conquered by the Chinese but had now thrown off Chinese rule. And her expedition was so successful that she came home with eighteen ships full of loot. But far more important than that plunder was the fact that Jingo Kogo had established Japan's first contact with the mainland and that by way of Korea Chinese culture began to come to Japan.

Japanese fleet attacking Korea, on an expedition similar to that of Empress Jingo Kogo. The Koreans have roped their ships together and anchored them before the harbor to withstand attack. (Painting.)

Korean noble riding before a closed carriage drawn by bullocks. (Ssang-yang tomb, 6th century A.D.) It was from Korea that Japan first received the benefit of ancient Chinese culture and civilization.

Thus it was that Buddhism came through Korea to Japan, and it was this event which started the islanders on the road to progress and enlightenment. Before this time the religion of Japan had been Shin'toism, two Chinese words meaning "the way of the gods." It was a simple worship of primitive gods and spirits, such as the sun, the wind, the waves, and the storm, war and hunting, emperors and ancestors. The gods were supposed to have an invisible soul or double which dwelt in some such object as a mirror, sword, or tablet placed in a plain, simple wooden house or shrine. Shrines were found everywhere throughout the islands; in fields, half-hidden by the grain; in distant mountain passes; and beside the well-trodden roads. The Emperor was the High Priest of the gods and made prayers for the nation and the people. Once a year, there was an impressive rite of purification called *O-Harahi*. Pieces of paper were cut to resemble human forms; the sins which the people had committed were transferred to these paper persons, and they were taken out to sea and sunk beneath the waves.

It was in the year 552 A.D. that a Korean prince sent to Japan a gold and copper image of Buddha, books explaining his teaching, and a letter saying: "This doctrine is hard to understand, but marvelously excellent. It furnishes men with treasure to their heart's content. Every prayer may be fulfilled, and every wish granted." The Emperor welcomed the gifts, and gave the image and books into the keeping of the noble Soga family. Shintoism continued to be the religion of most of the Japanese, however, and at first only a few accepted the new teachings.

But the number of Buddhists slowly grew and Buddhism greatly encouraged art and learning. Japan at this time was a small nation of farmers, fishermen, and hunters. It had no writing of its own and therefore no literature. Now, however, the Japanese took the Chinese ideographs, adapted them to syllabic writing and so devised a script of their own. The introduction of images and pictures laid the foundation of Japanese art, and almost every branch of industrial and artistic development was enriched by the coming of Buddhism. The bare simplicity of the Shinto temples gave way to a warmth of coloring and a splendor

of gilding and lacquering in the Buddhist shrines, and there was a sort of religious urge toward the making of beautiful things.

And now instructors came from China and Korea to teach the Japanese more of the advantages of civilization; and the Japanese journeyed to China to receive knowledge from the enlightened people under the Tangs. Chinese and Koreans taught the Japanese in calendar compiling, geography, magic, tile- and brick-making, pottery, the casting of metal, and many other crafts.

Koreans like those who aided Japanese civilization in the 6th century A.D. Costumes and attitudes show how strong was Chinese influence. (From the Tomb of the Two Pillars, Kokuryo.)

Shoguns and Samurai

Prince Sho-to-ku Tai-shi, head of the Soga family and guardian of Buddhism, the new religion of Japan. (A painting, Imperial Household.)

However, with all this growth of Buddhism in Japan, the Soga family, to whom the guardianship of that new religion had been entrusted, kept growing more powerful until they became the actual rulers of the land, leaving the emperors as puppets only. And after the Sogas other noble families fought each other to gain supreme power until at last in 1192 the Emperor Ta′ka-hi′ra bestowed on the leader of one of these families the title of Shogun or Generalissimo, thus creating a position which was to last for seven hundred years, finally becoming hereditary in one family and making these military leaders, the shoguns, instead of the emperors, the real rulers of the whole island empire of Japan.

It was at this time that the Japanese began to look on fighting as a business whereby men might earn a living and so arose the *samurai*, a large class of professional soldiers. Men of indomitable courage, able to perform the most marvelous feats of arms, these samurai took their greatest delight in sword play and won their greatest fame as swordsmen. But they were also expert in the use of bows and arrows and spears. And they developed the art of *jujitsu*, so a man might defend himself if he was caught without weapons by using a scientific sort of wrestling which disabled an opponent by turning against him his own strength and weight. Thus the Japanese, in contrast to the common people of China, who were by nature peaceful, developed a warrior class and a great sense of glory in warfare.

Such was Japan for hundreds of years straight on down to modern times. Her Heaven-born emperor, living in seclusion and seldom seen, was regarded with awe by the people, but was in fact a voiceless puppet while the nation was run by the shogun, a dictator, who pretended to act in the name of the god-emperor. Governing through docile lords known as daimyos, each in charge of a district, the shogun, with all those loyal samurai at his command, could enforce whatever he would. And it was most useful that the emperor should remain as a god to the people, for thus the shogun spoke for a god and the daimyos spoke for a shogun who spoke for a god. And so it went all down the line—no man could think of disobeying his superior, for that superior spoke for another superior, who spoke for a god. The result was blind obedience from the man below to the man above and the acceptance of any injustice or misrule rather than to revolt or even criticize a superior which in the last analysis meant to strike at the gods.

But if Japan through all those centuries made no advance toward a more liberal and democratic government, she advanced steadily in all the arts from the year 710 when Nara was established as a permanent capital. At Nara the Japanese built a beautiful city with parks and temples, graceful shrines and court buildings. And in literature they began to produce the most beautiful poetry.

Warriors of the Fu'ji-wa'ra family who governed Japan in the name of the Emperor after the Sogas.

The Poetry of Japan

Peafowl and Peonies. (Painting, Boston Museum.) Love of such beautiful things, of birds and breezes, flowers and trees, moonlight and starlight, is seen in Japanese paintings as well as in their charming little *tanka* poems of thirty-one syllables and the tiny *hokkus* of only seventeen syllables. See *Little Pictures of Japan.* The early poetry of Japan, however, was spirited and warlike in contrast to the peaceful poetry of early China, indicating an essential difference between the two peoples. "The Japanese," said their countryman, Yo-ne No-gu-chi, "were from the beginning both poets and warriors." See p. 169.

In Japan there was a wealth of sunshine, of flower-bloom and bird-song, and the people loved these beautiful things. They loved trees and breezes, butterflies and birds, moonlight and starlight; and they loved these little things so much that they always wrote poems about them.

Anyone might write verses in Japan—that is anyone who listened with all his heart to the song of the nightingale among the flowers, to the voice of the frogs in a star-lit pool, and the music of the wind, singing in the trees. Like little dewdrops were their poems, no more in size than the smallest drop of water; but reflecting all the shine and color of the sun, and they were written on embroidered screens, on cups and plates, on painted fans—anywhere in fact. Farm-girls standing knee-deep in the muddy water of the rice fields, made verses as they worked. Fishermen, fishing with cormorants by the flaming light of torches, made verses as they fished. Porters, with packs on their heads, up to their necks in tall grass, made verses as they trudged. Indeed, in no country of the world were people taught to love poetry as truly as in Japan.

Often the Japanese held poetry picnics. When a householder had an especially fine flowering tree, a cherry perhaps, all pink with a wealth of bloom, he invited his friends to a party. They came in their holiday-robes and clattering wooden sandals; they walked about the tree and admired it; they drank in its fragrance, and tea was served to them under its branches. Then each sat down and wrote a poem, and after he had read it to the others, he fastened it to the tree.

> Months and days I've wasted
> Doing some useless thing,—
> How few the hours that have been well spent
> Viewing the flowers in spring!

The early-blossoming plum tree was called, "the elder brother of the flowers," but it was the cherry blossom that was most dearly loved in Japan. The cherry blossom was the national flower, and the Japanese loved it so deeply that it stood to them as a sign for Beauty itself. When the lovely pink petals began to fall from the trees in the spring, they imagined that all nature sorrowed and sighed to see them go.

> When cherry blossoms fall,
> So sorrowfully men sigh.
> Who knows,—perhaps the soft spring showers
> Are tears of the sorrowing sky!

For many years the emperors of Japan entertained at garden parties on the beautiful hills at Yo-shi-no when they were a cloud of pink at cherry-blossom time. As many as ten thousand people thronged at once to that lovely spot— lords and ladies in splendid garments swarming over the hillside, even the poorest of men and women trudging from the city slums, a pilgrimage of two hundred miles and all the way on foot—just to view the cherry blossoms.

Two Women in a Spring Breeze, a print by Ha-ru-no-bu, alive with the vigorous swirl and graceful sweep of the wind. Japanese artists loved the wind and Japanese poets were called Friends of Moon and Winds.

Someone among that multitude, struck dumb by the beauty of the sight, once stammered in halting words:

> Oh this! Oh this!
> I have no words! I can but say
> "Flower-mountain, Yoshino!"

Another cried:

> I thought I saw a great white cloud, but no!
> I looked again and lo!
> 'Twas blossoms fluttering down from Yoshino.

Greatest of the older poets of Japan was Hi'to-ma'ro, who lived about 737 A.D. He was an orphan who said of himself: "No father or mother have I, but the moon and winds obey me, and in poetry I find my joy." True indeed it was that Hitomaro was the friend of moon and winds; he knew what they said, he heard their secret voice, and he turned it into poems of magic words that others, too, might understand.

> In the ocean of the sky,
> Borne on rising waves of cloud,
> The moon ship
> Goes a-gliding by
> Through a forest of stars.

Thus sang Hitomaro, dwelling like many another among the Japanese poets, with night and silence, solitude, dreams, and moonlight.

The thrilling beauty of moonlight as expressed by the famous Japanese artist, Hi'ro-shi'ge.

As time went on, the poets of Japan came to be called Friends of Moon and Winds, and so they were in very truth; for these were the things they loved,—moon and winds, birds and blossoms, frogs and crickets, butterflies and bees. Their hearts were as full of wonderment and adoration as the hearts of little children.

Truth and beauty, said the Japanese poet, need no explanation. Real poetry is the voice of Spontaneity, as simple and natural as the growth of a flower. It is not in word but in life and feeling. To sing the stars and the flowers is to sing Life itself.

> Eternity, rolled in love,
> Bids the visible world to sing.

Ko'ma-chi, beloved Japanese poetess. (By Harunobu.) "Real poetry," said Basho, greatest of Japanese poets as he wandered with his students through the countryside during the seventeenth century, "is to lead a beautiful life. To live poetry is better than to write it." And whenever he saw a young follower give way to a fit of anger, or otherwise act unworthily, he would gently say to the youth: "But this is not poetry."

The Western poet often preaches and theorizes about life but the great Japanese poet makes his readers *feel* life itself, the pulse of universal being. The Westerner is intellectual; the Chinese and Japanese are emotional. The Westerner approaches truth through reasoning, the Japanese through feeling. As Greek needs Jew, and Jew needs Greek, so the Western attitude needs the Eastern for completeness, for any real grasp of the one Universal Spirit. Says Yo-ne No-gu-chi in *The Spirit of Japanese Poetry*, "My mind thinks on the real spiritual freedom which will soon become a perfect idealism like a broader day born from the mixed souls of East and West."

But poetry was not the only form of Japanese literature, although it was the most universal. All forms of writing had become popular, and much of this writing was the work of the ladies at court. Among the most important literature of these women were novels and diaries giving intimate and interesting pictures of court life and intrigue. Indeed, so personal were these novels that the Japanese called them *mono-gatari*, or "gossip-things"; and great was the delight of the demure, soft-spoken Japanese women when a group gathered together in the still afternoon to listen to the reading of "gossip-things" by one of their number. *Pillow-sketches*, another work of a Japanese woman, was an amazing record of impressions of life and its daily problems. Two perfectly delightful chapters were entitled "Things I dislike heartily," and "Things I am fond of." Then, too, there were the *No* plays, a form of lyric drama which grew out of religious dances.

Painting was first brought to Japan by Chinese artists, and the island kingdom gave it such enthusiastic interest that it developed rapidly. The two most common forms were *makimono*, or long horizontal scrolls, and *kakemono*, or hanging scrolls. With the introduction of the Zen form of Buddhism, Japanese artists produced the most exquisite landscape, flower, and bird paintings of the nation's history.

The Repulse of the Mongols

In 794, six years before Charlemagne was crowned Emperor of the West, the capital of Japan was moved from Nara to Kyo'to. The first name for Kyoto was *Heian-kyo*, "the city of peace," and it was patterned after the Chinese city of Sian, the capital of the Tang emperors. It was not at this palace of Kyoto that the Hojo Regents ruled, however, but at the Shogun's city of Ka'ma-ku'ra. And to Kamakura there came to the Regent To'ki-mu'ne in the year 1268, a letter from Kublai Khan of China demanding tribute and homage. Tokimune paid no attention to the letter and sent no reply. Kublai Khan could not understand such indifference to the mighty Mongol power. Again and again ambassadors were sent to the island, but always the Regents refused to listen to them, and always they came back empty handed.

Kublai prepared for war. The Koreans were ordered to build a thousand ships and assemble an army of forty thousand men; and in 1274, the Korean army, reinforced by twenty-five thousand Mongols, set sail for the invasion of Japan. The first attack was upon the island of Tsu'shi'ma in the strait between Korea and Japan. There was only a small garrison of two hundred Japanese stationed on this island, but these worthy warriors fought gallantly until the last man

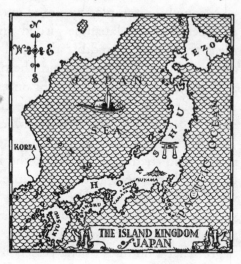

THE ISLAND KINGDOM of JAPAN

died. During the night, the coast was swept by a fierce sub-tropical gale. The Mongol invasion was abandoned, and the fleet sailed for Korea. One vessel ran aground and several sank, so when the expedition returned home, over thirteen thousand men had been lost.

Kublai Khan immediately redoubled his preparations for invasion and conquest on a larger scale than before. Ships were built in such numbers that the Chinese poets describe the hills as in mourning for their stricken forests. Every conceivable kind of war engine was constructed, and two great armies were assembled. One army of Chinese and Mongols had their meeting place at a southern port opposite the island of For-mo'sa, the other army of Koreans and Mongols gathered in Korea. Altogether, Kublai Khan had prepared a force of almost two hundred thousand warriors and a navy of three thousand five hundred ships. There was to be no question about the conquest of Japan this time.

The Korean fleet sailed nearly a month before that from China, and made a landing at the island of Tsu'shi'ma where it awaited the laggards. Day by day the Japanese attacked and harried them; three thousand men died from sickness, and the Koreans were preparing to withdraw when the Chinese fleet hove in sight. The united force now took the island of I'ki and once more landed on the sandy coast of Kyu'shu.

Meanwhile, temples hummed with prayer and grew dim with clouds of incense as the Japanese girded on their weapons and went forth to meet their foe. Incredible deeds of daring were performed. The Japanese did not wait to defend themselves, but attacked bravely by sea and shore. So furious were their onsets, and so deadly were their flashing swords at close quarters, that the enemy were compelled to lash their ships together and lay planks between them to concentrate their forces.

In fifty-three days of combat and fighting, but little progress was made. And then disaster struck the Mongol forces. Let Marco tell the tale: "It happened, after some time, that a north wind began to blow with great force, and the ships of the Mongols, which lay near the shore of the island, were driven foul of each other. It was then determined to set out to sea. The gale, however, increased to so violent a degree that a number of the vessels floundered. The other ships did not suffer from the storm, and returned home to the great Khan."

That ended the Mongol attempt to conquer Japan. But from that time on Japan was cut off from China and went on her way alone without help or hindrance from other peoples. Thus, like China, she remained for centuries shut in by herself, untouched by any contact with Europe, so she also had to face in our own times and without preparation her adjustment to the modern culture of the West.

Japanese nobles in armor hiding among the sand dunes of the coast, eager to sacrifice themselves in a sudden charge against the overwhelming hordes of Kublai Khan. (Imperial Palace, Tokyo.)

VI

Around Africa to India

(1415–1498)

The Polos Return to Venice

For seventeen years the three Polos served Kublai Khan faithfully. Many were the difficult missions they performed for the Mongol monarch, and great was the favor in which they were held. All three amassed such riches as were beyond their wildest dreams. They lived in luxury, with servants and slaves at their command. But royal favor and prosperity bred envy in the hearts of Mongol chiefs and Chinese nobles; and Kublai Khan was growing old. Time enough had been spent in this glamorous land; it would be fool-hardy to remain

Chinese emperor like Kublai Khan. (7th cent.)

until their protector died, and their jealous enemies gained control.

One day, therefore, when the great Khan seemed unusually cheerful, Nicolo seized the opportunity to throw himself at his monarch's feet, and beg that he and his family might be permitted to depart for home. At once the Khan's mood changed. Frowning darkly, he demanded what reason they could have to endure the hazards of a dangerous journey on which they would probably lose their lives? If gain was their object, he was ready to give them double what they possessed. If honor, he would gratify them to the extent of their desires. But because of the regard he bore them, he positively refused permission to depart.

The Polos were greatly disturbed, but they could not permit the Khan to know how uneasy they were. With the patience of true merchants artfully waiting to bring opposing bargainers to their terms, they bore the refusal with outward good grace, determined, nevertheless, to seize the first opportunity of making their escape.

Now it happened that soon there came to the court of Kublai Khan at Pe-king', an embassy from the Il'khan of Persia, the Mongol Empire established by Kublai's brother, Hu-la-gu'. The wife of the Ilkhan had died, and in a letter written on her deathbed, she had begged her husband to take his new wife only from her own family in China. The Ilkhan agreed and at once dispatched three nobles and numerous attendants to the court of Kublai Khan with the request that his Emperor should make the selection of his bride. Kublai was greatly pleased, and under his direction, choice was made of a beautiful young girl named Ku-ka-chin'. Though but seventeen years of age, Kukachin had been trained in all the graces of a highborn lady, and the ambassadors of the Ilkhan gave their hearty approval of the choice.

Arrangements were promptly made to return to Persia overland by the route the envoys had followed when they came to the Great Khan, and Kublai added a numerous and splendid suite of attendants to do honor to the bride. Kukachin and her escort departed in a blaze of glory, and the incident was quite forgotten, when suddenly, after a year had passed, the gallant band reappeared before the gates of Peking. Fresh wars had broken out among the Tartar nobles, and after traveling eight months, the envoys had found the country so unsettled and dangerous that they could progress no further. Much against their wills, they had been forced to return to Peking.

The Polos saw their opportunity. Marco had just come back from a successful expedition to the Indies, and had reported that the sea voyage was eminently safe. The ambassadors of the Ilkhan were anxious to get home. The Polos and the Persians, therefore, reached an agreement, and the young Queen begged the Khan to send her to Persia by sea in the safe keeping of the Polos. With all the progress made in many different ways, the Mongols were still landsmen, knowing little of navigation;

but the Venetians were as much at home on sea as land, and would insure the safe delivery of the little royal bride. Kublai Khan was tricked. The crafty Venetians had placed him in a position where he could not refuse the request they made without offending the Ilkhan. The Great Khan gave his consent, but exacted their promise to return.

Accordingly fourteen great ships, with four masts and nine sails, were prepared for the impending journey. Each was amply manned with crews and stocked with provisions for two years. Every facility for the voyage was provided with a lavish hand, and to the Polos the Khan gave rubies and precious jewels, as well as tablets of authority which would serve as passports and letters of unlimited credit.

The voyage was long and adventurous. Skirting the shore of China, the little fleet sailed south to the island of Java, then across the Bay of Bengal, between Ceylon and India, and gradually moved westward until they arrived at last at Or'muz on the Persian Gulf. Two years were spent on the journey, and six hundred members of the expedition died along the way; but in spite of difficulties, Ku-ka-chin' was safely escorted to the Persian court, and wept when she parted from her guardians. Moreover, she found that in the three years spent in adventurous way-faring to join her husband-to-be, the old Ilkhan had died, and she had the good fortune to marry his son and get a young husband in his stead!

The arrival of the Polos in Persia, on their homeward journey to Venice. (15th cent. miniature.)

Remaining in Persia nine months to rest and refresh themselves, the Polos now took up the remaining journey to Venice. Word had reached them during their voyage that Kublai Khan had died; and thus released from their promise, they resolved never again to return to China. The wealth they had amassed had been exchanged for jewels, and these were safely secreted about their bodies and clothes. Luxury and magnificence could now be purchased in Venice; nevermore would they go exploring.

Thus it happened that late one afternoon in the year 1295, there stepped ashore in Venice, a bedraggled, weather-beaten trio, their faces bronzed and leathery, their garments strange and foreign, all their bearing marked by the manners of the Mongol; even the bundles they carried were bound in Eastern cloths, and they had almost forgotten their native Italian tongue. The youngest member of the trio, a bushy-haired, black-bearded fellow, led the way across the piazza. Dusk was already falling and torches began to flare like fireflies along the canals. Venice had changed much during the twenty-four years since they had last seen it, and they had difficulty in finding their old residence. At last, they entered the courtyard, and the dogs of Venice barked loudly as they knocked on their own front door. The Polos had come home!

But the venturesome merchants had long been thought dead, and the distant kinsmen, who now occupied the house, refused to admit these extremely suspicious-looking strangers who thus demanded entrance when the door had been shut for the night. The newcomers had to force themselves bodily into the house, and only after long argument and discussion did the Polos convince their kindred.

The older Polos now settled down to enjoy their wealth and leisure and the companionship of friends. But Marco was still hearty, a vigorous, active man just in the prime of life. Not for him was the settled life. Three years later, equipping a war galley, he sailed off as commander in the navy of Venice; but in an unfortunate battle with a rival fleet from Genoa, he was taken prisoner with seven thousand of his countrymen; and it was while he languished in jail in Genoa, with time hanging heavy on his hands, that he dictated to a fellow prisoner, a scribe called Rus'ti-ci-an'o, the story of his travels and adventures in the East.

The Isles of Venice, with a boatyard busy upon a new vessel for wares from the lands visited by the Polos. (15th cent. woodcut.) Modern explorers have proved beyond question the truth and accuracy of Marco Polo's report of his travels. General Sir Percy Sykes, who spent twenty-five years in Asia, patiently traced out the western part of the Polo's route and verified Marco's descriptions by personal observation. Another Englishman, Captain John Wood, explored the Himalayas and the "Roof of the World" five centuries after Marco had passed that way, only to prove again the truth and remarkable accuracy of the memory of this observing young Venetian of the Middle Ages.

Before a year had passed, a truce was signed by the rival cities, all prisoners were released, and Marco returned to Venice where he married and settled down, his household growing lively with the arrival of three little daughters. But almost no one believed the stories he told his friends; and though scribes copied the book he had dictated to Rus'ti-ci-an'o, they would not vouch for its truth, but were very careful to say that they had copied the work only because they found the tale so interesting. Slowly, nevertheless, the story of Marco Polo was spread all over Europe. A romantic adventure, indeed! Everyone enjoyed its descriptions of wealth and power, its strange people with stranger customs, its queer beasts, stones, and fruits. But whether its marvels were true or the most entertaining fiction, no one really knew and to the people of Europe, China and the Orient remained vague, unknown lands, mysterious, veiled in romance. Western noble and merchant-prince wore splendid silks from China, diamonds from Gol-con'da and jade from far-off Kho-tan'; they walked on carpets from Persia, and seasoned food with spices from Java and Ceylon; but they knew nothing of the lands from whence these came.

The Closing of the Caravan Routes

There came, as years passed by, a day when the rich supply of jewels, silks and spices suddenly diminished. Prices soared sky-high, and still the demand for all these luxurious goods of the East continued unabated. What had checked the supply? Merchants haunted the markets of the Eastern Mediterranean, impatiently awaiting the arrival of caravans. They waited now in vain. The only goods of the East were in the hands of Arabs whose seamen had brought them from India. These shrewd traders demanded twice and thrice the amount formerly paid by Italians for goods from the Orient. And they received their price; for Europe demanded her luxuries. But what had caused this change? Slowly the Venetian and Genoese merchants learned that events come to pass in the East had rendered the caravan routes unsafe.

It was due to Genghis Khan and his powerful line of successors that Asia had been kept peaceful and open to trade with the West. Brute conquerors though they were, holding their conquests by force, the Mongols had swept away all religious and political barriers that endangered communication. From China to the Russian steppes the *Yassa* kept the peace; while the *yam*, the Khan's post system, made it possible for merchants to pass in safety over routes from end to end of the then-known world. Under this exchange between the East and West, culture had sprung up anew. Mohammedan science and skill were carried to the Far East; Chinese inventions were brought to the West. In the ruined gardens of Islam, architects enjoyed a silver age under the Mongol khans; China blossomed in literature; Christian Crusades to Palestine came at last to an end; for the Mongols permitted Christians to visit the Holy Sepulchre unmolested and in safety. The Mongol Empire, despite its history of force, had compelled the world to peace, for the first time bringing together the two ends of the earth and civilizations utterly diverse.

But all this was to end. The Mongol Empire reached its height under Kublai Khan; and even during his time, there were signs of renewing feuds in the vast expanses of Central Asia. Kublai died in 1294, and with his death the power and importance of the Mongols swiftly passed away.

In China, his successors continued for a time to rule, but their power was steadily weakening. In 1355 a Buddhist priest raised an army; Korea joined the revolt; Pe-king' was taken; the Khan fled, the Mongols were driven out, and in thirteen years, a new dynasty, the Mings, were established in China, and the priest who had led the revolt became the emperor of the land. In Turkestan, Central Asia, and the Gobi Desert, the lesser khans or chieftains asserted their independence, fought, and quarreled with each other, robbed the caravans, slew the merchants and travelers, and put an end to trade overland by way of the caravan routes. A great black curtain rolled down again cutting Europe off from Asia, confining Western commerce to the Mediterranean ports, and engulfing the East in its pristine veil of remoteness and mystery.

If only the road to the East were open! The Mohammedans jealously guarded the caravan routes of Syria. Venice and Genoa controlled the Mediterranean, and suffered no ships but theirs to traffic with the ports' of Palestine and Asia Minor. Where could enterprising merchants of other nations find a route which would reach the land of their heart's desire, and make the fabulous riches of the Eastern World their very own?

Long caravan of camels, mules, and horses, bearing spices from the East. Mohammedan merchants, shown in cloaks and turbans, grew enormously wealthy from this commerce. (de Bry's *India* 1599.)

Frightful tales of death and danger were told by sailors of the Sea of Darkness (Woodcut, 1555.)

The people of Europe knew little about the world beyond the lands bordering the Mediterranean; the monk, Cosmas, living in the sixth century, had described a flat world that hung in space. Cosmas based his description on the Bible wherein Moses had likened the world to the tabernacle of the Lord. Of this mighty tabernacle, the earth is the floor, the four walls of Heaven are glued to the extremities of the world and to the domed roof, and stretching across the great dome is the firmament wherein are the stars and the waters of the sky. A great ocean stream completely surrounded the earth, closing it in on all sides, and beyond its borders no one dared venture. The "Green Sea of Darkness," the name given the Atlantic, was a part of this ocean stream, and all shrank from sailing it. It was believed that if a ship ventured far to the west it would meet with black fog, so thick that it could not be penetrated; if south, that the sun would grow hotter and hotter until the sea boiled and the land became too hot for any living creature to set foot on it. Then, too, this dreadful sea was inhabited by horrible monsters, sea-serpents, and dragons which could swallow up ship and crew easily. No, the "Green Sea of Darkness" offered no opportunity for a new route to the East.

But the desire for the wealth and commerce of the East was great; and by the fifteenth century, certain men had begun to express doubt regarding the existence of Cosmas' world and the terrors of the encircling ocean.

Monstrous beasts, large enough to destroy great vessels, were believed to inhabit the unknown seas.

Among these men was a certain Prince Henry of the narrow little kingdom of Portugal. And of all the great deeds which the world afforded, none seemed so worthy to him as to discover the secret of the Sea of Darkness.

Strange, horrible, and fantastic were the terrible creatures of the Sea of Darkness. This illustration from Munster's *Cosmographiae Universalis*, published 1544, shows sailors throwing barrels to a whale to turn it from their ship, a serpent curling over a vessel, and a man caught by a gigantic crab.

From his stone tower on Cape St. Vincent, Prince Henry sought to dispel the ignorance of seamen concerning the Sea of Darkness. The instrument on the table is the astrolabe used in navigation.

To this end Prince Henry built high on the sacred promontory of St. Vincent, a sturdy stone tower whose windows looked far out over the Atlantic Ocean. There he gathered around him learned mathematicians and astronomers from all parts of Europe; and for long hours each day he studied and experimented with astrolabe and compass, seeking to find new and better instruments for the use of his sailors.

From prisoners captured in North African wars and from merchants, Henry learned that south of the Sahara Desert in Africa, in the region of the Sen'e-gal' River, there was a fertile, prosperous land from which came gold, ivory, and slaves. The Mohammedans called this *Bdad Ghana*, Land of Wealth, and this became Guin'ea to the Portuguese. Moreover, he was told that the Senegal River had its rise in the same lake as the Nile; and Henry believed that if the mouth of the Senegal were discovered, there would be a water route right across Africa to the Red Sea and the ports of Arabia, India, and China!

No living person knew anything about the African coast, however, farther than a great cape named Boj'a-dor'. Beyond that shoulder of land were treacherous shoals, baffling winds, and terrible currents, it was said; and Arabian legends told of a hand of Satan which reached out of the water to clutch and destroy helpless vessels. Nevertheless, Henry was determined to explore the coast beyond Cape Bojador, and he sought out brave and daring mariners, offering them riches and favor if they would sail their vessels past this point of land.

For twelve fruitless years he sent his mariners steadily down the African coast, and in all that time none of them ever dared pass beyond the Cape. Henry received them back patiently, listened to their stories, rewarded them, and then sent them down to search again. Each time he made his request more urgent and promised greater rewards. At last, one day, in the year 1434, he sent for a captain by the name of Gil Ean'nes and bade him go out in God's Name, nor dare to return until he had passed Cape Bojador and could bring a truthful account of what lay beyond.

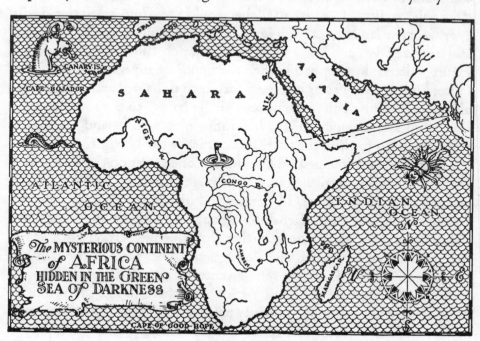

With one tiny caravel, Gil Eannes started on his perilous quest. Southward he set his course, then westward until the surf roared and the water churned the sand and he knew that he had reached Boj'a-dor'. Fear gripped the hearts of Eannes and his companions and they would fain have turned back to safety. But stronger than their fear of the unknown, was their fear of Prince Henry's displeasure; so tremblingly they gave themselves up to the currents and drifted far out into the Sea of Darkness.

To their surprise no black fog came up to swallow them. No sea-monsters appeared. No evil spirits descended upon them. And when they judged that wind and currents had carried them far to the south of Bojador, they trimmed their sails and set their course to the eastward. And behold! after some days' sailing, land ahead, and about them a sea as easy to navigate as the waters of Portugal.

They landed on this unknown shore, and gathered plants to take back to Prince Henry, for they saw no sign of people or houses. This was not the rich and fertile land of Prince Henry's dreams, but at least it was a habitable country, free, as far as they could see, from spirits or devils. Nor were the land and sea too hot for human beings to bear. So the old stories were false, and brave men might now defy the dangers of Bojador! Henry's determination had broken the bonds of superstition and ignorance; his untiring efforts had persuaded men to hazard and explore, and although he himself never went on a single voyage to the southland, his leadership and encouragement, his unflinching resolve and his patient insistence won for him the title, Prince Henry the Navigator.

Great was the rejoicing in the staunch, stone tower on the wave-swept coast of Portugal when the caravel returned, and many were the honors and rewards showered on Gil Eannes and his companions. During the years that followed, ship after ship sailed around Bojador and crept down the African coast, each a little farther than the one before; until at last the great desert was passed and Portuguese sailors reached the rich and fertile land of Guinea. Later vessels ventured even farther south to the swamps and jungles of tropical Africa, and there found the primitive Negro living in elemental simplicity amid strange gods and spirits, with ceremonies and customs utterly unknown to Europe.

The Negroes of Africa

Cut off completely from North Africa, by the vast expanses of the Sahara Desert, were the great equatorial jungle forests of tropical Africa, ever green, as if carved from the heart of an emerald. Two great rivers watered this torrid land of evil smelling swamp. The turbid Niger River, a huge web of mud and water, rising in the foothills of the Kong Mountains, flowed over treacherous sand-bars into the grey Atlantic. A thousand miles to the south lay the giant Congo in the very heart of the rain belt and luxuriant jungles. Together, these two great rivers produced hundreds of miles of tangled trees and feathery foliage, so thick that they could be crossed only by narrow footpaths.

Here on the West African coast between the Niger and Congo, there had dwelt from time immemorial the shiny, black Negro, in all his ignorance and primitiveness. Broad-faced, flat-nosed, and thick-lipped was the frizzly-haired African native. Living ever in a hot, damp climate, he had become listless and indifferent to progress, and forgotten by Europe and Asia; for centuries he and his tribe had lived and died uninfluenced by Mohammedan or European.

Chieftain of the Ben-in' tribe of Negroes on the West Coast of Africa, bearing spear and carved scepter. (Bronze statuette, Field Museum, Chicago.)

When the startled Portuguese came upon them in their journeys down the coast, these people of forest and bush lived as they had always lived, in insignificant hamlets,—mere specks in an impenetrable jungle. Their villages were built in small clearings from ten to fifty miles apart, and the only roads between them were narrow, forest paths beset at every step by the spirits of their ancestors. Several related groups formed a village quarter, and each village was governed by a priest and a chieftain.

Ben-in' chieftain'wearing the coral strands about his neck which indicate rank, and also wide coral anklets. On his head is a coral crown; in his right hand is a carved wooden image scepter; in his left, a thunderbolt; below are two tamed leopards, and on the base are beheaded enemies. (Bronze, Berlin.)

There was little order in which the houses of the villages were built. A chief suddenly determined to found a new settlement because the old one had become bewitched. He selected a new site. A large space of open ground with a shade tree in the center of the settlement was reserved for "palavers," gatherings, and dances. Nearby were the chief's huts, marked by a roof coming low down so as to form a veranda.

Both four-sided and round buildings were erected on the Western Coast. In certain districts rectangular, wooden frame-work houses of wattled bamboo and palm bast, with mud squeezed between, were set up quickly, and skulls of animals were stuck on the gables as trophies of the chase. At other places well-built, grass-thatched huts, with elaborately decorated walls, stood singly on a plantation, or were arranged in an oblong group around the house of the chief. Curious domed and windowless houses of sun-baked clay were built in still other sections.

The pride of every village, and the hub around which native life revolved, was the tribal council house. Here the tribesmen whiled away idle moments, held tribal dances, councils of war, and "palavers,"— those long, endless arguments and discussions which the Negro so loved.

Here were stored all articles of common ownership, such as war canoes, tribal fetishes, dancing masks and signal drums, and the more grisly relics of human skulls and heads of vanquished enemies, which were usually displayed in small holes or windows constructed for this purpose. The council house was always the most ornate and decorative building of the village, varying from a few poles driven into the ground with a covering of palm-leaf thatch to elaborate, two-storied buildings adorned with grotesque, symbolic paintings done with gay vegetable dyes and colored

Bronze, Benin plaque showing armed men before the single doorway of the tribal council house. (Berlin.) It was before such tribal houses that stories were told, and the American Uncle Remus tales of *Br'er Rabbit* were known in Africa for centuries. See these stories in *My Book House*, Vol.III, p.123; Vol.IV, p.128.

mud. On the upper story of the council house was the secret ceremonial tribal chamber which no woman was allowed to enter on pain of death.

By day both men and women were busy hunting, fishing, farming, weaving, or making pottery. If idle, they passed the time in sleep or gossip. But at night the moon cast its spell, and a story-teller was asked to recite. All knew the tales, which had been told and retold for countless generations, but not all could relate them dramatically. This was the special accomplishment of the story-teller, a man with the memory and skill of a great actor; and all the tribe followed with breathless interest, familiar accounts of beasts and gods.

Constantly with the African native was his religion. The simple-souled Negro believed that the bush, with its soft green twilight, dark shadows and quivering lights, was peopled everywhere by good and bad spirits, and supernatural beings and ghosts. But he also believed that over and above these spirits was a Creator, or Supreme God, although this God did not touch his life closely. However, between the great over-God and mankind were thousands and millions of lesser spirits whose favor must be courted. They were everywhere,—in the air, in the caves, in enormous rocks, in hollow trees, in dark forests; the spirit world was made up of the souls of all the dead that had passed since the world began.

Ben-in' chieftain and warriors in the elaborate ceremonial dress worn when performing human sacrifice. (16th cent. bronze.) Such work shows that the Negro, like all other races, is capable of developing a highly interesting culture of his own.

These spirits were everlastingly longing and seeking for places to rest. In their search for a home they were helped by the native *oganga*, the priest, or witch-doctor. He it was who had the power to conjure the free, wandering spirits into the narrow limits of small, material objects. At his command, the spirit entered a tree, a stone, a block of wood, a clod of mud, a piece of jagged glass, or a rusty nail. The abiding place of the spirit might be any curious object that struck the fancy of the Negro *oganga*: the curling tails of bush cats, nuts, snail shells, the bones of animals, the teeth and claws of stealthy prowling leopards, or sticks roughly carved to represent the human body. Any object in which a spirit lived was called a "fetish" by the Portuguese sailors, from the Portuguese *feities*, a luck charm. Native words, however, were *gree-gree* and *monda*.

The fact that the spirit of a departed soul passed into a tall, majestic African cotton-tree made it sacred at once, and it was immediately worshiped because of the spirit which dwelt within it. The Negro never worshiped the object itself, but always addressed himself to the spirit within. If anyone broke a branch from the tree containing the spirit, however, he dishonored the spirit inside.

Bronze head of Benin chieftain wearing so many strands of coral that the neck is stretched, the eyes bulge, and the head is held so stiffly it can hardly be moved.

If the tree fell so that it killed a man, it was believed that unintentionally, the Negro had selected a tree containing a spirit, and that this spirit had caused the death, rather than the falling tree. And to confirm this view the witch-doctor was sure to report that the spirit had appeared to him, complaining bitterly of the annoying busy-bodies who had disturbed its peace and quiet.

Other fetishes were thought to possess some of the power of their original owner. The hair of a lion worn by a man gave him the courage of that animal, and a piece of tiger's claw brought a ferocious spirit. It was this belief that led to cannibalism. A brave enemy eaten by his conquerors gave the eaters the bravery of the dead man.

Oganga, or medicine man, in costume. (Field Museum.)

Powerful spirits lived in the fetishes. Nothing was too small or insignificant for a dwelling place. Before starting on a hunt, the Negro rubbed medicine into his weapons to strengthen the spirits within, talking to them, telling them what care he had taken of them, and reminding them of the gifts he had given them. If the hunter then returned empty-handed, or if the warrior, wearing a fetish on his black shiny breast to turn aside an arrow, came back wounded, the Negro did not lose faith in fetishism, but he did lose faith in that particular fetish. Going to the wizardous *oganga* or fetish man whom he had paid for concocting the now disappointing amulet, he told of his failure. To which the shrewd *oganga* replied: "Yes, I know. You have an enemy who possesses a fetish containing a spirit more powerful than yours. Yours is no longer of use. It is dead. Come, pay me, and I will make you a charm containing a still more powerful spirit."

Fetishes were found on every path in the African jungle, at every ford, on every house-door. They hung as amulets round every man's neck; they guarded against sickness, or inflicted it if neglected; they brought rain; they filled the waters with fishes willing to swim into the fisherman's net; they "smelled-out," caught, and punished thieves and witches; they gave the owner a bold heart and confounded his enemies. There was nothing the fetish could not do if it were but the right fetish.

The *oganga*, the witch-doctor and maker of fetishes, was the leader at certain ceremonials called "customs." Among some Negro tribes there was a Yam Feast custom, or thanksgiving for the new crop. All the natives assembled under the shade of the grove adjoining the fetish hut for the festivities. Bullocks and rams and cocks were killed, and their flesh was mixed with boiled yams and palm-oil. A portion of this mixture was placed on the heads of fetish figures, and the remainder was thrown about the fetish hut as a peace-offering. Then began the monotonous beating of tomtoms, the rumble of enormous hollow bamboo drums, joined by the noise of a dozen blacks madly blowing their elephant tusks. A dance, by nobles adorned with weird, fantastic headdresses, continued three or four days, rousing all to a frenzy of excitement.

All other pastimes paled before the attractions of the dance. The dance provided an outlet for the Negro's dramatic instinct and religious fervor. It expressed the native's confused sense of the power of the supernatural, which so completely enfolded him; it expressed the delight of joy in life, of love, and of all the deeper, keener feelings so far beyond his means of expression.

Dressed for the "customs" and the dance, the Benin chieftain was attended by boys and bodyguards. (British Museum.) See story of spirits in *My Book House*, Vol. VI, p. 132.

Headdress of a Sen'e-gal' dancer. (Field Museum.)

Every event, either in the life of the family or that of the tribal community, was celebrated by dancing. Occasions of rejoicing or grief, such as births, marriages, successful hunts, the entertainment of visitors, deaths, funeral rites, and the thousand and one religious observances, all had their special dances. No noon-day sun was ever too hot, no rain too heavy for zeal to flag and dampen the spirits of these ardorous performers. Hour after hour, the dance continued with a monotonous chant and an accompaniment of drumming tomtoms which threw the dancers into frenzied excitement. Each dance showed a beautiful feeling for true rhythm. Every atom of the body moved with a wave-like ripple running down the muscles of the back and out along the arms to the quivering finger-tips.

Although dancing was carried on during every hour of the day, and at all seasons of the year, it was by the enchanting light of the full moon that the black forest-people were bewitched and possessed. On occasions when the people of a village had gathered together to give a series of dances, the scene of dark figures painted in grotesque white, red, and yellow, gracefully weaving in and out, became one of weird beauty.

Some of the oldest dances held enshrined within them traces of beliefs and fancies which had faded from every other record. Such was *Ejame*, a solemn, grave dance, never given save during the funeral rites of very great chiefs. Seven men danced in the center of an immense circle formed by the other performers standing some distance away. Each took special care to leave space between himself and his neighbors; for should the aura of one overlap that of any other, both would die.

It was forbidden for any of the performers to raise their eyes. From the beginning to the end of the dance, each kept his eyes glued to the earth at his feet. Three of the dancers wore rattles round their necks and bore spears. The songs sung during this dance were so old that their meaning had long ago been forgotten.

Another peculiar dance was called *Okpata*. When this was danced, two jaunty little wooden fetishes were trotted out from the back of a fetish house and placed on a stone. Only one man danced to the music of an orchid-fibre stringed harp; then lo! the fetishes began to bend up and down, and skipped and hopped around on the stone in true marionette fashion. None, but those familiar with the mysteries of the dance, were allowed within several yards of the stone.

Sculpture in bronze and carving in wood and ivory flourished in certain of the West African hut-villages on the distant tributaries of the Niger and Congo rivers. These arts were the product of long days of dreamy indolence in the shade of enormous, thick-leaved trees, and were a part of the Negro's expression of religious feeling and tribal organization. Usually the sculpture and carvings represented the tribal conception of the spirits which they worshiped. Some tribes had learned the art of casting bronzes, and these pictured their chiefs and attendants with ornate coiffures and huge ringed collars. Other tribes embellished great elephant tusks with boldly carved, grotesque human and animal figures, ornamented their wooden signal-drums, and chiselled ivory face masks with fearsome heads.

Stiff, angular, wooden fetishes like those made to move about in the *okpata* dance.

Benin warriors in full array, with shields and swords.

Certain Negroes living on the Congo were skillful and artistic smiths, and made such a terrible knife that other tribesmen called them "the-people-of-the-throwing-knife." These people also made sculptured portraits of their chieftains and wrought bows and arrows and spears taller than man. Their neighbors on the Congo practised scar-tattooing and tooth-filling for beauty's sake, and ornamented with carving, utensils, cups, staffs, tobacco-pipes, stools, wooden head-rests to keep the coiffure from being damaged during sleep, and musical instruments, and wove baskets and mats. Helmets were also woven.

The greatest works of art of the Negroes, however, were the terrifying masks representing human and animal forms. These were worn by the witch-doctors to transform them into something mysterious and supernaturally powerful enough to talk to spirits and to announce their messages. Many of these masks were elaborate affairs made of hard wood covered with skin or leather, and adorned with horns and human hair. Occasionally they were made of metal, ivory, horn, stone or plaster, and trimmed with huge fringed beards of knotted straw, frayed-out, bushy string, and glittering, jingling ornaments. Often the artist added metal rings, and inserted beads, shells, stones and bits of metal for eyes.

There were many occasions when the Africans disguised themselves in masks of the most grotesque ugliness. Especially was this true for the ceremonials connected with one of their great secret societies. The Negro was fascinated with the idea of a secret society, and many were the organizations of a mysterious nature to which only the chosen were admitted. There were secret societies for men and for women; some practised murder, some animal and human sacrifices. All were mysterious, and had incantations with dances and rites at which everyone was transformed by a fanciful head-dress.*

As the Portuguese moved slowly farther and farther south beyond the Congo they came upon a new kind of natives, the small, yellowish-brown Bushmen, the people-with-a-wrinkly-skin. Once upon a time the Bushmen had been nomadic hunters in tropical East Africa, but many ages before they had been pushed into the southernmost end of this vast, mysterious continent. In former days the Egyptian pharaohs had greatly prized these cunning dwarfs; and whenever they could be captured and brought back from the south, they were taught to dance before them with many queer antics.

Benin headdress for sacrifice.

The heads of the Bushmen were adorned with peppercorn tufts of hair; their ears were lobeless, and they decked themselves with ornaments of shell and ostrich eggs. Unprepossessing in appearance were the Bushmen, and every man's hand was against them. They wandered about restlessly in clans under a chief who was little more than a war-leader.

*Most appalling and awesome of secret societies was Voodoo. The word means *fearful*, and Voo'doo was a powerful, fearful spirit who had entered into the body of a snake. Worship of the Voodoo snake took place only in remote places in the depths of darkest night. The worshipers assembled stealthily. Then came the mysterious rites. First, there was prayer to an actual, living snake; this was followed by wild, emotional, orgiastic dancing; and the climax of frenzy was reached with the sacrifice and eating of a human child. The worship of the Voodoo snake is still continued in Africa; and in the remote regions of Haiti and Cuba, Voo'doo-ism is today a powerful living religion.

The tiller of the soil. A bronze casting of a field worker made by the Da-ho'mey tribe, West Africa.

But little removed from animals were the Bushmen, a silent, furtive race without home or habitation. They secured fire by friction, lived under rude wind-screens, made merry on a mead of fermented root-juice and honey, lived on roots which their wee women dug up with digging sticks, and the game that the men brought down with their tiny, poisoned arrows. They had no fields to till, and knew nothing about agriculture, pottery-making, weaving, or other simple arts which were common everywhere throughout this vast continent where a primitive people were beginning to develop a civilization suited to the nature of the country.

The Bushmen believed in the use of charms against witches, and they prayed to the moon and stars. Their language was full of queer clicks and had no plurals, and their numbers stopped at three. Nevertheless, they made up for these shortcomings by their great skill in painting and carving in which they rivaled and resembled the painters in the cavernous rocks of Altamira in Spain and Southern France. In the huge rock shelters of South Africa, these wild and tiny men drew wonderfully powerful, spirited scenes of the chase, battle, the dance, and pictures of animals made vivid with vegetable colorings.

A musician and calabash carrier. Dahomey tribe.

Two or more colors were sometimes used. The head of a buffalo
might be white and the body
brown. The lion was never represented because of a fear of offending the formidable animal. In
some places where the rock was
very smooth and hard the Bushmen drew an outline of a figure
and then chipped away the surface.

Da-ho'mey hunter using blow pipe with thorns
touched with a poison to make them deadly.

But of all the natives that the
Portuguese encountered, as ship
after ship crept farther down the
coast, the most primitive of all were the merry, carefree, little Pygmies
who roamed the great forest-jungles of the Congo. Carefree were they,
because they had no settled home, but wandered from place to place,
living on wild vegetables and what-
ever animals they might capture
with their tiny bows and poisoned
arrows. The Pygmies were restless
wanderers; they had no dress or ornaments, no customs, laws, or religion; they did not even have a
language, but adopted the speech
of the more advanced tribe they
happened to be nearest. They had
no thought for the morrow, but
gorged themselves when game was
at hand and starved when it was
gone. Truly, of all the queer and
hitherto unknown people the Portuguese found, as slowly and cautiously they explored the coast, the
strangest of all were the Pygmies.

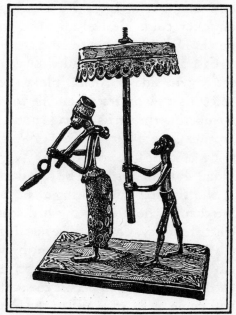

Dahomey chieftain under umbrella of rank.

Vasco da Gama Reaches India

In the fifty years following the passage of Cape Boj'a-dor', Portuguese ships made frequent voyages to the west coast of Africa, bringing back slaves, and gold, and ivory; and the wealth of the tiny kingdom grew enormously. But the wealth to be won in spices and silks from India was far greater than any from Africa, and the final goal of all these venturesome voyages was never completely lost,—a way must be found to India. And then Bartholomew Di'as explored the last bit of western coast, rounded the southernmost tip of land, and opened the way!

It was in the year 1486 that this sturdy seaman left Lisbon on an African voyage. Passing the farthest point that vessels had landed, Dias dared advance onward. Still to the south he sailed, struggling with wind and weather, until the wind changed, driving his ships south, ever south with half-reefed sails and no sight of land. Long days and longer nights passed to find the boats still drifting in an unknown sea, knowing not what an hour might bring forth. At last the great wind ceased to blow and it became icy cold. He had sailed to the south of South Africa. Steering north, Dias now came to land again where he saw cattle and cowherds.

East along the coast sailed Dias, coming to anchor in Al-go'a Bay on the eastern side of Africa. He wished to venture farther, but with one voice his crew protested; and he was compelled to turn back home. Remembering the perils he had endured, he named the southern tip, "the Stormy Cape"; but the King of Portugal, overjoyed at his news, refused to name it the Cape of Storms. Was not this the long-sought passage to India? Rather, it should be called the Cape of Good Hope.

Shortly after this exciting event, a letter was received from one of two merchants whom the King had sent overland through Egypt to learn where India lay. One of these merchants, Pedro de Co'vil-ham', had actually reached India; but, returning by way of Africa, he had been detained in Ab'ys-sin'i-a, half-guest, half captive, until his death. His letter was most encouraging. "If you persist to southward," he wrote the King, "Africa will come to an end. When the ships come to the Western Ocean, let them ask for So-fa'la, and they will find pilots to take them to Mal'a-bar."

To Malabar! To India! There
was a thrill in merely sounding the
names. A fleet must sail at once!
All necessary plans were pushed
with dispatch. Soon ships and
supplies were ready; and on July 8,
1497, the Portuguese gathered at
the seaport town of Be-lem' to witness the departure of the first expedition to sail by sea to India.

Great numbers of excited people
pushed and jostled each other
through the narrow streets as they
accompanied the procession of departing seamen from the chapel to
the crowded shore. At the head
rode the leader of the expedition,

Bold Vas'co da Ga'ma, discoverer of the water
route around Africa to India. (Portrait, Lisbon.)

noble and military in bearing, and gorgeous in his fine velvets and glittering sword. Behind him no less splendidly arrayed, walked his captains; and then came the liveried members of his crew. All carried
lighted candles in their hands. Priests and friars followed after, chanting
a solemn litany. Mass had been said the evening before, and all night the
men had held vigil in a little chapel by the sea built for mariners.

Then out through the blazing sunshine, out over the choppy water,
rode the San Gabriel, flagship of the squadron. High on her quarter-
deck stood a man of middle stature, strong and well-knit. Rosy were his
cheeks, and thick and brown his beard. He watched the other vessels fall
in behind him, and turned to give quick, firm orders. He was Vas'co da
Ga'ma, chosen by the King to be captain-major of the Indian expedition.

Charts and maps of the coast, his helmsmen had aplenty, and a pilot of
Dias' voyage around the Cape steered the flagship. But da Gama, with
great experience as a navigator, and with an urge for adventure in his
heart, had conceived a wise and courageous plan by which to avoid the
dangerous, hindering shoals and currents of the customary coastal route.

After leaving the Cape Verde Islands, he boldly set a course to the southern tip of Africa. Circling far out through the unknown South Atlantic, he sailed straight over the open sea, far from any land, where no one had even thought to go before!

Weeks went by; the endless waves rose and fell. Ever and ever again, the men watched the sun come up out of the sea, trail its way across the vast sky, and drop back again into the illimitable expanse. No land ever broke the weary view. Shut within the narrow limits of the tiny vessels, the sailors chaffed at the endless monotony of the dreary, heaving ocean, the boundless sky, the other vessels. They seized upon the stray passing of a lonely heron, a whale, or a seal as a matter of great moment and recorded this eventful happening in the *Roteiro*, the log-book.

Months passed; at last the blue-gray haze of land. Joyously the pilots drew the little ships together. Their glad crews ran up all the gay bunting and in honor to da Gama fired a salute from the bombards. He had been right in his calculations; he had safely steered the ships forty-five hundred miles through unchartered seas. Ninety-six days had they sailed with never a sight of land. No other voyage on record compares with it. Little they dreamed that during the voyage they had come within six hundred miles of the land soon to be called South America.

On a fair November morning the boats drifted into a bay which da Gama named Saint Helena. Here all landed and all set to, with a will, laying in water and wood, patching and mending sails and getting everything tight and strong for the difficult passage before them. Then, once more, out upon the open sea, with the "Cape of Storms" to be rounded.

Many of the crew were seasoned men who had been with Dias on his eventful voyage, and they well knew the task they had to face. On November 18, the Cape was sighted; but although the ships tacked, and returned again and again, contrary winds held them back. Suddenly a heavy squall began to darken the sky and whiten the waves. The boats tossed and pitched violently; and the wind, blowing in fitful gusts, soon burst with fierce suddenness. Then the expected storms swooped down, breaking with such a fury that the seas rose toward the sky and fell in heavy showers which flooded the vessels. Darkness fell upon the world.

The Portuguese battle bravely against raging seas and bitter cold, rounding the Cape of Good Hope.

Alarmed at the force of the storm, the sailors stayed the masts and shrouds, because, with the raging of the seas, the ships seemed every minute to be going to pieces. It was impossible to prepare food, and soon with fear and hardships, the crews grew sick. During a lull in the storms they clamored to put back to Portugal, but sharply Vasco da Gama answered that he had vowed as he left the bar of Lisbon not to turn back "one span's breadth" until he found India. In spite of their panic, however, the sailors were disciplined, experienced seamen; and driven by a stern commander, they fought and struggled to make headway. At last the wind dropped and fell astern; the sea moderated. Wearily then, the worn fleet doubled the cape of Africa and sailed out upon the Eastern Ocean. Thankfully, masters and men fell upon their knees and gave praise to the Lord for delivering them from death.

In the long, drawn-out weeks, in which the vessels pushed their way up the East African coast, da Gama's sorely buffeted little fleet met with other storms and high seas, with hurricanes and sudden calms, with contrary currents which carried them back until they thought never to proceed again. But fresh breezes always sprang up astern, filling the ragged sails, and before the tired sailors were well aware of the change, the winds were roaring about them with a rush, as they were swept forward.

Missing in a storm the much-desired harbor of So-fa'la opposite the island of Madagascar, the battered fleet made frequent landings on the eastern coast for provisions and water, touched at the hostile Arabian ports of Mo'zam-bique' and Mom-bas'sa, and so came to still another Arabian trading post, Me'li-ni'di, a garden city of white washed houses set midst cocoa palms and fields of maize and herbs on the edge of a beautiful curving bay of sparkling blue water.

The rajah, the governor of the city, though Mohammedan, was friendly, and sent them a pilot who would guide them to the Malabar coast of India. Rejoicing greatly, they at once set sail straight across the Arabian Sea. For twenty-three days, the worn and grubby ships crept eastward. At times the seas and winds were gentle; at others, the ships were tossed and torn by chill and crashing storms. At length a watchman's cry rang out, "Land ho!" And there on the horizon rose the dim, far-away outline of mountain peaks.

For a moment, da Gama and his men gazed in speechless wonder. Then shouts of joy broke loose. India, land of enchantment! The goal of their dreams where was to be found the riches of the fabulous East. Two days later the fleet anchored outside the harbor of Calicut. Just two hundred years after Marco Polo told the story of his travels through the fascinating East, Europe reached India!

When the Za'mo-rin, the ruler of Calicut, learned of their arrival, he seemed hospitable and ordered them to his palace some distance away. A pilot was sent to the ships; the fleet was moved to better anchorage a little north of Calicut, and da Gama and his officers were conducted to the royal audience. As they left their ships, the Portuguese saw waiting on shore a magnificent escort of two thousand men. They were impressed and a bit subdued; and as they passed through the streets of the city, they were amazed at the wealth displayed on every hand. The very natives thronging the streets were decked with jewels, they reported upon their return. The women wore gold necklaces and bracelets, and "rings set with precious stones on their toes." People watched from every roof and window. Music of drums, trumpets, and bagpipes lent a gay and martial air to the parade. Evidently this was an ancient and civilized nation.

VASCO de GAMA'S HAZARDOUS VOYAGE AROUND AFRICA TO INDIA.

Arrived at the palace, da Gama found the Zamorin in a courtyard, richly spread with various silks, reclining on a couch covered with a cloth of green velvet under a gilded canopy, and beside him were many silver jugs and an enormous gold basin full of betel-nuts which he chewed. "He was a very dark man," wrote the chronicler of the expedition, "half-naked and clothed with white cloths, from the middle to the knees: one of these cloths ended in a long point on which were threaded several gold rings with large rubies which made a great show. He had on his left arm a bracelet above the elbow, which seemed like three rings together, the middle one larger than the others, all studded with rich jewels. From this middle ring hung a pendant stone which glittered; it was a diamond of the thickness of a thumb; it seemed a priceless thing. Round his neck was a string of pearls about the size of hazel nuts, the string took two turns and reached to his middle; above it he wore a thin, round gold chain which bore a jewel of the form of a heart, surrounded with larger pearls, and all full of rubies. In the middle was a green stone of the size of a large bean, which, from its showiness was of great price, which was called an emerald. These jewels and another pearl belonged to the ancient treasury of the kings of Calicut.

"The King had long dark hair, all gathered up and tied on the top of his head with a knot made in it; and round the knot he had a string of pearls like those round his neck, and at the end of the string a pendant pearl, pear-shaped, and larger, which seemed a thing of great value.

Surrounded by luxury, with gold, precious jewels, and slaves beyond number, the haughty Za'mo-rin receives the dauntless da Gama, who had found a new way to the wealth and wonders of India.

His ears were pierced with large holes, containing many gold earrings.

"Close to the King stood a boy, his page, with a silk cloth round him. He held a red shield with a border of gold and jewels, and a boss in the center of a span's breadth of the same materials, and the rings inside for the arm were of gold; also a short drawn sword of an ell's length, round at the point, with a hilt of gold and jewelry with pendant pearls. On the other side stood another page who held a gold cup."

Gold, pearls, rubies, jewels,—hundreds of retainers! The wealth and splendor of the East dazzled the eyes of the Europeans. Breath came fast and hearts beat high with inner excitement, as quick, covetous glances took in the lavish display. India! Land of dreams! Of silks and spices! Reached at last by the Portuguese by direct water route from Europe!

VII

India, Land of Wealth and Splendor

(From about 3300 B.C. to about 1650 A.D.)

Ancient India

The India which the Portuguese found, when they arrived in Calicut in the year 1498 A.D., had long been the home of intelligent, enlightened people, who had a record of settlement reaching back five thousand years to the time when the Sumerians were dwelling in Mesopotamia in their clay-brick cities of Kish, Ur, Larsa, and Nip-pur'. Although the rough seamen of da Gama knew very little about this glamorous land, India was a mighty peninsula cut off from the rest of the world by the sea and the towering, ice-bound Hi-ma'la-yas. Pear-shaped, fertile, watered in the north by two great rivers, the Indus and the Ganges, it had been occupied in ancient times by primitive, wild tribes of hunters, dwelling in forests and trees, with only crude stone tools to aid them. Short, dark, almost Negroid, these savage Das'yus tribesmen wandered like dusky shadows over nearly all the habitable portions of the land. Only in the northwestern corner in the valley of the Indus, had thriving cities arisen bustling with all the life of a people highly gifted and forging steadily forward in the march of civilization.

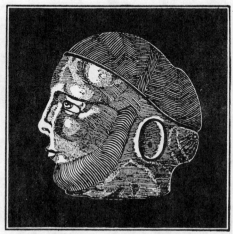

Hither, to the fertile plains stretching in rich green verdure along the banks of the Indus, a dark-skinned, curly-haired people, much like the smooth-faced Sumerians, had come in the dim, distant ages long before 3300 B.C.

Pottery head of a man of the ancient Indus civilization with wavy beard. (Mu-hen'jo Daro.) Compare with Sumerians, Vol. II, p. 88

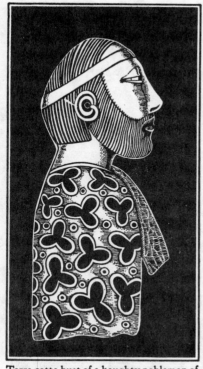

Terra cotta bust of a haughty nobleman of Mu-hen'jo Daro who lived about 3000 B.C. His elaborate tunic is embroidered.

Journeying from some unknown part of the Mediterranean lands, they had come to India by way of Ba-lu'chi-stan', and like the colorful Cretans and other fellow members of the Mediterranean race, they worshiped the Mother Goddess. Enslaving such as they could of the primitive inhabitants and driving the rest from the land, the invaders settled by the Indus, beginning to till the soil and line the river valley with the patchwork strips of their fields.

For two thousand years thereafter, these people dwelt in the well-watered, fertile plains of the Indus; and since they had no powerful enemies, they occupied time and thought with making their lives more comfortable. Magnificent cities arose, walled, built of baked clay brick, and having long, straight streets lined with comfortable homes and massive temples erected to the glory and honor of the gods. Ha-rap'pa and Mu-hen'jo Daro, splendid among these cities, were well supplied with water, and their handsome well-paved avenues and strong, substantial buildings were all kept clean and pure by means of arched underground drains that were, for the time of their making, marvels of construction. In their beautiful clean cities, the active, industrious people of the Indus civilization went peacefully about their business as students, builders, craftsmen, and merchants.

Exquisitely carved seals, with written characters of the Indus civilization. (Muhenjo Daro.)

Priests on the temple roofs, scanning the moon and stars, studied and understood the mysteries of the sky. Below in the temple-chambers, they worked at the picture-writing, which they had managed to discover independent of all other nations. Carpenters built strong ships for commerce or for pleasure; jewelers wrought gold and silver into beautiful ornaments; craftsmen cut fine seals carved of stone or ivory and showing greater skill than the great seal-makers of Sumer; and down among the potters, men discovered the potter's wheel. Squatting about on the ground, they deftly fashioned the clay into beautiful vessels as they turned the wheel before them, ornamenting their wares with geometric patterns, with bands of leaves and flowers or fantastic figures of animals, painted in black or red. And amid all this swarming life of an

Pottery figure of the Mother Goddess of Mu-hen'jo Daro. In costume and workmanship it is like the Sumerian images.

ancient Indus city, two-wheeled carts, drawn by bullocks, bore the produce of the fields within the gates of the industrious, flourishing cities.

Enterprising merchants from the Indus traded with the cities of Sumer before the dawn of history; and once trade routes had been opened, Indian commerce with foreign nations continued throughout the ages. Shal'ma-ne'ser IV of Assyria received presents of two-humped camels and humped oxen from Bactria and India, and beams of clear, fragrant Indian cedar

Two vases from Muhenjo Daro with fish and geometric designs in black on a red background.

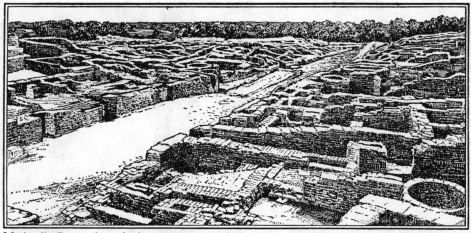

Mu-hen'jo Daro, where dwelt prosperous people in a city with well-paved streets, lined with substantial, clay-brick houses. (Photograph) Thus far only two cities of the ancient Indus civilization have been excavated under the direction of Sir John Marshall, Director-general of Archaeology in India, although many other sites remain. At Muhenjo Daro, three cities have been found, built one upon another, the earliest dating from about 3300 B.C. and the latest from about 2700 B.C.

graced the wonder palace of Neb'u-chad-nez'zar of Babylon. Wares from India were imported into Babylonia even in the days of Solomon the Magnificent, before 900 B.C.; and rice and peacocks from India were a common food in Greece in the time of the poet Sophocles.

Remarkably like the Sumerians were these people of the Indus, and great had grown their settlements throughout the broad river valley when, about 2700 B.C., for some mysterious reason, they abandoned their splendid cities. Why they went no one knows. The cities show no signs of fire or violent destruction; but the inhabitants moved south and east and mixed with other dwellers in India, till gradually, their civilization vanished altogether.

But shortly after this strange desertion of the Indus cities, a band of Semitic adventurers found their way to Southern India and the tangled tropical jungles along the coast of the Dec'can, where they developed a second center of better, more comfortable living. Possibly these Semites were a part of those desert hordes who swept across the fertile lands of lower Mesopotamia, and under the mighty Sargon, mastered Sumer and Ak'kad; but whoever they were in fact, they quickly made prosperous settlements in this warm and fruitful region, and soon luxurious cities rose where once again people lived in magnificence and wealth. India's gold and pearls, conch-shells, pepper, diamonds, beryls, and fine cotton goods were in great demand abroad, and the Semites of India naturally took to commerce and sea-faring and flourished on their trade.

It was, however, in Southern India alone, that wealth and luxury flourished in the days of that civilization which was known as the Dra-vid'i-an. Throughout the rest of the continent, tribesmen and savages roamed in constant search for food; and only where stray wanderers, from the one-time prosperous cities of the deserted Indus Valley, had come and settled down, was the struggle for life somewhat lightened by the help of a few old tools whose use had been almost forgotten.

Such was India when an important change began to come to pass. From about 2000 B.C. to 1400 B.C., waves of white-skinned people, calling themselves Aryans, singing hymns of praise to their nature gods, tramped through the grim, perilous northwestern passages of the mountains to the smiling land below. Long had the wanderers traveled from their homeland in the vast plain south of the Carpathian Mountains in Central Europe. Growing too numerous for even this wide-spreading grassland to support them, many had been forced to migrate; and

Wandering Aryans, tramping through perilous mountain passes, see the fertile Indus Valley.

once started on their travels, they had spread in all directions. A part mixed with the brown-haired Alpine race and became the ancient Persians; some became the ancestors of the Hit'tites, the pale-faced Kas'sites of Babylon, and the white-skinned, Asiatic Mi-tan'ni. Others straggled down into Greece, destroying the Cretan and My'ce-nae'an civilizations; still others swept into Italy and reared the city on the Seven Hills that became Imperial Rome. And, last of all, they came here to India. In many waves of migration they swarmed into the valley of the Indus and so in time they came to be called Hindus after the name of that river.

Not for centuries did these Aryans become a nation in India. Instead, they continued to live in large tribal groups. Each father of a family was the priest of his own household, and the chieftain acted as father and priest for the whole tribe. At greater festivals, however, the chieftain selected someone specially learned in holy offerings to conduct the sacrifice in the name of all the people. Women held a high position as wives and mothers; marriage was sacred with them and husband and wife were both the rulers of the home.

In their *Ve'das*, or sacred hymns of praise, a group of over a hundred books of hymns, prayers, charms and chants, they set down all that is known of them. Existing at first only orally, these Vedas were gathered together about 1200 B.C., but were not written down until centuries later. The *Rig-Veda*, the oldest of these hymns, speaks of the Aryan's scorn for the broad-nosed, dark-hued people whom they drove from the land. These primitive tribesmen were called "disturbers of sacrifices," "gross feeders on flesh," "lawless," "not sacrificing," "without gods and without rites." It was the Aryans who gave them the name of Das'yus, or enemies.

But the Aryans could not long be kept in the valley of the Indus. Pushed on from behind by later arrivals of their own race, they spread eastward through India to the smooth, fertile, river valley of the Ganges, and southward into broad, wide-spreading plains. The Dasyus were enslaved, or forced farther south into mountains and forests remote; and the last remnants of the splendid Indus civilization were lost.

Cheerful, freedom-loving, sing-ing songs of praise, the Aryans made gods of all the powers of nature. They praised the Hima-layas as "Him whose greatness the snowy ranges and the aerial rivers declare"; and high amid the mountains lay the paradise of de-ities and heroes where the kind and the brave forever dwelt. Because the Aryans in India had the same forefathers as the Greeks, the Ital-ics, the Vikings, and the Teutons, they all believed in a sky-god who ruled from the skies of India, Greece, Italy, Scandinavia and Germany. This same god was called Zeus by the Greeks, Jupiter by the Italics, and Thor by the Teutons and Vikings. But no-where was the sky-god so adored, nowhere was he as splendid and powerful as in the hymns of the *Rig-Veda*. He was known as In-

Indra, god of the sky, astride an elephant up-rooting a tree. (From a monastery at Bhaja.)

dra, god of the thundering sky, hidden away in the storm-cloud, caus-ing the earth to tremble with terror, and all the forests to shudder. A mighty fighter, big of bone and large of limb, golden-haired, broad-chested,—a mace-bearing hero was he, who loved to drink the intoxi-cating Soma-nectar enjoyed by the gods. In one fight-engendered thirst, great Indra drank thirty lakes. Greatest of exploits was the mighty Indra's conquest of the serpent-demon, Vrit'ra, imprisoner of rains. Against this curse the great god hurled thunderbolts, and clove the demon in twain, thus rending the clouds asunder and loosening the torrents to water the sun-parched fields of the Aryans.

Aryan nature gods: U'shas, the Dawn, opens the gates of the sky for Sur'ya, the Sun. At right appears Ag'ni, Fire, the friend of men. (From an imaginary Hindu illustration to the ancient Vedic hymns.)

Among the companions of Indra were the Mar'uts and Ru'dra, gods of the whirlwind and dispensers of rain, who made the rock to tremble; the Horsemen, the fleet outriders of the dawn, bringing the first rays of sunrise; the Lords of Luster; the Solar Orb, Sur'ya; the Wind, Va'yu; and the Sunshine, or Friendly Day. Moreover, there was Var'u-na, calm and serene, god of the heavenly ocean, the power of law and order in the universe. A shining bright array was this collection of Aryan gods.

Slowly, as the Aryan tribesmen settled through all Northern India, towns began to spring up; the numerous tribes drew together into sixteen or more tribal kingdoms and states, each with a king at its head. Then it was that the haughty Aryans, proud of their white skins, decided that they must do something to keep their race, their speech and their religion from being entirely swamped by the great mass of their Negroid subjects. To prevent intermarriage with the darker people and to preserve their customs unchanged, they felt obliged to draw the color line. Thus they began to form men into castes, or classes of society, who could not marry outside their own caste. The word for caste in Sanskrit, the speech of the Aryan invaders, was *varna*, meaning color.

Among the old freedom-loving Aryans in the valley of the Indus, each householder had been a husbandman, warrior, and priest; but gradually certain gifted families, who composed the Vedic hymns or learned them by heart, were always chosen by the kings to perform the great sacrifices. In this way a priestly class of Brahmans grew up, the highest caste in the land. They were tall and fair; and down through the ages they became the philosophers, lawgivers, and poets of their race, swaying the minds and receiving the homage of peoples and nations.

The bronze-cheeked, large-limbed, fighting companions of the kings formed the second caste, the Kshat'ri-ya, or warriors. As the Aryans had added to their territory, some of the warriors had received a larger share of the land than others, and had forced the vanquished Dasyus to cultivate their fields. Thus there grew up a group of warriors, freed from labor, and now the Kshatriya also became the governing class.

The Vai' syas, or herdsmen and landowners, became the traders and merchants, and formed the third caste in the land, and all these three upper castes were of Aryan white descent and were honored by the name of "Twice-born." All three wore a thin cord hung from the left shoulder to the hip, and all worshiped the same bright shining Vedic-Aryan gods.

The fourth caste, the Sudras, were the conquered, down-trodden Dasyus. They were the laborers, the hewers of wood and the drawers of water, and they were scornfully spoken of as the "Once-born," non-Aryan castes to be kept separate from the whites.

A Hindu Brahman, tall, stately, with well-formed features. From left shoulder to waist is the three-strand cord of the "Twice-born."

To make the caste system absolutely rigid and to give caste the force of law, Man'u, a great Aryan lawgiver, drew up a code of laws, sometime between 1200 B.C. and 500 B.C., which gave the government and customs of India a definite form. The *Laws of Manu* were written so simply and plainly that everyone could understand them; and they told each person exactly what were his rights, what his duties to family and king, and what services he must perform to the gods. The laws forbade intermarriage between castes, and even prohibited them from eating together; they likewise regulated such matters as the cut of clothes, the shape of ornaments, and the architecture of houses. Everything that was confused during the early times was given its proper place and order. And this strict system of castes made the Hindus, the Aryans of India, different from their Aryan brethren in other lands.

As the centuries passed, each of the castes was divided again and again until there were between two and three thousand castes. Lower than the Sudras were the *Pariahs* or outcasts, who were looked upon as another race of beings, altogether outside the pale of society. These "untouchables" were forbidden the use of public roads and bridges, and were not even allowed to draw water from the public well. So defiling was their touch that most Hindus would rather die than to accept their help.

In the early days, the Brahmans had a long struggle with the Kshat'ri-ya caste before they won their proud position as head of the Hindu

people, but afterward they taught that Brahma, the Creator, had made them the leaders. They said that in the beginning the Brahman proceeded from the mouth of the Creator, the Kshatriya from his arms, the Vai'sya from his thigh or belly, and the Sudra from his feet. Caste, therefore, was of divine origin.

Dasyus, or "untouchables," lower than any caste, fit only for the meanest duties, beneath notice, or consideration.

"All things change, all things cast off their old forms and assume new shapes," taught the Brahman. "As a goldsmith, taking a piece of gold, turns it into another newer and more beautiful shape, so does the soul, after having thrown off this body and dispelled all ignorance, make unto itself another newer and more beautiful shape. . . ." The teaching that at the death of a person the soul passed into some other creature, either human or animal, was known as the transmigration of the soul. Everything in this life, said the Brahmans, was a result of

The great god, Brahma, the soul of the universe. (15th century statue from the Deccan.) The soul within all living beings was believed to change its outward form with successive lives until it merged with Brahma, the Universal Soul.

actions performed in a previous existence, and only by gradually building up a good record in life after life could final salvation be secured.

As early as 500 B.C., the Brahmans arranged a system of philosophy, and a hundred and fifty years later they compiled a Sanskrit grammar. In their long, priestly robes, they studied the movements of the heavenly bodies, and learned to chart the moon's path through the heavens, to divide the zodiac into twelve signs, to measure time by weeks, months, and solar years, and to follow the movements of the planets. They developed geometry, discovered trigonometry and algebra, and gave the world the decimal system while the unfortunate Roman school boy still struggled with his clumsy, awkward, Roman numerals. They were also the first to win through the mystery of the square and the cube root.

The departure of Rama, the great hero of India, driven into exile by the jealousy of a Queen. An incident in the *Ra-ma'ya-na*, the epic poem of India, written in Sanskrit before 500 B.C., describing the conquest of India and Ceylon by the Aryans. (Retold in part in *My Book House*, Vol. X, p. 175.)

But the Brahmans were not merely the composers and keepers of the sacred books, the philosophers, and law-makers, they were also poets. They did not write history; but they told the tales of the ancient wars and the lives of the Aryan heroes in mighty epic poems. In the famous *Ma-ha-bha'ra-ta*, they sang the chronicles of the Delhi kings, the struggle grim and grand between two noble families; and in the *Ra-ma'ya-na*, they related the story of the Aryan advance into Southern India. To the Vedic poems they added prose works, called the *Brah'ma-nas*, explaining the duties of the priests; the *Sutras*, telling of laws and ceremonies; the *U-pan'i-shads*, treating of God and the soul; and finally, the *Puranas*, or ancient, prehistoric legends and sacred traditions of the gods.

The Brahmans, therefore, were the writers and thinkers of India, the counsellors of Hindu princes and the teachers of the Hindu people. The low-caste Sudras were more and more trampled upon by their tyranny; and even the royal warriors, the Kshat'ri-ya, were compelled to bow to their authority. But the priestly supremacy of the Brahmans was challenged in time by a new religion, the great religion of Buddha.

Buddha, the Enlightened
(About 600 B.C. to about 543 B.C.)

More than five hundred years before Jesus was born, and about the same time that Confucius was giving the Chinese his ideal of the superior man, a Hindu prince of the Sak'yas tribe named Sidd-har' tha Gau' ta-ma was growing to manhood in his father's kingdom beneath the foothills of the majestic Himalaya Mountains. All the good that life seemed to offer, Gautama enjoyed. At nineteen, he married his beautiful and bewitching cousin, whom he had won by a contest of arms over rival chieftains and suitors for her hand. He lived in luxury with wealth and servants innumerable at his command; he hunted, played, and went about in a sunny world of gardens, groves, and irrigated rice fields.

But in the midst of this gay, carefree life, a strange discontent seized the Prince. Even as a child, he had been torn by sorrow and suffering, and now it seemed to him that the life he was leading was not a true life, but a holiday,—a holiday that had lasted too long. The world was filled with sadness, with sickness, and with sorrow; and pain, misery, age, and death came in time to all. Rebellious against such conditions, but knowing not what to do, he went one day in his chariot to see the plowing of his father's lands. In the great heat, the laborers, young and aged, still must toil and toil, endlessly in the sun. He saw them struggling with all their might; and the oxen toiling also with no reward whatever. These things tortured the Prince, and he thought: "This world is built in pain, and its foundations are laid in agony. If there be a *Way*, where is it? I am bound indeed in the deepest dungeon of despair."

Gau'ta-ma, the prince, in his chariot, surrounded by slaves and courtiers. (Engraved water-jar.)
Amid such luxuries, Gautama first felt the necessity to seek the way to a more lasting peace and joy.

Then slowly passing down the road toward home, he and Channa, his chariot driver, saw one of the wandering Brahman holy men, carrying a bowl in his hand and wearing a coarse saffron-colored robe.

"Who is this person?" asked the Prince. "For his face is calm, and his eyes bespeak a soul at rest. And what is this bowl in his hand?"

Even as he spoke, the stranger answered him with grave salutation: "Great lord, I am a religious wanderer, who shuddering at the problems of life, seeing all things fleeting, have left the fetters of my home behind to seek some happiness that is trustworthy and imperishable, that looks with equal mind on friend and enemy, and does not regard wealth or beauty. Such is the only happiness which will content me!"

The sorrow-laden Prince was amazed at this voicing of his own thoughts, and asked eagerly: "And where, O wise man, do you seek it?"

"Great lord, in solitude, in the quiet of deep words," was the reply. "There, in the quiet dwells Enlightenment. And I carry this bowl that the charitable may bestow an alms of food; and this is all I ask of the world. And now pardon haste, for my way lies onward to the mountains where enlightenment awaits me."

The Prince went his way, and as he entered the city, news of great joy was brought to him; he learned that a son had been born that day. But the words of the strange beggar still stirred him, and the pain of suffering people moved him much more deeply than any personal joy. That very night, at the age of twenty-nine, he gave up wealth, happiness, and family life. Leaving the palace, he donned the robe of a beggar and made his way southward to a place of hermits and teachers.

Buddha, the beggar, receiving alms of food. (Fresco, Ajanta.)

There in the quiet of the solitudes dwelt a number of holy men, gathered to study the ancient philosophies of India. But though Gau'ta-ma remained long with these earnest students and learned all that could be found in the *Vedas* and *U-pan'i-shads*, he was not satisfied with their teachings and practices.

For a time he wandered from saint to teacher, listening eagerly to their sayings, practicing their rules, but always feeling that even these holy ones had not learned how to avoid the pain and sorrow of life.

Then he resolved to put to test the Hindu idea that knowledge may be obtained by fasting, sleeplessness and, self-torment. With five companions, he went to a gorge hidden away in the dense jungle of the mountains, there to give himself up to fasting and terrible penances, thinking that perhaps the soul might spring free from the almost utter destruction of the body. He set

Buddha worn to a skeleton as he seeks peace and enlightenment by torturing the body. (Central Museum, Lahore.)

himself to meditation, daily lessening his food until it became a tiny morsel, sitting mute and motionless, and controlling even his breath. So still he sat that the birds moved about him unafraid, and his fame spread "like the sound of a huge bell hung in the canopy of the skies."

At last he swallowed only a grain of rice; his arms and legs were like dried reeds and his spine like a plait of hair. But instead of earning peace of mind by six years of fasting and self-torture, he sank into despair. Torn by doubts as to whether all his penance availed anything, the haggard hermit fell senseless to the earth. When he recovered, the mental agony had passed. He felt that the path to salvation lay not in self-torture, but in preaching a higher life to his fellow-men.

Amazing and horrifying the five companions of his fast, he demanded
ordinary food and refused to continue his tortures, realizing quite
clearly that whatever truth a man might reach was best reached with
a healthy body. But such an idea was unheard of; his companions
promptly deserted him. The boom of the great bell ceased! Gau'ta-ma
the Wonderful had fallen! He was no longer a saint!

But earnest seeking had not been in vain. When his thin, weak body
had been nourished to greater strength, Gautama returned to his task.
Seeing before him a large and noble broad-leaved Bo tree of the fig
variety, he seated himself beneath it with folded hands and feet. Then
he turned his mind from outward things and directed them inward,
resolving never to leave that spot until he had entered upon Enlightenment or Buddhahood, which would enable him to attain salvation.

It was a night of terror and temptation. Visions of his life of love,
luxury, and power beset his body. Delirious dreams and delusions fell
about him; demons with flaming weapons whirled threateningly about.
But love and deep compassion for the sorrows of mankind held him
firmly to his purpose. He sat all night in profound thought; and when
the darkness thinned, and the east became faintly gray, he received
complete Enlightenment, and cried aloud this song of victory:

Many a house of life
Has held me, seeking ever that which wrought
The prison of the senses; sorrow-frought,
Sore, was my ceaseless strife.
But now,
Thou builder of the body-prison, now
I know thee! Never shalt thou build again
These walls of pain,
Nor raise the roof-tree of deceits, nor lay
Fresh rafters on the clay.
Broken the house is, and the ridge pole split:
Delusion fashioned it.
Safe, pass I hence, deliverance to attain.

Gautama was free! He had cried that the prison of his body was built
by delusions of the senses and he had found a way of deliverance from
pain and sorrow for himself and all mankind. Henceforth he was called
"the Buddha", or "the Enlightened One!"

Seeking his five companions who were still torturing their bodies to secure holiness and knowledge, he sat down under the shade trees, cross-legged, with hand uplifted, gravely explained to his listeners what he had learned in that moment of enlightenment; that all suffering came from evil and selfish desires, — sensual desires, desires for power and wealth, for personal blessedness. But by constant meditation and by control of the mind, he declared, a habit of thought could be reached in which man would cease to desire anything selfish, and there would come to him perfect peace and joy. This state Buddha called *Nirvana*.

Buddha, the Enlightened, with right hand upraised, seated in characteristic attitude of meditation with feet twisted across legs, explaining to his disciples that the remedy for all evil and suffering consists in meditation, control of the mind, and relinquishment of selfish desires. (Wall painting from Turkestan. Museum für Völker-kunde, Berlin.)

Perfect peace, Buddha taught, could be reached by the Eightfold Path of Right Understanding, Right Thought, Right Speech, Right Conduct, Right Living, Right Effort, Right Mindfulness, and Right Rapture.

After five days of teaching, the eyes of Buddha's companions were opened. News of his message spread swiftly; about him gathered young men, nobles wearied of luxurious lives, eager to hear of joy and the ending of all sorrow, and unlike the Brahmans, Buddha preached not to a few of the sacred caste, but to people from all ranks of life.

People of all castes and stations listening to Buddha. Women and nobles have arrived by elephant or horse, priests and poorer people by foot. One of many frescoes from the A-jan'ta caves, painted in the 4th century A.D., with remarkable skill and understanding, and representing the height of Indian art.

Many of Buddha's first converts were common men, and among the earliest were women. After three months, he had gathered around him sixty disciples whom he sent forth to the neighboring states saying: "Go ye now, and preach the most excellent law."

When Buddha died in 543 B.C., all India was not yet ready to receive the simple message of the Master; and when the influence of his earnest eloquence was gone, the purity, the simplicity and the daring of his teaching was gradually lost. As the years passed, many myths grew up around his memory. He became the savior of mankind, the wise, self-contained teacher who held every desire in leash, the remote, emotionless, rotund, jeweled figure sitting cross-legged in changeless contemplation! He was a god! He was one of a series of divine Buddhas of the past and of Buddhas yet to come! And thus, under the influence of myth and legend, many of his clear simple teachings were lost.

The Development of India

Divided into a great number of small kingdoms, each governed by its own ruler called *rajah*, India went its way, practically unknown to the great world which lay beyond the ice-bound Himalayas. Then suddenly, unexpectedly, nearly three hundred years after the death of Buddha, there appeared the first of a long series of foreign invaders. Alexander the Great, of Macedon, having conquered Persia, marched his troops across Parthia and Bactria, pushed his way through the bleak, perilous gorges of the Hindu Kush Mountains, and in May, 327 B.C., saw before him the shaded forests, and fertile valleys of India!

In the spring of the following year, he descended into the lowlands, crossed the Indus, advanced without a struggle through northwestern India, and so came to the Hy-das'pes River. Here he erected a bronze pillar, bearing the inscription: "Here Alexander halted."

Alexander found India divided into petty kingdoms so jealous of each other that many were eager to join him in an attempt to overthrow their enemies. He fought a great battle on the Upper Indus against a local king, Porus; but the overwhelming numbers of Porus, strengthened by powerful elephants, went down in defeat before the spirited charge of the Greek phalanxes. The Indian Prince himself was wounded; but when he humbly tendered his submission to the conquerors, Alexander left him in power as the governor for the Greeks.

Alexander then marched southeastward towards the Ganges; but yielding at length to the clamor of his men, he retraced his steps to the Hydaspes, whence he and his army floated down the river to the sea, stopping here and there to fight a pitched battle with the natives. A longer halt was made where the five branches of the Indus came together, and here a town was built, a Greek garrison and governor were left behind, and these laid the foundation of lasting Greek influence in India.

Horseman of Alexander attacking an elephant-mounted Hindu warrior. (Poros medal.)

During his two years' campaign in northwestern India, Alexander subjugated no provinces; but he made alliances, founded cities, and planted Greek garrisons until all the land swarmed with Greek adventurers. Much of Greek civilization was brought to India and native artists soon showed scenes from the life of Buddha after the manner of the Greeks; Indian craftsmen copied Greek models in sculpture and building; Greek coins were made; Greek myths colored Indian thought; and exquisite Greek faces and profiles even found their way into Turkestan, China, and Japan.

Now, of all the many states in Northern India, the kingdom of Mag' a-dha, on the Ganges, was by far the strongest; and not long after Alexander left India, there came to the throne of Magadha, a fiery warrior, named Chan'dra-gup'ta. Anxious to extend his kingdom and increase his power, Chandragupta launched his armies westward; Greek garrisons and Indian princes alike fell before his headlong rush, and the last traces of Alexander's campaign were destroyed. Chandragupta was now master of all North India from sea to sea, and he ruled from the Indus, south to the Vind'hya Mountains. He was the first great Indian emperor.

So great was the power of this King, that Se-leu'cus, the Greek general who took Persia and Asia as his empire upon Alexander's death, gave Chandragupta his daughter in marriage and stationed at the court of the Emperor, as ambassador, a Greek philosopher named Me-gas'the-nes. This learned envoy from Greece used his leisure time in writing a trustworthy, life-like account of the court and the people of India.

The capital city, wrote Megasthenes, was twenty-five miles in diameter, and sheltered a great population within its massive, timber stockade. Sixty-four gates pierced this wooden wall, and five hundred and seventy towers rose above its battlements. The narrow, twisting streets were lined with mud-houses, lime-plastered to shed the rain, flat-roofed, and having coarse awnings spread above mud porches. Dull without and poorly furnished within were the houses of the common folk, but set apart in better quarters were the dwellings of craftsmen and merchants, built of unbaked brick with comfortable verandas and cool rooms grouped about a courtyard.

Powerful, wealthy King Chan'dra-gup'ta is borne in a golden litter to the palace gates to give justice.

The royal palace itself was a stately, impressive group of brick and wooden buildings, standing in a wide park, surrounded by an elaborate garden. Its pillars were carved and gilded, and their shafts were set with clinging, golden vines in which birds of silver played. The grounds were adorned with majestic evergreens, and flowering trees, and shrubs. Shady walks led through deep groves, and half-tame deer roamed at will, while birds of bright plumage flashed and flitted everywhere.

The King never slept twice in the same room, lest an assassin's dagger find his heart. Early each day he went forth to hold public audience at the palace gate. To the roll of drums, Chan'dra-gup'ta came forth, borne in a golden litter studded with jewels. Rubies and emeralds clasped the spray of peacock feathers in his silken turban; he was clothed in robes of rich muslin edged with purple, crusted with gold embroidery, and stiff with pearls. His hair hung long and loose; his cheeks and upper lip were shaved smooth, and his chin-beard was perfumed.

A Hindu king with standard riding his royal elephant and followed by a mounted umbrella bearer. (2nd century B.C., stone relief, Barhut.)

For a body-guard, the King had a group of brown-limbed women from the hills clothed in gaily-colored, quilted cotton corselets, and armed with spear and shield or with seven-foot bows and long reed arrows tipped with iron. He dismounted from his lowered palanquin in the gateway and seated himself on a wooden throne, its carving picked out with lacquer in many colors. The fairest woman of the realm fanned him and held an umbrella of state to shield his head from the burning sun, while another tasted Persian wine from a golden pitcher before she offered it to the King. Skillful slaves appeared to knead his limbs, and very much at ease Chan'dra-gup'ta heard the reading of petitions.

When the audience was ended, Chandragupta returned to his apartments where the Amazons of the Guard held faithful watch. He dined alone on curried rice heaped with rich meats; his chair and table were miracles of intricate carving; his golden bowls and cups were studded with precious stones. In the afternoon he received the heads of his departments of state, the ministers of war, of public works, the treasury, agriculture, the mint, and foreign trade.

Fond of amusement, fierce and cruel, Chandragupta was nevertheless an able, conscientious ruler. Reservoirs and lakes, made by his orders, furnished water to feed the fields through a network of canals maintained by royal engineers; special officers surveyed the lands and saw that every farmer had his due share of irrigation privileges. Excellent roads were maintained throughout the empire, and even the pleasures of the people were under the care of the king. He ordered that taverns and wine-shops should be supplied with every convenience, with abundant perfumes and garlands of flowers.

In 257 B.C. Chandragupta's grandson, the good and able A-so'ka, came to the throne of the highly organized kingdom of Mag'a-dha, ruling it wisely for forty years. In his youth Asoka had been a conqueror, extending his empire far to the south till it embraced all India as far as Nellore. In the north, the wild mountainous lands of Kashmir and Ne-pal' were also added to his realm, and even the people of the lower slopes of the snow-capped Himalayas were compelled to pay tribute.

But in the ninth year of his reign, Asoka was stricken with remorse and horror at the misery caused by the evils of his campaigns of conquest, and he foreswore war forever. The teachings of Buddha had captured his heart; he became a devoted follower of Buddhism, and strove to rule according to the teachings of the great Master.

From his palace at Pa'ta-li-pu'tra on the Ganges, Asoka issued a series of edicts dealing with the organization of his empire, with morals, and with religion. He had these edicts carved in the speech of the people upon the highly-polished surfaces of tall columns which he ordered placed over the whole of his empire so that they could be read by all. Each pillar was crowned by a capital in the form of a deeply carved bell of Persian design bearing an abacus adorned with lotus and honeysuckle, and lifelike animals sculptured in high relief. These animals symbolized the preaching of the Word in every corner of the realm; the lion was chosen for the north; the elephant for the east; the bull for the west; and the trusty horse for the south.

Stone capital erected by A-so'ka, showing four lions, back to back, upon an abacus. (About 242–232 B.C., Sarnath Museum.)

The *stupa* at San'chi. This enormous stone dome with carved gallery and umbrellas was erected in the 3rd century B C. in the Deer Park, where Buddha told his former companions of his Enlightenment.

A-so'ka was the first ruler to use stone as a building material, and his builders made lavish use of the Aryan *stupa*, a hemispherical dome set on a drum, built to enshrine a relic of Buddha. Stupas of stone were built at places sacred to the four events in Buddha's life: his Birth, his Enlightenment, his First Sermon, and his Death. In the hands of Asoka's architects the stupa became a huge dome of solid brickwork with a flattened top, crowned by a stone umbrella. A gallery ran around at the level of the drum where pilgrims could walk and meditate.

Asoka felt it his duty to convert all mankind to Buddhism, and missionary monks were sent to the independent kingdoms of the Dec'can, developing under native Dra-vid'i-an cultures, to Ceylon, and even to the Hellenistic countries of Syria, Egypt, Macedonia, and Epirus. And the stupa which Asoka made an emblem of faith, spread with Buddhism everywhere. It became the *dagoba* of Burma and Ceylon, the *pagoda* of China, Japan and Korea, and the terraced pyramid of Java. Gateways to the stupas, made of square stone pillars with triple cross-beams of stone, were the inspiration for the dainty *torii*, the temple-gateways of Japan.

The influence of Asoka was as lasting as it was wide-spread. He made Buddhism a state religion; his rule was just and enlightened, and he worked wisely for the real needs of man. High among the names of kings, stands that of Asoka, the greatest ruler of India.

The Spread of Buddhism

One of the earliest missions of Asoka was the sending of his son to the beautiful, luxuriant, pear-shaped island of Ceylon. The missionary prince came in the reign of King Tissa in 250 B.C., and Tissa promptly entered into an alliance with Asoka and did all he could to foster Buddhism. His court followed its King, and the people followed the court, and quickly Buddhism became the religion of Ceylon.

A legend relates that King Tissa asked King Asoka for a branch of the sacred Bo tree under which Buddha grew to enlightenment, requesting that his daughter, the Princess, bring it to Ceylon. The Princess was willing, but the King feared to profane the tree; whereupon the tree itself, detached one of its branches which planted itself in a golden vase made by a goldsmith of the gods. This was then carried to Ceylon with a retinue of celestial light, music and flowers; and great were the ceremonies and rejoicings at its planting. A tree believed to have grown from this branch still stands in Ceylon, tended throughout the ages by a company of monks; thousands of worshipers visit it, and the most sacred possession of many a pilgrim is a leaf from this tree.

Dagoba in Ceylon, built by King Tissa about 247 B.C. to enshrine a Buddhist relic. (Photograph)

But Buddhism spread much farther than Ceylon. During the early centuries of the Christian Era, important Hindu colonies had been established in the long, lozenge-shaped Malay Peninsula; in the balmy island of Java, land of emerald ravines and sparkling rivers; in the rainy, palm-fringed island of Sumatra at the equator; and in the warm, moist island of Borneo where queerly tattooed, brown-skinned natives counted to twenty on their fingers and toes. Here a Hindu felt as much at home as in his own native land, and to these lands now came Buddhism.

To the smiling, garden-island of Java, Buddhist colonists carried their art of sculpture and building, and here their faith resulted in the great picture-Bible of the Buddhists, the colossal temple of Bo'ro Bu'dor, or Many Buddhas. Begun in 850 A.D., by unknown master-chisellers, fashioned and adorned by the hands of faith to hold a long lost relic of a Buddhist saint, it arose in terraced splendor. The terraces were lavishly carved with sculptures of life-sized figures of Buddha sitting cross-legged; realistic reliefs pictured the whole story of Buddha's life, so that the devout pilgrim ascending from terrace to terrace beheld in pictured form the story of Buddha's path from worldly honors to enlightenment.

Bo'ro Bu'dor, the wonderful Buddhist shrine in Java begun in 850 A.D. Built in the form of a stepped pyramid, its terraced walls bear exquisite reliefs of incidents in the life of Buddha. (Photograph)

Temple of A-nan'da, "the Endless," at Pagan, Burma, with its thousand cloud-capped towers and crowning pinnacle, containing four enormous statues of Buddha thirty feet high. (Photograph)

To the north of the island of Java, in the mountainous, forested land of Siam, lived the short, slightly slant-eyed Siamese. These black-haired, olive-skinned natives, with lips and teeth stained red from chewing juicy betel leaves, long followed the customs of their forefathers. Their dead were embalmed in large jars before cremation, their boys were married at seventeen and their girls at fourteen; they dressed in kilt-like garments, ate their simple food of rice and fish with their fingers, and took the greatest delight in cock-fights and fish-fights. But in time the light-hearted Siamese were also converted to Buddhism, and here, as in all Buddhist lands, ornate monasteries, gilded-roofed temples, and pagodas of teak-wood rose like miracles from the jungles.

Still another settlement of Hindu colonists had been made in Cambodia in Farther India, or Indo-China, in the southeastern corner of Asia. Here lived a short, brown-skinned people closely akin to the Siamese, but mixed with fair-skinned Indo-Aryans and slant-eyed Mongolians and Chinese. The early Cambodians had believed in a religion of serpent worship, but the Hindus brought Brahmanism to the land, and established a powerful line of kings known as the Khymers.

Ang'kor Vat, the temple of awe-inspiring beauty, built in the jungles of Cambodia, Siam. This marvel of mystery, symmetry and grace, with its conical-pyramidal towers, seven-headed, hooded cobras, and miles of carved statuary and animated relief, still breathes the spirit of its builders. (Photograph)

Hidden away in the jungle, the Khymer kings built a wonder building of the East, the Temple of Ang'kor Vat, beautiful with Eastern carving, fascinating and mysterious. In form, the temple was made up of conical, pyramidal towers, pointed arches and ribbed vaulting; it was different from all other buildings, and no one knows from whence the Khymers received their ideas for it. Every inch of the galleries of Angkor Vat was richly carved with scenes from the heroic epics. Master artists transformed the lifeless stone into living, moving images, expressing the cadenced sound of marching troops, the slower movement of huge elephants, and the eagerness of mounted riders. Strange rites to the sacred snake of Cambodia were sculptured in a riot of movement and mystery; and many were the figures of gracefully grouped dancing girls.

Angkor Vat was complete save for the chiselling of a single pillar when Buddhism was brought into Cambodia; and, today, images of Buddhism stand serenely beside those of an older faith.

Buddhist monks also found their way to the mysterious, windswept mountain-land of Tibet, northeast of India. But here Buddhism became mixed with sorcery, and ancient Hindu beliefs, and was called La'ma-ism. A Grand Lama, or Da-lai' La'ma, the living Buddha, was the ruler of this strange land; and scattered throughout the countryside were little spinning wind-wheels and water-wheels on which short prayers were inscribed. Every time these spun, it was thought that a prayer had been made. There were also many flag-staffs bearing beautiful silk flags on which were written: *"Om Mani padme hum,"* "the jewel is in the lotus." Whenever the flag flapped, still another prayer had been made; thus the Buddhist teaching of the path to peace had become deeply buried beneath superstition and form.

Long after Asoka's death, the Hindu Brahmans, who had always feared and hated the new religion, succeeded in driving Buddhism from all India with the exception of a few remote border states. But Buddhism won greater triumphs beyond India than it could have made in the land of its birth. It created a literature and a religion for all the East. It was a mighty stimulus to the creation of great art; and nearly one-half the inhabitants of the world still follow its inspiring teachings.

Monks of Tibet, in fearsome masks, dance to the dreadful demon-goddess of disease. (Photograph)

The Golden Age of Hinduism

After Asoka, the rulers who governed in the palace of the Emperor were weak and peaceful men, well content to leave the cares of government to their favorites and officers, and to live in luxury and idleness. For two hundred years there was peace in the land. Then, suddenly in the year 20 A.D., swarms of barbarian Mongol tribes, clothed in skin, and fighting with bone-tipped javelins, burst through the mountain passes of the Hindu Kush, blotted out the border states, and rolled down upon the fertile Indian plain.

The invaders drove out the Hellenistic rulers in Parthia and Bactria, and opened the way for trade with Rome during the great peace of Caesar Augustus. All of northwestern India fell into their hands, and their kingdom expanded until it reached to the Ganges. But after a time, the Hindus revolted against the cruelties and oppressions of these barbarian savages, and under a second Chan'dra-gup'ta, they broke the power of the Mongol kings and established the rule of the Guptas; and then it was that Northern India reached the height of its glory.

Under the reign of the Gupta emperors, the land had peace, and the arts of peace flourished. Science was studied; sculpture was perfected; and painting, hitherto crude and uneven, blossomed with a warmth which inspired the beautiful cave frescoes at A-jan'ta. Buddhist abbot, dramatist, and poet were encouraged to create a literature wholly Indian in thought and feeling; and court scribes wrote down in the flexible Sanskrit, the tales told round fires of dung and brush in bleak mountain passes, in far-lying caravanserais, or in thronged market places.

But although Buddhism was the court religion, it had never driven Brahmanism, the older Hindu religion, from the land; and now Hindu temples, magnificent and glorious, were erected throughout India, and dedicated to the Hindu gods: Brahma, the Creator; Vishnu, the Preserver; and Siva, the Destroyer. Even though the Gupta kings were outwardly Buddhist, the shrewd Brahman priests, who still held the devotion of the millions and filled the temples with the treasures, must be favored and permitted to do almost as they pleased.

The three most important gods of Brahmanism. Left to right, many-headed Brahma, the Creator, upon the sacred lotus; Vishnu, the Preserver, whose breath created the world; and blood-thirsty Siva, the Destroyer encircled by flames, dancing upon the corpse of the demon Tripura. (Musée Guimet.)

Fa Hsien, a yellow skinned Chinese monk, who came toiling over the Himalayas in the fifth century to secure Buddhist books, noticed that the land was rich and prosperous; charitable institutions were numerous, and rest houses for travelers were built beside all the highways. The people in general followed the Buddhist rule of life but they were still divided into castes, castes, and more castes.

As a part of the caste system, the Hindu was born into his trade. Every noble had a goldsmith among his household servants to make jewelry and plate for his family; for jewelry played an important part in the costume of the men as well as the women, and was used not only for personal adornment, but also for palace hangings and the trappings of state elephants. The general shape of an ornament or design might be suggested by a bird with outspread wings, but the artist never thought of making a true representation of the bird-form. The aim was to use the essential parts only to get decorative beauty. "To wear a real bird . . . would be barbarous; to imitate a real bird closely . . . would be idle; but all that is beautiful in the general idea of a bird, —color, form, and poise can be suggested."

In the art of weaving the Hindus also reached a high state of perfection. The most common material was cotton which the Hindu wove into superb muslins and cloths. Many of these muslins were so sheer that they were given poetic names, such as "Running Water," or "Noon Day Ease," or "Morning Dew" because the cloth was scarcely visible; and when these delicate muslins were embroidered, they had the effect of exquisite lace. Coarser cotton cloths were used for garments, turbans, hangings, and bedspreads, and from their native names are derived many of our own words for cotton fabrics, such as chintz and bandanna.

But the making of a Cashmere shawl from the beautiful, soft, silky undercoat of the sleek-headed Cashmere goat was a greater thing than the mere weaving of a piece of muslin. Twenty men often sat around the loom like an orchestra! Journeyman and apprentices, born weavers all, they had a vision of the beautiful design; but the master who had woven it hundreds of times, visualized the finished shawl to the tiniest detail. One held the red threads flashing like tongues of flame, another the blue, others the russet, the green and the purple. The master with a small cane in his hand, mumbled a short prayer and then the weavers began—first the red, then the green, and then the purple. Toil without song was unknown in India, and the weavers sang:

> What are you weaving?
> We are weaving the little garment of a child.
> What are you weaving?
> We are making the dress of a bride.
> What are you weaving?
> We are making the chaplet of the dead.

So the gamut of life was sung as the threads went into the shawl. Day in and day out, the looms hummed faster and faster, and the voices became higher and higher. The master touched this weaver and that with his stick and each responded as if inspired. The colors began to appear with such beauty, it seemed as if the sun had been torn into ribbons and was being woven into a pattern. Slowly this flow of color took shape and form. Week in and week out, the weavers wove and sang, till the body of each man became as taut as a full-stretched bow.

Hindu artists express their innermost feeling of beauty in the weaving of an exquisite Cashmere shawl, each striving so earnestly to express perfection that something of life itself entered into its making.

The master stood over all as an eagle circling over his prey, the threads were a rainbow of colors, the weavers gave a terrific cry! The shawl was finished, an exquisitely beautiful Cashmere shawl! And then it was given a name: "The True," "The Well-Made," "The Pride of the Maker," or "The Pride of the Possessor."

All his life the Hindu artisan, potter, goldsmith, and weaver had been taught to work *unconsciously* in order to attain perfection. A potter could make any kind of pot or vase if people never asked him *how* he was making it, for he was too busy *creating* to answer questions. The whole effort of the Hindu race was directed toward the attainment of unconscious wisdom, natural, unforced, spontaneous.

The upper castes lived with a gorgeous display of gold and gems, of silk and costly cloths. Wealth increased with the constantly growing trade in gold and silver, precious stones, fine silks, spices, drugs, rare teak, and sandal woods. Treasures from India reached China, all the countries of Asia, and Alexandria; and trade followed the caravans, winding slowly through the passes of Afghanistan to the glittering courts of the Moslems and the imperial palaces at Constantinople.

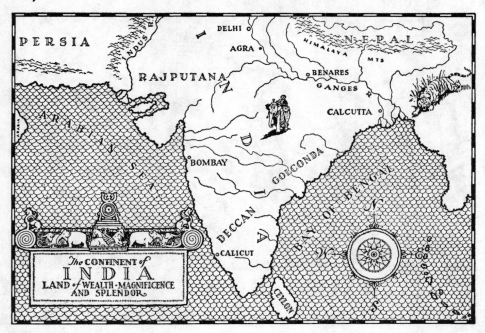

But, unexpectedly in the fifth century, the Golden Age of the Guptas came to an end, and all India was paralyzed by an invasion of the merciless, savage, blood-thirsty Huns. Beaten off, in raid after raid on China, these most barbarous of all Mongol tribes had darted through the northwestern mountains and laid waste all Northern India. The prosperous Ganges Valley groaned under the smoke of burning cities; peace-loving males were put to death, and their women carried away to slavery; marauding bands of Huns spread terror far and wide. At length, a deliverer arose. Ya-sod-har'man, a powerful, handsome rajah of the warrior caste of Central India, aided by a number of native princes, combined the forces of India and freed the land from its barbarous oppressors.

Again there was peace and Northern India, recovering from the ravages of the Huns with most amazing quickness, slowly went to sleep. The people grew careless, forgetful, and slumbered for generations, lax with long years of ease. Then suddenly, rudely awakening, came the thundering hosts of Islam bearing fire and sword.

The Mohammedans in India

With the sword, the Mohammedans had wrought the will of the Prophet, and had spread their faith among the infidels of Central Asia; with the sword, they had won wealth and glory and power. They had taken Afghanistan; and now the fanatical Mohammedan Ghaz'ni-vites made their first swoop into the deep, calm land of India. Under Mahmud, the Turkish King of Ghaz'ni in Afghanistan, the Khyber Pass opened like a sluice-gate to let through turbulent floods of burly-bosomed Mohammedans, aflame with zeal and greed, their hoarse throats resounding with the unforgettable Mohammedan war cry of *"Allah Akbar!,"* "Victory or Paradise!"

Mahmud of Ghaz'ni, leader of the first Mohammedan invasion of India.

Mahmud made seventeen invasions into India, and swept like a pestilence across the fertile, northern plains, from the Indus to the Ganges. Immense stores of treasure and jewels, money, silver-ingots, a pavilion of silver, a canopy of Byzantine linen reared upon pillars of glittering gold were the prizes of these Holy Wars. The booty was placed on display at the court in the palace at Ghazni; and there the awe-struck Mohammedans saw precious jewels, unbored pearls, rubies shining like sparks of iced wine, emeralds, and diamonds. All the world came to Ghazni to gaze upon the incredible wealth of India.

Such rewards quickly kindled the desire to carry on the pious work of converting the infidel Hindu to Mohammedanism; and in 1191, there came another Afghan host into India under Mohammed of Ghor. The first on-sweep of the Moslem scimitar mowed down the tangle of petty chieftains who attempted to defend their lands, but the Rajputs were born soldiers and again made a mighty stand against the invading foe.

The Rajputs were the proud and haughty Kshat'ri-ya caste of ancient Vedic times; they had provided India with her warriors, her nobles, and her monarchs. *Raj-putra* meant a king's son, and these "king's sons" had faced and fought every enemy that had come to their land. Each clan was led by a hereditary leader, and formed a separate community bound by the strongest ties of military devotion and pride of race. The chivalry of Europe was strained and artificial beside the stern, straightforward code of honor of the early Rajputs; and no roundel of troubadour or challenge of knight-errant ever roused more enthusiasm than did the ardent love songs and war songs of Rajput bards.

These were the warriors who fought for India, and utterly defeated Mohammed of Ghor in a battle in which Mohammed barely escaped with his life and his scattered hosts were chased for forty miles. But Mohammed would not admit defeat, and gathered together his wrecked army for another attempt. Strengthened by new hordes of Afghans, Turks, and Persians, he again marched into India, ravaging the Indus Valley and extending his conquests east to Ben-a'res. The defeated Rajputs, rather than submit to the Unclean Raiders, migrated in a body to the hills and deserts bordering the Indus and there founded the military kingdom known today as Raj'pu-ta'na. Soon the entire northern plain lay under the Mohammedan yoke.

Mohammed of Ghor was no religious knight-errant like Mahmud of Ghazni, but a practical conqueror. He wanted lands and provinces, rather than wealth and slaves, and he organized all Northern India under skillful Mohammedan generals who, upon his death, set themselves up as the Sultans of Delhi. These Delhi Sultans were known as the Slave dynasty, because the founder of the house had been a handsome, educated Turkish slave of Mohammed of Ghor, and they ruled India with a display of lavish pomp and splendor.

A hundred years later, another Afghan conqueror, called "the Shelter of the Gods," extended Mohammedan rule deep into the South, winning the whole of the Deccan. With pitiless fury the Afghan Sultans shattered Hindu temples, destroyed sacred images, and ruined every building devoted to native worship. But they were dependent on native

War-loving, fanatical Mohammedans make themselves masters of India with their capital at Del'hi.

Hindu craftsmen for the erection and adornment of their own temples, mosques, and tombs; and thus the Mohammedan dome, pointed arch, and minaret united with native Hindu forms to produce a new and beautiful architecture in India.

All India was now under Moslem sway or in fear of Moslem conquest, and the sea-borne trade of India was almost entirely in the hands of the Mohammedan Arabs. Many Hindus were converted to Mohammedanism, as all government offices were given to Mohammedans, and they alone could be admitted to rank in the army; moreover, the Mohammedans erected colleges and charitable institutions for the instruction of their children and the care of their poor; even the Moslem idler was cared for, since he was one of the privileged of Allah. To turn Moslem had great advantages. The Mohammedans were the masters; the Hindus were merely the taxpayers who gave of their gold whenever a Mohammedan official demanded it.

Meanwhile India had felt the onset of its most terrible invader, Timur the Lame, or Tam'er-lane', the "Earth Shaker," the "Scourge of the World," who had swept down from the mountain plains of the Northwest and sacked the city of Delhi in a savage, merciless raid.

Tamerlane
(1336–1405)

In Transoxiana in western Turkestan, near the borderland of Persia, a wide-shouldered, long-limbed Mongol prince named Timur grew to manhood. With companions as hardy and vigorous as himself, he lived continually among his beloved horses. He and his friends matched their steeds in the clover meadows across the caravan road to Sa-mar-kand'; with their bows they hunted quail and fox; and their trophies they kept in a castle of their own among rocks. Here, too, they played at siege in a game of mimic-war, with Timur always the leader.

Until Timur was thirty-four years old, he fought for the honor and success of his tribe; and, in the eyes of his people, he became a hero who had suffered in their cause; for it was in one of these battles of warring clans that he was wounded by an arrow in the leg, and henceforth he was known as Timur the Lame, or Tam'er-lane'.

Warrior of Tamerlane. (Persian painting.)

Skilled in warfare and crafty was Tamerlane. In 1369, he made himself ruler of Central Asia, with his capital and throne at beautiful Samarkand. Here Alexander the Great had tarried; here Genghis Khan had quartered his horde a hundred and fifty years before; and now Tamerlane was master. Silk robed merchants, saddlers, porcelain makers, horse-merchants, and slave-traders, all thronged to greet him, calling him "Lion," and "Conqueror," and "Lord of Good Fortune," but seldom did they dare go before him for judgment; for Tamerlane was patient only with those who served him in war.

A fertile kingdom, five hundred miles in length and breadth, had Tamerlane won by his strength of arms; and though this might have satisfied a lesser man, the heart of the Mongol was aflame with the lust of conquest and he was determined to subdue the world. Within a few years therefore, he advanced into Russia, broke the power of the Golden Horde; and swinging through the broad steppes, looted the people of bars of gold and silver, white ermine skins and black sables, mule-loads of woven-cloth and silver foxes. Holy Moscow trembled once more at the approach of the Mongols. The Russian Grand Prince and the army took the field with little hope, and a miraculous image of the Virgin was drawn in procession through the streets, between lines of kneeling people who cried as it passed: "Mother of God, save Russia!" It was to this image that the Russians believed their deliverance was due;

but Tamerlane turned aside at the river Don because Moscow, with its fifty thousand inhabitants, was no more to him than a roadside village, and swept around the Caspian Sea to storm the rock-nests of the war-like Georgians.

Then Tamerlane decided upon the conquest of Persia. Leading his armies by way of As-tra-han', he levelled all the cities which held out against him, and blotted out a nest of Assassins who had escaped the massacre of Hulagu Khan. Shah Mansur, Prince of Fars, or Persia proper, was one of the most stubborn and dangerous of Tamerlane's enemies, and the Persian stood firm as a rock within Shi-raz', city of rose-bow-ers and gardens. But in spite of heroic resistance, the city was taken, the Prince beheaded, and all members of his family chained and put to death.

Another Mongol soldier. (Painted 1430 A.D.)

Tamerlane's army attack a walled city in their unchecked conquest of Central Asia and Persia, storming it behind special shields. (Miniature)

From Shiraz, Tamerlane next advanced to the Persian Gulf. Here the wealth of Or'muz, rich in Indian trade and pearl-fisheries, was seized, and demanded henceforth as yearly tribute. Bagdad, no longer the heart of the Mohammedan caliphs, once more felt a conqueror's heel; and the valley of the Tigris and Euphrates, the ancient Land of the Two Rivers, from the mouth to the source, bowed to his obedience.

Tamerlane was now undisputed master of Central Asia, Persia, and the vast lands north of the Arabian and Caspian Seas. For twenty-two hundred miles the great Khorassan road ran through his domains, and cities untold paid him tribute. Up and down the post roads, couriers carried messages to their master, and dispatches to him from generals far beyond the borders. Throughout every province, and even in caravan cities outside the empire, spies sent their reports.

Whatever happened was always told truthfully; for anyone who falsified a report was killed at once. Tamerlane's soldiers received their pay from the army treasurers, and were not allowed to levy tribute on the populace; but waste land and property left without heirs belonged to the throne, though taxes were only collected after harvest.

Tamerlane's next conquest was the rich land of India, and when he first decided to attempt it, his princes and generals murmured: "Ind hath many ramparts. The rivers! and the mountains! and deserts! and the soldiers clad in armor! and the elephants, destroyers of men."

"Ind," said a Mongol lord who had been there, "is a land of sudden heat, not like our heat, but breeding sickness and sapping strength. There, the water is bad and the Indus speak a language that is not like ours. What if the army should linger there too long?"

"With the gold of Ind," said another, "we could subdue the world."

But the anger of Tamerlane was more feared than the terrors of India. Spies had arrived who told him that the land was torn by "commotion and civil wars"; and he knew already that the empire beyond the mountains was the treasure-house of Asia. "My object in the invasion of Hindustan," said Tamerlane "is to lead a campaign against the infidels, to convert them to the true faith according to the command of Mohammed, and to purify the land from the defilement of misbelief."

Ninety-two thousand strong, the armies of Tamerlane marched through the gorges of the Khyber Pass, descended terrifying precipices in pursuit of the infidel tribes; and Tamerlane himself was let down a mountain on a portable scaffold. The Indus was crossed at Attock, and there the attack of the "Lame Firebrand of the World" began in earnest.

It was at this point that Tamerlane became aware that his soldiers were so terrified by stories of invincible elephants, that to calm their fears, he supplied them with claws of iron to throw before the alarming beasts.

In a march of death to Del'hi, the ferocity of Tamerlane and his Mongols broke all bounds. The countryside was stripped and ravaged of every vestige of life, worship, and industry; not a village was left unburned, not a man or woman remained unslain.

An encampment of the army of Tamerlane during his descent into India. (MS. illumination, 1529 A.D.)

Only when he came upon the shrine of a Mohammedan saint did Tamerlane pause, and because of the honor shown a holy one did he spare the populace. After gravely intoning a few prayers, he pressed on, carrying his flaming sword ever forward, and grimly massacring a hundred thousand captives. Helpless country folk fled for protection to the Rajput fortress where they overcrowded the cities and were herded together like sheep beyond the walls, to be slain by the invincible invaders.

As if fascinated by some unholy spell of terror, the people of India yielded to the conqueror without a blow; but the nobles and warriors refused to submit without a struggle. Under the walls of Delhi, they gathered an army of ten thousand horse, forty thousand foot soldiers and more than a hundred elephants. But the seasoned warriors of Tamerlane quickly broke the ranks of the defending army, scattered the elephants with flame throwers, and made a triumphal entry into the capital.

The streets of Delhi were clogged with the bodies of the dead, but Tamerlane passed them unheeding while he went to view the architectural wonders of the city. That evening a feast was held in honor of his victory, and a pyramid of seventy thousand skulls graced the banquet board. On the last day of 1398, the victorious leader left Delhi after giving "sincere and humble tribute of grateful praise for his victory" in a beautiful mosque of marble on the banks of the river. Tamerlane next crossed the Ganges, and after a great massacre at Mee'rut, skirted the foot of the lofty Himalayas to make his way back to Samarkand laden with booty.

Enemy heads cast to the ground as in the slaughter at Delhi

The conqueror had finished with India. He made no move toward organizing the empire he had won, but leaving anarchy, famine, and pestilence behind him, he simply quitted the land. While still loitering on the banks of the Ganges, he had been told that disturbances had arisen in Mesopotamia, Georgia and Anatolia under the leadership of Baj'a-zet', the turbulent, courageous Sultan of the Ottoman Turks, who had built up a kingdom in Asia Minor, and was now barring further conquest. Tamerlane set forth at once for Western Asia. Here he made war upon the Mam'e-luke Sultan of Egypt, sacked Aleppo and gave Damascus to the flames. But during the destruction, he ordered that plans be drawn of a curious dome, shaped like a pomegranate, which had caught his fancy. Swelling out from the base, the dome tapered to a slender point; and this bulbed dome of Damascus, destroyed

Baj'a-zet', Sultan of the Turks, attended by dwarfs and Janissaries in his magnificent and luxurious palace. (Persian MS.)

in the fire, became the pattern for Tamerlane's later buildings and those of his descendants. Transported in another century to India it formed the crown of the Taj Mahal and the palaces of the Moghul emperors.

After the destruction of Damascus, Tamerlane mustered his strength to meet the armored hosts of Sultan Bajazet at Angora. There the Turks were badly defeated and routed, and Tamerlane took the proud Sultan prisoner, flung him in a dungeon, and loaded him down with chains. Then he reaped the fruits of victory by occupying Bru'sa, capital of the Ottoman Turks, Ni-cae'a, and Smyr'na in Asia Minor, and by taking the personal treasure of Bajazet, even to his women slaves.

So completely had the Turks been crushed that no second battle was necessary. The Mongol horsemen rode down to the shore of the Bosphorus and looked across to the gold domes of Constantinople; they galloped over the long buried ruins of Troy, where Helen once held court; they drove out the Christian Knights of St. John from Smyrna; and then they returned home.

The kings of Europe were astonished, bewildered, and quite fearful at this upheaval on their threshold; and Henry III, king of Castile, sent ambassadors to Tamerlane to learn more about the scourge of the East. The leader of the mission was Henry's chamberlain, the good Ruy de Gon-za'lez de Cla-vi'jo, who sought the Mongol conqueror even to the distant city of Samarkand where he was courteously received.

"Lord Tamer was seated in a portal," wrote Clavijo with trustworthy accuracy, "in front of the entrance of a beautiful palace, and he was sitting on the ground. Before him there was a fountain where red apples floated and which threw up the water very high. The lord was seated cross-legged in silken embroidered carpets among round pillows. He wore a robe of silk with a high, white hat on his head, and on the top of the hat was a spinal ruby with pearls and precious stones around it."

Tamerlane had made Samarkand the wonder city of Asia. He had adorned it with whatever had pleased his fancy in other lands; he had peopled it anew with captives and scientists and philosophers. In it, he feasted magnificently, and there the wondering Clavijo beheld courts covered with flowers and ripe fruit. Litters, flaming with precious stones, moved through the streets bearing singing girls, escorted by lute players, and tigers and goats with golden horns that were not beasts, but other fair girls thus attired by the skinners of Samarkand. Clavijo wandered through a castle higher than the mosque towers, built of crimson cloth by the weavers; he visited Tamerlane's grandson, Pir Mohammed, richly dressed in "blue satin embroidered with golden wheels"; he saw elephants fight and Tartar princes arrive from India and the Gobi, bringing gifts to their lord. Then, abruptly, he was dismissed without seeing Tamerlane again, and sent back home.

And now Tamerlane summoned a council of princes and amirs.

"We have conquered all of Asia except China," he told them. "We have overthrown such mighty kings that our deeds will be remembered always. You have been my companions in many wars, and never has victory failed you; thither to China you shall go with me."

Forthwith a mighty army of picked men was equipped and the great horde began its march, but as the host crossed the Jax-ar'tes River, Tamerlane was seized with a sudden illness. He died within a few days, and the army returned at once to Samarkand.

Like the conquests of Genghis Khan, the victories of Tamerlane changed the history of Europe as well as that of Asia. He opened again the transcontinental trade routes which had been blocked for a hundred years, the Golden Horde was crushed, and the way opened for the Russians to make themselves a free people. The petty kings of Persia were exterminated, and the Ottoman Turks weakened and scattered. The Church of Islam never recovered from the destruction he wrought; and the fanatical zeal for forcing the world to accept Mohammedanism **very** soon disappeared.

Tamerlane holds audience in the beautiful palace gardens of his gorgeous capital of Samarkand, Central Asia. (Martin, F. R., *Painting and Painters of Persia, India and Turkey*.) Here Cla-vi'jo was courteously received by the invincible conqueror of the Eastern world. See *Narrative of the Embassy of Ruy Gonzalez de Clavijo to the Court of Timour at Samarkand, 1403–06*. Translated by Clements R. Markham, Hakluyt Society.

Gypsies in Europe, restless, care-free, colorful wanderers, driven from Asia Minor by Tamerlane.

A curious result of these Mongol disturbances was the appearance in Europe of drifting, happy-go-lucky groups of a strange people called Gypsies. They came first to Greece about the end of the fourteenth century; and because they were thought to be Egyptians, they were given the name Gypsies. They had been drifting about Asia for some centuries before the massacres of Tamerlane drove them across the Hellespont, and now they spread slowly across Europe to live in commons and by hedgerows in the wild woodlands and neglected patches of a civilized world. The Germans called them "Hungarians" and "Tartars," the French gave them the name of "Bohemians"; but no one ever knew whence they really came.

Tamerlane was dead, and all Asia slept the sleep of exhaustion. Delhi was a city in ruins; for thirty-six years India had no government. Dazed, depopulated, she lay ravaged and despairing. A whole generation had to pass ere men could be found with hope enough to face the future again. But Tamerlane's enormous empire had been an empire of conquest only; on his death, his domains fell apart, and it was not until the time of his great-grandsons that a real empire was established. Then it was that the Mongols came again into India, and the empire they founded was the Empire of the Great Moghuls, famous for its wealth and luxury.

The Great Moghuls

It was in the year 1526, that a Turkoman prince, called Ba'ber, the "Panther," with the blood of Tamerlane and Genghis Khan flowing in his veins, was tempted by the wealth of India to enter this southern land. Five times he invaded India, and finally the immense armies of the Sultan of Delhi were defeated with the help of artillery, a new weapon only then coming into use in Europe, and hitherto unknown to India.

Baber then set himself to the task of subduing the land, and establishing himself firmly as its ruler. His terrifying artillery was needed again, however; for he still had a worthy foe in Rana Sanhram Singh, king of the fiery Rajputs and hero of a hundred fights. But once more the flaming cannon conquered, the flower of India's chivalry was slaughtered, and the heads of the high-spirited nobles of Raj'pu-ta'na were heaped in a ghastly pyramid before the Mongol leader.

Thenceforth, Baber was master of India, though he loved not this land which he had won with his sword. Nevertheless, he made the city of A'gra his capital; and there in a beautiful garden, the Garden of the Eight Paradises, where bloomed roses and narcissuses and red oleanders, he directed his officers, received reports from ministers, and composed those verses in Persian in which he so delighted.

Baber, first of the Moghul emperors of India. (Miniature, Calcutta.) "Moghul" was the Arabic spelling of Mongol, and was the name given to the line of emperors descended from Baber. The Moghuls were a mixed race from Central Asia, half Turkish, half Mongol.

The Emperor Akbar, greatest of all Moghul rulers, whose magnificence captured the imagination of Europe, riding in state upon a gaily caparisoned royal elephant. (India Office.)

But although Baber had conquered India, he did not live long enough to organize his conquest and to establish the reign of the Moghul emperors. This task remained for his grandson, Ak'bar. Sallow, black-eyed, sturdy of figure, Akbar became Sultan of Delhi and Agra at the age of fourteen, and at once began a series of whirlwind conquests which extended the frontiers of his empire in all directions and won for him the name of Akbar the Great. Unlike Baber and Tamerlane, Akbar was not merely a conqueror, but also an organizer who established a strong government for his empire. Like the Buddhist king, Asoka the Great, who had said that conquest by the sword was not worth calling conquest, Akbar felt that the king should be the center in which caste, and creed, and even race should disappear, leaving nothing but equal rights and justice for all.

Akbar found India split up into numerous petty Hindu and Mohammedan kingdoms. The earlier invasions by Turks, Afghans and Mongols had left a powerful Mohammedan population in addition to the Hindu states, and each of these Mohammedan conquests had also left a petty kingdom ruled by its own king. Akbar reduced these Moslem states to provinces of the Delhi Empire; he won the support of the Rajput princes by marriage, and then gave them positions of honor.

His friendship with the Hindus, and his interest in their literature and religion made him many enemies among the pious Mohammedans. But Akbar saw clearly what was to prove for centuries down to modern times to be the great stumbling block in the way of India's progress. He saw how the jealousy of Hindus and Mohammedans and the rigid system of castes was keeping the country split up and preventing its unification. So he decided to found a new religion, in which Indians of all creeds could unite, a worship of the Sun. Of this new religion, Akbar himself was the prophet, and every morning he worshiped in public the Sun whose good and kindly influence even the crudest mind could grasp. But instead of worshiping the sun, the people worshiped Akbar; and when at last he died, his religion perished with him.

It was under Akbar that the Mohammedan-Indian architecture, beautiful in decoration and soaring lightness, reached its perfection in the masterpieces of the palaces of the king at Agra and Fat'e-hpur Si'kri. Akbar removed the capital from Delhi to the Moghul city of Agra,

Akbar was greatly interested in building, and often visited the many new structures under construction. (Miniature)

The Royal Salute. A Hindu painting of the ceremony performed for an emperor such as Akbar. As the Emperor approached the walled city, the people gathered, and a mighty cannon roared a welcome.

the center of the Afghan sultans; and in gratitude for the birth of a son, he made a peerless city out of the little village of Fat'e-hpur Si'kri, calling it "the City of Victory."

In Agra were the many buildings of the Palace, stately groups of public halls, set about courtyards and gardens fed by cool fountains. Every morning after a conference with his ministers in a Private Audience Chamber, Akbar was borne to the *Diwan-i-Am*, the Hall of Public Audience, where he proclaimed before the people the decisions of his Privy Council, and where justice was done in the sight of all. Hither streamed the folk from the lower city, squatting under the burning sun, to hear Akbar's wisdom and to see his judgment executed; and hither flocked blue-coated, wide-trousered Mohammedans in close white turbans; red-hatted Parsis, worshipers of fire; yellow caftaned Jews; shaven Hindus in white *dhotis* falling from the waist, and Bengalis in embroidered caps and wide vests. Now and then from behind the tracery of stone screens above the roof, a flash of color betrayed the presence of harem women watching the place of judgment.

When the Emperor finally rose to go, the multitude prostrated themselves and rose again, scattering with a swirl of many-colored robes. Sword-bearing eunuchs and women guards escorted Akbar into a scented garden, set with spreading trees and flowering shrubs. Here only one of his Council, A'bul Fa'zl, a learned Persian historian, was privileged to attend him.

Akbar laid the foundations of a supremely beautiful civilization in India. His reign created a united country from an unhappy jumble of warring races and creeds, and he governed it wisely and justly. He was a brave soldier, a great general, a wise administrator, a benevolent ruler, and a sound judge of character. Those who followed him on the throne continued to rule the Moghul Empire with strong and able hands, and under the Moghuls, there was prosperity, peace, and plenty. Agriculture and industry created such abundance that trade flourished between India, Western Asia and Europe, providing great revenues to fill the treasury to overflowing.

Akbar receives officials and ministers in his Audience Chamber. At his left is his son. Prince Jahangir. (Miniature, Paris.)

The Taj Ma-hal', one of the most perfect of buildings, and the glory of Moghul India. (Photograph)

Akbar's successors were likewise interested in erecting exquisite buildings and planned forms even more noble than before. His grandson, Shah Je-han', erected the masterpiece of India, a building which only the Greek Parthenon can rival in perfection. This was the Taj Ma-hal', or Gem of Buildings at Agra, built as a tomb for his beloved wife, Mum'taz Mahal, a name meaning "Exalted of the Palace." Mumtaz died in the full bloom of her youth, happy with the promise of her husband that he would build an immortal monument in her memory.

The Taj Mahal is a monument of wondrous beauty, dazzling in the whiteness of its exterior. Within, the walls are everywhere covered with floral designs beloved by the Persians; and the sunlight filters in through marble screens, intricately wrought, and as delicate as lace. The Taj, with its graceful dome, its slender minarets, its lacy trellises of fine marbles, stands in the midst of a beautiful Persian garden where fountains play in cypress avenues and quiet pools reflect the pure beauty of its majesty. Here in beauty and grace, the beautiful young wife is buried.

Under the Moghul emperors, painting also developed to lofty heights, and the making of jewelry became even more important and artistic than before. All Moghul emperors loved ornamentation; Akbar had left an enormous collection of jewels; Jahangir's jewels included priceless diamonds, pearls, rubies, emeralds and jade, as well as jeweled sword-hilts, drums, brooches, aigrettes, saddles, lances, chairs of state, wine-cups and rings. With Shah Je-han' jewels were a passion, and a crowning example of the jeweler's art was his pure gold Peacock Throne studded with gems and covered with rubies. Pillars of emeralds supported a roof surmounted by two peacocks ablaze with precious stones; between the peacocks was a tree set with diamonds, rubies and pearls; and three jeweled steps led to the Emperor's seat. Mid these dazzling splendors, clad in white garments and turban of gold-cloth stiff with priceless gems, the Moghul emperors ruled India.

There came a time, however, when feeble rulers sat on the throne of Agra, and the descendants of Akbar became puppet kings. The Moghuls had lost their vigor, the days of India's greatness had passed. Meanwhile, the Portuguese had followed Vasco da Gama to India. And after them came the Dutch, the English, the Spanish and the French to establish trading posts or try to seize parts of India. But maintaining these various positions became so dangerous and difficult that at last all save the English gave up struggling to do so. Thus the English alone of all European powers remained in India and in time they came to rule the whole land, making it a part of the mighty British Empire they were creating.

The famous gold Peacock Throne, made for Shah Jehan, grandson of Akbar. (Moghul Miniature.)

SUMMARY

SUMMARY OF VOLUME SEVEN

IN THE thirteenth century Western Europeans began to feel a great interest in lands that lay far to the east, lands of which they knew little or nothing, so in this volume we take up those eastern countries, Persia, China, Japan and India, as well as Russia, which had all been developing outside the main stream of Western culture. And we start with the story of Marco Polo, that young adventurer from Venice who set out with his father and uncle, bent on getting through to the mysterious, golden, far away land of China. Journeying by horseback with a camel caravan, these three Polos rode all the long distance from Syria to Persia, then over the snow-capped Himalayas and the dangerous Gobi Desert to China, thus establishing for Western Europe its first actual contact with the Far East, where lay so many rich countries offering Europeans enormous opportunities for trade. In those days China was ruled not by the Chinese, but by that magnificent Mongol, Kublai Khan, whom the Polos found in his splendid summer pavilion built of gilded bamboo with its columns carved in the shape of dragons. And for seventeen years they remained in the service of the Great Khan, while Marco traveled through the vast empire the Mongols had conquered, seeing the interesting sights he described in the book he wrote after his return to Europe.

Save for Japan all the eastern countries whose histories we take up had been linked together by the conquests of these Mongols. Fierce wandering people called Tartars by Europeans, the Mongols were akin to the Turks but utterly different from the Chinese and they had lived in the Gobi Desert in movable tents called yurts, which they took about on carts that were often twenty feet wide and drawn by twenty-two oxen. So strong were these wild men that they could ride eighty miles a day on horseback and their great chieftain, Genghis Khan, the grandfather of Kublai Khan, had forged them into a terrifying host of warriors. Then he had set out and conquered all Asia from the Pacific Ocean to the Caspian Sea and from the Arctic regions south to the borders of India. When he died in 1227, Genghis Khan had left his sons not only the greatest empire ever conquered by one man but also the most powerful army on earth. And his sons and generals had continued to make more conquests while one of his grandsons pushed on from Asia into Europe. This man was Batu the Splendid, who always wore gold-embroidered clothes and whose great felt traveling tent with its roof of gold was so glittering and gorgeous that his army was called the Golden Horde. With this Golden Horde Batu had entered Russia in 1236 and subjugated the country. So this brings us to the story of Russia and how and why it always faced east instead of west, remaining outside the culture of Western Europe.

LYING IN THE eastern plains of Europe and bordering Western Asia, Russia stretched from the frozen marsh tundras of the great white North, southward through virgin forests of birch and pine, to those enormous seas of grass, the vast, silent, treeless steppes. Into this vast land there came in early days the brown-haired, gray-eyed Slavs, who settled in villages, building log houses with elaborately carved and gaily painted porches projecting from the second story. A merry people, they gathered often to celebrate picturesque festivals, singing songs to their old Slavic gods, dancing their old folk-dances in honor of the coming of spring after the long cold winter, telling tales of the lovely Snow Maid or the nymphs who dwelt in forest and field. Gradually they built up trading posts with Kiev on the Dnieper River their most important settlement while Novgorod far to the north was the second town of importance. Scattered in little groups between Kiev and Novgorod, the Slavs lived to themselves, having little contact with the rest of Europe, for they were hemmed in by savage foes—to the north the Finns, to the south roving Turkish tribes, and to the East the Mongols who were then wandering the Gobi Desert.

It was thus that the Slavs were living when the Vikings, those Norsemen who raided all Europe in the Middle Ages, bore down on Russia also. Coming first to trade, they remained to settle there. Then in the year 862 the Slavs around Novgorod, who were always suffering from raids of the Finns, invited Rurik, the Red, the red-haired leader of those Norsemen who had settled near Novgorod, to become their ruler and drive out the Finns. So Rurik, though he was loath to accept this offer, "for dread," as he said, "of the beastlike manners of the men of Novgorod," finally went to their aid. Driving out the Finns, he became the ruler of all the Slavs and Norsemen who lived around Novgorod. And his successor, advancing southward, captured Kiev, transferred his court to that place, and at last united all the country. Thereafter the land was called Russia in honor of Rurik, the Red, and under Viking leadership an infant Russian nation began to take form at last.

During the next hundred years, the Norsemen slowly melted into the Slavic population, so by the year 980 when Vladimir became Grand Prince of Russia, he and his country were wholly Slavic in language, in customs and religion with no trace of the Nordic remaining. Vladimir had won his throne after a bloody civil war in which he had slain his brother and to celebrate this victory he placed before his palace statues, not of Nordic, but of Slavic gods, including Perun, the god of thunder, whose huge figure with a head of silver and long mustaches of gold, guarded the portals of his dwelling. And to these Slavic gods he savagely sacrificed a thousand human lives. His grandmother Olga had been a Greek Christian but Vladimir was at first determinedly set against Christianity. Though the highway to Italy, as well as the one leading off to Constantinople and the bright light of Byzantine civilization, both went through his capital, Kiev, Vladimir had no more interest than his people in those distant countries. He wished to remain just Slavic and Russian. However, the Russians were unlike other primitive people in that they had no priestly class, for the head of each household offered sacrifice for his family to such gods as he chose and there was no unity in their religion. So Vladimir slowly began to see that if he would hold his people together, he must give them some definite creed and a set form of worship in which everyone could join. Therefore, he sent ten men out into the world to investigate the Roman Church, the Greek Church, the religion of the Jews and that of the Moslems and to report to him which of these religions would serve his purpose best.

Traveling about on this business, his envoys decided that the Jews thought too much of their sins and the Moslems had too little gladness, while they saw no beauty in the Roman Church and did not like the fact that the Pope was considered above all emperors and kings. But when these shy, uncouth, gray-bearded Russian elders, in their long coats and fur-brimmed hats, came to beautiful Constantinople they were dazzled by its glory. And the Byzantine emperors, Basil and Constantine, two brothers who were ruling together, took them to the beautiful church of Sancta Sophia, where the Patriarch of the Greek Church had arranged a service so magnificent that the envoys did not know whether they were in heaven or on earth. Impressed beyond words, they reported to Vladimir that Greek Christianity was the proper religion for Russia. So Vladimir decided to accept Christianity from the East, not from the West, but with true Russian pride, he made up his mind not to humble himself by requesting the rite of baptism into the Church. He would get it the Russian way. By force of arms and threats, he would make the Byzantine emperors beg him to be baptized as a Christian! So he set forth with an army and captured the Byzantine city of Korsun, then he sent word to the emperors that he would come and take Constantinople unless they sent him their sister Anna to be his wife. Aghast at the very thought of wedding their sister to such a barbarian, the emperors still dared not refuse this request with that savage army of Slavs all ready to descend upon them. So they replied that if Vladimir would receive baptism as a Christian they would send Anna to him. Defiantly Vladimir answered: "First send me your sister, then will I receive baptism." Thus the emperors had to send Anna to him, though she herself wept bitterly when she left them, for this barbarian whom she was to marry already had eight hundred wives.

Then, having successfully used his threat to get himself baptized and wedded to Anna, Vladimir gave Korsun back to the emperors and returned with his new wife to Kiev. There he ordered the idols about his palace to be cut to pieces or consumed by fire while he had Perun, the god of thunder, tied to the tail of a horse and lashed with rods as he was dragged off and cast into the Dnieper. Then he ordered every man, woman and child in Kiev to appear the next morning at the river. And when they gathered there, he sent them all into the water to be baptized by the priests who had come to Russia with him and Anna. In this manner all were baptized into Christianity, still knowing nothing whatever of what Christianity meant. However, Vladimir really tried after that to absorb at least a few Christian ideas. He put away all his wives save Anna and he set himself to see that noblemen's sons got the fundamentals of education. He started building churches also, and sent out missionaries who converted many people in the country along the river. After his death in 1015, he was canonized as a saint and to the peasants who sang of him as Fair Sun Vladimir, he became a national hero, the great King Arthur of Russia.

But despite the efforts of Vladimir and later rulers to Christianize Russia, heathenism still lingered in far corners of the land where the people continued for centuries to celebrate their beloved pagan festivals. Moreover, being richly gifted with fancy, the Russians, when they did accept Christianity, adorned with imaginative trimmings all such Bible stories as they now told and retold. Having no copies of the Bible and being, in addition to that, unable to read, they mingled Bible stories with their own ancient legends. And that has been the Christianity of the Russian peasant through the ages down to the twentieth century, for not until then were these sturdy, simple, hard-working peasants, ground down by their rulers and the upper classes, ever permitted to learn to read.

With the Princess Anna much besides Christianity came to Russia, for Anna brought with her to Kiev Byzantine craftsmen who introduced Byzantine art and architecture into the land. Now the Russians began to make icons, those flat paintings of saints, often framed in silver or gold, which the Greek Church used, in contrast to the statues and rounded figures in paintings used by the Roman Church. And they began to build beautiful churches in the Byzantine style, churches adorned with brightly colored mosaics and crowned with domes. But the Russians had too much imagination to continue forever just copying Byzantine art. Soon they were changing and adapting it, building, instead of the low round domes of the Byzantines, those bulbous, onion-shaped domes which are purely Russian. And they began decorating their churches with carvings of fabulous monsters, twisted into interlaced designs, which also appeared on the beautiful manuscripts made in Russian monasteries and became in time characteristic of a national Russian art.

But even as the Russians grew more race-conscious and truly Russian, they grew also more withdrawn into themselves, more exclusive of foreigners. Their nearest neighbor to the west was Poland, which was Slavic just as Russia was, but Poland was Roman Catholic, while Russia was Greek Catholic. And as Poland grew in power she began to fear greatly that great Russia which covered so vast an expanse and lay at her own back door. Russia was fast asleep, a great sprawling, ignorant giant, and Poland saw to it that no knowledge should come from Western Europe to waken that huge colossus and stir him into sudden consciousness of his own tremendous power.

Then in 1236 Batu the Splendid bore down on Russia with his Golden Horde of Mongols. Looting, burning, killing, they laid all Russia waste, then swept on into Europe. The Poles could not stop them, neither could Henry, Duke of Silesia. Slaying Henry in battle, the Mongols cut off his head, stuck it up on a spear and filled nine sacks with ears which they cut from the heads of dead foes. They ravaged Bohemia, the land of the Czechs, where King Wenceslaus was unable to halt them, they defeated King Bela of Hungary, burning his city of Pesth, and lastly, turning south, they sacked the fine cities along the Adriatic. Then Batu had word that his father, the khan, was dead and being obliged to return to Asia for the election of a new khan, he led his Golden Horde, laden with the spoils of twenty-two countries they had ravished, back through Russia to Asia. All Western Europe he had found too shut in by mountains to suit him, but he had been vastly pleased by the enormous flat stretches of Russia. So, after the new khan was chosen, Batu returned to Russia and established a permanent kingdom there with Sarai on the Volga River as his capital city.

For the next three hundred years Russia remained in bondage to the Mongols while the real Russia, the Russia of the Slavs, retreated to the swamplands surrounding Moscow, which stood on a hill above the river Moskwa in the province of Vladimir-Suzdal. Here Prince Yuri Long Arm had set up a country estate in the depths of primeval pinewoods. On the hill called the Kremlin he had built a stout oaken wall to enclose both the wooden lodge where he feasted his friends and the little wooden settlement around the old church of St. Savior of the Pines. But as more and more Russians came flocking to this wooden fortress, Moscow began to grow and the Metropolitan of Vladimir, the highest dignitary of the Russian Church, moved to the Kremlin, thus making Moscow the center of Russian Christianity. So the Kremlin grew ever more splendid until it was no longer a simple wooden fortress but a city with churches and palaces, a fairy town of white buildings, gilded onion-shaped domes and tall turrets enclosed within a white wall. And as Moscow grew, her rulers kept acquiring more land and more power until by the end of the fifteenth century her princes, working for the Mongols as tax collectors, had become so powerful, that they made themselves hereditary grand dukes. Then in 1547 Grand Duke Ivan IV did what his forebears had never dared do. Heretofore, the title Czar had been used only by the Mongol khans, but Ivan had himself crowned as Czar of Russia, thus becoming the first Russian Czar, and so weakening the waning power of the Mongols that they began to withdraw from Russia.

Well-educated and a great admirer of Western culture, Ivan still had within him a strong strain of cruelty which amounted almost to madness at times and could make him not only kill the son he loved in a fit of fury, but also slay thousands of the people of Novgorod whom he suspected of plotting rebellion against him. For this reason he is generally known as Ivan the Terrible, yet he succeeded in uniting Russia and holding it together. Moreover, he started Russia's advance to the east by his conquests in Siberia, an eastward march which was to continue through the centuries until Russia reached the Pacific, finally owning far more land in Asia than in Europe and becoming in truth a huge colossus overpowering in size. Ivan also tried to spread out to the west and to import skilled workmen from Germany to teach his people the trades and crafts of Western Europe, but in both these attempts he was balked by his neighbors, the King of Poland and the Emperor Charles V of Germany, who had no wish to see Russia advance any farther in their direction or grow more powerful through taking on Western learning.

Like the Mongol khans, Ivan was an absolute ruler, an autocrat whose will was law. Batu had held that since he had conquered Russia the land belonged to him alone and all the khans after him had held as firmly to that idea. All lands, all property were theirs, solely theirs. There was no private owner-ship of anything in Russia. Regularly the nobles had to present the khan with precious gifts as an acknowledgment that the land they held was his and every Russian could be called upon at any time for any service the khan required. As to the peasants, they could never own the land they worked. It belonged to the khan, to whom they must pay every year one-tenth of their harvest and one-tenth of all increase in cattle or other stock. Even the horse or ox with which the poor peasant ploughed his land could be taken from him in the name of the khan. And three centuries of absolute obedience to the Mongol master formed a habit of thought slow to change. Having almost no contact with Western Europe, where many ideas of freedom were developing, the patient, good-natured Russians grew ever more accustomed to the ancient law of the Mongols, which the Russian czars took over with an autocracy equaling that of the khans. No man, woman or child had any rights of his own, all must submit to the State, whether represented in the person of khan or czar. Thus when the Russians disposed of their czar after the first World War, the communistic state they founded, with all property belonging to the State and a dictator heading the government, was the natural outcome of their own history.

NOW SHORTLY AFTER Batu settled in Russia, other Mongols had turned on Persia where the Arabs, after their conquest of the land, had developed a distinctive culture based on old Persian patterns. These Arabs had made Bagdad, which was the capital of the Moslem empire, a wonder city of beauty and they had visited India, China and Africa long before Europeans did. From these far countries so much wealth in gold dust, ivory, jewels, cinnamon and slaves flowed into the laps of the caliphs at Bagdad that they lived in a golden haze of luxury and splendor. Best known of all these caliphs was Haroun-al-Raschid, whose magnificent court, far outshining that of his powerful contemporary, Charlemagne, was forever glorified in that glamorous collection of Arabian tales called "A Thousand and One Nights." But when Haroun-al-Raschid died in 809 Arabic power declined. Egypt broke away under her own Moslem rulers and the Persians regained control of Eastern Persia. Then the caliph at Bagdad, fearing Persian disloyalty, formed for himself a bodyguard of Turks, appointing as their commander a Turkish officer with the title of sultan and from then on these Turks, arrogant and overbearing, assumed more and more power over the weakening caliphs, until they actually ruled the land.

This was the Persia into which the Mongols burst under their savage leader, Hulagu. And even warriors as fierce as the Turks could not stand against the Mongols. In 1258 Hulagu took the beautiful city of Bagdad, looted it, ruined it and murdered nearly all its inhabitants. For three hundred and fifty years after that the Mongols ruled Persia. Then the land was seized by Turkoman Turks, who were finally driven out by Shah Abbas, one of the greatest rulers of the Persians. But in 1598 when Shah Abbas was trying to modernize his army he summoned two Englishmen, Sir Anthony and Sir Robert Shirley, to aid him in training his soldiers and from that time on, while the Turks every now and then tried to get a foothold in Persia, it was to be European nations, England, Russia and France, who kept competing with each other to gain concessions, influence and power in that rich country which is now known as Iran.

THE MONGOLS had only recently conquered Persia when the Polos passed through that land on their way to China where the great Kublai Khan was ruling. And of all the countries conquered by the Mongols none was more interesting than China. The history of this ancient nation went back to some four thousand years before Christ, when the Sumerians were creating their culture at Ur in the Land of Two Rivers, far to the west in Asia. Then a migrating people of unknown origin but perhaps akin to the Sumerians came and settled in China in the valley of the Hwang Ho or Yellow River. On all sides these primitive Chinese were surrounded by hostile wandering herdsmen, including the savage forefathers of the Huns, the Turks and the Mongols, but despite these foes they began to till the soil and develop as farmers. Settling in little family groups, they lived in villages around a well and the oldest man in each family told the others what to do. No one lived or worked for himself alone, everything he did was for the family as a whole. Thus the family became the basis of Chinese life and from the exalted position of the oldest man in the family ancestor worship arose, for this meant that family ties were not broken even when the oldest man died. His spirit still lived on to exercise authority and protect the family from harm. The Chinese also believed in one supreme God, Shang Ti, the Most High God or Heaven, and in spirits of the hills, the rivers and the stars, whom they worshiped by burning sweet smelling wood.

At some time in that dim distant past they discovered the use of the silkworm and started the weaving of silk. Moreover, they invented their own system of writing by simplifying pictures into groups of lines, thus forming ideographs which stood for ideas as well as things.

Early Chinese history is all embroidered by legend, but with the coming of the Chou dynasty, or family of rulers, in 1122 B. C., the history of China became a record of facts. During the nine hundred years of Chou rule China changed very greatly. Spreading out from the basin of the Yellow River, the Chinese conquered and occupied much more land. Then while most of the people still loved farming, raising the rice and other grain on which they subsisted, others went to the growing cities as merchants or craftsmen and these gifted craftsmen began to develop that exquisite refinement in art which was to produce the beautiful pottery, porcelains, bronzes and carved ivory for which the Chinese are famous. However, the Chou emperors reduced the farmers to a condition little better than that of serfs, who spent their lives in poverty laboring to support their wealthy masters. Dwelling in miserable hovels, the poor lived in sharp contrast to the idle luxurious nobles and the rich. The home of any wealthy man was a whole magnificent group of one story buildings built around many little inner courts and shut in by a wall. Usually made of wood, the buildings were richly carved and painted in vivid colors, while their steep tiled roofs, curving upward at the corners, extended beyond the houses, resting on pillars and so forming pleasant galleries where one could sit to enjoy the flowers in the courtyards. Certainly, the rich lived grandly on the labors of the poor and this fact was to continue for the next three thousand years. Patient, long-suffering, hard-working, the farmers tilled the beloved little fields which they had inherited from their ancestors. Often they suffered famine when crops were bad, sometimes they starved to death but always they were uncomplaining, courteous and polite. Submissively through the centuries they paid over to greedy masters and venal tax collectors, who kept a huge share of the taxes they collected, all too much of the produce from their small farms, for they were a peace-loving people, taking life as it came and having no thoughts of revolt.

The nobles, however, were no such lovers of peace. What they wanted they took by force and by the later years of Chou rule they had grown so powerful that they no longer heeded the emperor. Acting as little independent rulers, they fought with each other and kept the country divided. Then amid all this strife Chinese philosophers sought to restore peace and happiness to the land by introducing new ways of thinking, and the first of these great philosophers was Lao Tze, who founded the religion called Taoism. Born about 604 B. C., Lao Tze wrote a book about the Tao which meant the Way —the way to serenity and joy, the way for a man to bring his spirit into harmony with the actual laws of the universe, the way to virtue, unstudied, unself-conscious virtue. Lao Tze defined God by the one word *Spontaneity*, that is, the prompting to right action that speaks within men's hearts and needs no compulsion from outward restraints and elaborate regulations.

Quite different were the teachings of the next great philosopher, Confucius, born in 551 B. C., for Confucius sought to save society by a return to the ways of the ancients and this meant not only emphasis on moral training, but also the complete regulation of human conduct in accordance with the ceremonies, rituals and customs that had come down from the past. Gathering his material from writings of the ancients, Confucius put forth five books, offering no philosophy of religion, no attempt to define the nature of God, but designed solely to preserve for his people a detailed knowledge of old Chinese rules of conduct. By this means he hoped to develop what he called "the superior man," one who sought not riches or fame, but was modest, reverent, sincere, polite, and self-possessed. And his influence on the Chinese people was tremendous. Gradually his ideals became the ideals of the nation and every Chinese gentleman strove to attain the standards Confucius had set for becoming a "superior man." But the continuance of ancestor worship of which Confucius had approved and the constant care to do only what Confucius sanctioned developed in the Chinese people an unquestioning belief in the perfection of the past which made them resist all change and proved for centuries to be a serious bar to progress.

Both Lao Tze and Confucius had tried to show rulers and people the way back to peace, but the rulers refused to heed them, so war between the nobles continued, causing so much misery and destruction that for the first time in Chinese history, many men abandoned farming to earn their living by fighting in the armies of the rival nobles. Then with all the land in confusion, Huns, Turks and Mongols swept into Northern China where they intermarried with the Chinese and formed a people of mixed blood, who were taller and stronger but less cultured than the pure-blooded Chinese to the South. But finally in 249 B. C., the able Chin deposed the last Chou ruler, made himself emperor and united all the land, which was henceforth called China after him. Putting down the warring nobles, Chin took away their land and divided China into provinces governed by men whom he appointed. Then he encouraged the peasants to return to farming and it was he who connected the separate fortifications which had existed along the north-western frontier by building the Great Wall of China to keep out the raiding barbarians.

The next great dynasty was that of the Hans who ruled China from 202 B. C., to 220 A. D., and this was a glorious period for China. It was one of these Han emperors who thought up the idea of a civil service, appointing officials only after they had taken an examination to prove their fitness for the position and so making worth and ability instead of wealth or position the standard for selection to governmental posts. Under the Hans there was also a great revival in literature and art and a great expansion in trade as they made the caravan routes to the west safer for merchants to use. By 36 B. C., when Mark Antony was in Syria, ruling the eastern part of the Roman Empire, China's silks and her other beautiful products were beginning to reach that part of the world and Chinese merchants were experiencing their first contact with even the outskirts of Western civilization.

It was also due to this increase in the safety of travel that a third religion, Buddhism, came to China brought by missionary monks from India. This religion had originated some five hundred years before with a young man named Gautama, the son of an Indian rajah. Renouncing his wealth, his family and his inheritance, Gautama had left home in the robe of a beggar to go off and consider in solitude how men might be delivered from the pain and sorrow of life. And after six years of struggle and meditation he had at last gained what he believed to be true enlightenment. Therefore, he had taken the name Buddha, which meant "The Enlightened." Then he set out to teach men what he had learned, often sitting cross-legged under a shade tree with his face benevolent, passionless, calm, looking as he talked like the many statues by which he has so often been represented. Buddha taught that by constant meditation and control of the mind, men could lose all selfish desires and passions and live in a state of perfect peace and joy which he called "Nirvana." And to attain this peace they must follow the Eightfold Path of Right Understanding, Right Thought, Right Speech, Right Conduct, Right Living, Right Effort, Right Mindfulness and Right Rapture. Such a religion of passionless, spiritual calm and benevolence appealed to the Chinese and in time became an integral part of their life and thought, having a profound effect both on Taoism and Confucianism.

When the great Han dynasty ended, China again experienced centuries of anarchy and disorder during which North and South China separated, with the South remaining wholly Chinese under Chinese rulers while the North was governed by Mongols, Turks or Huns. Then in 618 the powerful family of the Tangs once more united all of China, so the second Tang emperor, Tai Tsung, ruled over the largest empire ever governed by a Chinese. His beautiful capital, Sian, to which came ambassadors from Korea, Japan, all of Asia and even from the far away Byzantine Empire, was one of the most civilized and enlightened cities of the world, for the Tangs were great patrons of all the arts. Under them the Chinese made their finest glazed pottery, their most beautiful statues in bronze and their loveliest figures carved out of ivory, jade or other precious stones. Then, too, the greatest of Chinese painters, Wu Tao Yuan, brought the painting of landscape to new heights and the most brilliant of the Chinese poets, Tu Fu and Li Po, sang their songs for the Emperor. Sitting on the velvety lawn of the palace gardens, they struck their lutes and sang of the beauty of all the visible universe, of flowers and clouds and sunsets, meantime directing thought with the magic of their words to a beauty beyond this beauty, a glory beyond human sight. Musicians, poets and painters all gathered at the palace of the Emperor and there the first Chinese dramas were presented, with actors wearing carved wooden masks. And to the glory of the Tangs it was under them that the Chinese invented printing, published the first printed book and contributed to the world an invention which was to affect the whole course of history.

But with the end of Tang rule in 907 disorder once more engulfed China and the empire was again divided into two parts. It was still divided in 1223 when Genghis Khan swept into the land with his savage hordes, and such of China as he did not conquer was conquered by his grandson Kublai Khan. In 1279 the last of the Sung emperors, who had been ruling in South China, cast himself into the sea and Kublai Khan became Emperor of all China. This was the time when the Polos entered his service and they remained with him for the greater part of his successful and brilliant reign. At Peking, the present Peiping, Kublai Khan built a beautiful city as a new capital and though he ruled the land as a conqueror, bringing in Mongol troops and Mongol officials, he loved and encouraged Chinese culture, becoming at last far more Chinese than Mongol. Moreover, he kept the trans-Asiatic caravan routes absolutely safe from robbers, so for the first time Western Europeans began to venture into China.

The Mongols governed China until 1368. Then they were driven out and replaced by the purely Chinese dynasty of the Mings who let the caravan routes again become unsafe and under whom a sentiment so anti-foreign developed that European merchants and Christian missionaries, who had been coming into the land, took their departure, leaving China to herself. However, the Mings were great builders. Yung Lo, the third emperor of this line, made Peking his capital and the palaces and temples which made that city one of the loveliest capitals of the world were largely his work. Nearly all city and frontier walls, paved roads, bridges, palaces, temples and pagodas which still exist in China were constructed by the great Ming builders. And in the latter years of that dynasty when Europeans had found a sea route around Africa to China, they began to return to the land both as merchants and missionaries.

The last dynasty to rule China was that of the Manchus, Mongolian invaders from Manchuria who adopted Chinese customs and governed the land from Peking. Under their rule which lasted from 1644 right down to modern times more and more foreigners came as traders to China. From Portugal, Spain, England, France, Holland, Germany, Russia they came, all anxious to get the fine Chinese silks, brocades, teas, embroideries, rugs, carpets, pottery, bronzes and delicate ivory figurines. And in 1784 came the first ship from the United States, to be followed by many more in the era of the great American clipper ships. But while the Chinese permitted Christian missionaries to enter the interior of their country, they allowed European merchants to do their trading at one port only, Canton. Never able to deal with foreigners on a basis of equality, always regarding them as inferiors, the Chinese hemmed European merchants in at Canton by the most cramping restrictions. Growing ever more restive under these restraints, the English at last fought two wars with China but for the very bad reason that they demanded the right to sell opium in that country when the Chinese government was trying to stamp out the use of that terrible drug. By 1860 when the last of these wars ended, China had been forced to cede the island of Hong Kong to Britain and open four more ports besides Canton to foreign trade. Then began a mad scramble between various European countries to gain rights and concessions in China while Russia and Japan aggressively took whatever Chinese land they were able to seize.

Naturally all this increased Chinese hatred of foreigners. In 1900 it culminated when the strong-minded old Empress Dowager, instigated by the band of men called Boxers, ordered all foreigners slain. So scores of Europeans and thousands of Chinese Christians were massacred, while as many as could took refuge in the legation quarters and the Catholic Cathedral in Peking. Then an international expeditionary force captured Peking, forced the Empress to flee, and dispersed the Boxers. However, the Empress, reversing the position which she had held for so long, soon decided that she could no longer avert the influx of foreigners into China. Returning to Peking, she set herself to be friendly toward them.

After that Europeans could come and go freely in China and many Chinese students flocked to Europe and to the United States, eagerly bent on acquiring Western learning. But with that learning they acquired also Western ideas of freedom which seeped from them out through the people of China. So the Chinese began to change. More and more they resented their venal officials, their fighting warlords, and the unjust treatment of Chinese farmers, who had so often starved in periods of famine and always been robbed by tax collectors. When the Empress Dowager died reform was in the air and revolutionary societies of Chinese both in and out of China were demanding a better, more liberal government. In 1912 men like the great Sun Yat-sen pushed aside the little boy-emperor, who was the last of the Manchus, and established a republic, aiming at a free, democratic government and a higher standard of living.

But the poor in China had suffered too long. Reforms that were centuries overdue all demanded settlement at once. And the way of gradual reform, with one thing at a time accomplished, was far too slow for the radicals, especially the young Chinese. So many left their homes to gather in distant gorges, mountains and hills, where they dreamed of solving their problems all at once by accepting the Russian ideas of communism. Then all land, all property, all means of production would be owned by the State and everyone would share in the common earnings from industry. To people so long ground down as these Chinese peasants that seemed a magnificent dream. So they failed to see that communism, since it had to be administered by men, who are always open to greed, dishonesty, cupidity and inordinate desire for power, was only the road toward worse forms of tyranny, toward the setting up of dictators, reigns of terror and a continuance of the old unjust order by which the industrious support the lazy. In time the Chinese Communists grew so powerful that they broke forth in the first great warlike outburst ever shown by a naturally peaceful people. Gaining control of the whole Chinese mainland, they drove the Nationalist government under Chiang Kai-shek to the Island of Formosa, forcing the people, whether they would or no, to accept communistic government.

SUCH HAS BEEN the interesting history of China and now to turn to Japan. Compared to the Chinese, the Japanese had come to their land very late, only a few hundred years before Christ, and they did not all belong to one race as the first settlers in China had. Some of them, Korean and Mongolian people called Yamato, came from the West, another group, the Malayans, came from the East and both these groups had to fight the fierce hairy Ainu, who were the natives of the land. So it was from the mixture of all these races that the Japanese were descended. A nation of farmers, fishermen and hunters, who had not yet discovered writing, they long remained a simple, primitive people. Their religion was Shintoism, the worship of spirits such as the sun, the moon, the wind and the waves, and they believed their islands had been created by the gods. Over the earth-people in Japan the Sun goddess had ruled until the Storm gods created such disorder there that she sent one of her descendants down from Heaven to drive out the Storm gods and rule the land. This man was Jimmu Tenno, the first Emperor of Japan, and thus it was that the Japanese through all the centuries down to modern times have believed their emperors to be celestial beings, sons of the Sun and her husband the Moon, and sent down from Heaven to rule them.

Not until around 200 A. D. did the Japanese begin to reach out beyond their islands. Then, according to legend, a woman, the Empress Jingo Kogo, saw a vision of a land awaiting conquest in the west. Seeking to learn whether the gods wished her to go and conquer that land, she went to the seashore to bathe, praying as she dived in the water, "If I am to go may my hair be parted by the waves evenly on either side." And when she came up her hair was in truth evenly parted in the middle. So she set forth for Korea on the mainland, which had long ago been conquered by the Chinese but had now thrown off Chinese rule. And her expedition was so successful that she came home with eighteen ships full of loot. But far more important than that plunder was the fact that Jingo Kogo had established Japan's first contact with the mainland and that by way of Korea Chinese culture began to come to Japan.

In 552 A. D. a Korean prince sent the Emperor of Japan a statue of Buddha, made of copper and gold, together with books explaining Buddha's teachings, and the Emperor welcomed these gifts, giving the statue and the books into the keeping of the noble Soga family. Then as Buddhism spread among the people, it started them on the real road to progress. Teachers came to them from China and Korea, teaching them Chinese arts and crafts. Soon the stark simplicity of the ancient Shinto temples was giving way to the splendor of color, of gilding and lacquer-work, which adorned the Buddhist shrines, and the Japanese were waking up to a longing for beauty and knowledge. From Chinese ideographs they devised their own system of writing and with that they began to write poetry, beautiful poetry, about the trees, the breezes, the butterflies, the moonlight, all the natural things they loved. Taking on Chinese civilization, they adapted it with a native ability they are still showing to grasp and use the ideas of foreigners. By 794 when the capital of the empire was moved to Kyoto, many Japanese were traveling to China and learning much from the master workmen of the great Tang dynasty there.

However, with all this growth of Buddhism in Japan, the Soga family, to whom the guardianship of that new religion had been entrusted, kept growing more powerful until they became the actual rulers of the land, leaving the emperors as puppets only. And after the Sogas other noble families fought each other to gain supreme power until at last in 1192 the Emperor Takahira bestowed on the leader of one of these families the title of Shogun or Generalissimo, thus creating a position which was to last for seven hundred years, finally becoming hereditary in one family and making these military leaders, the shoguns, instead of the emperors, the real rulers of Japan. Meantime, all these family feuds had made the Japanese look on fighting as a business whereby men might earn a living and so arose the samurai, a large class of professional soldiers. Men of indomitable courage, able to perform the most marvelous feats of arms, these samurai took their greatest delight in sword play and won their greatest fame as swordsmen. Thus the Japanese, in direct contrast to the peaceful Chinese, developed a warrior class and a great sense of glory in warfare.

Such was Japan when the Mongols conquered China and Korea. Then in 1274 Kublai Khan decided to seize Japan also. Forcing the Koreans to furnish most of the ships and men, he sent forth a mighty expedition. But a little garrison of two hundred Japanese, all fighting to the death, held his soldiers off from an island in the strait between Korea and Japan and that same night a violent storm forced his fleet to turn back to Korea with a loss by shipwreck and in battle of 13,000 men. Determinedly Kublai Khan prepared a new force—200,000 warriors and 3,500 ships. There was to be no question this time about the conquest of Japan. And his Mongols and Koreans now succeeded in landing on Japanese soil, but the Japanese attacked them so furiously, both by sea and on the shore, that in fifty-three days of fighting they accomplished nothing. Then another fierce storm blew up, so many ships foundered and the rest sailed off for China.

That ended the Mongol attempt to conquer Japan. In all of Asia, save for the western coastlands, Japan was the only country that was never under Mongol rule. But from that time on she was also cut off from China, from whom she had learned so much. Without help or hindrance from any other peoples, she went on her way alone.

Thus Japan remained for centuries little changed from what she had been in the seventh century. Her Heaven-born emperor, living in seclusion and seldom seen, was regarded with awe by the people, but was in fact a voiceless puppet while the nation was run by the shogun, a dictator, who pretended to act in the name of the god-emperor. Governing through docile lords known as daimyos, each in charge of a district, the shogun, with all those loyal samurai at his command, could enforce whatever he would. And it was most useful that the emperor should remain as a god to the people, for thus the shogun spoke for a god and the daimyos spoke for a shogun who spoke for a god. And so it went all down the line—no man could think of disobeying his superior, for that superior spoke for another superior, who spoke for another superior, who spoke for a god. The result was blind obedience from the man below to the man above and the acceptance of any injustice or misrule rather than to revolt or even criticize a superior which in the last analysis meant to strike at the gods.

Yet when the first European ship, a Portuguese vessel, reached Japan in 1542 to be followed soon by Spanish, Dutch and British ships, the Japanese, unlike the Chinese, readily welcomed these strangers from the West and all the new ideas they brought, suddenly seeing a chance to emerge from the cramped-in life they had led for so many centuries past. For a time they let foreign traders come and go as they liked and they permitted Christian missionaries to make many converts among their people. But when the Spaniards began to boast that priests and merchants were but the forerunners for Spanish galleons and armies and that Spain would soon rule Japan as she now ruled Mexico and Peru, the Japanese were stricken with fear. Well enough they knew the hideous story of the Spanish conquest of Mexico and Peru. So they ordered the Spanish out of the land and watched the Portuguese very strictly, though many among them still wished to keep some contact with the big alluring world beyond Japan. Then at last in 1637 a rebellion among certain of the Japanese, who had long been abused by their overlords, was laid by the government to the Christian Japanese because it occured in a district where there were many Christians. So when they had crushed that rebellion they forced the Portuguese and British to leave, allowing only the Dutch of the Dutch East India Company to remain and confining them to one place where they were hemmed in by the strictest restrictions.

Thus Japan slammed the door on the West and she kept it shut until the American, Commodore Perry, arrived off her shores in 1854 when a treaty was negotiated which reopened Japan to foreign trade. Then the Japanese, so little changed since the seventh century, had to try to absorb in a rush the ideas which the West had been accumulating for the past twelve hundred years. By a revolution in 1868 they did away with the shoguns and the samurai and tried to achieve a constitutional monarchy with the emperor at its head. But the habit of blind obedience, so ingrained in the mass of the people, still permitted a few all too powerful men to direct affairs while the emperor remained a god and a figurehead. And this situation continued until Japan entered the second World War with her surprise attack on American warships, bombing them as they lay anchored at our Hawaiian base, Pearl Harbor. That war ended in her defeat, in the occupation of Japan by American troops and in a real attempt on the part of the United States to lead Japan forward on the actual road to democracy.

RETURNING NOW to the Polos, we find them in 1295 again at home 'n Venice where Marco put forth his fascinating account of his adventures, thereby greatly increasing the interest of Europeans in the rich and magnificent East. However, when the Mongols were driven out of China and replaced by the purely Chinese dynasty of the Mings, with hatred of foreigners flaring up in the land, the trans-Asiatic caravan routes to China, Persia and India, which the Mongols had kept safe, were again left unprotected. Robbers fell on the caravans, slew the merchants and seized their goods until overland trade with the East was ended completely. If the Western world was to have access to the treasures of the East, someone must find a way to get there by sea. For years the Portuguese kept sending fleets to push farther and farther down the coast of Africa, hoping to get either through or around that continent. Then at last the King of Portugal sent Vasco da Gama forth and Da Gama, rounding the Cape of Good Hope, finally reached India in 1498, two hundred years after Marco Polo had left there. After that many European ships began to follow Da Gama's route to the East and this drew India into world affairs, so we need to know something of India also.

IN THE EARLIEST DAYS that huge peninsula, cut off from the rest of the world by the sea and the towering ice-bound Himalayas, had been inhabited by primitive wild tribes of hunters, who were black of skin like the Negroes. But before 3300 B. C., a people resembling the Sumerians had built fine cities in Northern India, only to vanish mysteriously in time, leaving no record of where they went. Meantime, Semitic adventurers had found their way into Southern India where they developed a second fine center of culture. Then at last around 2000 B. C., waves of white-skinned Aryans from Central Europe, wanderers from the plain below the Carpathian Mountains, began to roam down into India. These people were the Hindus and their religion was Hinduism. Many gods they had, including Vishnu, the Preserver, Siva, the Destroyer, and Indra, god of the thundering sky. But above all they believed in Brahma, the Creator, the life and soul of the universe. Everyone's soul, so they believed, would pass on his death into some other creature, either human or animal, according to whether he had been good or bad on earth, until at last, by gradually building up a good record in life after life, he would be merged with Brahma, the great universal soul.

Slowly these Aryans settled through all Northern India, finally building up at least sixteen little states, each with a king at its head. But in so doing they had to conquer the broad-nosed, dark-skinned natives of the land whom they despised and called Dasyus or enemies. Proud of their own white skins, they felt that something must be done to keep their race, their speech, and their religion from being entirely swamped by the great mass of their Negroid subjects. So they invented the system of castes to prevent the two races from intermingling and to keep their customs unchanged. The word for caste in Sanskrit, the speech of the Aryan invaders, was *varna*, meaning color, and these white men made the conquered black Dasyus into the lowest caste, the Sudras or laborers. Above them were three other castes—the herdsmen and traders, the warriors, and the highest caste, the Brahmans, who were the priests, the lawgivers and the poets. Then Manu, an Aryan, wishing to give the caste system the force of law, drew up a code of laws which not only forbade intermarriage between the castes, but even prohibited them from eating together. After that each of the castes was divided again and again until in time there were between two and three thousand castes, with every man born to a certain caste and a certain trade or work, from which he could never escape. Lower than the Sudras were the Pariahs or outcasts, who were looked upon as scarcely human. Altogether outside the pale of society, these "untouchables" were forbidden the use of public roads and bridges. They were not even allowed to draw water from the public well and so defiling was their touch considered that Hindus preferred to die rather than accept their help. It was in this manner that India developed that rigid caste system which was to be such a stumbling block on her road to progress.

The Brahmans were the undisputed leaders of Hindu religion until Gautama, that great Indian thinker who founded Buddhism, gained his "enlightenment" and started introducing a second religion into the land. From the very beginning the Brahmans hated and feared this new religion but in spite of them Buddhism spread until the kings themselves became Buddhists, built beautiful Buddhist temples and sent Buddhist missionaries to China, Burma, Java and Ceylon. This was the golden age for Indian culture in sculpture, architecture, painting and literature. And wealth increased with the growing trade in gold and silver, precious stones, fine muslins, cashmere shawls, spices, teakwood and sandalwood, so the upper castes lived magnificently, wearing garments of costly silks adorned with diamonds, rubies, pearls and every sort of glittering gem. But for all the growth of Buddhism, it had never wholly displaced Brahmanism in the land and at last the Brahmans, who had never ceased in their hostility to the Buddhists, succeeded in driving Buddhism out of all India except for a few remote border states. The Brahmans, however, were not to enjoy for too long their sole rule over Indian thought, for Moslems, hearing of the wealth of India, began to invade the land and finally one of them, Mohammed of Ghor, led a host of wild warriors into India. By 1191 A. D. he had conquered all the northern plain and a hundred years later another Moslem extended Moslem rule to the south, until all India was under the yoke of the Moslems. Thus India now had a third religion, Mohammedanism, claiming an ever growing number of adherents.

At about this time the Mongols began making raids into India and at last in 1398 came the most savage of all the Mongols, Timur, the Lame, or Tamerlane, whose name was a terror to all of Asia. Sweeping through India, looting and killing, he took the city of Delhi and sacked it. Then he was off bent on further conquests, so he never established a permanent Mongol rule over India, but in 1526 one of his descendants, Baber, a Moslem, who was ruling a Turkoman tribe, came in force and conquered India, making his capital at Agra. And since Moghul was the Arabic spelling for Mongol, Baber and the Mongol emperors who succeeded him were called the Great Moghuls. Under these Great Moghuls India was very powerful even down through the days of early American history, and under them, too, a fine Mohammedan-Indian architecture arose, of which the finest example is the Taj Mahal erected by Baber's grandson, Shah Jehan, as a tomb for his beloved wife. But finally the descendants of the Great Moghuls lost all their vigor and the days of India's greatness passed.

Meantime, Spaniards, Portuguese, English, and Europeans of other different nations had tried and sometimes temporarily succeeded in gaining possession of parts of India or in establishing trading posts there. But maintaining these various positions became so dangerous and difficult that at last all save the English gave up struggling to do so. Thus the English alone of all European powers remained in India and in time they came to rule the whole land, making it a part of the mighty British Empire they were creating. And with India all split up by her different, antagonistic religions, by her numerous jealous rulers of petty states and by her destructive system of castes, she was long held together only by British rule. But through the centuries her people grew ever more resentful of foreign domination and in modern times this resentment culminated under the preaching of passive resistance put forth by her great leader, Mahatma Gandhi. So after the second World War, her people threw off British rule and tried to solve their difficult problems by emerging as two separate states, the Hindu state of India and the Moslem state of Pakistan.

AND NOW with the story of India we end this volume of explorations in the East, whereby we have tried to gain some knowledge of those Eastern countries which we need to understand as in this ever enlarging world the East becomes a part of our own present history.

THE
STORY OF MANKIND

A Picturesque Tale of Progress

By Olive Beaupré Miller

Assisted by Harry Neal Baum

EXPLORATIONS

PART II

THE BOOK HOUSE FOR CHILDREN
TANGLEY OAKS EDUCATIONAL CENTER
LAKE BLUFF, ILLINOIS

PRINTED IN U.S.A.

CONTENTS

This summary and those in the other seven volumes, if read consecutively, give an interesting picture of the whole sweep of history during the period covered in the eight volumes, with the meaning of events conveyed clearly and the *significance they have for us, brought down to the world of today.*

LIST OF MAPS

I

Land in the West

(1000–1492)

Adventurous Northmen

Many years before the Portuguese had discovered the route to India, the Vikings, sailing from Norway, had found distant lands in the West. Hardy mariners, who lived on the sea, asking only if they died on land to be buried in a ship, they sailed through fog and ice, laughing at towering seas and the sharp bite of howling winds. In the ninth century A.D., they found the island of Iceland, a weird land of ice and fire, where volcanoes flamed among glaciers and the brilliant Northern Lights gave unholy beauty to the night. Here they established a colony that continued for five hundred years.

Now about the year 982, there lived in Iceland a sturdy old Viking by the name of Eric Thorwaldson. Having quarreled with certain of his neighbors, he was outlawed for three years from Iceland and embarking at once on his vessel he turned his face toward the sea. Intending to seek some islands of which he had heard reports, he sailed far to the westward and stumbled at length by chance on the rocky coast of Greenland where he stayed for three long years, exploring the great barren land.

ADVENTUROUS NORTHMEN
FIND UNKNOWN LANDS
IN THE WEST...

The discovery of Vinland by Leif Ericson about 1000 A.D., a painting in the National Gallery, Oslo. The records of the voyages of Leif Ericson and Bjar'ne Her-julf'son, and an account of Viking settlement in America were long told orally, and passed to each generation until preserved in two ancient Icelandic *sagas*, *The Saga of Eric the Red*, and *The Vineland History of the Flat Island Book*.

"It is well," he said with shrewd wit, "to give the country a pleasant name to induce people to go thither!" So in spite of its bleak appearance he called the new land Greenland, speaking of it on his return in such glowing terms to the Icelanders that when he set out again it required all of twenty-five ships to bear the settlers who went with him. Eleven of these vessels were lost in the stormy seas, but survivors from the other fourteen began to build up Greenland, making houses of stone since the little trees on the island were only stunted bushes, and supporting themselves by dairying, hunting the walrus and seal.

Now in those days a roving sea-captain by the name of Bjarne Herjulfson, came to visit his father in Iceland, but he found his father had gone, emigrated to Greenland. Weighing anchor at once Bjarne set out after him. Scarcely had he left Iceland when his ship was swallowed in fog through which he drifted for days, not knowing whither he went. Then suddenly the fog lifted and he saw looming out of the mist a pleasant land of low hills richly covered with timber. This he knew could not be the desolate, treeless island where his father had settled, so he put out to sea again and sailed until he reached Greenland.

The truth of the matter was that Bjarne, first of all Europeans, had seen the coast of North America, but his father's farm was lonely and few people heard his stories of mysterious land to the south. Some years later however, Bjarne told the same tales before the King's court in Norway and here there were many bold listeners to hear what he had to say. About the year 1002 Eric Thorwaldson's son, the enterprising Leif Ericson, decided to set out and seek the new lands Bjarne had seen. Westward his black ship sped, the Viking crew shouting for joy as they plied their mighty oars, steering by sun and stars across the angry sea. First, after many days, they sighted a barren country without any grass or trees, Labrador or Newfoundland perhaps, and here they went ashore calling the place Halluland or Stone-land, thus being the first Europeans to land on the American continent. Next they came to a low-lying, plentifully wooded country which they called Markland or Timberland, and lastly they went ashore somewhere in New England, where they found abundance of grapes. This land seemed so pleasant to them that they called it Vinland or Wineland, and they remained there through the winter returning again to Greenland some time in the spring.

Interior of a Viking log house like those built in America by the colonists from Greenland. It had a central hearth for cooking and heating and no windows. The only light came through a small opening in the roof where the smoke escaped. (Open Air Museum of Norse Antiquities, Oslo, Norway.)

Leif Ericson never went back to visit the land he had found but his brother-in-law, Thorfin Karlsefne, set out a few years later, taking Gudrid, his wife, together with five other women, 165 men and plenty of grain and cattle, to settle permanently in Vinland. They stayed for three years in the land and Thorfin's young wife, Gudrid, gave birth here to little Snorri, the first white child born in America. But the Indians of these parts, Skrellings, the Norsemen called them, frightened one day by a bull bellowing in the settlement, became deadly foes to the colonists, so the settlers had to give up and go back home to Greenland.

After these events for some 300 years men of Greenland and Iceland paid occasional visits to the continent of North America, especially for the purpose of getting there the timber which was so badly needed in their desolate treeless homeland. In the year 1362 one party even ventured as far inland as Minnesota. Ten of the men were massacred near Kensington in that state and the rest left in old runic letters engraved on a tablet of stone the story of the tragedy which befell them there.

Earliest drawing of the inhabitants of America, under a crude shelter of boughs. Vikings called both Indians and Eskimos *Skrellings*, or scrubby little people. (Wood cut, 1497–1504, British Museum.)

(We are) 8 Goths (Swedes) and 22 Nor-
    wegians on
(an) exploration journey from
Vinland through the Western regions.
(We) have 10 men by the sea to look
after our ships 14 days-journey
from this island; year 1362.
We had (our) camp by two skerries
one days-journey north from this stone.
We were (out) and fished one day
When we returned home (we) found 10
    (of our) men red
with blood and dead. Ave Maria!
Save (us) from evil!

The only direct record of Norsemen in America. In 1898 a farmer near Kensington, Minnesota, found this stone engraved with runes. Scholars called it a forgery and for years it formed a step for the owner's granary. Then H. R. Holand translated it. Light hair among the Mandan Indians, North Dakota, suggests that Norsemen who escaped the massacre may have married natives.

As time passed, the Norsemen abandoned Vinland, Iceland and Greenland. Even rumors of their voyages seem not to have seeped out in Europe save that in the year 1112 the Pope appointed Erik Gnupsson Bishop to Greenland and Vinland, thus showing that these lands were known at least in Rome. The rest of Europe in those days slept in a kind of lethargy while kings and rulers tried to put down the feudal princes. In the 15th century, how-ever, something vital occurred to wake men out of their sleep. Europe had discovered India; but only the Portuguese were profiting by the route they had found to the Golden East. Men of other na-tions also must find a route to India. All Europe began to wake up and turn its gaze toward the sea.

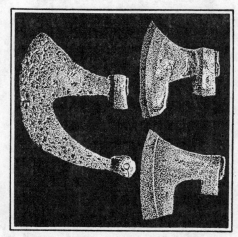

Interest in the Kensington Stone brought to light these battle axes all unearthed in Minnesota. Mr. Holand visited 26 European museums to prove these finds were Scandinavian axes of the 14th century. *Kensington Stone* by Holand.

Christopher Columbus

Almost five hundred years after the Norsemen discovered America, another daring voyage was made far out on the wide Atlantic and again land was found in the west. This later journey, however, unlike the voyages of the Norsemen which had been haphazard sailings and discoveries made by chance, was the outcome of a definite, carefully thought out plan to prove that the earth was round and that by sailing west one could reach the East and thus find a route to India. The Norsemen had believed Greenland to be a part of Europe. They did not know it was an island off a newly discovered continent. Never dreaming of a world that was round, they felt no scientific urge, no vision of a great idea in their wild and stirring adventures. The voyage five hundred years later was something altogether different. Christopher Columbus risked his life and all that he had to open a route to India by proving a scientific fact, a fact which as yet existed only as a theory in the minds of a very few scholars, being to most of humanity the wild dream of a madman, worthy of laughter and jeers. His journey was therefore far more an adventure of the mind than had been those discoveries made by the sturdy Norsemen.

Columbus was born in Italy in the busy port of Genoa somewhere about the year 1446. His father was a weaver by trade and when Christopher was a small boy, he helped comb out the wool which his father wove into cloth. As soon as he was old enough he was sent to the wool-weaver's school in Genoa and there he learned to read and write, and to do simple sums with figures.

Christopher Columbus (about 1446–1506), the best portrait. (Naval Museum, Madrid.)

The busy harbor of Genoa, which so fascinated young Christopher. (Painting, City Hall, Genoa.)

But sometimes, the lad forgot about wool and school. Gleefully then, he spent his hours down at the wharves watching the ships come in from marvelous Alexandria across the Mediterranean, or from those wondrous, distant ports of Antwerp, Bristol, Dieppe, and Lisbon. It was curious to watch the ships come a-sailing out of the dim distance. In they came, rolling gently in the harbor swell; down dropped their flapping, painted sails, and soon anchor chains rattled against the mooring posts; and the bump and thud of heavy casks and bales dumped upon the cluttered quay filled his ears. Wide-eyed with eagerness, young Christopher listened to idling sailors tell marvelous tales of romance and great adventure. Those were exciting days upon the seas; and thrilling, indeed, were the stories of brave encounters with plundering Saracens, of swift treasure-snatching, of trading in curious, far-off ports.

The wide-eyed, sturdy boy longed to see these strange sights and do the brave things his sailor-friends did. He yearned to become a seaman, a strong, swaggering sailor going far and wide in a fine ship over the big blue sea; he wanted to visit those foreign ports in the strange, mysterious corners of the world reached only after many days of sailing.

Strange people believed to inhabit unknown lands: Monopes with one leg; Ypifagus, a headless man; Cyclopes, the one-eyed. (From a 15th cent. French MS. on Natural History.)

So strong was this longing for adventure, so keen the call of the sea, that when Christopher was only fourteen, he did become a sailor. And then, indeed, came strenuous times for the sturdy, growing boy. He was trained for a life of seamanship; he learned about vessels and rigging, winds and stars and tides, about maps and sea-charts; he probably even worked with some of the noted Italian draughtsmen in the drawing of these maps. In thirteen years of sea-faring, he grew to be an expert in the art and practice of navigation, and far and wide he sailed, all over the Mediterranean; south, along the coast of Africa; north, as far as England, and possibly even to Iceland.

Meanwhile Christopher's brother, Bartholomew, had gone to live in Lisbon; and, giving up voyaging for a time, Christopher came there to join him. Together the brothers earned a modest living by making charts on soft parchment in gay colors of red, green, and blue. They also sold books in their little shop in a steep street near the bustle and commotion of the harbor; and here in Portugal, Christopher came close to that eager, adventurous spirit of exploration which seemed to stir the whole land. Africa had not yet been passed, India had not yet been reached, but here Christopher heard constantly, exciting tales of adventure.

Striding back and forth over the white sands, the thunder of the surf pounding in his ears, Columbus remembered all the stories he had heard of men who had ventured out upon the sea to hunt for distant islands in the Atlantic.

Map of the World known to ancient seamen and travelers, drawn by Ptolemy about 150 A.D. Russia was practically unknown, and Northern Europe and Asia are called Scythia; China was forgotten.

Storm-blown sailors were always coming back with tales of having seen distant shores; and even Columbus knew that there were many indications of lands across the ocean in the West. He himself had seen a piece of driftwood curiously carved in no recognized fashion; and there were those great pieces of cane which he had seen in Lisbon. They had been washed ashore on the Canaries, and must have come from some unknown place, because they were unlike anything in Europe. Moreover, the people of the A-zores' had one time found upon their shores queerly shaped canoes dug from single logs; and then there were those bodies of strange, brown, broad-faced men which had been washed ashore on the island of Flo'res. Most certainly, there must be islands far across the Atlantic in the West. Where were they? How could they be reached?

Columbus began to study, to read, and to question. He talked to Martin Be'haim, a German scientist, and learned that this student of geography believed that the world was round and had made a globe.

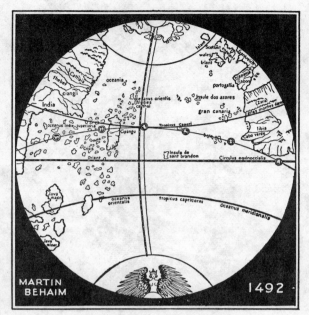

MARTIN
BEHAIM　　　　　　　　　　1492

Globe made by Martin Be'haim of Nuremberg in 1492, showing
a round world with Japan, China, and India lying in the Atlantic directly west of Europe. (Am. Geo. Soc., New York.)

He learned that scholars believed Asia was very large, much larger, indeed, than it later proved to be; and from all this knowledge, it did not appear to him to be unreasonably far across the Atlantic to the treasures of India and China. Moreover, these were heathen lands, and should be Christianized. Slowly his plan began to take definite form; he would sail across the trackless waters of the western ocean to the lands of India and China.

But such a voyage would be a supreme accomplishment worthy of great consideration; he would take the matter to no less a person than the King. It was accordingly a well-thought out plan which Columbus finally laid before King John of Portugal, and it is said that the King, having made copies of the charts which were presented to prove the truth of the idea, hastily fitted out an expedition to sail westward. But the sailors of Portugal met with a violent storm and turned back before sailing many leagues, loudly declaring that the whole idea was false and that no new lands lay to the west. King John, therefore, refused further consideration to the plan.

The refusal was a hard blow to Columbus. He believed so thoroughly in his ideas, he had supported them with so much proof that he had never thought they could be cast aside. Moreover, so completely absorbed had he been in the study of his project that he had earned no money in many months, and now he was sadly in debt.

Columbus, however, believed that his idea was right; and instead of bowing dumbly to failure, he journeyed straight to Spain to lay his plans before the Spanish monarchs. Arriving in Cor'do-va in 1486, he found their "Most Catholic Majesties," Ferdinand of Aragon, and Isabella of Castile, fighting against the Moors, determined to drive all the Mohammedans from Spain and form a united Christian nation.

But Columbus talked so enthusiastically about his idea to everyone he met that at last he interested a powerful duke who lodged him in the establishment of Alonso de Quin-ta-nil'la, the Treasurer to the Crown of Castile, there to await the monarch's pleasure. And when after months of weary waiting, he was at length received by the Queen, the only encouragement she gave him was to listen thoughtfully to his words.

Isabella thought well enough of the plan to ask Columbus to appear before a royal committee for questioning; but that was all. The committee hemmed and hawed, and shook their heads; they would not believe that his plan should be seriously considered; they said that his statements could scarcely be true: no one had actually proved that the world was round. Such a belief was contrary to reason and the Bible.

The committee of Queen Isabella arrogantly reject Columbus' plan. (Painting, Orsini Gallery, Genoa).

A few influential people in Cordova did listen sympathetically, however, and the confidence of Columbus spread to others. One new friend, Di-e'go de De'za, prior of a Dominican convent, helped Columbus put his visionary ideas into more systematic and convincing form. Diego brought learned people to talk to him and the whole matter was discussed sympathetically from every angle. He gave Columbus important books so that he could quote authorities for his statements, and he had him present his ideas to a great Florentine astronomer. The Florentine sent Columbus a map, and a letter stating definitely that the plan of reaching the East by sailing westward was quite possible and practical. With such support, Columbus was more than ever convinced that his idea was sound and practical. All he asked was to be allowed to go and venture all in proving it.

The wars of Ferdinand and Isabella against the Moors were now coming to a triumphant end. Still the Queen did nothing. Endless waiting, and neglect! Always the same reply: "Wait!" But now Columbus had enough of waiting; the years were passing; not yet had he started on the mission for which he believed he was divinely chosen. He would leave Spain to her wars and take his plan elsewhere. His brother, Bartholomew, had already set out to present the idea to Henry VI of England; and since that mission might turn out unsuccessfully, he himself would take his project to the court of France. Greater to Columbus than all disappointments was his determination to prove his vision true.

Returning from Huel'va, whither he had gone to get his son, Diego, Columbus stopped one night at a convent, high on the rocky slopes above Pa'los. The prior of the convent, Friar Ju'an Pe'rez, questioned his guest about his journey and Columbus talked eagerly of his theories. Perez was astounded at a matter of such magnitude. He bustled about hunting books and maps, delighted to have such interesting matters discussed in his quiet monastery. He, too, was something of a cosmographer, and he realized perfectly what Columbus proposed to do in sailing over the unknown ocean, down the curve of a supposedly round world to the rich but heathen countries of India and China. He saw the value of the enterprise both to state and church; Spain must be the nation to

To the convent at Pa'los, Friar Pe'rez brought friends and learned men to talk with Columbus, and it was here that the wealthy ship owner, Martin Pin-zon', decided to aid him. (Painting, Huelva, Spain.)

sponsor the finding of this route; any man who thought of seeking it, must certainly not take his plan to Spain's great rival, France.

The good friar accordingly sent for a friend in Palos, Garcia Her-nan'-dez, who was an expert in cosmography and astronomy, and Hernandez nodded his head learnedly when he heard Columbus' arguments. He, too, agreed that Spain must not lose this opportunity. Between them they became so keenly interested and eager that Columbus again took heart, and welcomed Perez' plea to be allowed to write Isabella.

Off went the little letter, so confidently written; but once more the answer was: "Wait." After more weeks had been passed in study and argument and plan, however, Perez was finally asked to come to the Queen so that she might learn more about his views in this matter. Suspense was at its height; but at last came a messenger from the friar saying that the Queen had listened with good purpose and Columbus was to have three ships equipped for the expedition "that he might go and make discoveries and prove true the words he had spoken!"

The Voyage to the West

Months passed in securing ships and men. Indeed, many of the sailors volunteered to go only to escape the jails. But a wealthy merchant of Palos, Martin Alonso Pin-zon', had become so interested in the voyage that he had agreed to go as captain of one vessel, and take his brother as captain of another. With this encouragement, the crews were finally gathered. Three ships were to make the voyage; the Pinzon brothers were to command the *Nina* and the *Pinta*; and Columbus was to take as his flagship the *Santa Maria*. At last, all was ready.

The fleet sailed at dawn on August 3, 1492. Upon the quay at Palos in the cool, soft light, Christopher Columbus bowed his uncovered head. Friar Pe'rez rested one hand upon the seaman's shoulder; the other he raised in final benediction. The noisy crowd hushed; shouts, and the cries of the crews died away; families clung to their men in terrified farewells. Most of Palos thought it a wild fatal voyage; nothing but disaster could come of sailing far away from land into that terrible Sea of Darkness, and they did not expect ever to see their loved ones again.

Columbus leaves Palos on his venturesome voyage. (A painting in the Provincial Museum, Cadiz.)

"We departed on Friday, the third of August, in the year 1492, from the bar of Saltes, at eight o'clock; and proceeded with a strong sea-breeze until sunset, towards the south, for sixty miles, equal to fifteen leagues; afterwards southwest, and west, southwest, which was the course for the Canaries."

Thus simply Columbus recorded in his journal the departure from Palos. Within a month he reached the Canaries, where he made repairs, and reprovisioned his vessels. From here the ships set out upon the great undertaking of sailing directly west "by which course," Columbus wrote, "unto the present time we do not know for certain that anyone has passed."

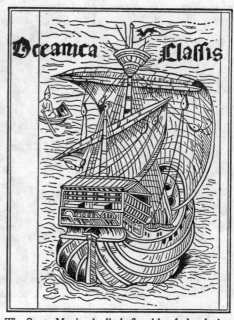

The *Santa Maria*, the little flagship of the daring explorer, a drawing made by Columbus. (1494.)

For days and days thereafter, the journal entries began with the statement that they sailed west because it was their course. Could any words reveal more clearly the reason for Columbus' power? There was no other thought in his mind than to proceed along the way he had chosen; he had striven steadily for his plan in the slow years past, and he would keep to his course now with the same strength and purpose.

But no sooner had the boats left the Canaries than the men grew restless. They began to realize what it meant to have no reassuring coastline near at hand. No longer could they even hope to come upon familiar islands. On and on must they sail day after day, night after night, over that utterly unknown ocean, and that endless waste of waters. Their little ships seemed woefully alone on the monstrous forbidding sea. They wondered if in truth they would ever see land again. Columbus saw their growing panic and tried to calm and comfort them.

Private cabin of Columbus on the *Santa Maria* where he slept, ate, and worked during the long voyage across the Atlantic.

Gravely he felt his responsibility, but no fears or qualms must hinder his purpose now. He assured them that soon they would come upon the new land he searched for; he reminded them of the wealth and honor due them for helping discover it. Then, he decided that they would not feel so far from Spain if they did not know how far they journeyed, and thereafter, he kept two reckonings, announcing on a bulletin board, a lesser one, each day, than the actual one he entered in his secret log-book.

The voyage was a constant struggle for Columbus, not only in matters of navigation involving brilliant seamanship, but against the vivid fears and sad discouragements of his company. He must be constantly alert to find ways to subdue rebellious mutterings on the part of his crew, and to make the men more hopeful. Night after night he paced the decks in the cold watches, hearing the calls to man this rope or that, hearing the wash of the waters and the restless creaking of his ship. Every little happening he promptly turned to a sign of hope; every unfavorable event was made into something less alarming.

Weeks passed. Still the great, empty horizon lay unbroken in all directions. Each day brought something which Columbus read to his crews as a promise of the nearness of land. A little crayfish was found in some floating weeds; it was "a sure sign of land." The tunny fish killed by the company on the *Nina* was supposed to have come from the west. They saw a ring-tail, a bird "which does not sleep at sea."

Two pelicans came on board, "a sign of the neighborhood of land." "It drizzled without wind, which is a sure sign of land." They caught a bird which was like a jay; "it was a river bird, not a marine bird." They saw a whale, "an indication of land, as they always keep near the coast." Little birds settled on the rigging of the ships and began to sing. They flew away at daybreak, "which was considered a strong indication of the approaching of land, as these little birds could not have come from any far distant country."

These signs helped to convince the crews for a little while only; soon they were constantly murmuring among themselves. They were terrified at the great expanse of sea; they had gone much farther than anyone had ever gone before; provisions would give out; they would turn back.

Columbus was desperate. He would have died rather than give up the voyage. He strode up and down among the men, a greater sailor than they, and they knew it. He persuaded and cheered them; he bullied and over-awed them with his reasoning. He told them they would be punished; he recalled all of the favorable signs they had seen; he reminded them of the rich land ahead and the wealth that would be theirs. And the ships continued steadily on their way.

On Thursday, October eleventh, a higher sea arose than they had encountered during the whole journey, but the waves passed unnoticed when certain encouraging signs appeared: sandpipers, a green reed, and pieces of wood. The men found a small pole in the water which appeared to have been worked with iron; there were bits of cane; a small branch floated by, covered with gay-colored rose berries.

Cramped under deck amid ropes and tackle were the quarters of the fifty-two fearing men who sailed on the *Santa Maria.*

After evening prayers that night Columbus talked to his men. He told them he now knew they were near the Indies and asked them to keep a good look-out from the forecastle. To the one who first sighted land he would add a silken doublet as reward, in addition to the ten thousand gold pieces promised by Ferdinand and Isabella.

At ten o'clock, standing on the poop, trying to see through the darkness, straining his eyes, Columbus thought he saw a light. It burned unsteadily, and he could not be sure. Sharply he called Pero Gu-tier'rez. Did he see a light yonder? Pero peered in the direction where Columbus pointed. Yes! That was a light! Columbus called Roderick San-chez' of Sebovia to them. Did the King's inspector see anything out there in the darkness? No! There! A light? Couldn't he see a light? Neither could Gutierrez nor Columbus see it now. Yes! there it was again! Someone must be carrying it from one house to another, or perhaps some fisherman was raising and lowering it. A sailor from below suddenly called out: "Light! Land!" then the flame completely disappeared.

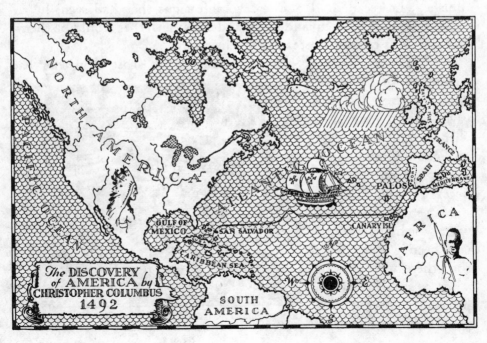

The earliest picture of the landing of Columbus drawn in 1493 immediately after his return to Spain with news of his discovery. At left sits King Ferdinand in Europe; before him in the ocean are the ships; and beyond, is the island with its palm trees and unclothed natives. (British Museum)

At two o'clock in the morning of October twelfth, a dark mass spread itself on the moonlit waters two leagues away, and when dawn came, there before them lay the low shores of an island. There at last was land! Land with green grass, and rocks, and stone and sand! Growing green trees covered it, a smooth blue lake lay in the middle. Land, solid and firm, after sea-weary weeks of weaving waters. A boat was quickly lowered from the *Santa Maria*, and Columbus was rowed ashore.

Columbus takes possession of San Sal'va-dor' in the name of Spain. (A painting in the Capitol.)

Great numbers of naked inhabitants swarmed the land, and rushed down to the shores, amazed and delighted at the sight of the ships, which they supposed to be strange white birds bearing gods.

Columbus leaped ashore bearing in his hand the royal standard of Spain. He had donned a rich scarlet cloak over his bright steel armor, and he towered tall, impressive, and joyous over all. Then came the two brightly clad Pinzon brothers, each carrying a white banner bearing a green cross and the monogram of Ferdinand and Isabella. When all were landed, the whole company fell on their knees and kissed the ground for joy, thanking God for the great mercy they had experienced. Then Columbus with drawn sword and solemn words, took formal possession of the land and gave it the name, San Sal'va-dor'. Columbus, too, had found land in the West and found it not by chance, but in proof of a great idea, logically reasoned out.

II
Ancient America

(From before 20,000 B.C. to about 1500 A.D.)

The Peopling of America

Columbus was positive that the island which he named San Salvador was only a bit of land lying off the coast of Asia. Three other voyages of exploration he made in the neighborhood of his first landing, but despite the fact that he found very little gold and no jewels or spices, Columbus died believing that he had discovered a new route to the wealth and splendor of the East. However, other adventurous seamen and explorers, following in his path, learned within a few years that this land to the west was not Asia but a new and hitherto unknown country divided into two great continents. Then honoring the Florentine explorer, Americus Vespucius, they began to call these continents North and South America.

In these new lands the explorers found a people different from any they had ever known. Their hair was straight and raven black, they had high cheek bones, prominent noses, and bronze or copper-colored skins. And the men decorated their bodies with painted designs.

Inhabitants of America, a woman and child, and a warrior with bow and flint-tipped arrow. One of the earliest drawings of Americans made by John White in 1585, now in the British Museum. America was named for Americus Vespucius, an adventurous Florentine merchant, who made several voyages to Brazil. A famous geographer suggested that this country be named America after him, and gradually this name was given to both northern and southern continents.

31

Columbus had called these people Indians because he was so sure that he had reached some outlying part of India. So now we come to the story of our American Indians and what had been happening on our continent before Columbus ever landed on our shores. White men seem to believe that history began in North and South America only when white men arrived here, but the fact is that these two continents had countless centuries of interesting history behind them before white men ever appeared on the scene.

Long before the dawn of history, even before the glaciers drifted south in the last of the four Ice Ages, roving Mongolian tribesmen began to come into North America by way of Bering Strait, crossing from what is now the northeastern tip of Russia to the present Alaska. And these Mongolians were the ancestors of the American Indians. They did not come all at once but in many separate waves of migration which went on for hundreds of years.

Driven off their hunting grounds in innermost Asia by the pressure of other more fierce and savage hunters, these wandering Mongolians were forced up into Siberia in a desperate search for food. There they lived miserable lives in a cold, barren land, where they often found nothing to eat for days. Thus they came at last to the very tip end of Asia and looking out over Bering Strait, they saw across the dark sullen waters a country that seemed to them to have less ice and snow. It lay only some fifty miles away and the strait was scattered with islands. So these hungry, half-frozen people, hoping that that new land over the water might offer them more food and be less bitterly cold, crossed the strait from island to island, using boats which the fisher folk of that region had learned how to make out of skins.

The country across the water did, indeed, prove to be a better place. It was not quite as cold, and there were many animals to hunt; the tribesmen found deer in abundance, and the fishing people speared fish with their harpoons in bays that teemed with life. So attractive was the new land, that some went back to tell friends about it, and soon there was a constant passage from Asia to the foreign shore, and back again.

Desperate Asiatics, driven by cold and hunger, crossed Bering Strait in prehistoric ages, and so began the peopling of America. Dr. Alec Hrdlicka, of the Smithsonian Institute, Washington, D. C., found on the southern slopes of the Himalaya Mountains certain little-known Tibetan tribes so closely resembling the American Indians that if found in America no one could possibly take them for anything but Indians "in physique, in behavior, in dress, and even in the intonation of their language."

In time so many people came to the new land, and the families already there grew so rapidly, that there was not enough food for all. Then some of the younger and more adventurous pushed farther south and inland. They found the country warmer to the south, and the deer in such enormous herds that they settled there at once. But, before long, even this new region grew too crowded, and other daring people again set out to search for new homes, plunging bravely through vast forests, where they lived on roots and berries as well as meat; and even venturing out upon broad grasslands to follow wandering herds of bison. Slowly, steadily, in the course of centuries, the newcomers spread out all over the enormous continents which lay before them; and thus it was that America was peopled by Mon'gol-oid tribesmen from Asia in the dim, distant ages before the year 20,000 B.C.

In prehistoric times before the Fourth Glacial Period, the continent of North America was bound to Europe and Asia by great masses of land. On the west there was land across Bering Strait and the A-leu'tian Islands to Asia, and on the east, Newfoundland, Labrador, Greenland, Iceland, the British Isles and the Scandinavian Peninsula were all united in one great mass to the mainland of Europe.

The newcomers were men of the Early Stone Age with only stone tools and weapons, and they knew little of any of the comforts of life. They had developed a language, however; they knew how to make fire by rubbing together two pieces of wood; they had invented spears and spear-throwers; they knew how to weave coarse fibers into nets, and they had recently learned how to make canoes. Moreover, they had tamed the dog for companionship and as a help in hunting. With this meager store of knowledge, these ancient Americans lived for centuries just like the men of the Early Stone Age in Europe, hunting constantly for food, moving about the country as the herds traveled from place to place, living under trees, in caves, or crude shelters, feasting when the hunting was good, and grimly bearing hunger when no animals were taken.

But in time the land grew cold. The summers were shorter and the winters longer; the sun was hidden by dense, black clouds; sleet and snow fell constantly; enormous glaciers of clear green ice formed, and moved relentlessly southward. America was in the grip of another Ice Age. This was the fourth time that ice had covered most of the continents; three times in the past had the land been stripped and torn by devastating ice-sheets; but in the beginning, when the earth first appeared from beneath the seas, America had been warm and tropical. Great plants with wide-spreading leaves grew to enormous heights, and even the rushes and mosses were fifty and seventy-five feet tall; ferns grew as far north as Greenland, and Wyoming was thick with giant palms.

In these early days, a land bridge bound America to Asia across Bering Sea; and in the North Atlantic, another mass connected Labrador with Greenland and Europe. Strange animals passed freely back and forth across these land bridges, and all the queer, unusual beasts found in Europe were equally at home in America. Upon the muddy banks of the rivers in what is now Wyoming lived an animal twenty-five feet long called the Stegosaur or Plated Lizard. Down his back, in a double row, were great, bony fins, three feet high; and his long, heavy tail bore a long line of sharp spikes. Enormous dinosaurs, measuring sixty-five feet from small, snake-like head to tapering tail, lived in the warm, moist regions of Arizona and Montana; and elephant-like mammoths and mastodons dwelt in Florida. Throughout the land roamed savage sabre-tooth tigers, woolly rhinoceroses and fierce cave bears, together with other animals utterly different from those which are now on earth. There were herds of little wild horses less than two feet high and having three toes on each foot, the ancestors of horses as we know horses today.

Prehistoric America, when the continents were moist and tropical, and strange beasts roamed the land. (Restoration in Field Museum, Chicago.) The enormous animals are huge, rhinoceros-like *Unitalheres*, long since passed from earth; and the small beasts are little horses, less than two feet high and little larger than dogs. They had three toes and lived in the warm, humid regions of America thirty million years ago, but moved away to Europe and Asia before the land-bridges were broken.

Then, too, there was the great ground sloth, bulky, slow and silent, and with great claws a foot in length.

These, and many other strange animals, lived in America in the very earliest days; but each time that the continents had been covered with ice, many had died or moved across the land bridges to other continents. First to leave were the vast herds of wild horses, primitive camels, and small elephants; and shortly after, the land bridges to Asia and Europe were broken, so America was cut off from other lands.

Many of these animals had long since vanished when the Mongolian wanderers reached America. But some still remained. One day a band of hunters in New Mexico surrounded a herd of bison unlike any on earth today. Killing thirty with flint spears, they stripped off the flesh and left the bones. Then the glaciers, creeping southward, covered these bones and their recent discovery tells us that men were living in America before the last Ice Age more than 20,000 years ago.

Stone Age men in America kill thirty bison near what is now Folsom, New Mexico, 20,000 years ago. (Restoration, American Museum of Natural History, New York.) The pit containing the bones of the bison and flint arrow heads carefully chipped by Stone Age Americans was discovered only a few years ago, and proved beyond question that men lived in America in the dim ages before the Fourth Glacial Period. (For Europe in prehistoric Stone Ages, see Vol. I, pp. 15-17.)

Ground sloth driven from Gypsum Cave, Nevada, by a prehistoric American. (Southwest Museum.)

In Nevada, when the cold grew too great, these men of the Early Stone Age drove from their caves the shaggy, reddish ground sloths and settled in these shelters themselves. But, after a time, the giant sloths succeeded in driving out the men, and returned to the warm, cozy caverns until forced to give place once more to the superior cunning of people driven to desperation by the cold. In time, however, the glaciers and ice-sheets began to melt. In this last Ice Age in America, only the region as far south as Kentucky had been covered, and many people and animals remained alive and strong. As the land grew warmer year by year and the barren plains and mountains began to be covered with shrub and forest, some of these men and beasts moved back north again in the constant search for food. So America was once more peopled both in the south and in the north and the climate everywhere was much the same as it is today. But now these ancestors of our Indians had been separated from their Mongolian forebears by so long a stretch of time and so many all-absorbing events that they knew nothing about their Asiatic origin. To them America was their native land and it was here in America that they would now work out their own approach to civilization, having no knowledge of either Europe or Asia, from which they were wholly cut off by vast stormy stretches of sea.

The Basket Makers
(From about 3250 B.C. to 500 B.C.)

For thousands of years the people in America drifted about aimlessly, here and there, wherever food could be found. They lived on roots and berries; they hunted and fished; and slowly they gathered into groups or tribes for success in hunting or for protection against their enemies. The strongest, most warlike people seized the best hunting grounds, and the warmer and more pleasant dwelling places; and they fought vigorously to keep others away from these favorable regions. As the centuries passed, groups or tribes were spread throughout both continents; and, sometime before the year 15,000 B.C., one of the earliest bands reached the highlands of Mexico. There it was that agriculture was discovered when a sharp-eyed tribesman noticed that some seeds of grain spilled beside their shelter had sprouted and grown more seeds.

For a time, only the tribesmen of the Mexican highlands knew about agriculture; and far to the north, in what is now the Southwest of the United States, a primitive, peaceful people continued to live as they had for centuries. There, under burning skies which seldom dropped rain; on painted deserts of strange yellows, dull reds, and whites; in the throbbing purple haze of sun-baked mesas and canyons of grotesque form, these people managed to find enough food to satisfy them. Other wandering tribes from the northern plateaus or the eastern plains spurned this uninviting land, and the desert dwellers were left alone to hunt for squirrel, rabbit, deer, and mountain sheep; or to gather birds' nests, grass seeds, wild berries, and tender plants. For clothing they wore the skins of the beasts, and for shelter they had trees or projecting rocks.

But after many centuries of such simple living, strange tribes straggled into the Southwest bringing the seeds of a cultivated plant that some fellow-tribesman had developed in Mexico. This was corn, or maize, and the growing of maize wrought a great change in the life of the Southwestern people. Having learned to plant the seed, they now had to stay near by and guard it against animals while growing, and against the raids of strange hungry tribes after it had ripened.

Thus it came about that the wanderers wandered no more; but settled down in this land of painted deserts, and began to develop better ways of living. They came to be known as the Basket Makers because they had baskets for everything: baskets for pots and pans, baskets lined with clay and ashes for carrying water, baskets for storage bins, and even baskets for babies. These baskets were all made of yucca plant fibers or wooden splinters coiled and bound together with fiber cords, and often they were painted with black in designs of whirls and zigzags, or other patterns.

A Basket Maker warrior with his dog stands before White Dog Cave, Southwestern America, where he lived almost five thousand years ago. Sandals, beads, baskets, stone spear tip and flint knife are taken from remains found in the caves.

And now that the Basket Makers lived for years beside their little fields of corn, the larger animals left the region. Skins big enough for coverings could no longer be found to protect the people from the cold winds of winter, and so an inventive leader thought up a new kind of blanket. As the smaller animals were caught, their hides were cut into strips and placed in a huge basket-tray, until there were enough for a blanket. Then the women were set to tearing apart yucca leaves, and when all was ready, the furry skin strips were twisted around the yucca fiber so that the hair stood out in little swirls.

After all the skin strips had been twisted, two stakes were set in the ground six or eight feet apart, and the men took the heavy fur ropes and wound them one above the other, flatly and evenly, back and forth around the two stakes. When all the ropes had been woven, the strips were fastened together with twined threads of yucca cord, and when the piece was removed from the frame, there was a fine, warm, fur-cloth blanket. Men in America had for the first time used their wits to meet the necessities of life with things thought out and planned for, rather than merely seized by superior force or cunning.

Such blankets were used only in winter, however; in the blazing heat of summer no one bothered much about clothes or coverings. The men wore breech-cloths and strings of stone and abalone shell beads, bartered from traders who came from the sunset sea; and the clothing of women was a twelve-inch skirt made of yucca fiber string. Men and women, children and aged people, all had sandals, however; for the cactus spine-strewn desert and the hot, burning sands made a foot covering necessary. These sandals were woven from yucca plant fiber or milkweed fiber; at first, all were made with square toes, but later scalloped-toe sandals were fashioned; some had little feather decorations, and often there were fringes on the toes. Stockings were also worn by the Basket Makers, and these were made from the hair of the women carefully knitted with bone knitting needles.

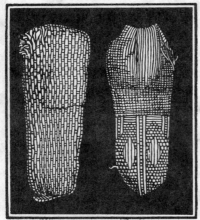

Woven yucca fiber Basket Maker sandals found in ground of caves where these people buried their dead. (Peabody Mus.)

But although they had learned about maize and planting, and how to make baskets, sandals, and fur blankets, the Basket Makers were still primitive people of the Stone Age. Their only possessions were stone knives and axes; grooved, wooden war-clubs; a few extra flint spear-heads; some digging sticks; and a needle made of deer bone. Some of the more important families also had a squat, stone pipe or two for smoking tobacco incense to the gods; and all the women had little feather-decorated bags made of yucca thread or hair string. This was all, however; the Basket Makers continued to live in the simple, flimsy structures of branches and twigs they had learned to build beside their fields; and caves were used only as hiding places, storage places, or as burial places where the dead were laid, wrapped in their heavy fur-blankets, and surrounded by weapons, baskets of food, and their only domesticated animal, the dog. At times they even made separate burials for their dogs, and one grieving

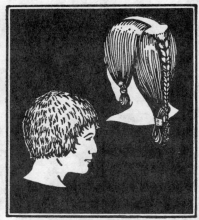

Basket Maker hairdress. The man at right wears his long hair in a braid and his head is shaved in an unusual tonsure; the woman at left has bobbed her hair to make a strong rope. (Peabody Museum.)

Basket Maker placed, in a dry sandy cave, carefully wrapped mummies of a large yellow dog and a small black and white dog who had been his friends and companions in life. And with these faithful animals, he buried two deer bones painted red, that the dogs should not go hungry on their journey to the next world.

Thus the Basket Makers continued to live for centuries. In time they learned how to make crude bowls of baked clay; but these were used only for cooking; for all other purposes they still clung to their baskets. And then some more thoughtful leader had a new idea. It seemed to him a foolish thing for the people to leave all their baskets, robes, and other treasures in the frail brush-shelters where storms often ruined everything. Why not have stronger, better protected dwellings? Why not build homes in caves? And so this leader dug a large hole in the sandy floor of a dry cave and lined it with slabs of stone to make the floor and lower walls of a dwelling. Then he found branches of trees which he made into poles for the upper walls and the roof, covering them with cedar bark; and when the building was finished, it was a strong substantial room tucked away in the protecting shelter of the cave where it would remain for years undamaged by the elements.

Basket Maker hut built partly into the ground. The part above the surface is made of bark-slabs, and the roof is covered with clay. Remains of such a hut have been found in Mesa Verde National Park.

Many of the Basket Makers followed the example of this leader and built other huts in caves, but some there were who still liked dwelling in open places. Everyone, however, saw how much better the bark-slab house was than their flimsy brushwood huts; and these new houses soon appeared everywhere,—down in the valley bottoms near the fields, up on the mesa tops, or in a canyon on some slight rise of ground where the winter snows melting away would leave them high and dry.

Wherever the house might be, a hole ten or twelve feet across was dug in the ground and the sides smoothed carefully and coated with a plaster of mud. If the soil were sandy and yielding, the sides had to be strengthened with stone slabs; and often the walls of the hole were carried higher by building them up with layers of large lumps of clay, or with upright poles wattled together with withes and coated inside and out with mud. Roofs were made by leaning light poles against the walls, and covering the spaces between with twigs and bark. And then when the twig roof was covered with clay, it was practically a cave in the open.

The Cliff Dwellers
(500 B.C.—1250 A.D.)

Year after year the Basket Makers lived peacefully and contentedly
in the Southwest; and for centuries they remained a solitary group, left
to themselves by the wandering inhabitants of this vast land, until
sometime before the year 500 B.C. Then new tribes moved into the
Southwest from regions much farther south, and brought with them
many things that were unknown to the Basket Makers. They brought
seeds of squashes, beans, and cotton; and from the fleecy, white cotton
puffs they wove a soft cloth, much better than yucca fiber cloth; they
knew how to tame the wild turkey and how to make jewelry of turquoise and shell and bone; moreover, they brought with them a new
weapon, the bow and arrow, unknown to the Basket Makers.

The peaceful Basket Makers did not resist the coming of the new
people; there was land enough for all, and the Southerners were welcome. The newcomers settled quietly, therefore, and lived and married
with the ancient dwellers. Gradually they took over the farming patches
and the best of the cave shelters and homes of the older people; and in
time, the long-established Basket Makers died out and disappeared.

One thing these newcomers learned from the old ones was the making of clay pottery; but having learned it, they made much better bowls
than their teachers. They watched the Basket Makers coil their long
bundles of wooden splinters, or fibers, one on top of the other, and they
copied the idea and made their clay baskets very much the same way.

Prehistoric drawings of primitive, Stone Age Americans on the rock walls of Frijoles Canyon, N. Mex.

Duck hunting scene from bowl of earliest Cliff Dwellers. The men have feather headdresses, and the humps on their backs are game bags. At right, a hunter blows a whistle to lure the wild duck flying above within the shooting range of his companion. (Mesa Verde National Park Museum.)

Then, with a stick or a piece of shell and some water, they smoothed the outside. And after the clay vessel had dried in the sun and had been baked in the fire, they painted a design on it in black just like the designs on the baskets of the Basket Makers, or with dimly-remembered forms of the feathered serpent-god of their old land in the south.

One strange thing about these new people was their custom of tying infants so close to hard boards at their backs that the soft, pliable skulls were flattened. In other ways, however, they carried on most of the customs of the earlier people; although soon they began to build their one-room slab dwellings in small, rectangular clusters of two or three, or large groups of fifty or more,—a village all under one roof.

Because game was scarce in this settled region, the savage tribesmen from the north and east did not bother these farmers until it was learned

Early Cliff Dweller cotton shawl in which a child had been wrapped for burial. The intricate design and expert workmanship show an art even finer than that of the modern Navaho. (Arizona State Museum.)

that hidden in their cave storehouses were supplies of corn and berries and roots; and that they had beautifully woven shawls and fine ornaments of shell and bone, and turquoise mosaics. Then hunger and greed moved these restless, war-loving tribesmen, who raised no grain of their own, to swoop down on the defenseless village people, killing the men, running off with women and children, and stealing the stores and treasures.

The Southwestern desert dwellers had never been fighters, and now they were helpless to defend themselves or their homes from these merciless raiders.

Cliff Palace, Mesa Verde National Park, Colorado. (From photographs.) Cliff Palace was discovered in December, 1888, by Richard and Alfred Wetherell, two ranchmen who were hunting cattle. Suddenly, their horses stopped on the edge of a steep canyon; and as the ranchmen looked across, they saw an unbelievable, white fairy-city built high up in the opposite cliff, beneath its jutting top. Stirred by the magnificence and beauty of their find, the Wetherells named their discovery Cliff Palace.

They fled, therefore, and took refuge in caves high up in the steep walls of the canyon cliffs. Here in places almost impossible to attack, they built themselves new homes; and because these homes were in the cliffs, they came to be known as Cliff Dwellers. In the steep walls of the canyons, they dug out rooms from the soft, red sandstone or built little houses in natural caves or on narrow ledges; and here they fled for safety when watchers at their lookout posts gave warning that enemy raiders were approaching.

It was almost impossible to reach these hiding places; even the Cliff Dwellers themselves had difficulty in getting to them in the beginning. In the steep, almost perpendicular cliffs, they cut small toe-holds and hand-holds with their stone hatchets, and by reaching above their heads to make new holds, they gradually reached the shelf or cave they desired, which was often hundreds of feet above the canyon floor. Afterward they made ladders or cut notches in tree trunks which they placed against the cliffs; and when these were drawn up, no one could reach their refuge.

As the wild, roving tribes harassed the region more and more, and learned of these hiding places, and of the stores of food hidden away in the cliffs, the people gathered closer together for protection, and began to live permanently in their cliff homes. When the families living in each cave grew larger, and others gathered into the same cave, new houses were added to the old ones and more spaces in the cave were walled off. Houses were even built on top of one another, until the cave was filled to the roof with hundreds of rooms, the upper dwellings reached by ladders from the roofs of the houses below. The walls, dividing the rooms of the different families, were made of carefully cut stone blocks laid with clay mortar in regular layers, and plastered with yellow mud smoothed by hand. Often a small hand print could be seen in the walls, for it was the women who built the home. The men helped only in carrying the larger stones, and the women erected the walls and plastered them. And because of this, the woman owned the home, and not the man; when a man married, he went to live with his wife in her home, and the children belonged to the mother and took the mother's name.

Cliff Palace as it is today. Built snugly under an overhanging ledge with the canyon dropping sharply almost 1000 feet, Cliff Palace was a fortified city. The circular structures at the edge were *kivas* covered and hidden underground; toward the cliff were the dwellings and watch towers.

Cliff Palace as it was in the days of the Cliff Dwellers. (A reconstruction from the ruins shown on the opposite page.) Through the open window of the house in the foreground can be seen a painted fresco of red lightning and spruce trees, copied by the author from one of the dwellings at Cliff Palace. The city was begun in the year 1073 A.D., and its exact date can be given because Dr. A. E. Douglass, of the University of Arizona, has been able to work out a system of dating these pueblos by means of the tree rings found in the wooden beams. *Pueblo* is a Spanish word meaning "city" and the name was given to the Cliff Dwellers because their crowded dwelling places were really villages or cities.

In the small, open spaces of the canyon valleys or on the high tops of mesas, the Cliff Dwellers raised their crops of maize and beans, and only ventured beyond their canyons to gather firewood or to hunt.

The great building age of the Cliff Dwellers began in the year 919 A.D., in the erection of a moon-shaped settlement called Pueb'lo Bo-ni'to, in what is now New Mexico, and continued until about 1250 A.D.; but it was in the canyons of Mesa Verde in Colorado that they made their finest houses. Here, high up above the ground in a sheer perpendicular cliff, they built the fairy-like Cliff Palace in an enormous open cave that was as long as a present-day, city block and as high as a five-story building.

Balcony House, a good example of a perfectly fortified cliff dwelling at Mesa Verde. Built on a narrow ledge, at the edge of a precipitous, almost perpendicular cliff, it could be entered, when the ladders were drawn up, only through two narrow slits in the rock at either end of the ledge.

Here, too, were Spruce Tree House, Balcony House, Square Tower House, and Farview House. At first there were only a few rooms for a small number of families in Cliff Palace; but as more and more people came into the cave, other rooms were added until all of the uneven floor space was covered with homes except for an open terrace along the edge of the precipice. Here, women sat at their work making pots or baskets, as in a city-square, looking out from their airy perch to the ground below or up the curve of the canyon with its splendid rocky walls. The front part of the cave was only one story high, and the doorways were often in the roofs, so that the people had to climb up ladders and go in through trapdoors in the flat roofs. A good many of the houses had two stories, however, and some had as many as five. The doors of these upper rooms opened upon the flat roofs of the rooms beneath, and the whole house-village was thus built up in steps.

Small windows and T-shaped doors pierced the walls of the upper stories. The lower part of these doors was just wide enough to permit two legs to squeeze through; but the upper part was wider so that shoulders loaded with water jars, food, and fire wood could pass easily.

In time of attack, the lower part of the door was covered with stone slabs, so that enemy arrows could not reach the family within; and the defenders shot their own arrows from the wider opening above.

Built, underneath the terrace, where workers and idlers sat along the front of the cave, were a number of secret, ceremonial chambers called *kivas*. All the people of the village were divided into families, or clans; and each clan had its own kiva where the leaders and priests met, and where the young men of the clan slept until they were married. The kiva was for men only; no woman was ever permitted to enter it; and the only entrance was by a ladder through a small hole in the roof.

At the bottom of the kiva near the fire-pit was a hole called the *sipapu*. The legends of the Cliff Dwellers said that man had been created deep down in the earth, and it was from the earth that he had struggled upward into the light of day. The gods also lived within the earth, and to the earth, men returned at death to be welcomed by the gods. The sipapu represented the hole from which man came into the world, and was the most sacred part of the kiva.

Most important to the Cliff Dwellers was a great tower built high up above the ceilings of the other houses. Here a watchman stood constantly on guard. Through an open window, he could see all the canyon and much of the surrounding country; and when, in the distance, his sharp eyes noticed clouds of dust piling up, he watched closely, tensely. Were they caused by wind, animals, or enemies?

Balcony House, Mesa Verde, showing its exceedingly difficult approach. Beyond the tower may be seen an entrance, so narrow a single person could just squeeze through.

CRANE

Cliff Dwellers running to their homes at the sound of alarm. Wild turkeys were kept in rear room-pens for meat, and in other rooms were stores of grain, water, and fire wood.

Steadily the cloud approached. Enemies! Boom-boom-boom! sounded the great drum in the watch-tower as the man struck vigorous, sturdy blows; and the sound went resounding throughout the canyon, echoing against the steep, sandstone walls! Quickly the men came running from the fields; children scampered in from berry patches or carried up the wild turkeys to their pens in the rear of the cave; and mothers waiting on the terrace hastily counted their families as they fled up the long notched poles. When the last one was safely home, the ladders were all drawn up, the lower doors blocked and the raiders found the valley deserted.

Although most of the time the Cliff Dwellers were thus forced to fight wild outsiders, there were times when they had opportunity for trading with them in peace. From far-distant Mexico, wandering merchants brought copper bells and macaw feathers to exchange for turquoise, and shells from the Pacific Coast were traded for pottery. Cliff Dweller pottery was always in demand; the women had developed great skill in molding and painting pottery, and the bowls of the dwellers in different canyons had their own traditional shapes and decorations.

South of the Cliff Dwellers were brethren who built their community houses in the valleys of the Salt and Gila rivers of Colorado, instead of in the steep walls of canyons. They, too, were farmers, and had not only learned how to store the extra rainfall in reservoirs made by hollowing out spots in the rock, but had also learned to build irrigation ditches. Here in a large city, with thirty-six, great, many-roomed buildings, water was supplied from the Salt River nine miles away by a canal thirty feet wide. The walls and the bottom of the canal were plastered with clay, and fires had been made in the canal to bake the clay hard. Side canals distributed water to the fields, and gates were arranged to regulate the flow, so that two hundred thousand acres of dry desert land were made into fertile fields for growing food.

In seasons of poor hunting, the wild wandering tribes surrounding these farms were tempted by a vision of jars filled with corn from the harvest. Eagerly, they raided the villages, often creeping up so suddenly that they took the valley dwellers by surprise and there was no time for defense; if surprise failed, they laid siege to the well-fortified dwellings until the water supply diminished and the exhausted dwellers were compelled to surrender before their children and old folks became too weak.

Pueb'lo Bo-ni'to, New Mexico, begun in 919 A.D., an enormous community dwelling or apartment house in several stories, hidden in a beautiful canyon, but not built into cliffs. (A reconstruction.)

Enchanted Mesa, a beautiful buff-rose tableland of rock, rising abruptly 430 ft. from a waste of sandy desert. (Photograph by the author.) It was to such towering and almost unscalable tablelands that the people of the Southwest retreated when driven from their canyons and cliff dwellings. Enchanted Mesa was reached in ancient times by a rock ladder; and once, so legend relates, all its inhabitants, save three sick women and a boy, were below working the fields, when a terrific storm arose. The rock ladder was split from the face of the cliff, the sick women were isolated, and never again could the homeless people find a way to climb back to their dwellings on the top. The wrap worn by the woman is copied from an ancient Cliff Dweller blanket recently discovered in a grave.

By force or by guile they overpowered the unfortunate communities; then men, women, and children were killed or enslaved; and off went the bandits with supplies of food, turquoise jewelry and other valuables.

Constantly and unceasingly harassed by these savages, the people from cliff and valley dwellings gave up the struggle at last, abandoned their homes and fled. Over the entire southwestern region, they moved about restlessly, seeking always more difficult and remote places of refuge. In time, they settled in the central part of the region, on steep, wind-swept mesa tops of towering rock amid an ocean of sand. Here they shut themselves away from their dread enemies, and here they guarded their old arts and protected their old customs and traditions.

The Mound Builders

Far to the east of the Cliff Dwellers, in the rolling valley-lands of the Mississippi, dwelt another ancient people, a tall, strong, intelligent race who decked themselves with necklaces of highly polished stone beads or breast ornaments of bear claws. Living in little villages with lodges made of bark and wood, they differed from all other tribes in that they built earthen mounds above the bodies of their dead and because of this custom they are called Mound Builders.

Portrait of a Mound Builder with long, straight nose, slanting eyes and hair cut severely straight. (A pipe from Dickson Mound, Lewistown, Illinois.)

Devoted in family affections, one group of these people lived near Lewistown, Illinois. When a number died all at one time from pestilence or some other cause, their friends buried them with remarkable tenderness, each husband and wife together with their faces turned t o w a r d each other, and where there was a baby, it lay between the father and mother, provided with a tiny jar exactly like the larger ones provided for its parents. The care with which the heads were arranged and the baby snuggled in so cozily, present a picture of a race with deep-seated human feelings.

Burials at Dickson Mound reveal deep family affection. Husband and wife face each other and the baby, tucked in between, has a tiny toy jar like the larger jars of his parents.

Monk's Mound, Cahokia Mounds State Park, Illinois. This great truncated pyramid bears sufficient resemblance to Maya structures in Yucatan to give reason for assuming that the Mound Builders had intercourse with the Mayas or were perhaps migrating Mayas. See pages 108, 111.

Not all the mounds of these people were burial places, however; they also erected great mounds for religious ceremonies. Near Portsmouth, Ohio, was the awe-inspiring form of a serpent writhing along a cliff, while the huge Monk's Mound in Illinois was a flattened pyramid covering a far greater area than the Great Pyramid in Egypt.

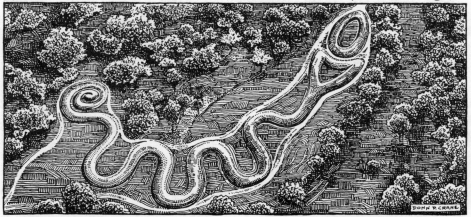

Great Serpent Mound near Portsmouth, Ohio, a ceremonial mound enclosing an altar between its jaws. Worship of the serpent is one resemblance Mound Builders bear to Mayas. See pages 112, 115, 118.

One of the largest cities built by these ancient people arose at Wickliffe, Kentucky. Standing high up on the only bluff in the district round about, this city overlooked the broad, green, deeply wooded valley where the Ohio River flows into the Mississippi, and far down these two great waterways from the depths of primeval forests and the plains of the Middle West or up from the Gulf of Mexico boats could come to Wickliffe. Thus there arose at this cross-roads of ancient civilization, a very populous city of some two or three thousand people, a commercial and religious center, whose fame was known far and wide. Thither adventurous travelers brought pottery and jewelry, copper, lead and mica from all the distant parts of the known and unknown world and there lived men and women come from such far away districts that they differed in religious beliefs and had drifted, as men do today, into their great metropolis, the big city of their times.

Near the meeting point of the rivers, there towered up a look-out mound where men could overlook all the surrounding country and watch the canoes and log dug-outs that passed on the water below. Mid the cluster of huts built of poles and thatched with split-cane and grass, rose the wooden walls of a temple, likewise shaggy with thatch, and through the lanes of the town, men, women, and children, dressed in skins or cloth, went about the business of life. Some went to fish or

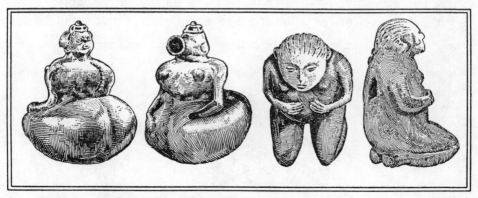

A man and woman of Wickliffe as shown in clay water jars. The man has his hair slicked back pompadour and whoever made the woman must have had a sense of humor; her head is on hindside before, her face looks out over her spine with vertebrae showing like a row of buttons, the back of her head is above her bosom. From Wickliffe Mounds, the Ancient Buried City, Wickliffe, Ky.

Earthen jars, Wickliffe. Left a saucy pig's snout or opossum, next a beautiful serpent. Last a woman's head, hair parted in the middle and done in a knot at the rear. Mound Builders preceded the Indians in the Mississippi Valley and may have lived here when Caesar ruled Rome.

hunt; some, carrying hoes made of flint, went out to till the fields, for the town was a peaceable place where the chief pursuit was farming; and some made interesting pottery, gracefully proportioned bowls, pitchers and curious vessels in picturesque effigy shapes, an owl, a pig's snout, a serpent, or even a queer human figure. Here an old man carved a pipe out of a gray-green soapstone, making it in the shape of a graceful little duck and another man polished stone or shell into beautiful beads. A woman sat in a doorway weaving threads of plant fibre into long strips of cloth while a second woman nearby was busy with beaten herbs, roots and jars of crushed berries, dyeing the woven fabric, making it purple, yellow or a beautiful shade of red. There was trade in

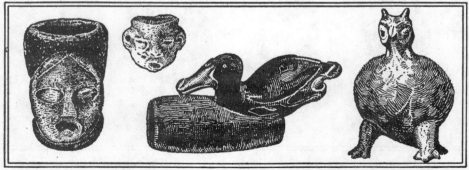

To the right an owl water-jar of tannish yellow and white clay, the symmetry of its modeling indicating an artistic people. To the left three pipes. The figure of the duck, made of polished steatite, a gray-green soapstone, is particularly beautiful in carving and design. All are from Wickliffe.

the city, too, with travelers from far and wide bartering the goods they brought. Colorful heaps of melons, squash, beans, potatoes, tomatoes, bright red peppers and corn were heaped up for exchange, and from the little houses rose the odor of bear-meat cooking, or perhaps of wild-turkey or venison. In the temple the people gathered to say prayers to the gods or to bring them offerings of food, of clothing or tobacco, while before the three sacred altars, shut off by a rail from

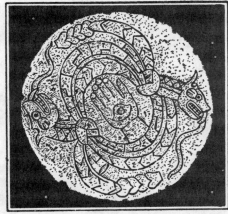

A ceremonial disk from Moundville, Alabama, showing a design of rattle snakes encircling a human hand with an all-seeing eye in the palm.

the people, the shaman or high-priest conducted the rites of the service.

At times, too, there was a funeral. Arrayed in his finest necklace of shell-beads or polished bear's claws and provided with pottery jars for use in the after-life, the dead was borne to the temple by a procession of friends and kinsfolk and after the services there, the procession wound its way to the burial mound. Laying their dead on the ground and covering them over with earth in layer after layer of burials, as was the Mound-Builder's custom, the people had heaped up a cemetery that was an imposing mound. Some of these processions laid their dead out at full length and covered them soon after death; others burned their dead, leaving only ashes in the mound, while still others, having previously left the body exposed on a high scaffold or a tree till the flesh had dis-

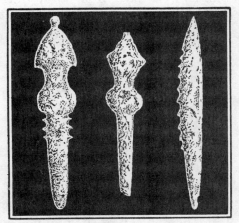

To the left two ceremonial scepters. To the right a sacrificial knife. These were found buried together at Wickliffe as though they were the complete ceremonial objects of a *shaman* or priest.

The Mound Builders' city, Wickliffe, Ky. A funeral party starting from the Temple Mound at the left wind down the path behind the Council House toward the Burial Mound at the right. Houses are made of a wattle-work of split cane supported on upright poles and plastered with clay. The temple and larger houses are finely thatched with split cane and grass. At the bend behind the temple the Ohio and Mississippi Rivers meet opposite the modern town of Cairo, Illinois.

integrated, brought only the bones of their loved one, done up in a bundle or basket to lay away in the mound.

These three varied kinds of burials show that the people at Wickliffe so differed in their customs they must have had three religions, since men dispose of their dead in accordance with what they believe about a future life. In their temple were three altars, too, so doubtless in ages past the people had come from such widely separated districts that they worshiped three different gods whose service within this temple was united in one religion. On a certain solemn occasion the people burned their temple in a fiery ceremonial. Perhaps it was fire they worshiped on one of the altars and the flames were an offering to the fire-god. For while the building burned, they heaped clay on the flames and buried the ruins of their temple to a depth of four or five feet, then on top of the mound thus raised, they built a second temple. In time they burned that temple too, buried it like the first one and built a third sacred structure on top of their temple-mound.

Today one may see the hard-beaten clay floor of their temple with its row of three sacred altars. One may see, too, the council house with its doorway and three fire-places and the holes where stakes had been driven, not only to support the roof but to hold fast the furniture or benches. In the burial mound itself lie the city's men, women and children. Here is a pottery maker surrounded by her tools, here a warlike male enclosing a human skull, like a trophy, between his feet. In general,

A Mound Builder portrayed in clay, with ears pierced for earrings. Red paint remains on his cheeks. Metropolis, Illinois.

however, there are few warlike implements buried at Wickliffe. The Mound Builders seemed to have been a peaceable people of more than usual capacity for tender human feeling. Artistic, intelligent, strong, they lived for unknown centuries in the valley of the Mississippi, merchants, travelers and craftsmen, expressing their feeling for beauty in everything they made. Where they went no one knows. The Indians the white men found in the Mississippi Valley may have been their descendants; but if so it is strange that these Indians knew nothing of their predecessors. They had no legends of who had built the mounds; and little remains in their lives of the Mound Builders' culture or customs. More probably the Mound Builders vanished as many tribes seem to vanish, overcome and absorbed by tribesmen more numerous and savage, but certainly they were related to the Indians of later times, being either migrating Mayas wandering north from Central America or some other Mongolian tribe who crossed the straits from Asia.

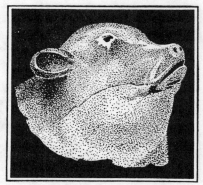

A bear of baked clay from Metropolis, Illinois, evidence of the artistic skill of the Mound Builders.

People of Plain and Forest

From the river valleys of the Mound Builders to the sun-baked lands of the Cliff Dwellers, the country spread out into far-reaching, grass-covered plains. Here grazed great herds of shaggy, bow-backed bison or buffalo; here multitudes of plump little prairie dogs dug their burrows; snarling packs of fierce, hungry wolves roamed restlessly; and the nights were made hideous with the howling of lean, sleek-flanked coyotes. And here, as elsewhere, people gradually found their way.

The people of the plains were nomads and hunters, and the buffalo supplied them with food, clothing, and shelter. Every part of the animal they used; the meat was food, the hair they made into ropes and strings, the hide they cut up into small pieces for clothing, or sewed to other hides to make a great tent or tepee as protection from sun and storm. And since the buffalo were constantly roaming over the prairie in search of pasture, the plains people were ever moving, too.

Wherever the prairie was split by a river, the plains people pitched their camp, and the women set up the slim, pointed, cone-shaped, skin tepees in a rough circle. Over a framework of long, slender saplings they stretched dressed buffalo skins laced together in the middle. Some were newly made, others were patched and weather-stained by countless seasons of storm and sunshine and by almost constant travel.

Bison, tepees, and people of the plain. A buffalo skin painted by the A-rap'a-hoe Indians of Oklahoma and Wyoming, showing how these tribes of the plains had developed a life suited to following the buffalo herds. The tribes of the forest dwelt in the region east of the Mississippi to the Atlantic.

A temporary village of tepees. Meat is hung on the drying racks, and women are scraping buffalo hides. (A drawing made about 1835 by George Catlin, one of the earliest students of the plains people.)

Each round shelter ended in a sheaf of crossing poles, and from a wide, dark opening in the center arose curling wreaths of blue smoke. Often the skin walls were ornamented in gay colors with angular figures of warriors and the heroic deeds they had performed; here, too, were pictures of the number of enemy slain and captured.

But, although hunting was the main source of food, and there was no true farming, there were seasons when the buffalo herds remained in favorite pasturelands, and then the plains people established quite permanent villages and raised crops of maize, squash, and beans. Nuts and grains and roots were collected; and berries and fruits were dried for use during the winter. It was also at these times that tobacco was grown.

The people of ancient America used tobacco only in certain ceremonies; it was an offering to the gods, and its smoke was an incense which relieved distress or disease, lessened danger, and brought help in time of need. Only the men of the tribe were permitted to plant the tobacco and care for the growing crop, and only the men could smoke it in stone or pottery pipes to call upon the favor of the gods for the welfare of the tribe. These pipes were holy and sacred; they were carved and ornamented and decorated with feathers; and the shafts which ran from mouthpiece to bowl were the pathways of the spirits. One such pipe was believed to have come from the thunder god himself.

A village of the forest people, showing wooden lodges or huts, corn fields, and native dances. (A drawing by John White, 1585, now in the British Museum.) Hiawatha, the Iroquois chieftain of the On'on-da'ga tribe, who ruled about 1450, lived like many of the forest people in such a lodge and was a real person transformed by legend like King Arthur into the heroic Hiawatha of Longfellow's poem. See *My Book House*, Vol. IX, page 89 for *Hiawatha's Fasting, A Legend of the First Indian Corn*. Among the most famous forest people were the five Iroquois tribes: the Mohawks, Oneidas, Onondagas, Senecas, and Ca-yu'gas. Later the Tus'ca-ro'ras joined this League, which was then known as the "Six Nations." They were an inventive people who wove cone-shaped baskets for fish traps, made birch canoes, and fire drills. The wampum used by these Indians was made of spiral beads from fresh-water shells, polished smooth and strung on fine strands of skin. It was a sign of power and authority, and was used as money and to bind treaties. When a tribe was defeated in war, its wampum was a prize surrendered to the victors.

East of the Mississippi, and continuing to the Atlantic, the country changed in character, and was broken up into beautiful rolling river valleys, everywhere covered with thick, sun-flecked forests. Here, too, dwelt vigorous, active tribesmen. All the forest people were hunters; they lived in small lodges built of saplings, and nearby in little clearings among the trees, they raised maize, squash, and tobacco.

Women were held in great honor by the forest people, and worked with the men in perfect harmony. Confidence and trust governed all, and home life was peaceful, sacred, and very happy.

Much of the life of the forest dwellers was spent in fighting other tribes who tried to take their hunting grounds and their stores of food and grain; and under the leadership of a brave and good man named Hiawatha, five of the tribes living in the vicinity of what is now New York State, united in a League of Nations to keep peace among themselves. Hiawatha also taught his people agriculture, and legend related that he arose to heaven in a white, birch bark canoe.

All over the vast continent of North America people dwelt in tribal groups with ideas and customs very much the same,—the forest people, the plains people, the people of the Southwest, those of the Pacific Coast and those of the great Northwest, who built tall totem-poles, kept records on walrus tusks, and drove their painted boats to the edge of Eternal Snow. The only difference was due to the nature of the country where they lived, and the manner in which they found food.

Typical art of the Indians of the Northwest Coast, a wooden plaque, portraying the adventures of a mythological being. (Natural History Museum, New York.) Only among the northwestern and southwestern tribes of North America did feeling find expression in true art. Plains people, forest people and the Digger Indians of California never developed any distinctive artistic expression. This plaque, painted in brilliant colors with strength and vigor, shows a bold and impressive figure composed of block-like parts, so characteristic of the Indians of the Northwest, as used on their totem poles and high-prowed war canoes.   For characteristic art of the Indians of the Southwest see pages 206–210.

Eskimo record of a walrus hunt. The men in large skin boats have attacked this enormous beast of the seas with their stone spears, and one boat has been overturned. (Heye Museum, New York City.)

Some were more peaceful than others, some had developed the arts of weaving, painting, carving, and building to greater heights, but all were Stone Age people with no knowledge of metal or the wheel.

Nevertheless, the people of Ancient America had progressed far beyond the knowledge of their primitive ancestors who ventured from Asia across the cold waters of Bering Sea so many thousands of years before. They had discovered agriculture and developed many new plants; they had learned basket making, pottery making, and how to weave fine cloth. And in addition to all this they had developed a religion that was wholesome, pure and satisfying.

Such were the Indians who settled in what are now the United States and Canada. But they were very few in number compared to those who for thousands of years had been going on south into the warmer lands of Mexico, Central and South America. And the most brilliant civilizations ever built up by Indians were the work of those tribes who kept moving southward after they crossed from Asia.

Reindeer pulling loaded sledges over the frozen land of the northwestern tribes, a realistic carving on a walrus tusk, showing vigor and skill. (From Point Barrow, Alaska. Heye Museum, New York.)

III

The Brilliant Civilization of the Mayas

(From about 3500 B.C. to 1490 A.D.)

Migrating Mayas

In earlier volumes we have told the stories of the various nations of Europe and Asia and now we complete our knowledge of the peoples of the world by learning the background which has produced our neighbors in Mexico, Central America, Peru and other parts of South America. Descended from various American Indian tribes who had attained a magnificent culture before they ever saw a white man, these neighbors of ours are highly proud of that fact, particularly our nearest neighbors in Mexico, and to understand them fully we need to know the greatness of their past and how deeply they cherish the memory of it today. Therefore, we take up now the story of those Indians who continued to roam southward for century after century, led by the lure of a warmer sun and a milder climate or by the pursuit of game, and stopping for years in some sheltered valley where hunting was good and enemies few.

These people were short but strong. They had straight black hair, high cheek bones, and brown eyes in slanting eye-sockets, like those of the Mongolians, while the color of their skin had a slight reddish tinge and varied greatly from light yellow to a dark brown.

Archaic pottery figures of the earliest dwellers in Mexico with slanting eye-sockets indicating Asiatic ancestry. Bodies are painted, and the woman with baby wears armlets. (From Tepic and Jalisco.)

Primitive, half-savage, still in the Early Stone Age, they kept pushing southward, ever southward, for the whole of five thousand years. By that time they had long since forgotten any connection their forebears had had with Asia. So many centuries of having to adapt themselves to conditions of living in America, conditions utterly different from those existing in Asia, had changed and altered them until they had become Americans, the original native Americans, with no memory of that country from which their ancestors had come. And all the great civilization which their descendants were to build up was developed without any contact with either Europe or Asia. It was created by these Indians alone, by their own great talents and abilities, a true American civilization, in contrast to the European culture which white men eventually transplanted to the New World.

Some time around the year 15,000 B. C., the earliest bands of these wanderers reached the highlands of Mexico, and following the usual custom, they settled down to remain there as long as the hunting was good. But on that pleasant plateau beneath great snow-capped volcanoes they made an important discovery. They found that grain was good to eat and that by planting seeds they could raise it. Thus agriculture began and with it the whole life of the people changed. No longer were they mere wandering hunters depending on chance for food. Now they became a settled people, tillers of the soil, with fields to be sown and harvests to be gathered. And as soon as they stopped their roving they began to want permanent homes, so they started building villages near the fields where they worked every day, making their houses of stones and clay.

Then came the most important discovery in the history of ancient America. Some inquiring tribesman, experimenting with seeds of different grains, united the seed of the plant called *teocentli* with that of an unknown grass and so developed maize or corn. From this discovery, which gradually spread to the other tribes, all the culture of the Indians arose. All their art and architecture, all their religion, science and learning were based on maize which was first developed in the highlands of Mexico.

Little pottery figurines of the now important goddess of fertility, naked or slightly clothed, and with elaborate headdress, much like similar Asiatic figures. (Amer. Mus. Nat. Hist.) See Vol. II, p. 241.

As maize became the common, life-sustaining food of the people, their manner of living changed again. Containers were necessary to keep the corn in storage until it was needed, so pottery was invented. Then other seeds and grains were experimented with until more than forty plants, utterly unknown in Europe and Asia, had been developed here. It is to these Indians that we owe pumpkins, squash, beans, corn, potatoes and tomatoes. They learned, also, the use of cotton, how to make it into thread and weave the thread into cloth. Thus they could at last secure even their clothing from the soil and were no longer obliged to go out and hunt wild beasts in order to have their skins to wear.

With all these changes, interest in the forces of nature on which the people were dependent for raising sufficient crops, created new explanations, new beliefs concerning the gods. Most important to the growing of maize was fertility and germination, and the goddess of fertility was now worshiped with renewed devotion. Having learned how to mould and bake clay for pottery, the people moulded little images of the goddess of fertility, showing her naked but with a most elaborate headdress or turban, and with hands upon knees, hips, or breasts. These little figures were only from two to five inches high, but whether the goddess was represented as standing or sitting, all were carefully painted to give them the color of flesh. Countless numbers of these images were made from clay, and the people even tried a crude kind of sculpture on stones whose natural shape somewhat resembled a human figure.

Many were the prayers that arose to the fertility goddess when the seed had been placed in the earth, but as the tiny green shoots broke the surface of the ground, the help of other forces of nature must, likewise, be sought. Then prayers arose to the rain god, the sun god, and the wind god. All these gods of agriculture had now become especially important; images were made to represent them; they were worshiped with prayer and offerings, and new rites and ceremonies were invented to please them and persuade them to be kind.

When food thus grew more plentiful, families grew larger and the land became more thickly settled. The people lived in one-room huts, rectangular or round, made of saplings and branches bound together with fiber vines, and sometimes coated with clay. Roofs were thatched with layer upon layer of thick, broad leaves, and these simple shelters were all that was needed in the pleasant semi-tropical climate of the Mexican highlands. The maize fields lay round about on all sides of the huts which were grouped together for companionship and security, and the men, when not working in the fields, spent their time idling, experimenting with painted designs upon pottery, moulding new forms, chipping stones for spear points and cutting out great knobbed war clubs. They discovered how to make sounds from flutes and learned the intoxicating effect of rhythm sounded by drums, thus adding music to their religious ceremonies. The women used their spare time in weaving, and many became so expert that they could make a wonderfully soft and fine cotton cloth in which they wove brilliantly colored geometric designs.

Designs woven into garments by earliest dwellers on the Mexican highlands showing great variety and skill. (Copied from figurines.)

For the first time since man had lived in America, all of life was not spent in a constant struggle for mere existence.

Gradually a priest class arose. Certain men with quick minds learned easily the prayers required by the gods, and some few there were whose chanting of ceremonies seemed to be more pleasing to the mysterious powers of the universe, and to bring better results on earth. Such men were greatly respected, their advice was sought, and soon the priests became the rulers of the people.

Priests and gods were good to the dwellers on the highlands. They had leisure and freedom from want, and in order to show their gratitude, they banded together and erected a

Figure, possibly an early priest, with curly beard, tall, conical hat, and elaborate woven garment. (From a grave, Jalisco.)

pyramid to bear a temple to their gods. This earliest pyramid in America, known as the Pyramid of Cui-cuil'co, is still standing near the town of Tlal-pam', about twelve miles south of Mexico City. When it was completed, it was fifty-two feet high, and measured four hundred twelve feet around the base. It was a solid mass of heaped-up earth, and its sides were faced with uncut pieces of stone. The temple was built upon a flat, stone paved platform at the top, and had the same form as the ordinary dwellings. And here, amid much blowing of flutes and pounding of drums, the images of the gods were installed.

For thousands of years the people lived happily in the highlands, farming their fields, developing the maize plant, and worshiping their gods. Not far from the pyramid and temple, their priests and most important families were buried in a prehistoric cemetery. Just under the surface, in a layer of coarse gravel, their skeletons have been found surrounded by bowls, pots, and dishes of baked clay, knives of volcanic glass, and little baked clay figures, some undoubtedly supposed to represent gods buried with the dead to guide and protect them in the next world, others probably intended to be portraits of the buried person.

Portrait figures of the dead, and images of the gods, with turbans or headdresses of the Archaic Civilization, buried in the cemetery near the Pyramid of Cui-cuil'co and preserved in the lava.

But when many thousands of years had passed here in the Mexican highlands, some of the people of this Archaic Civilization moved. Their priests had learned from other bands of similar folk living in the lowlands to the east on the Gulf of Mexico, that there the climate was warmer and the maize crops greater, and many were eager to try this more favored land. After they had gone, a volcano, ten miles away, let loose a flood of lava which encircled the now deserted temple pyramid, burying its base and covering the neighboring cemetery, so that both have been preserved exactly as they were left by the people.

Coast Dwellers

The travelers were delighted with their new homes on the east coast. Here the climate was warm and caressing, the sun shone brilliantly, the soil was rich and fertile, rainfall was plentiful, and the planted maize grew luxuriantly. Truly, this was a delightful land, a land of no grief or trouble, and so happy were they at finding it, that "no grief" was the name they henceforth called themselves. In their language *Ma* meant *no* or *not*, and *ya* meant *grief* or *trouble;* Ma'ya, therefore, was the word they used to describe themselves, and Mayas they and their neighbors have been called since that time.*

Maya is pronounced mä'yä: Not all authorities of Ancient America admit that the Mayas came to the east coast of Mexico from the highlands, whither they had journeyed from the north. Dr. Sylvanus G. Morley, of the Carnegie Institute believes that the Mayas were the original people on the east coast, coming directly from the north. To this theory J. Eric Thompson, of the Field Museum, Chicago, agrees. Dr. Herbert J. Spinden, of the Brooklyn Museum does not commit himself. The outline here given is advanced by Dr. Thomas Gann, of the British Museum, in *The History of the Maya*, p. 10, and is followed because it seems to be logically correct and can be supported by a number of reasons, especially by the general agreement regarding the development of the maize plant on the highlands of Mexico.

Pottery figurines, probably of the goddess of fertility. These figures, from Nicaragua and Panama, were made when maize was carried to these regions by migrating tribes. (Amer. Mus. of Nat. Hist.)

This march from the highlands of Mexico to the low east coast near the Pa-nu'co River Valley was possibly taken some time around the years 3000 B.C. or 2000 B.C. The Ma'yas found the land thickly covered with a jungle growth of trees, vines and bushes, which had to be cut, stacked, dried, and burned before the fields were clear enough for planting. When this had been done, the farmers passed over the cleared places with a bag of maize seed and a planting stick. Loosening the earth in a circle with their sticks, they made a hole in the center, dropped in a few grains of maize, and covered them by kicking up the loosened earth in a little hill. Not one of the people of Ancient America knew about the plough; everywhere, throughout the vast continents wherever agriculture spread, the planting stick was always used.

Having even more leisure here than they had had on the highlands, the Mayas now devoted themselves to improving their carving and weaving. No longer content to select soft stones with a natural resemblance to the human figure, they experimented upon wood and other substances. Soon a very hard, rare stone known as jadite became their most valuable material, and men worked for months with sharp pieces of flint, fashioning jadite and other more common stones. Meanwhile, the priests, the most intelligent people of the Mayas, turned their thoughts to a study of the sun, the seasons, and the heavens. Agriculture was the very life of the people; if, by study, they could learn the will of the gods of earth, sky, and water, they would know exactly the right time for planting the maize, they would know when to expect rain; they would live and work in harmony with the gods.

Soon questions arose among the priests. They had known for years, of course, that the sun rose and set each day, that the moon waxed and waned at certain periods; but now they learned that the sun had still another movement, that an evening star shone in the west and a morning star in the east. And then the questions the priests asked themselves were, How long was the year, or the revolution of the earth about the sun? How long the waxing and waning of the moon? How long shone the morning star and the evening star? Some system of mathematics or counting was necessary before these questions could be answered, and some method of writing must be found before they could be recorded. So the priests turned their thoughts to counting and writing, and among the Mayas on the east coast of Mexico, there was developed sometime before the year 613 B.C., an accurate method of recording dates and events. Steadily the Mayas were advancing to a high state of civilization.

But again there was a movement of people. The coast plains were becoming crowded; families grew rapidly with peace and plenty, and more and more fields were needed to support them. Among the priests there had grown up an adventurous, inquiring spirit, a desire to explore and to learn. The southland called to all the more active and intelligent, the warm, luxuriant southland where the gods smiled kindly, and maize grew luxuriantly. And so began again the journey to the south.

Travel was slow, and many and long were the halts of the migrating Mayas. When their supply of maize ran low, they stopped, cleared the forest of tree and bush, planted new fields, and waited for the harvest. Every halting place meant a stay of at least two years. But there was no hurry; life was easy and simple, and everyone was content. Babes were born, grew to manhood, married, had children of their own, and were buried on this long, leisurely search for a new home. In the year 100 B.C., the travelers arrived in the neighborhood of what is now Vera Cruz. Here some one among them lost a prized possession, a little jadite statuette carved into the figure of a Buddha-like priest wearing a penguin skin. Safe and secure in its hiding place, the lost treasure lay unseen until a few years ago when its discovery told that the ancient Maya had passed this way one hundred years before the birth of Christ.

Steadily the journey southward continued. The attraction of unknown places, the charm of the southland still beckoned, and the generations that had grown up on the journey knew no other life. The priests, however, knew that greater progress in agriculture, learning, and the arts could only come with settlement, and as the people continued to travel through forest and swamp, they began searching at last for a permanent stopping place.

The Mayas had undoubtedly followed the coast line, and passed through what is now Mexico into British Honduras when the march was all at once turned inland to Gua'te-ma'la. And there at last, on a small hill beside a water hole in the dense forest, they established the city

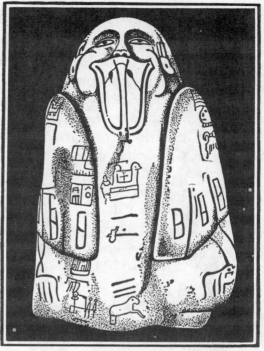

Jadite statuette of a Maya priest wearing a penguin skin found at Vera Cruz and bearing a date corresponding to 100 B.C. Dr. Herbert J. Spinden, the first thorough student of the Maya calendar, has shown that this calendar originated some time before 613 B.C., when the Greeks were just beginning to settle in city-states and Italy was controlled by the Etruscans. The Mayas, however, must have been developing a high civilization for many centuries before this time in order to work out such a complicated thing as a calendar, and to make it the most accurate the world has ever known.

known as Uaxactun (Wah-shack-toon'). Here a stone column was carved, bearing the date 68 A.D. If this marked the time of their arrival, one hundred and sixty-eight years had been spent in making the journey from Vera Cruz and some two hundred and fifty years had passed since they left the Panuco Valley; but since the date-column had been cut from a still older stone, their arrival was undoubtedly somewhat earlier. The year 68 A.D. is, nevertheless, the first definitely known date to mark the beginning of the Maya Old Empire in the south.

The Old Empire in the South

In the lush, green lowlands of Central America, the Mayas quickly developed a civilization that in sculpture, art, and astronomy placed them high among the nations of the world. All worked together under the direction of the priests, and the life-giving maize grew so abundantly that there was time for everyone to think of making the finer things that satisfied their inner craving for beauty and improvement. The region was rich in limestone, easily carved when wet, and this was at once seized upon to pave the hill and adorn it with stone temples, plazas, open courts, monuments, and dwelling places.

He who stood on the hill had a magnificent view of city and countryside: below was a circle of thatched houses; beyond lay a green ring of maize; and then came the deep, dark, encircling forest.

Here the Mayas lived for more than five hundred years; and in these long centuries of peace and plenty, certain customs, habits, and ways of living developed which set them apart from all other settled people.

Elaborate stone Temple of the Cross at Pa-len'que, Central America, an impressive, richly adorned pyramid temple with ornate, false roof. (Reconstruction, National Museum, Washington, D. C.)

Interior of the stone palace at Pa-len'que. Long, narrow rooms, with high vaulted ceilings and walls, adorned with intricate stucco reliefs surround an open court. (Reconstruction after Maudsley.)

The usual clothing for men was sandals of hide and a waist-girdle which passed between their legs and hung down back and front. The ends were elaborately embroidered with colored threads or feather mosaic work, and so also was a kind of square mantle worn draped over the shoulders. Men of wealth and position wore more elaborately decorated clothing, and, in addition, they decked themselves with feather mosaic headdresses, armlets and leglets, jade breast-ornaments and belts, necklaces of engraved stone, and sandals studded with jade.

The feather headdress was a sign of rank and was made of the brilliant plumage of the quetzal bird found only in the highlands of Guatemala. Cloaks of feathers were also worn at special ceremonies, and Maya craftsmen created marvelous masterpieces of color and design.

Other forms of ornament which the Mayas delighted to wear were nose, lip, and ear plugs. Both men and women wore these, and the wealthy people had them made of precious jade, most elaborately carved. The poorer people who could not afford jade or were not permitted to wear it, had to content themselves with common plugs of pottery, painted with elaborate designs. Tattooing was common among them, and on special occasions the men painted faces and bodies red.

Maya women in usual costume of a skirt from waist to ankles, carrying their babies with elongated skulls on their backs. (Dresden Codex.)

Women ordinarily wore only a skirt from waist to ankles. The upper part of their bodies was tattooed or stamped with paint by clay seals. Sometimes they, too, painted themselves red; and, in addition anointed themselves with sweet-smelling salves. Children went naked until they were four or five years old, but a few days after birth when their skulls were still soft, their heads were bound between two boards so that they would grow upward in the shape of a sugar loaf. Another mark of beauty to the Mayas was squinting, and a small object was often tied to the hair of a child so that it would hang down between the eyebrows and so cause a squint. Hair on the face, however, was considered ugly, and mothers often scalded the faces of their sons with hot cloths to prevent the hair from growing.

One of the greatest delights of the Mayas was dancing. It was the men alone, however, who did most of the dancing; for women held a much lower position than men. Women were not permitted to attend the big feasts in the temples; they even ate apart from their husbands at home; and when a woman met a man coming along a path, she would step off, modestly turning her back until he had passed.

Maya woman kneeling before a god. (Yaxchilan.) Her ceremonial robe is richly embroidered in geometric designs and has a short tasseled fringe.

As always, however, woman was the homemaker among the Mayas. It was she who prepared and cooked the maize. It was she who shelled the ear, placed the grains in a solution of lime and water over night, cleaned and ground them between rubbing-stones in the morning, and baked the maize meal into round cakes. It was she who invented new maize dishes and combined the meal with meat, beans, or calabash seeds.

Meat for the Maya family. Left, a turkey caught in a trap; right, hunter bringing home a deer he has shot. (Troano-Cortesianus Codex.)

The Mayas also raised sweet potatoes, tomatoes, squashes, and beans, and had plums and pears for fruit. For meat, they hunted the wild boar and deer, raised a breed of dogs for eating, tamed the wild turkey or kept herds of deer. On ceremonial occasions they used a drink called *balche*, made from honey of a stingless bee, kept in long wooden tubes as hives; but their favorite beverage was cocoa, spiced with chili.

With such abundance ever at hand, families increased rapidly; and the population was still further enlarged by other bands of archaic people from the highlands of Mexico. In wider and wider circles stretched the growing fields of maize about the temples of Ua-xac-tun', and soon the priests ordered the founding of another city.

Maya priest in feather headdress and elaborate costume in a ceremonial sowing of maize. (A sculpture in relief from Pi-e'dras Neg'ras.)

Main plaza of the city of Tik'al, founded after Ua-xac-tun' became too large. Tikal became the most important of all Maya cities in the south, and had nearly a hundred pyramid temples and public buildings of stucco-covered limestone. In this reconstruction from the Buffalo Museum of Science, a religious ceremony is in progress and a long procession of priests is climbing a temple pyramid.

Fifteen miles to the southeast of Ua-xac-tun', there grew up the city of Tik'al, afterward to become the largest and most important of all Maya centers in the south. The earliest date recorded here was 185 A.D. From Uaxactun and Tikal came other cities, and as these increased in size, they, too, aided in founding new centers until the region was swarming with a host of busy, thriving places of trade and learning. Cities arose not by tens and twenties, but by hundreds; all were independent, ruled by their own priests, but all formed a kind of loose confederation.

Of all Mayan cities in the south, Co-pan' in Hon-du'ras, three hundred miles from Uaxactun, was by far the most magnificent. Here streets, courts, and courtyards were paved with stone or cement; a drainage system ran underneath the buildings; and in the very center of the plain was a great temple plaza, placed so that it faced the four points of the compass, carved and painted with human and grotesque figures, designs of feathers and hieroglyphic writing. Many of the most beautiful statues and sculptures of the Old Empire were erected here.

Ua-xac-tun', in addition to its stone paved capital with the magnificent array of temples, courts, and monuments, had, to the east, a second group of stone buildings and altars raised on great pyramids and all grouped around a large central court. Here the whole arrangement of pyramid, court, and temples was a huge sun dial. Daily astronomer-priests mounted to the top of the pyramid to watch the sun rise behind three temples opposite and from the relation of sun to pyramids, they determined the solstices and equinoxes which marked the seasons.

Each of the three temples contained a rectangular, hollow stone altar in which people and priests placed beautiful objects of jade and pottery as offerings to the gods. Here, too, were performed human sacrifices to these lords of the universe. Held firmly by lesser priests, the human victim was placed so that his body lay over the hollow altar, then with quick stabbing slashes, the breast was pierced with a sharp stone knife, the heart was torn out, and the thirsty gods drank of the sacrificial blood.

Beautiful white stone terraced pyramid adorned with great carven faces at Uaxactun. From the top of this pyramid the priests of the Old Empire determined the solstices and equinoxes by noting the position of the sun over the three small pyramids at the rear. (Largest pyramid from a photograph.)

Intricate sculptured relief from the Temple of the Foliated Cross, Pa-len'que. The cross itself represents the maize plant and the face of the maize god may be seen carved upon it. Two priests, beautifully carved in profile, make an offering. The border is formed of glyphs or word-signs. (Maudsley.)

Pi-e'dras Neg'ras and Pa-len'que, founded somewhat later than Co-pan', were especially famous for their sculptures. The most perfect statues, reliefs, and ornamental decorations of the splendid Maya civilization adorned these cities. Sculptural decoration was used everywhere; in the interior of buildings, along the facade outside, on altars and carved slabs of stone called stelae; and all this splendor of sculpture was developed from that slightly raised work which is called relief. In showing figures in profile, that is, in complete sideview, or in representing the human body in three-quarters view, Mayan skill was almost perfect. But the decorative use of relief sculpture caused the body to become simply a part of an ornamental pattern covered with scrolls and hieroglyphs and it is difficult to separate it and to observe the perfection of its form. At Pi-e'dras Neg'ras and Palenque, however, the Mayan artist succeeded in producing entire sculptured figures standing out in the round, almost completely free from the block of stone, although one of the most perfect and beautiful of these sculptures is combined with a less-important figure in relief.

These magnificent cities with their massive stone temples, spacious courts, and broad plazas, erected at the cost of infinite patience and labor, all showed how very important religion was in the life of the Mayas. The Mayas believed that there was a constant, unending struggle between the gods of life and the powers of darkness. Although a certain good god might watch over a tender young tree and care for it, just behind him, awaiting his opportunity, lurked an evil god ready to root up the tree and destroy it. So it was all through life; and all the many religious ceremonies were performed either to keep the evil gods from causing trouble, or to praise the good gods so that they would not forget their most faithful worshipers.

A priest in feather headdress and long robes worships before a figure of a god; one of the finest Maya stelas, combining the flat of relief-carving and the round of sculpture, the sitting figure being so rounded as to stand out almost free from the stone. (Piedras Negras.)

It'zam-na, chief of gods and creator of all things, represented as a wrinkled old man with only one tooth. (Dresden Codex.)

Chief of the gods was It'zam-na, the creator and father of all, the inventor of writing, the founder of Mayan civilization, and the god of life and light. He was represented as an old man with a high forehead and a prominent beak-like nose. His face was wrinkled, his mouth had only one tooth, and sometimes he was shown with a beard. The sun-god had a wife who was the moon. Once she was as bright as the sun; but then people complained that they could not sleep because there was no darkness at any time on the earth. So the sun, quite willing to help them, promptly attended to the matter by plucking out one of his wife's eyes! Since then the moon has not shone as brilliantly, people can sleep undisturbed, and all are satisfied!

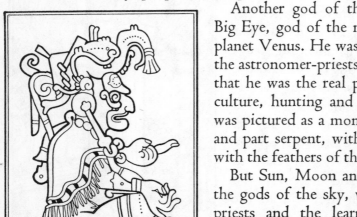

The Sun God, closely associated with the creator god because the sun brought life and growth to all things. (Dresden Codex.)

Another god of the sky was Lord Big Eye, god of the morning star, the planet Venus. He was the great god of the astronomer-priests, and they taught that he was the real protector of agriculture, hunting and fishing. Big Eye was pictured as a monster, part dragon and part serpent, with a body covered with the feathers of the quetzal bird.

But Sun, Moon and Morning Star, the gods of the sky, were gods of the priests and the learned people; the farmers and peasants had their own special earth-gods who were not so distant and remote, but were nearer and dearer to them, and more comforting.

Although there were great numbers of these earth-gods, four principal ones were especially important as the gods of the directions, and each had its own particular color: red for the north, white for the south, yellow for the east, and blue for the west. All the earth-gods were called *Mam*, meaning "grandfather," for the earth was old. It had been from the beginning, and the earth-gods were old too, old in years and wisdom. They were the grandfathers, and looked after their grandchildren, the people of the soil. They sent the crops; they watched over the animals in the forest and permitted

Yum Kaax, Lord of the Harvest, bearing a maize plant, one of the most important gods and most kindly. (Dresden Codex.)

their grandchildren to hunt them. They were kind gods who were good to the people, only asking prayer and incense in return for blessings.

The earth-gods were also gods of rain and thunder and lightning. They sent the rains to nourish the crops, and when, as sometimes happened, they were angry, they hurled their thunderbolts from the mountain tops. As gods of the rain, the earth-gods were called *Chacs* and the Mayas pictured them as holding a small calabash of water, a bag containing wind, and a drum. From his calabash of water, the Chac sprinkled rain on the earth; opening his bag, he let out the wind and forced it back again; he caused the thunder by beating his drum. The Chac of the south was considered unlucky and a death-dealer.

The Death God, *Chac* of the south, a skeleton figure who sent the hot, parching winds from the south. (Dresden Codex.)

The Maize God, an exquisitely sculptured bust of a young man, wearing the maize plant as a headdress. (Copan.) The prayer to the earth gods on this page is a modern Maya prayer; no ancient prayers exist, but this short simple plea is undoubtedly of ancient origin.

As they were the gods of the soil, a simple prayer to them was made when the forest was felled to prepare the land for sowing. "O God, my mother, my father," chanted the Maya farmer. "Huitz-Hok, Lord of Hills and Valleys, Che, Lord of Forests, be patient with me for I am about to do as my fathers have ever done. Now I make my offering to you that you may know that I am about to trouble your very soul; but suffer it, I pray you. I am about to dirty you, to destroy your beauty. I am going to work you that I may obtain my daily bread. I pray you suffer no animal to attack, nor snake to bite me. Bid the trees that they fall not upon me, and suffer not the axe or knife to cut me."

Beloved by both priests and people was the maize god. Sculptures and pictures showed him as a handsome young man wearing a growing maize plant as his headdress, and there were countless representations of this favorite deity in all cities of the Maya Empire of the south. He was Yum Kaax, lord of the harvest fields and god of agriculture. But by himself the beautiful god was helpless; he was at the mercy of the gods who controlled the rain and the drought; most often he was under the protection of the rain god, but at times he suffered persecution by the god of death who controlled drought and famine.

The Mayas believed in a future life beyond the grave where each was rewarded or punished according to his life on earth. Evil-doers were condemned to the underworld called Metnal and ruled by Ah Puch, god of death. Metnal was a dank, gloomy cold spot and existence there was endless. Those who had led good lives on earth went to a heaven where there was feasting and dancing, rest and enjoyment in the shade of an enormous tree. Suicides also went to heaven and were greatly respected, being under the guidance of a special goddess.

But although all these gods were important and controlled the life of man on earth, they did not explain how man had been created nor tell about the earth on which he lived. These were questions which troubled the Mayas as they did all peoples and the following tale arose.

An offering to the Sun God, represented by a carved shield. (Temple of the Sun, Palenque.) The priest at right is considered the most perfect figure in Maya sculpture for his dignity of pose, and treatment of shoulders in profile. The lower figures in three-quarters view are also perfectly carved.

The Story of Creation

The earth was once a huge cube covered with water, and at the four points of the compass, which were its four corners, there were the legs of the great vase which was the sky. In this vase grew the Tree of Life, and the flowers of this tree were the souls of men which entered into the bodies of the people as they were created. Above hung heavy clouds carrying those rains on which all growth and life depended. Here the creator gods, the *Mams*, assembled. The world existed, but there was no light or life so long as the surface of the earth was completely covered with water. So the gods took council with one another, and after long deliberation, decided upon creation. "Earth!" they cried, and the earth appeared. Out of the waters it raised itself up. Then the creator gods formed mountains and valleys, plants, animals and birds.

Unfortunately, the birds and animals could not speak to thank their creators nor praise them, and after one blunder the gods made a race of men of wood. The wooden men, however, were irreverent and mischievous, and in despair, the gods caused a flood to destroy them. Birds attacked the wooden men, eating their bodies and tearing out their eyes; even the dogs turned on their former masters to kill them.

Glyphs, or word and numeral signs which formed the written language of the ancient Mayas. (Copan.) The Maya Story of Creation is from Villacorta, A., and Rodas, F. *Manuscrito de Chichicastanango* (*Popol Vuh*) a collection of myth, legend and history of the Qui-ches', a Maya tribe of Guatemala, written before the coming of the Spaniards and translated into Spanish shortly after the Conquest (1521) by a native who had learned from Spanish priests how to write the Mayan language with European characters. It is interesting to note that all the primitive races of man, in all parts of the world, have creation myths and flood myths which bear a striking similarity. See Vols. I and II for Egyptian, Babylonian and Hebraic stories; Vols. III and IV for Greek and Roman stories; Vol. V, p. 215f. for Norse tales, and Vol. VII, p. 140f. and p. 185f. for Chinese and Japanese stories.

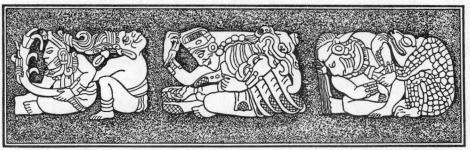

The glyph figures show typically clothed Mayas in various poses and attitudes, and mythological beasts. The men are not priests, but common people without elaborate ceremonial garments. (Copan.)

The wooden men fled to the house tops and climbed the trees, but the flood swept up and the few who escaped became small monkeys, the ancestors of those that play today in the forests of Guatemala.

Now after the flood, there lived a terrible being known as Vu-kub Cak'ix, whose body was made of gold, silver, and precious stones. He was boastful and irreverent, and the gods sent to earth to deal with him two divine brothers, Hun-a-pu' and Xba-lan'que. Hunapu, who afterward became the sun god, found the monster in a nance tree and shot him in the mouth. Vukub Cakix was only injured, however, and falling from the tree, he rushed upon the brothers to slay them. In the struggle, he tore off the arm of the youth who had shot him, and immediately strode home with it to his wife who withered it over a fire, chanting spells against the young hero, hoping to cause his death.

In order to recover the arm, the two brothers now joined two sorcerers, and seeking their enemy in disguise, they offered to cure his damaged mouth. Delighted at the hope of relief, the monster willingly submitted to the cure which they prescribed, but as soon as they had the monster down on his back and tied, they removed his teeth and put out his eyes, and this at last caused his death. Then the hero hunted up his arm, fixed it in position, and was again sound and whole.

But though the dread being was dead, he left behind two sons who were determined to destroy the slayers of their father. These two sons, were giants, terrific earthquake gods. The divine brothers, therefore, decided to build a strong house as a retreat and fortress against them.

With the aid of a number of youths, they were busy dragging along a very heavy tree trunk to set up in a hole which they had dug for a corner post, when they fell in with Zi-pac'na, one of these terrible giants. The giant offered to help them and the youths persuaded him to get down into the hole. Then they threw logs down on him until they thought he was dead. The giant was in fact still alive, but in order to make the youths believe that they had killed him, he gave some of his hair and nail-parings to the ants to take up to the surface of the earth. Seeing these, the youths, indeed, believed him dead and prepared a great feast of rejoicing. But in the midst of the feast, the giant caused a mighty earthquake which hurled all the youths into the sky where they became the loose cluster of stars known as the Pleiades. Only the two divine heroes, Hunapu and his brother, escaped his rage unharmed.

Foiled in this first attempt to destroy the earthquake giant, the brothers learned that Zipacna was very fond of crabs, and at once they made an enormous clay crab which they placed in a large cave under a mountain. When the giant sought the crab, the brothers threw down the mountain, turned him to stone, and so destroyed him. The other giant they killed by means of a fowl baked in poisoned mud.

Thus the metal monster and his sons, the earthquake giants, were destroyed, but still the world was without people. Once more the creator gods assembled to make men to praise them. "They made their flesh," said the legend, "of the produce of the yellow and white cobs of maize, and their arms and legs they made from the cobs themselves. These were our forefathers. Four in number were the men whom they created."

These new beings were intelligent, they spoke and acted with reason; but then the gods decided that they were too intelligent; they knew as much as their creators! Accordingly, to remedy this, "they covered their eyes with a cloth by order of the Heart of Heaven, covering them as the breath covers the surface of a mirror. Thus their eyes became clouded and they could only see what was near them." Afterward, causing a deep sleep to fall on the four men, the gods created four women from them. Then, at last, the sun rose, for until this time the world had been in darkness. And thus was created the world and all things on it.

Ceremonies and Customs

Such was the story of creation told to the Mayas by their priests and the Mayas believed it implicitly; for they were deeply religious and loved and honored their priests above all other people.

There were countless priests in all the cities of the Empire, and it was the priests who were the real rulers of the people. If the Mayas had been a war-like race, or compelled to fight other tribes to gain or keep their homes, the nobles would have become the leaders of the army and made themselves chieftains and kings. But the Mayas did not love warfare; in all the sculptured monuments and decorations of the Old Empire there were almost no battle scenes. Thus the priests remained the rulers not only of the common people but also of those wealthy farmers, manufacturers, and merchants.

The chief priest was known as the Ah Kin Mai. This position was kept in his family, and he was succeeded in it by a son or very near relative. A man held in high esteem, he rarely went abroad except in a litter, and he was called upon to preside only at very special functions. His most important duty was to teach the second sons of the nobility who entered the priesthood.

Monolithic monument nearly 20 ft. high, formed into a sculptured figure of a stately dignified priest. Erected in 232 A.D.

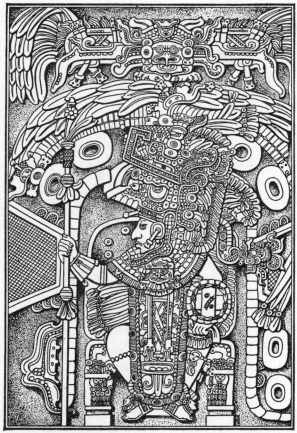

Chief priest, wearing a most elaborate feather headdress, and clothed in an embroidered garment reaching to his feet. He wears ear ornaments, armlets, leglets and sandals. (Tikal.)

Below Ah Kin Mai were the regular priests, known as *Chilans*, whose special duties were to preside at the sacrifices, interpret the wishes of the gods, and serve as doctors to the people. The *Nacons* tore out the hearts of the victims on the altar of sacrifice and served as military leaders; the commander of the fighting forces, being elected from among them; and the *Chacs* were other priests who assisted at the many sacrifices.

Human beings were sacrificed to the gods only at a few special ceremonies among the Mayas of the Old Empire; the most common sacrifices were animals, birds, fruits, deer, turkeys, dishes of maize and seed, or dogs bred especially for eating, a great luxury with the people and particularly pleasing to the gods. Each man offered according to his wealth and rank. A wealthy person was expected to offer his prized jade ornaments, but a poor man would make a simple offering of maize. All sacrifices were accompanied by the burning of copal incense or acacia gum, and the priest who presided was gorgeous in feathered headdress, square shoulder-mantle, girdle of cotton, elaborately embroidered, and decorated sandals.

An especially powerful sacrifice was that of the worshiper's own blood. This was secured by piercing the tongue, ear, or limbs, and passing a cord through the wound. Sometimes thorns were attached to the cord to make the wound bleed more freely, and such human blood, willingly given, when presented to the image of the god, was sure to influence that being favorably toward the one who made the sacrifice.

All religious ceremonies were not sacrifices, however; certain days and nights, held sacred to special gods, were celebrated with dif-ferent rites. New Year ceremonies were impor-tant because the fortune to be experienced dur-ing the year depended greatly on their proper performance. Fasting for this great occasion began long before the end of the old year, the last five days of which were considered ex-tremely unlucky. Since the year was divided into eighteen months of twenty days each with a total of three hundred and sixty days, a little five day month had to be added to complete the year. No work was undertaken then that could possibly be avoided, and neither men nor women went out of doors save to pray.

A blood sacrifice. Kneeling before a priest, bearing a feath-ered staff of office, the worshiper, clad in his most valued finery and prized embroidered costume, pricks his tongue with thorns inserted in a rope so that drops of his own blood may be offered to please the gods (Stone Lintel, Menche.)

New Year ceremonies. The statue of the presiding god being carried in procession through the streets of the city by a priest in a fierce animal mask.

On the first day of the month Pop, that is July sixteenth, the new year began for the Mayas. An image of the god of the old year was carried through the city, sacrifices and blood offerings were then made to it and the image of the god of the new year was carried to the east entrance to watch the city. On New Year's Day, likewise, the houses were cleaned and all household possessions renewed. Plates, beds, and mats were taken outside the city and thrown away so that none of the evil of the old year might remain. Even the temple utensils were removed and destroyed. Then wearing new garments, and with bodies painted red, all the men flocked to the main temple to witness the kindling of the sacred fire, which had been extinguished for the dying year.

During the first month of the year, the priests forecast the weather and made other prophecies concerning good and bad fortune, and all the people gathered in the city square to hear these read from the temple. Later in the year there was a feast held by hunters to the gods of the chase, a feast by fishermen to the gods of the waters, a celebration of the bee-keepers, and a very important festival in honor of all the gods when everything, from costly temple bowl to humble house broom, was painted blue.

The statue of the old-year god having been placed at the south entrance, opposite an image of the god of the new year, solemn sacrifices are made.

This was the time, too, when new idols were carved from wood by consecrated artists.

Many, likewise, were the ceremonies held in honor of the Chacs, the earth gods, and at one such feast, held by the older people to insure good rains and a good harvest, a great bundle of dried sticks was heaped in the central court of the temple. After incense had been burned, the bundle was lighted, and as soon as the flames mounted

God of the New Year before a pillar representing the five evil days of the Old Year. (All illustrations of the New Year ceremonies from Dresden Codex.)

high, the people began throwing into it the hearts of all the animals and birds they hunted or raised. If they had no hearts of certain wild animals, they made imitation hearts of copal to burn in the flames.

Two months later, the owners of cocoa plantations held a feast to their patron god, while warriors had their celebration in the following month of Pax. Then it was that Cit Chac Coh, the red mountain lion, the god of war, received honor. The commander of the fighters, the Nacon, was carried to the temple with great show, and offered gifts and incense as though he had been divine. For five days the ceremony lasted while the warriors feasted and danced war dances.

The day of birth was important, and the priests cast a horoscope to tell how the whole future life of the infant must be controlled and governed.

Priests performing upon musical instruments, before an altar. The queer curly-cues issuing from the instruments indicate sound. (Dresden Codex.)

Priest in enormous feather headdress and elaborate ceremonial costume standing before worshipers. Note the numerous masks. (Palenque.)

From the cradle to the grave certain things must be avoided, certain things were lucky or unlucky according to his birthday. When a boy was four months old, he was led to a small tree and an ax was placed in his hand. Then an older person guided him so that he went through the motions of cutting down the tree. Afterward he was made to go through all the actions that a grown man would perform in his daily work. These ceremonies were supposed to have power to make him a good farmer and a hard worker when he was grown.

When children were about twelve years old, they took part in another rite, a baptism called "rebirth" in the Maya tongue. This was the occasion for a feast of the whole village or community. Each child old enough to be baptized came to the village priest in turn, and received from him a little ground maize and copal-incense which he threw into a brazier. When all had finished, the brazier was given to a man who carried it out of town and threw it away. Thus all evil inherent in the children was supposed to be taken out of them.

The priest then blessed the children and sprinkled them with water using a short carved stick from which hung the tails of rattlesnakes. After this, each father took a special bone and gave his child nine sharp taps on the forehead. Then the bone was dipped in a bowl containing a mixture of many different gay-colored wild flowers, ground cocoa, and water collected from the hollows of tree trunks, and this was rubbed on the child's face, and between his fingers and toes.

Finally, the priest cut the cord which held a special stone on the forehead of each child. This stone had been worn since babyhood and its removal meant that the children were accepted as men and women. The boys were now made to smell a special bouquet of flowers and were given tobacco to smoke while their parents brought them special dishes of food. In the evening there was a general feast for parents and children.

Following this "rebirth," the girls were free to marry, and the boys went to live in a large house which all the young unmarried men used for sports and as sleeping quarters. They were now men and could take wives unto themselves whenever they saw fit. After marriage, the young couple lived

Another priest in slightly different ceremonial costume with shoulder cape. All figures have the typical flattened Maya forehead. (Palenque.)

with the wife's parents for five or six years, while the husband paid for his wife by working for her father and only when this had been done were the young people permitted to set up housekeeping apart.

Life was fairly simple and easy to these people of the jungle in the days of the Old Empire and many Mayas turned from farming to other work. Great numbers became expert potters and, although they knew nothing of the potter's wheel, they made exquisitely proportioned tripod dishes, bowls, bottle-necked vessels, and cylindrical vases. These were all decorated with serpents, monkeys, jaguars, birds, priests, gods, or geometric designs. Often they painted a background orange or yellow in color and on this designs were outlined in black, the details being filled in with delicate reds, browns, or whites.

Astronomer-priests assembled at Co-pan'. From the altar recording a date which corresponds to September 2, 503 A.D.

Wool was unknown, but very beautiful fabrics were woven from cotton and from the fibers of sisal hemp, or agave, and cactus plants. The designs of these cloths were colorful and intricate, sometimes of diamond-shaped open work, and often embroidered in a great variety of patterns in which men, gods, animals, birds, fishes, flowers, and geometric figures appeared. Some were dyed red, blue, or yellow; and gorgeous feathers were often woven into them. The weavers even understood the making of brocades and lace, and made many beautiful and elaborate pieces.

So expert did the Mayas become in manufacture of pottery and cloth and in the production of cocoa that these articles were eagerly sought by other peoples. In the course of time, a merchant class of traders arose, and Maya products were carried to lands both north and south; the interior of Central America was crossed with a network of well known commercial roads, and great sailing canoes were built to carry goods along the sea coast. The merchants had their own god of trade and travel, and they banded together in guilds like the merchants of the Middle Ages to keep good standards of workmanship.

Meanwhile the priests were making progress along entirely different lines. The study of the heavens had always been considered a religious duty, and observatories had been built at Ua-xac-tun' and at Copan for study. From their study of the stars, the priests now learned that there had been an error in the calendar, and in September, 503 A.D., a great meeting of astronomers was held at the city of Copan to correct this mistake and change the date from September 9th to September 2nd. The calendar developed by the Maya priests was a wonderful thing, far more accurate than the calendar used in Europe at the same time, and even more exact than that used by the world today.

From this constant study of the heavens, the priests also figured out a zodiac to show the progress of certain planets from one position in the sky to another throughout the year. They learned how to predict eclipses of the sun and moon, and twenty-five eclipse dates were noted in forty different cities. Since the calendar had first been put in use eleven hundred years before, on August 6, 613 B.C., it was from this early date that the priests figured every important event. Time was marked off in units for easy measurement; twenty *kins*, or days made one *uinal*, or month; eighteen *uinals*, or three hundred and sixty days made one *tun*; twenty tuns made one *katun*, and twenty katuns were one *baktun*. Twenty was the unit in Maya mathematics instead of ten as in Europe, and was arrived at by counting both fingers and toes.

Magnificent stone lintel of buff-colored limestone from Pi-e'dras Neg'ras (about 750 A.D.). The sculptor has portrayed a religious ceremony with worshipers grouped around a deity kneeling upon a rectangular altar in the center. The delicately carved left hand of the god rests upon the edge of the altar, and the right arm, now missing, was probably raised. The swirl of the great plumed headdress is magnificent and the tasseled fringe of the altar is carefully shown. The group to the right probably consisted of four figures, two adults and two children. The poses are naturalistic, the feet being especially well carved. To the left is a group of three standing human figures in natural postures with hands crossed over the breast in the Maya gesture of reverence. Below the altar is a row of seven seated human figures, admirably carved in perfect proportions and in naturalistic poses. The hands, feet, and even the finger nails are excellently portrayed. One of the figures is holding his foot; most of the others hold jars, fans, or other objects. The border is composed of hieroglyphs and the lintel as a whole is one of the most perfect examples of Maya sculpture at its best, comparing favorably with Grecian sculpture in naturalness, grouping, and execution, and showing the heights of expression reached by a naturally artistic people entirely shut off from all outside stimulus or influence.

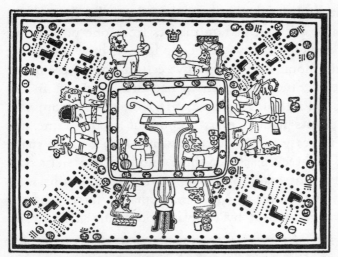

The Mayan Calendar. In the center is It-zam'na, God of the Sky, and his wife, under the heavenly tree. The band about them contains the 20 day signs of the month and the figures outside are in groups representing the four directions. At the top, or east, are Itzamna and his wife; at right, or north, is human sacrifice with the Death God and the War God. Other gods are in the remaining quarters and the border is composed of signs of the 260 day year. (Troano-Cortesianus Codex.) The Mayas also devised a calendar for their 360 day year.

When writing down their figures, the priests used dots in a row for the first four numbers, and a bar, or five dots run together, for the number five. By combining dots and bars, larger numbers were written. They invented ways of expressing zero which were in every day use in America at least five hundred years before the Hindus realized the need of the cipher and thought of a zero symbol for Asia and Europe.

Maya writing was ideographic, like the ancient Egyptian and Chinese. It developed from pictures used to express ideas or things, and a hieroglyph was used to represent each word. These hieroglyphs were written in books made of deer-skin or wood fiber; they were painted upon wooden posts and lintels; and were carved into stone monuments and buildings. Most of the books were lost, hidden away, or destroyed, and three alone are known today.* Sun and rain faded the paintings on wood; and only the stone carved inscriptions remain. Except for the dates on these monuments, the meaning of the hieroglyphs remains a mystery which hides the story of a wonderful race who developed a marvelous civilization in America thousands of years ago.

*These three remaining codices record astronomical and calendar calculations. The best preserved is the Dresden Codex which gives an account of the end of the world. It was written about 1000 A.D. and is now in the Public Library, Dresden, Germany. A more carelessly written codex is the Codex Peresianus, dating from shortly before the Spanish Conquest, and now in the Bibliotheque Nationale in Paris, France. The last codex, known as the Troano-Cortesian Codex, is poorly done and is now divided into two parts, each in a different museum in Spain.

The New Empire in Yucatan

For centuries the Mayas lived contentedly in the soft, abundant lands of the South. The jungle had been cleared of its dense, tropical growth, and now lay in planted fields of growing green that stretched mile after mile in all directions. Far flung cities, towns, and villages flourished on every side; lofty pyramid temples arose high above the thatched huts of the people, and great cities were adorned with stone-paved courts filled with elaborately carved monuments.

Thousands upon thousands of men, women, and children, priests, nobles, craftsmen, merchants, and farmers dwelt within the borders of the Old Maya Empire, and although they had nothing but stone tools to work with, they had gradually developed a remarkable civilization. Then suddenly, something happened. All at once they began to move. In the century between 530 A.D. and 629 A.D., group after group, in ever-increasing numbers, left their homes and their fields, their cities and their temples, and turning their backs on the wonderful civilization which they had been developing through many centuries, they now moved northward with their meager possessions into a wilderness of virgin forest.

A visit to a chieftain by a lower official, an exceedingly rare painting on an early Maya vase. (Nebaj.) The chieftain sits on a raised platform, and wears a headdress ending in a flower from which hangs a fish. The visitor offers a pouch containing copal incense. In the background are three attendants. There is no positive knowledge as to the real reason why the Mayas left Guatemala, and various archaeologists have advanced a number of theories including war, foreign invasion, intellectual and social exhaustion, pestilence, earthquake, religious reasons, and the exhaustion of the soil. Most students believe this last theory to be the most probable explanation of this mysterious abandonment.

The reason for this wholesale migration of a wealthy, civilized people was probably the exhaustion of the soil. The Maya method of burning the brush which covered the land led to the growth of such a thick, heavy sod that the tiny shoots of maize could hardly force their way through. Repeated crops of the same plants took from the land those foods needed to make bountiful harvests; and though the Mayas early formed the habit of allowing their fields to remain idle at certain seasons, there came a time when there was a steady lessening of the crops at each harvest time. And, to add to their discomfort, the climate changed. It became very much hotter, the rainy season was longer; and this caused the forest growth to climb so rapidly that it was more difficult than ever to keep the fields clear.

The priests urged the people to move to new lands and new homes. More than two hundred years before, groups of young, adventurous Mayas had left their homes in the region about Lake Peten and had moved northward into Yucatan; and now the leaders wanted others to go there also. Yucatan was not as fertile a land as Guatemala; it was dry, with a limestone soil, and it had very few rivers or lakes. Most of the low flat peninsula was undermined with subterranean streams; and it was only where the earth had caved in, leaving small wells open to the sky, that water could be drawn to the surface. Nevertheless, it was a new land with a soil that had never been planted, and any newcomers would find other Mayas living there to welcome them.

The earlier Mayan adventurers to Yucatan had been compelled to fight for their new homes there. There were Yucatecans already living in the land when the first Mayas appeared on the scene some time before 300 A.D.; and there were many years of bitter struggle before the invaders were able to establish themselves and live in peace. In time, however, small Mayan cities arose, Tu'lum on the eastern coast before 304 A.D., Ich-paa-tum' on the shores of Che'te-mal Bay where a stela was erected bearing the date 333 A.D.; there were settlements around Lake Coba, and at Ma-can-xoc'. Here were prosperous, happy Mayas who had developed into active, energetic pioneers, ready to fight for their lands, who would welcome their brethren from the south.

CITIES OF THE
ANCIENT CIVILIZATION
of the
MAYAS
IN CENTRAL
AMERICA

But the older Mayas objected. Living in the shadow of their great temples, surrounded by all the comforts of civilization, secure in the protection of their gods, rulers, and priests, they had no wish to leave peace and security and venture into the unknown wilderness of Yucatan. "Let well enough alone," they said. "True, our fields are no longer as fertile as they used to be, and our crops grow scantier year by year; but even so why change the surety, the convenience and comforts of life here for the known hardships and unknown terrors of those distant wilds?" Nevertheless, within a century, the last of the Mayas deserted the Southland, actually starved into movement.

Among the early groups of adventurers to the eastern coast of Yucatan, there had been a family or tribe, known as the It'zas. The name *Itza* meant *holy* in the Maya tongue, and many of the family were priests and learned men; but they were vigorous and active despite their priestly calling; and ever searching for more favorable lands, they moved west from around Coba and founded the city of Yax-hu'na about the year 350 A.D. Here they remained for a hundred years. But only ten miles north of the city, there were two large wells or *cenotes*; so, in 452 A.D., the Itzas moved to this spot and called their new home *Chi-chen' It'za*, which meant, "The mouths of the wells of the Itzas."

The two cenotes or wells of the new city were within a half mile of each other and were deep below the surface. They were simply great holes in the ground where the limestone crust had fallen through, opening some subterranean stream to the skies, and the largest was almost one hundred and fifty feet in diameter.

For two hundred and twenty years, the Itzas managed to exist at Chi-chen', but the struggle was hard and took most of their energies. The first settlement was made in the southern part of the present city, and over a hundred years passed before they were able to erect their first stone temples. These earliest buildings were different from those in the southern cities; the outer walls were built of shallow, evenly cut stones, smoothed level, and the decorations were carved on the stones before they were laid, after which they were fitted together like mosaics. The only remaining date of this early settlement appeared upon the door lintel of a small temple dedicated August 28, 619 A.D.

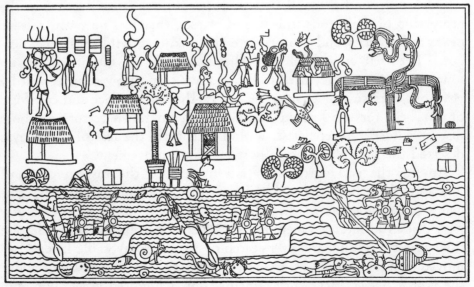

A Maya seacoast village having windowless, oval, white houses with blue doors and thatched roofs like modern Maya houses. Before the center house, fish are drying, elsewhere a woman watches a pot over a fire, another kneels to grind corn and men bear burdens on backs or heads. Boats paddled by naked oarsmen, bear warriors with shields and spears past fish, turtles, crabs and snails. (A fresco from Temple of the Warriors, Chichen, found on broken pieces of plaster and carefully reassembled.)

An attack on a Maya village by a rival Maya tribe. The ruler of the village is at lower right. There is great excitement in the village, and women with children or household possessions run between the huts while others sit numbly awaiting the outcome. (Fresco, The Temple of Tigers, Chichen.)

Possibly the city would have grown more rapidly now that massive stone buildings were being erected, but soon after 650 A.D., Chi-chen' It'za was abandoned by every one of its inhabitants. It was about this time that the Old Empire in the south was coming to an end, and among the many tribes or families who now made their way to Yucatan were the Xius, who at once began quarreling with the Itzas.

Whether this quarrel had been of old standing and the Itzas wished to avoid their ancient enemies, or whether their lands were beginning to fail and a long rest was needed; whatever the reason, Chichen was abandoned. The Xius settled near the Lake of Bak-hal'al on the eastern coast of Yucatan, and the Itzas moved to a city on the west coast.

But the Xius followed in the footsteps of the Itzas. They remained only a short time on the shores of Bakhalal, before they moved northward and took possession of the deserted city of Chichen. Even this could not satisfy them long; one hundred and twenty years later the spirit of restlessness seized them, and again they moved, following the Itzas to their new home on the coast. A truce was declared between the tribes, and for a time Itzas and Xius lived side by side in peace. Then suddenly, unexpectedly, the Xius rose against their enemies, seized **control** of the coast-town, and drove the Itzas from the land.

Yum Chac, the Rain and Thunder God, who dwelt at the bottom of the deep Sacred Well at Chi-chen'. (Dresden Codex.)

Expelled from their new home, the Itzas had nowhere to go. They "were under the trees, under the boughs, under the branches to their sorrow," reported the *Chronicle of Chilam Balaam*. Wandering in the wilderness for forty years, the Itzas now recalled the cool and refreshing wells of Chi-chen'. Like homing pigeons, they turned their steps thither and again settled in their ancient city in the year 964 A.D. Twenty-five years later the Xius also returned to a spot some distance west of Chichen and there began building a very beautiful city called Ux-mal'.

But before this had happened, Chichen had become the most important of all the cities of the New Maya Empire in Yucatan. The holy men had decided that Yum Chac, the Rain God, dwelt at the bottom of the largest well, and in this northern land the worship of the Rain God had become a far more important matter than it had ever been in the South. Pilgrims journeyed to the Sacred Well from near and far to offer their most prized possessions and to beg the Rain God to remember their fields and their harvests. Prisoners of war were sacrificed in its green depths, and Chichen became a holy city with the Itzas as its priests.

Many matters required the energy of more vigorous, active men, however, and no longer were priests the only important members of society, as they had been in the old days in Guatemala and the South. The Mayas had been compelled to fight for possession of Yucatan, and even after their settlement, there were frequent quarrels among the cities. Warriors, or fighting men, began to advance in power, and the most successful chieftains now became rulers called *baytabs*. Men told tales of the fighting *baytabs* which resounded with the ring of war.

A Tale of Canek the Chieftain

Now it happened that Canek, the eager young *baytab* of Chichen, was deeply in love with a beautiful maiden, the daughter of the ruler of a distant province. No longer were his thoughts on the coming hunt of the jaguar; the wild boar passed unnoticed and unharmed; a fawn, chased by the hunters, became snared close beside him, and seeing that its big, soft eyes were like those of his beloved, he set it free.

The days of the young ruler were filled with thoughts of love and longing. But one day as Canek sat in his chamber, a dusty runner came to the palace entrance and rattled the sounding shells before the curtains. Evil was his news; the powerful baytab of a neighboring province had taken that beloved maiden whom Canek so wished to wed.

For a while no raging jaguar robbed of his mate was more furious than the prince of the Itzas. Then, of a sudden, he grew quiet, cool and calm in manner as his warriors remembered him on days when he went into battle. With the coming of night came their orders. A storm was raging, and darkness surrounded the silent ranks of the swiftly marching warriors, though lightning played over the glinting points of the moving forest of spears as they neared the enemy's city.

Maya *baytab*, or chieftain, and his nobles in elaborate ceremonial war costumes. (Ball Court, Chichen.) *The Tale of Canek the Chieftain* was one of the best loved native legends gathered by a Spanish priest, Padre Cogolucco, who went to Yucatan immediately after the Spanish Conquest.

A chieftain of Chichen, such as Canek, with the head-dress of nobility, seated upon a jaguar throne, an indication of rulership. (Fresco, Temple of Warriors.)

There the ever-burning flames on the top of the temple gleamed redly, and black smoke went heavenward in increasing clouds as the priests burned great baskets of copal in honor of their ruler's marriage. The city was given over to revelry and feasting; even the watchers had drunk deep of intoxicating maize, and grumbled at the fate that kept them from the merry-making. They saw not Canek and his silent warriors as they came swiftly onward, melting into the darkness of the shadows, hiding from the lightning flash, and leaping ahead like deer when chance offered. Swiftly these black and moving shadows advanced, and sprang upon the watchers.

Merry were the wedding guests and well drunken within the palace. More than merry was the bridegroom who drank the deepest of all. Sodden was his brain, rebellious his limbs; but his tongue, though thick and clumsy, still responded to his call.

"As for the Lord of Chichen Itza," he mumbled loudly, "poor lean dog, let him take his pleasure howling at the moon tonight! But before I seek my wife in her many-curtained chamber, I must hear a lively song. Hallo there! Officers! Men! Lift your voices to the battle song!"

Drunkenly mumbling thus, he rolled on his side and fell asleep. With care-free abandon, unconscious of their fate, officers and men numbed and sodden with drink started singing the great war song of the Mayas, *Conex, Conex, Palache.* "Come on, Come on, ye warriors!"

But abruptly the drunken singing ceased. What was this before them? Silently the men of Chichen had filed into the chamber. At a signal from their master, they fell on their foes and slew them.

The deer-eyed woman, alone in her curtained chamber, heard the voices and the singing; then the muffled blows of fighting, the groans and sighs of the dying drove her to the carved stone entrance. Before she reached her doorway, the entrance-shells rattled, the curtains parted swiftly. "Star of the night! Star of my life!" cried the victorious Lord Canek.

Silently prince and princess quitted the hall, and never again did Chichen know its Lord Canek, nor any of his fighting men. In the passing of the night they vanished, the chieftain and the soft-eyed maiden, stolen bride of the drunken one who had thought to wed her in spite of the love of a bold, brave warrior.

But the memory of Lord Canek lived on in song and story, a legend of Chichen. One day, long after, a hunting band from Chichen marching many days, came upon a lake of shining water, wherein lay an island city, with houses and temples, and the carved fronts of many buildings like those in their own Chichen. From this island-city, warriors came to meet them, and here, they learned, was the city where Canek and his bride had found refuge and happiness. Here the young ruler and his soldiers had made themselves a new home; here they had built for themselves another city in the distant forest like their old beloved Chichen.

Maya in typical warrior costume with blue nose pendant, ear disk and breast plaque, with war club and protecting sleeve. (Temple of Warriors.)

Kukulcan, Hero and God

With the two cities of Chi-chen' and Ux-mal' growing greater and more powerful each day, the peninsula of Yucatan quickly became the center of the New Empire of the Mayas in the north. Manufacturing again became important; skill and art once more were honored; and powerful priests in gorgeous featherwork robes directed anew their time-honored ceremonies to the gods. Other cities arose in white and glittering splendor, and the broad peninsula was soon crowded.

Following the coast line, many of the migrating Mayas journeyed west and north to the neighborhood of Vera Cruz. Here they found brethren, the Huax'tec-an, who had not gone with their kinsmen into Guatemala. Others took to the sea. For years, the Maya merchants had used enormous trading canoes, hewn from single logs, but so large that they could hold great cargoes of cotton, pottery, and other merchandise, and needed thirty paddles to man them. It was in canoes such as these that the restless Mayas embarked, and the exact course of their further travels is not known. They arrived, however, at the lower Mississippi; for there, along the eastern shore of the great river are the remains of their settlements and many great earthen pyramids.

Two gold breast ornaments, a gold mask of a god, and a large collar of gold bells found at Monte Alban near Oaxaca, Mexico, where migrating Mayas carried their civilization. In 1502, on his fourth and last voyage Columbus met off Bon-ac'ca Island, in the Caribbean Sea, a Maya trading canoe large enough for sea voyaging; and it was in such canoes that some of the Mayas may have followed the coast of the Gulf of Mexico to the mouth of the Mississippi River from whence they perhaps made their way inland to be later known as Mound Builders. In *The Story of the American Indian*, by Paul Radin, Chapter V, "The Mexicans Conquer North America," there is a thought-provoking account of the northern spread of the ancient Maya civilization from Central America.

Not all the Mayas who went beyond Yucatan continued to follow the eastern coast, however. A large group turned inland and moved northward into the state of Oaxaca in southern Mexico, settling there and intermarrying with the people. This mixture of Mayas and natives led to two new civilizations, called the Za'po-tec' and the Mix'-tec. Among these new people, the old Maya language now became their language; Maya hieroglyphs were used in writing inscriptions and records; the Maya calendar of two hundred and sixty days was followed. Nevertheless, the Zapotec and Mixtec civilizations were different from the Maya, and those Mayas who settled in Mexico soon became quite changed from their

A Za'po-tec' gold breast ornament of delicate workmanship. The excavations of a Zapotec tomb at Monte Alban in Oaxaca, Mexico, by Dr. Alfonso Caso, Head of the Department of Archaeology of the National Museum of Mexico, gave much new knowledge regarding the Zapotecs and Mixtecs and revealed the fact that these people had developed a culture in some respects superior to that of the Aztecs and Mayas. Evidently the Zapotecs were the earlier people, and their tombs were used later by the Mixtecs. The recovery of objects of these ancient cultures from Monte Alban has been called the "richest archaeological find in America." Included in the treasure are jade and pearl objects, necklaces of gold, and gold masks of the gods of remarkable workmanship. Such objects were later the lure which tempted Spanish conquest.

brethren in Yucatan. At Monte Alban they buried in their tombs splendid jade and pearl objects, necklaces of gold, pearl, turquoise, and gold masks of their gods.

Gradually this changed form of Maya civilization, of Zapotec and Mixtec, was carried north and west by travelers and merchants until it was brought to a strange new tribe of people entirely different from the Maya tribes. These barbarians were the Toltecs, hardy, warlike invaders from the north, who had fought their way down into Mexico. Possibly they were Na'huas, the first adventurous arrivals of those later invaders, the Aztecs; but whoever they were, these savage and primitive fighters, eagerly took the changed form of Maya civilization which they found among the Zapotecs. And through the Toltecs, who still were in touch with tribes to the north, this Maya civilization was passed along from the valley of Mexico, beyond the Rio Grande to the people of the American Southwest.

Meanwhile the war-loving Toltecs had set about building up an Empire founded on conquest, and from their first settlement between the border of Vera Cruz and Oaxaca, they spread both north and south, and collected tribute of food, jewels, and precious metals. Great Toltec cities soon arose:—Cho-lu'la near Pue'bla, Te-o'ti-hua'can near Mexico City, Xo-chi-cal'co near Cuer'na-va'ca, and Tula, fifty miles north of Mexico City. In these cities, the pyramids were larger and higher than those of the Mayas, but they were not as well-built.

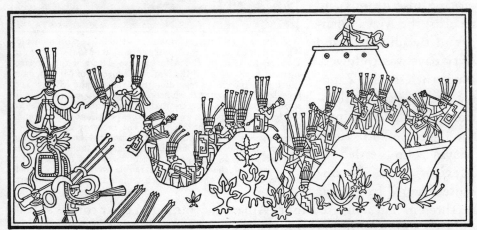

Invaders crossing mountains to attack the Itzas. Left, the Itza general; right, an Itzan horn blower with design indicating sound, standing on a pyramidal temple. (Fresco, Temple of Tigers, Chichen.)

Toltec temples at Te-o'ti-hua'can, near Mexico City. In the foreground is an enormous rectangular open court with row after row of altars guarded by carved and colored stone serpent heads; and in the background, the mammoth Pyramid of the Sun and Pyramid of the Moon. (Photographs.)

The temples which crowned the pyramids were also more poorly constructed. Adobe bricks were used in place of cut stone; vaulted ceilings were abandoned, and simple geometric carvings formed the main decorations. In spite of their simplicity, however, the size of these Toltec temples often made them most impressive. At Te-o'ti-hua'can, near Mexico City, the temple was enormous. A huge rectangular court open to the sky and surrounded by rows of altars with one large altar in the center, stretched off stupendously imposing toward the misty line of the mountains; and near this court towered great pyramids erected to the sun and moon with a city of dwellings for priests clustered about the whole. Most of the ideas of the Toltecs had been borrowed from the Mayas, but in religion, they still clung to ancient beliefs of their own, worshiping the sun's disk instead of idols of the gods, and regarding human sacrifice as absolutely necessary.

Three great emperors ruled the conquering Toltecs in their days of lordly power, and their merciless armies swept from Northern Mexico to Nic'a-ra'gua. Greatest of all Toltec emperors was Ku-kul-can', the most famous man of Ancient America. The name Kukulcan in the Maya language meant "feathered serpent," *kukul* being the word for the quetzal bird, and *kan* a serpent; Kukulcan was the same as the Mexican Quet-zal'co-a'tl, which also meant "quetzal-bird-serpent." Kukulcan and Quetzalcoatl were one person, the Emperor who was called by different names in different parts of the country. He was a Toltec, and after first conquering the southern neighbors nearest him, he advanced against the Mayas in Yucatan. In the fighting, however, the Mayas were victorious and Kukulcan was captured. Rejoicing greatly in the favor of the gods who had given them the power to triumph over so powerful an enemy, the Mayas carried the captured leader to the holy city of Chichen, there to be held a prisoner until the time came to be cast alive into the Sacred Well as an offering to the Rain God.

In the dim white light before dawn, the prisoner was dressed in the finest robes to be found. Beautiful feathered mosaic was his mantle; tall, graceful, vari-colored plumes adorned his head; his waistcloth was covered with exquisitely-worked embroidery in fanciful design; a jade breastplate of delicate workmanship hung from his neck; jade arm bands and leg bands were crowded together to make him still more gorgeous. Thus clad, Kukulcan was taken to the edge of the Sacred Well where the huge pool gleamed darkly below in its cup of cream-colored rocks, the sides overgrown with greenery and delicate lace of innumerable ferns.

Warrior-priest wearing a serpent-mask with long feather attachment, a sculptured relief at Chichen representing Ku-kul-can', the hero-god.

Priests in splendid ceremonial robes, like those who attended the daybreak sacrifices.   Right, three high priests with long, sleeveless robes, heavy capes or collars and stick nose-plugs carrying incense. Left, two lesser priests with serpent staves.   All have feather headdresses. (Temple of Warriors.)

Surrounded by great multitudes of chanting priests in their splendid ceremonial robes, almost hidden from sight in the clouds of smoke arising from countless swinging censers, deafened by the noise of shrill flutes and booming drums, the noble sacrifice stood tall and erect between two priests on the rocky brink of the opening.

The sky flushed a soft shell-pink, and slowly blossomed in rose. The chanting rose higher and higher, the drums beat louder and louder, the swinging censers were shaken in ever wider circles. And now the sun appeared. In a sudden blast of sound, song and music ended. The priests seized Kukulcan, swung him back and forth, and tossed him out into the center of the deep, dark, silent Well.

With an effort the prisoner straightened his body so that he plunged feet first into the shaded depths sixty feet below. Chanting and music arose once more; and after long prayers and ceremonies, the priests slowly withdrew. Such was the daybreak sacrifice to the Rain God.

But the prisoner had neither been killed nor stunned. Entering the water straight and true, he had shot deep into the cold, green pool. Instinctively he began treading water, and quickly he rose to the surface gasping for breath. Turning on his back, he rested and recovered from the shock of finding himself alive. Then with long, steady strokes he skirted the irregular, rocky edge of the Well until he found projections where he could draw himself up and rest.

No attention was paid to his movements by the chanting priests above who continued their ceremonies and slowly withdrew. But at midday the priests returned; Kukulcan was still alive. Sometimes swimming quietly in the silent water, sometimes resting on the rocky projections on the sides, he had passed the long hours.

Since the sacrifice had not been killed nor drowned by this time, the priests believed that the Rain God wanted him to live. Ropes were lowered, therefore, and Kukulcan was drawn to land. He had taken on divine rank by being offered as a sacrifice, and now he became a living god on earth. Honored and worshiped by the deeply religious Mayas, the Toltec chieftain became the ruler of Chichen and the most powerful lord in Yucatan.

Under the leadership of Kukulcan, the Mayas became even more active and prosperous. Their new ruler first conquered all the chieftains throughout the peninsula and organized Yucatan into a single united state so that all worked together. Then he founded the city of Ma'ya-pan and made it his capital, although Chichen remained the holy city of Maya religion.

A sphinx-like statue of Ku-kul-can', the hero-god of Chi-chen'. Not all authorities agree that Kukulcan, the Toltec leader, became master of Yucatan after escaping from sacrifice to the Rain God. The account here followed is from Gann & Thompson, *History of the Maya*, p. 81f.

Kukulcan, the feathered serpent hero-god, who probably ruled shortly before 1000 A.D. (Chichen).

All the conquered chieftains were compelled to live at Mayapan; and to keep peace in the land, Kukulcan brought paid soldiers from Mexico who were loyal to him alone. Then the new Toltec master gave the Mayas laws for their government, he encouraged manufacturing and commerce and began the erection of many fine buildings.

Towering to a height of one hundred feet, far beyond all other pyramids and buildings at Chichen, there now appeared the *Castillo*, a structure for the worship of Kukulcan as a god, the Temple of the Feathered Serpent. The pyramid itself was seventy-five or eighty feet high, faced with cut-stone beautifully paneled and terraced in sections. Stone stairways of ninety-one steps arose to the top on each side, and the main stair was guarded by two huge heads of feathered serpents, jaws open, fangs showing, and forked tongues extended. The bodies of the serpents ran up the mound on each side of the stairway to the little temple which crowned the platform, and the doorway of this temple was also guarded by pillars representing feathered serpents.

Here Kukulcan was worshiped as a wind god, a god of the air, and the bearer of civilization to the Mayas; he was a teacher and organizer who established cities, gave the people self-government, and aided them in all the activities of peaceful, happy living.

And now the Mayas began erecting many new temples and palaces carved with the feathered serpent, the symbol of Kukulcan. Columns were used more than before, and these, combined with lintels made of the hard *sapote* wood permitted the building of much larger rooms.

View of the city of Chi-chen' with the magnificent pyramid, now called *Castillo*, on the right. This temple to Kukulcan rises on an impressive stone-faced pyramid whose stairways of 91 steps are guarded by huge carved feathered serpents. To the left is one end of the ball court with the little Temple of the Tigers above (see page 117), and to the rear between these two structures is the splendid Temple of the Warriors. (See page 125.)   Few ruins in the Old World today surpass in beauty these splendid structures of the most brilliant and accomplished civilization of Ancient America.

Youths in the splendid magnificence of growing Maya cities, began to play a kind of basket ball called *tlaxtli* by the Mexicans, and probably introduced by the Toltecs of Kukulcan; and a fine ball court was built for playing the game at Chichen.

This court was almost two hundred yards long and forty yards wide. It was enclosed by high walls, and was in the shape of two capital T's placed base to base. At both ends of the court stood little pillared structures appearing to be boxes for judges or the royal party perhaps, and on top of one of the walls looking down into the court was the beautiful little Temple of the Tigers so called from the figures of jaguars carved in a line near the top. Here doubtless dwelt the idol of the court, to whom sacrifice must be made. The opposing teams at each end played with a hard rubber ball. Said an eye-witness of the game:

"They used a rubber ball and struck the ball with any part of the body; but he who could hit the ball with his hips was considered very dexterous; and to make the ball rebound better, they placed a piece of stiff leather on the hips. They played in parties, for a load of mantles or gold and featherwork, and sometimes played themselves away. He who could strike the ball through the hole thereby won the game and he had the right to the cloaks of all the lookers-on.

"It was very pleasant to see that as soon as ever the ball was in the hole, those standing by, took to their heels, running away with all their might to save their cloaks, laughing and rejoicing while others scoured after them to secure their cloaks for the fortunate winner."

Reconstruction of the ball court at Chichen showing Mayas playing the game called *tlaxtli*. The introduction of this basket ball game and the bow and arrow by the Toltecs is placed at this time by J. Eric Thompson in Chapter III, "The History of Yucatan," Gann and Thompson, *The History of the Maya*, and the chronology here followed agrees with the ideas of Herbert J. Spindon in *Ancient Civilizations of Mexico and Central America*. Dr. Morley and other authorities, however, believe that the *Castillo*, the Temple of Kukulcan, the ball court and bow and arrow belong to the later period of Toltec rule. The account of the game on this page was given by a Spaniard named Herrera who accompanied Cortez. It is quoted by Bernal Diaz in his *The Discovery and Conquest of Mexico*.

Sacrifice to the feathered serpent god on an altar in the form of the serpent. Stretched back downward, the victim is held taut by helpers while the priest stands ready to rend flesh and bone and tear out the living heart as an offering. (Fresco, Temple of the Warriors.)

For the first time the Mayas now began using the bow and arrow. This was also brought to them by the Mexican soldiers of Kukulcan; and although never taking the place of the spear, bows were used henceforth in all battles. And now, having brought peace and order into Yucatan, having set up a strong, central government, Kukulcan gave the control of the city of Ma'ya-pan to a noble family called the Co-coms'; and renouncing all wealth and honor, he left the country.

After departing from Yucatan, the noble lord returned to the highlands of Mexico where he reorganized that country, giving it a new and better government. He abolished the Toltec ceremony of human sacrifice and set up a center for his own religious ideas at Cho-lu'la, also erecting at Tula a temple with feathered serpent columns like the one adorning Chichen.

Quet-zal'co-a'tl's kindly religion did not long endure, however; it was too advanced for the bloodthirsty Toltecs to understand, and when he was no more obeyed, he left the land forever. Men said that he sailed away over the eastern sea on a raft of serpent skins to dwell in the land of the sunrise and that he had promised to return some day, to bring a new rule to his people. After he left, human sacrifice was again performed in ceremonies to the gods, but other of his ideas and reforms continued under the next invaders, the Aztecs who came from the north like the Toltecs, to swarm in and seize the land.

The League of Mayapan

Three cities in Yucatan were at this time larger, richer, and more powerful than any others, and after Kukulcan left the land, these cities formed a league to govern the peninsula between them. Chi-chen', Ux-mal', and Ma'ya-pan all agreed upon a joint rulership; and because Mayapan was the largest city and had been the capital of Kukulcan, it took the leadership and gave its name to the new form of government. For two hundred years, from 1004 to 1201 A.D., the league remained in power and there was peace and justice in the land for all. It'za-mal, another city of the Itzas, was also admitted to the league.

During these two hundred years of the League of Mayapan, merchants carried Maya cloth and pottery from Colombia on the south to New Mexico on the north, and Maya ideas and civilization were carried likewise to these regions. So important was this trade that all of Central America was crossed and recrossed with smooth, stone-paved highways running straight and true through forest and jungle mile after mile. Over these highways Maya cloth, pottery, metal work, and other articles were carried by bands of trudging porters who bore the burdens on their backs; for the Mayas had no beasts of burden and all their commerce and trade, their mighty building with stone was carried on by Maya men, small and slight of stature.

A Maya hut in the jungle with peasant wearing ear-plug and usual working garment. A warrior approaches through trees alive with animals. (Dresden Codex.)

Maya traveler clad in loin cloth, and walking with a staff, supports his bundle with a head band just as his descendants do today. (Fresco, Temple of Warriors.)

They carried articles of trade from inland-towns to the seaports where they were loaded into merchant canoes and transported to distant regions. And in return, the Maya merchants received pearls and emeralds from Colombia, and turquoise from New Mexico. It was through this trade with distant people who used gold and copper and who had learned how to make bronze that a knowledge of the usefulness and value of these metals reached the Mayas. At first gold was used only in making ornaments; but later it was formed into the shape of little bells and these became the money of the Maya merchants.

And now, with peace in Yucatan, and prosperity through agriculture and trade, art and architecture flourished anew. Great buildings of cut stone, elaborately decorated with sculptures, arose on every side. No town or village was so small and unimportant that it could not boast a pyramid temple, and even a chief's house built of stone.

All these buildings of the New Empire followed the same plan, and the only real difference in any of them was in the kind of roof. Buildings with flat roofs were used as dwellings, and buildings with arched roofs were temples and places of worship. The flat roofs were supported on beams of hard wood resting on walls and columns, but arched roofs were harder to build. The Mayas had no knowledge of the true arch with a keystone at the top; instead when the side walls of a temple had risen to a height of ten or twelve feet, the next layer of stone was lapped outward, the stones above were also lapped outward until a triangle was formed which could be capped by a single stone. This was called a false arch and it gave the temples the appearance of being vaulted. Thick, solid walls were necessary to support such an arch, and these vaulted ceilings limited the size of the rooms to a width of eighteen feet. All Maya buildings, therefore, had thick massive walls and rooms that were long but extremely narrow.

At Chichen, four new buildings of this kind were constructed during the League of Mayapan,—the House of the Dark Writing, the Red House, the House of the Deer, and parts of the Nunnery. The House of the Dark Writing was placed upon a little hill, and was a low structure only rising to a height of eighteen feet but stretching out a distance of one hundred and seventy-six feet, with few decorations. The Red House was elaborately carved with geometric designs and masks of the god Kukulcan; the lower parts of the Nunnery were also rich in beautifully carved stone work, displaying the plumed serpent along the walls, and at every corner, row upon row of fierce, grotesque masks of Kukulcan with eyelids and grinning jaws and a long, curling, trunk-like nose.

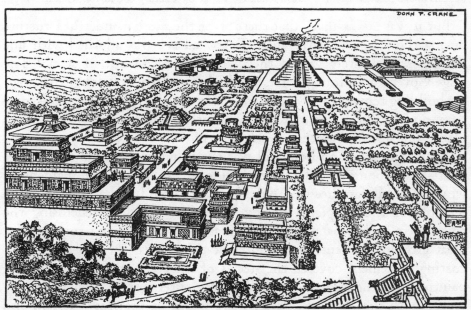

General view of Chichen. In left foreground, the Nunnery with two annexes; beyond it, The Red House, and at left the House of Dark Writing. In the center with round dome, the observatory, and beyond, the Pyramid of Kukulcan or *Castillo* with the ball court at the left and the Court of a Thousand Columns with Temple of Warriors at the right. In the distance is the Sacred Well surrounded by jungle, and scattered all about are the small thatched houses of the common people.

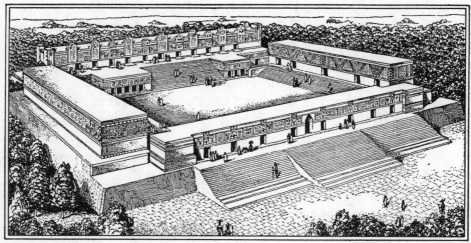

The Nunnery Quadrangle at Ux-mal', where lived the Maya Vestal Virgins. Every outer surface was carved and painted. (From reconstruction erected at the Century of Progress, Chicago, 1933.)

But it was at Ux-mal', that there arose the most wonderful structure during the League of Mayapan. Every surface was adorned with fine designs so delicately carved they were like lace-work in stone. The huge Governor's House, three hundred and thirty feet long, the longest building remaining in Yucatan, was covered with geometric decoration, and carved masks of Kukulcan, with his long curving nose, were placed one above the other at the corners.

Most elaborate and beautiful was the Nunnery Quadrangle, a huge court with rooms or cells on each side, where lived those maidens of wealthy, noble families whose duty it was to tend the sacred fire in the Temple of the Magician nearby. The four buildings enclosing the court were each separate, but the main structure facing south had a great arch in the center running right through to the inner court. A coating of cement covered the stones of the arch, and upon this were paintings in blue, red, and yellow. Every outer surface was elaborately carved with designs and figures; there was a basket work design, and one of lattice work; there were numberless carved masks of Kukulcan; there were portraits and bas-relief statues of gods, priests, worshipers, warriors, skulls, and animals; and even shields were used in a design.

The Governor's House at Uxmal. Carved masks of Kukulcan with his long curling nose (see page 128) rise one above the other at the corners. (Reconstruction, National Museum, Washington.)

Although the Nunnery Quadrangle was the dwelling place of the Maya Vestal Virgins, there were no windows to the little cells where they slept; windows did not appear in any Maya building. Instead, each cell had a doorway covered with cotton curtains or portiers, embroidered in brilliant colors; and beside the entrance was a string of shells which the visitor rattled to make his presence known. Through this doorway, reflection on the light-colored walls within gave a soft and indirect lighting, cool and pleasing in those hot lands.

But such wonderful works of architecture and art were possible only with peace, and soon war was to shake the passions and sap the energies of the Mayas. The League had lasted two hundred years, but the family of Co-coms' who ruled in Mayapan were greedy for greater power, and dreamed of absolute control of all the peninsula. Gradually they began to take more and more authority to themselves; taxes and tribute were increased, and when the people murmured and refused to pay, the Cocoms brought in Toltec warriors from Mexico to collect their demands by force. And then, with an army to compel obedience, they became bolder than ever. Chichen and Uxmal were treated as vassals, and the tax-gatherers even dared enter their lands.

Maya warriors in complete war costume, bowing before their chieftain before going out to battle, just as the men of Chichen saluted the "Very Red Man" before attacking the lord of Mayapan. The ruler at left is protected by the feathered serpent, and the warriors have a number of spears in their left hands, their throwing sticks in their right hands, shields at their backs and the usual breast ornaments, nose-plugs and ear-plugs. (Ball Court, Chichen.) The carvings and sculptures of the Old Empire showed very few scenes of warfare, but in the New Empire in Yucatan, battle and strife were frequent, and the warrior assumed a new importance. Legend relates that Hunac Cul attacked Chac Xib because the lord of Chichen stole the bride of the Mayapan ruler, but this is thought to be a later romantic coloring. An interesting story has been made of this legend, however, by Mrs. Alida Sims Malkus, which gives a good picture of Maya life and customs at Chichen.

The proud Maya spirit would endure no more. Weak though he was in fighting men, the "Very Red Man," the ruler of Chichen, conspired with his friend U-lil', governor of It'zam-al. They would combine their armies, make a surprise attack on the proud lord of Mayapan, and break his growing power. Disguised as merchants and pilgrims, secret messengers passed back and forth between the two cities; and about the year 1201 when the last details had been arranged, the "Very Red Man" gave a banquet to Ulil to cement their alliance.

But the tyrant of Mayapan was suspicious and alert. Spies were hidden both at Chichen and Itzamal; and although they failed to learn all about the conspiracy, they well knew that something was afoot and that this banquet in honor of Ulil was a menace to their master. Promptly they reported to the Cocom, and promptly the Cocom acted. Before the allies were prepared to attack, he hastily gathered his Toltec army and suddenly, unexpectedly, fell upon Chichen. Bravely, the men of Chichen rallied to the attack; but caught unprepared, overwhelmed by superior numbers and superior weapons, they were defeated; and the lord of Chichen, the "Very Red Man," died fighting valiantly and vigorously against the tyrant to the end.

Chichen Under Toltec Rule

No longer was Chichen permitted to remain a free, independent city. The Cocom ruler placed it under the mastery of one of his Toltec chieftains; he would have no more plotting against his power. The foreign Toltec rulers brought new customs and ideas to Chichen, and under their direction, the city became greater and more magnificent than ever. To the Toltecs, Kukulcan was a much greater god than he had been to the Mayas; he was the supreme god, and new temples and buildings to his glory now arose all over the northern part of Chichen.

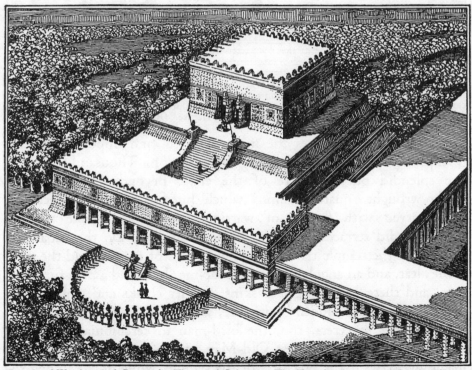

Temple of Warriors and Court of a Thousand Columns. The Temple, the most perfect building at Chichen, stands at one end of one of the most beautiful squares in the world. Its ruins have been restored by the Carnegie Institute acting in cooperation with the Mexican Government. The countless pillars of the surrounding colonnade have been placed in their original positions and the group now stands as an awe-inspiring monument of this most brilliant civilization of Ancient America, and an indication of the social, political, and intellectual heights reached by the Maya people.

Sanctuary at the top of the Temple of the Warriors. Columns are feathered serpents, the yawning jaws forming the base, the curved tail and rattle, the capital, and the body or column beautifully carved with feathers. Within is the altar supported by sculptured figures of men, and before the entrance is the reclining Chac-Mool holding a dish for incense. (Reconstructed from photographs.)

Of all these structures the most beautiful and imposing was the Temple of the Warriors adjoining the Court of a Thousand Columns, the splendid public square of the city. Beyond those thousand finely wrought square columns which lined the market place and were carved with figures of warriors, the great temple rose in four splendid terraces, gay with colored carvings. On the broad flat summit of the temple crouching stone figures of men upheld the great stone altar, and an angular woman, Chac-mool, upheld a dish for offerings; and there in their jaguar skins, feather cloaks and embroidered robes, priests, half hidden by incense, worshiped Kukulcan.

Sometimes sorcerers, too, the bird-man in ceremonial mask, the jaguar-man, or the toothless Old-Man-with-a-bone, performed their magic mysteries in the precincts of the temple, while down among the columns below wandered those bands of warriors in quilted cotton armor and elaborate feathered headdresses, whose portraits were carved on the pillars and gave the temple its name.

Great had the warrior class grown since those days in the Old Southern Empire when life was so peaceful and quiet that portraits of warriors never appeared among the temple-carvings. The Toltecs had made the land ring to the echoing rhythm of battle, and Chichen Itza was now a mighty city of warriors, temples, squares, and palaces surrounded by the little windowless white oval houses of the people as shown in the brilliant frescoes of the Temple of the Warriors.

It was these Toltec masters of Chichen, with their love for human sacrifice, who made a spectacular ceremony of honoring the terrible Rain God in the Sacred Well with the gift of a beautiful maiden. A sacred highway was built from the Temple of Kukulcan to the brink of the Well nearby; new temples were erected and two elaborately decorated dancing platforms.

Upon the still, sunflooded air, the chant of death began to swell softly over the slow pulsing of drums and lutes. A procession left the holy Temple of Kukulcan and advanced along the broad avenue of the Sacred Way toward the Well. The corn in the fields was withering, crying for rain. The Rain God was angry with his people, and must be satisfied, or famine would walk abroad in the land.

Carved and painted figures from pillars in the Court of a Thousand Columns, Chichen. Left, a bird-man in ceremonial mask. He wears a shoulder cape on which bits of jade are sewn, and a gaily colored kilt of feather-work with a bird's tail hanging from the rear. His leggings are horizontal bands of alternate red and yellow cloth. Center, a sorcerer, or jaguar man with tunic of jaguar skin, jaguar-mouth mask and leggings of snake skin around which are bound stuffed bodies of snakes. Right, Old-Man-with-a-bone through his nose, toothless, stooped with age, with wrinkled paunch and bent knees. Over his shoulders he wears a quilted head cloth; in his ears are long yellow pendants. He carries an ornate staff and a fan. (Photographs.)

Stone mask of Kukulcan, the feathered serpent god, a corner ornament of most of the buildings in Yucatan. The curved hook represents the snout; above may be seen the eye with eyeball, eyebrow and eyelashes; and below the powerful teeth.

Slowly the procession drew near. At the head was the high priest in embroidered ceremonial garments and elaborate feathered headdress. Behind, in a flower-twined bower borne by sturdy, sun-bronzed priests, was a lovely maiden, beautiful beyond compare, the most exquisite maid to be found in the land. Through every village and countryside, for weeks and weeks, a thousand priests had sought her, the fairest flower of Maya maidenhood to be the bride of the angry Rain God in the Sacred Well.

Following her bridal bower, filling the whole of the Sacred Way, came the Toltec ruler of the city, his nobles, the great warriors, and hundreds of priests, while on the far side of the Well a silent multitude gathered, composed of people from the city, and thousands of pilgrims who had come from afar.

The high priest entered the little temple standing on the brink of the Well. The chanting ceased, the drums were stilled. The priest recited prayers to the Rain God, and lighted sacred incense burners. As the fragrant, blue vapor curled upward, the chanting began anew.

Two powerful *nacons* lifted the maiden from her couch, their muscular brown arms forming a sling in which she lay as lightly as a leaf. They advanced to the edge of the Well. Slowly they swung the featherweight body backward and forward to the beat of the drums and the rhythm of the chant; backward and forward in an ever wider sweep, while drums and chant swelled to a roar. At a sign from the high priest the drums were suddenly stilled; the chant ended in a high-pitched wail. A last forward swing, and the bride of Yum Chac was hurled far out over the Well. Turning slowly in the air, the dainty body fell faster and faster till it struck the dark water below. An echoing splash, and all was still. The bride had found favor in the eves of her lord.

Sacrifice of the most beautiful maid in the Maya Empire to the Rain God at the bottom of the Sacred Well. Many interesting, artistic, and valuable objects of pure gold, jade, copper, and pottery have been recovered from the Sacred Well by Edward Herbert Thompson, the first American Consul to Yucatan. Mr. Thompson has devoted his whole life to awakening interest in the Mayas and preserving their civilization. For years he conducted archaeological research with the assistance of only the Peabody Museum and a few humble donations, but recently the Carnegie Institute of Washington, D. C., and the Mexican Government have undertaken to preserve the Maya ruins.

A shout of rejoicing arose from the multitude at this favorable sign. With eager joy the people tore off necklaces, pendants and jewels, and cast them into the Well. Gold and jade ornaments, beautiful pieces of pottery, carved wood, everything of greatest value was sacrificed to the Rain God. Pilgrims from Costa Rica threw jewelry and bells of gold into the water; holy men from northwestern Mexico flung, into the depths, turquoise-studded ornaments and beautiful pottery like cloisonne ware. All the civilized Western World was attracted to the ceremony.

Last Days in Yucatan

But though their Toltec rulers brought glory and honor to Chichen, the memory of their disgrace by Hunac Cul of Mayapan still ate the hearts of the Itzas. Led by the Xius of Uxmal, the other Mayas of the peninsula had kept up a little irritating warfare against the Co-coms' of Mayapan; but a hundred years must pass before Chichen was able to join the fighters and seek revenge for her wrongs.

There came a time, however, in the year 1451, when Chichen plotted anew with their brethren of Itzamal. A general uprising was planned, and this time the spies of the Cocoms failed to warn their masters. At a given signal, the whole peninsula awoke, seized arms, and marched from all directions upon Mayapan. Taken completely by surprise, the proud city was conquered despite the Toltec mercenaries; temples, palaces, and homes were sacked of their riches; the head of the lordly Cocom family, and all his sons, save one who chanced to be away, were ruthlessly slaughtered, and the city of the Cocoms was given to flames.

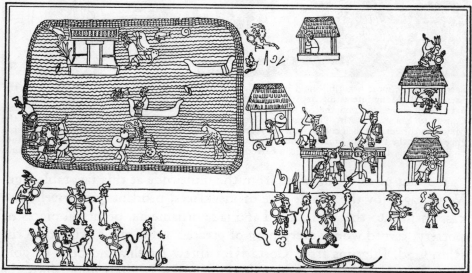

A raid upon a village by enemy tribes. The village is surrounded by cultivated fields, and on the road leading away from it, the victors are driving their captives, each with rope-bound arms tethered to a guard. The defeated are unclad and are painted in rings. (Fresco, Temple of Warriors, Chichen.)

The downfall of the Cocoms was a brilliant victory over tyranny, but a victory which failed to bring peace. A great restlessness seized upon the Mayas after the war, and they could not return to their cities and their labors in field and home. The Itzas, the ancient ruling family of Chichen, were the first to move. Gathering great numbers of their still loyal followers, they left the city of the Sacred Well and returned to the long forgotten southland of Guatemala, where they settled around

Maya warriors throwing spears tipped with fire-brands into an enemy village. (Fresco, Chichen.)

Lake Flores. The Xius, in turn, abandoned Uxmal; some moved to Chichen where they quickly established their leadership; others migrated to Ma'ni with the thought of erecting new temples and palaces, and building another wonderful city. But the war had exhausted the Xius and weakened their energies; Mani remained to the end a simple settlement of thatched huts with almost no monuments.

Meanwhile, the one remaining member of the Cocom family returned to his scattered, homeless people, and gathering as many as would follow him, he moved to the northeast coast and settled at a spot named Tib-u-lon', "We were judged." The new city grew steadily, and before long, the Cocoms were again important rulers. But fierce anger over the slaughter of his family rankled in the breast of Cocom, and this hatred was especially directed against Itzamal which alone came out of the war more powerful than before and had established a ruling house known as the Chel. With the Chel, the Cocom were ever at war. The Cocom controlled the salt deposits on the coast, and refused to allow the Chel to send there to gather salt; in return, the Chel erected a barrier to the game, cacao beans, fruit, and cereals from the interior which the Cocoms needed for food.

Exquisitely carved relief of warriors and priests in an important religious ceremony to the feathered-serpent god. The shrine of the serpent, in the lower panel, is attended by numerous priests; the serpent, rearing its head into the upper panel, there addresses the worshiping warriors. (Chichen.)

In spite of bickering and warfare, however, Yucatan steadily recovered from the effects of the slaughter. Twenty years of full harvests gave an abundance which allowed leisure for new works of art and science and for a time the Xiu family tried to take the place of the Cocoms and again unite the peninsula. But after twenty years of bountiful harvests, the land of Ma'ni suffered drought. The water holes shrank and dried. For many weeks no rain had fallen and the growing maize withered in the fields. The people were suffering. Something would have to be done quickly, or all would perish.

The Lord of the Xiu called a great meeting of all the nobles and priests and head men of Mani, and there it was decided to make a pilgrimage to the Sacred Well where a sacrifice of beautiful maidens to the Rain God might turn his wrath and bring life-giving rain to their lands. To reach Chichen from Mani, however, the people must pass through the lands of the Cocoms, and messengers were sent to ask passage. The Lord of the Cocoms granted peace; and he told the messengers that the people would be given a warm welcome.

Meanwhile, at the command of their lord, the Cocoms prepared for the expected guests. Along the line of march, arches were made of saplings tied together and bent to the ground, and around these were twined fresh vines and gay flowers. As the pilgrims reached each village, the chieftains and most beautiful maidens of the district came to welcome them, and gave rest and feasting with friendly songs.

When the procession reached the capital of the Cocoms, the whole city came forth to greet the Mani, and a feast to please the great was prepared. Wild turkeys, wild pigs, green corn, big potatoes, all made tasty and pleasing by fragrant herbs, were set before them. Then came religious games and dances, and at last the Mani were escorted to specially built palm-thatched huts beyond the city.

But in the chill light before dawn, when all the Mani were deep in sleep, silent forms surrounded the quiet rest-houses and the doors were blocked with thorny brush. Then flaming torches flickered, held close to the quiet huts. Red tongues of flame shot up each corner, and like snakes crept along the thatched roofs. The Mani awoke suffocating only to find themselves trapped. The morning air resounded with the shrill shrieks of women, and hoarse cries of men.

The Lord of the Cocoms stood forth, his sneering voice arising above the crackling flames and the agonized cries of the Mani: "Rest in peace brothers," he cried. "This is the warm welcome I promised you. Long years ago, I promised you such a welcome, but you had forgotten."

The blazing roofs sank; the cries of agony ceased. The evil Lord of the Cocoms was revenged.

Maya noble, like the Lord of the Cocoms, seated upon a jaguar throne, receiving the report of a chieftain. (Ball Court, Chichen.)

Among the Mayas, it was said that the Rain God was greatly angered by this unholy act, and was furious with his people. With an effort he withheld revenge, however, until another sacrilege at the Sacred Well burst the bonds that held him in check.

Then indeed the people of Yucatan felt the wrath of the Rain God. A great storm gathered; enormous clouds, as black as night, came rushing from the four corners of the heavens; a single bolt of lurid lightning split the sky. Then came the rain in such a tremendous deluge that the land was swept by death and disaster. When at last the storm was over, only a few houses were still standing; and of the mighty Maya people there remained only a shivering, terror-stricken remnant.

Maya warrior carved in relief on a doorway of the Temple of the Feathered Serpent high above the ghostly remains of a brilliant civilization abandoned to the ravage of the creeping, climbing jungle. (Photograph.) A monument at Tulum is believed to record the last date left by the Mayas, August 5, 1516, exactly 2129 years after they began to keep count of time.

Such was the Maya legend of a terrific hurricane which swept Yucatan, about 1475, tearing down dwellings, destroying fields and fruit trees, and leaving the people starving and miserable. Fifteen years later frightful plagues swept the peninsula; the Mayas suffered untold agony and died in droves like flies. Made desperate by want and suffering, most of the remaining people deserted their stone-built cities, and again turned their faces toward the south, leaving only a few weak, scattered groups behind.

So ended the brilliant civilization of the ancient Mayas.

IV
The Conquest of Mexico
(1519–1521)

Aztec Conquerors

During the greatest years of the New Empire of the Mayas in Yucatan, the people of Mexico, the land to the north of this low-lying, limestone peninsula, had become peaceful and settled. Mexico was a fair land. Its climate varied from the torrid heat of unhealthy jungle-coasts to the cool, bracing temperature of perpetual spring on the highlands. The tall majestic peaks of the Si-er'ra Ma'dre Mountains ran the whole length of both eastern and western coasts, and high among these mountains, upon a wide plateau, lay the fruitful valley of Mexico. The valley was dotted with glistening, shallow lakes and overshadowed by two snow-capped volcanoes, Po-po'ca-te'petl, "the Mountain that Smokes," and Iz'tac-ci'huatl, "the Sleeping Lady," with her three snowy peaks appearing like the figure of a woman lying down.

The beautiful green valley of Mexico, land of perpetual spring. The snow-capped volcano at left is Iz'tac-ci'huatl, "the Sleeping Lady"; at right is Po-po'ca-te'petl, "the Mountain that Smokes."

135

To this fair land came Toltec tribes from the north, establishing an empire there and ruling for five hundred years. The Toltecs took many ideas of culture and civilization from their neighbors, the Mayas; and when Ku-kul-can', or Quet-zal'co-a'tl returned from Yucatan to rule his northern Empire, the people followed his teachings to be pure and moderate in all things, to offer no human sacrifice, nor even the blood of animals; but to delight in offerings of flowers. Thus they had greater happiness than they had ever known.

As the years passed, many legends grew up about Quetzalcoatl, the hero who had walked the earth as a man. The Toltecs believed that they owed all their knowledge and progress to him. He it was who taught the Toltecs how to grow maize and cotton; he taught them how to weave cloth and how to plant according to the seasons so that there was always food and plenty; he was called the Fair God, and was described as being broad of brow, great-eyed, with long black hair and round beard, clothed in a robe of black bordered with crosses of white.

During his stay in the land, so the legend reported, the Toltec

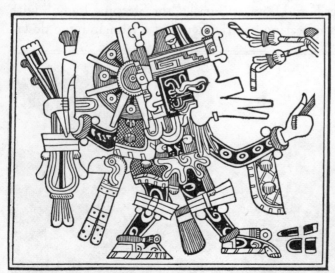

country was a glorious fairyland where white roses bloomed and fruit grew freely everywhere. The air was filled with the sweet melody of birds; the ripening cotton turned glowing red, pale rose, yellow, green, orange, and violet blue in the fields; glittering gold, shining silver, and many rare gems lay unnoticed upon the ground.

Toltec drawing of Quet-zal'co-a'tl, the Fair God. The Toltecs arrived in the valley of Mexico about 550 A.D., and were the first invaders speaking the Na'hua-tlan language, the mother tongue of the Aztecs.

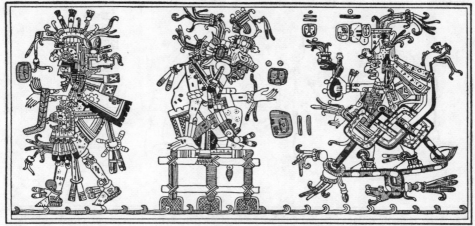

Toltec priests and sorcerers with tattooed bodies, feather headdresses, capes, and ornaments similar to the Mayas, but drawn without the sense of perspective of Mayan artists. (Fresco, Santa Rita.)

This was the Golden Age of the Toltecs. But the Golden Age was all too short; Quet-zal'co-a'tl, the Fair God, who had come to teach the ways of peace, left the land in sorrow when men turned their faces toward evil. Sailing in a wizard skiff made of serpents' skins he vanished over the sea to his home in the land of the sunrise; but ere he went, he promised that some day he would return with other white gods from the east, to take the land from the chiefs and govern again himself.

With the departure of Quetzalcoatl, all the splendor of the Toltecs vanished; and their empire fell before fierce, savage, northern invaders called Chi'chi-mecs' or Blood Suckers, who overran part of the high-lands, taking what they could understand of Toltec civilization. Many other tribes from the north also came at this time pressing into Mexico; and the warlike Chichimecs were compelled to fight for the valley with the People-of-the-flower plantation, the People-of-the-bridge, who built cities on the Mexican lakes, the People-of-the-winding-passages, the Maize-people, and the People-toward-the-land. Still another group of invaders was a miserable wandering tribe who wore patches of gum and feathers upon their ears and foreheads. These squalid, humble creatures were the Az'tecs, a flat-nosed, black-eyed, purple-lipped people, with copper-colored skin and thick, coarse hair.

The Aztec migration. Left to right: Original home of Az'tlan, a city on an island; crossing the lake; date of departure, "one stone knife," or 1168 A.D., and footsteps indicating the route; arrival at city of Col'hu-a'can where they join with eight other tribes indicated by name glyphs. (Boturini MS.)

According to legends of the Aztecs, they left their home in the north about 800 A.D., stopping here and there to settle for a time, and wandering for centuries in search of a new home. Weary and footsore from endless journeyings, they reached the edge of the salt Lake of Tez-cu'co beneath the snow-capped volcanoes about 1325 A.D. Here they were forced by the more powerful tribes already in the land, to huddle together on several small islands that dotted the surface of the lake. Perceiving that a thorny cactus plant had sprouted from a crevice in a rock jutting above the waters, the Aztecs marveled at this unnatural sight and even as they looked, a golden royal eagle with wings outspread to the rising sun appeared from the heavens, bearing in his talons a serpent. On the spiky cactus-shoot, the eagle came to earth, and this ominous occurrence the Aztec leaders hailed as a sign that here they should make their settlement. Accordingly, they established a little lake-village named Tenochtitlan (ta-noch-tet-lan'), "the Place of the Cactus Growing in the Stone," later to be called Mexico City after the Aztec war-god Mex'tli. The name Aztec, meaning "Crane People," was given to these humble settlers because they lived like cranes in the marshes, fashioning frail water houses of reeds and rushes; and living on insects and fish.

But although the Aztecs were subjects of a neighboring tribe called the Te-pa-necs', they were hardy fighters, and in time rebelled against the injustice of their masters. Led by their chief-of-war, King Itz-co-a'tl, who wore a long braid of featherwork hanging to his waist, they defeated the Tepanecs with terrible slaughter, and seized their capital city. Itzcoatl then led his Aztec warriors to other conquests; and under the following three kings, the despised lake-dwellers united the tribes of the valley into an Aztec Confederacy, which they ruled by fear and force, exacting tribute and homage from all.

Aztec armies conquered ever more widely; for the purple-lipped fighters found their greatest joy in battle. To them, war was the breath of life, and one great object of every expedition was the capture of victims to be sacrificed upon the altar of their bloodthirsty god of war, Mex'tli or Huit-zil-o-poch'tli. Every warrior sought prisoners for this sacrifice; even a king could not receive his crown until he had captured enough prisoners; and in all their fighting, the Aztecs sought rather to take prisoners for their gods than to kill outright in battle.

Valor and success in war were thought to be the highest of all honors, and Aztec sons were trained from childhood for the hardships and dangers of battle. Military orders and a degree of knighthood were established for famous fighters, and those who had won such honors were distinguished by having their hair bound and braided around a bright red thong.

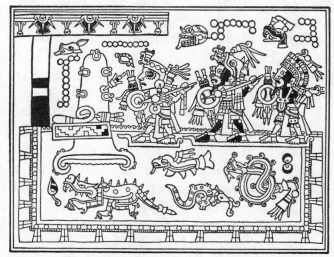

Fired with the zest and joy of battle, three famous chieftains standing in boats lead an attack on a city built on an island in a lake containing a ferocious crocodile, a flying fish and sea serpent. (Zouche Codex.)

Tiz'oc, Great Lord of the Aztecs, at left, is grasping a captive by the hair, and his principal sub-chieftains, at right, are shown in the same victorious position. (Sacrifice Stone of Tizoc, Mexico City.)

After twenty such brilliant actions, the soldier won the right to shave his head and to paint half his face red and the other half yellow; and even Chiefs-of-Men were proud to wear these honors. Magnificent indeed were the copper-skinned Aztecs as they marched into battle, wearing rich feather headdresses rising from wooden helmets, their quilted-cotton armor ornamented with gay colored feathers, and a garment of yellow macaw feathers reaching to the knees. For weapons they bore a sling, several flexible wooden bows, and a three-pointed dart which was the terror of all their foes.

At first, all that these Aztec warriors could do was to conquer and destroy, but when all the Mexican highland had been won, they began to take over the civilization of their enemies. Like the ancient Romans, the Aztecs knew how to organize and govern. The island capital of Te-noch-tit-lan' was made a magnificent place of stone pyramids, temples, and palaces, lining broad paved streets. It was divided into four quarters, each having twenty clans with a council of elders and a civil chief to rule them. Each quarter also had a war-chief called by such magnificent titles as Man-of-the-house-of-darts, Cutter-of-men, Blood-shedder, or Chief-of-the-Eagle; and these commanders received their orders and instructions from the King, or Chief-of-Men. The King was the greatest of all leaders in battle; he was chosen for his valor and power, and was compelled to remain forever holy and pure, lest he fall a victim to the watchful gods and be cast down from his throne.

Second only to the Chief-of-Men was the Snake-Woman, who represented peace; and when the King set forth to war the Snake-Woman remained at home to rule in his stead.

In the year 1450, there came to the throne in the capital city of Tenochtitlan, Mon'te-zu'ma I, "He-who-throws-arrows-toward-the-sky." No longer content to rule the tableland of which he was master, Montezuma crossed the snow-capped barriers to the east and conquered the interior tribes of Yucatan. The next king, A-hu'i-zotl, led his victorious armies westward to the Pacific; and when Montezuma II, the third ruler, came to the throne in 1502, he turned his restless warriors against the tribes of the eastern seacoast. Thus it came about that only two hundred years after the first Aztecs had built their rude dwellings on the shores of a salt marsh, their descendants, in a magnificent island city, ruled over all the rich lands east to the Gulf of Mexico and west to the Pacific Ocean, south to Yucatan and north to the Rio Grande. This was the Aztec Empire, and during the reign of Montezuma II it reached the height of its power and magnificence.

Aztec emperors who conquered surrounding tribes and established the Aztec Empire by the sword. Left, Great Lord Tizoc, who ruled 1481-1486, and extended Aztec mastery to the lands to the east. Following him, to right, the record of the death of Emperor A-hu'i-zotl in the year 10 Rabbit. (1502 A.D.) and the coronation of Montezuma II. The mummy of a human figure bound with ropes, with a crown on its head indicates the death of a ruler, a mummy being the Aztec hieroglyph for death. The right half of this drawing shows Montezuma II seated on a throne with a crown on his head, and a speech scroll issuing from his mouth, representing the Aztec word for ruler, *tlahtouani*, "he who speaks." Both figures are attached to the circle above giving the date, the year 10 Rabbit. At the extreme right is a glyph showing a shield with spears crossed behind it, the word-sign for war; below the shield is a temple in flames, the word-sign for conquest. This glyph with the one to the immediate left is another record of conquest and reads: "In the year 10 Rabbit, the Emperor Ahuizotl fought and conquered the city of Te-hu-an'te-pec." (From ancient Aztec hieroglyphic manuscripts.)

The Empire of the Aztecs

In the Aztec Empire, peaceful arts now flourished. Left, a wood carver; right, peasant woman weaving. (Mendoza MS.)

From his island city, Montezuma held the surrounding country in strict control and kept in touch with all parts of his kingdom by relays of runners. Trails and roads spread in all directions from the capital, crossing rivers, spanning deep ravines, and running straight and true to all the lesser cities. Not all the land was directly under the King; within the empire were many city-states and small republics with local rulers who were practically independent. However, every city and province had local judges appointed by Montezuma, and these judges had great power; they held office for life, and through them the King controlled his empire. So closely did he watch over his law-courts, making certain of honest judges, that he sometimes even visited them in disguise himself.

A strict and wise system of laws protected even the slaves from injustice. There were no lawyers in the courts; but each person presented his own case and brought in his own witnesses, and the testimony was written down in pictures by a law clerk. Crimes and disorders were severely punished even in youth. Young men who became intoxicated or who squandered their father's money were promply put to death; and from their earliest days children were taught self control.

An Aztec orchestra. Left to right: enormous log drum, a kettle drum, two pipe or flageolet players.

"Revere and salute thy elders," said the Aztec father when sending his son out into the world, "and never show any sign of contempt. Console the poor and unfortunate with kind words. Do not talk too much and never interrupt others. Eat not too fast, and show no dislike if a dish displeases you. When thou walkest, look whither thou goest, so thou mayest knock against no one. Live by thy work, for thou shalt be happier there-

Aztec education. Left, girl learning to spin; right, boy learning the use of fishing implements. (From the Mendoza MS.)

fore. Never lie. When thou tellest anyone what has been told thee, tell the simple truth, and add nothing thereto. Be silent in regard to the faults thou seest in others."

In writing, the Aztecs drew small colored pictures on skins, and on paper made from the pulp of the yucca. Each sign had a special meaning. A tongue stood for speaking, a footprint for traveling, and a man sitting on the ground for an earthquake. By this method the Aztecs wrote down their laws, and drew up their tribute rolls. In arithmetic a row of dots stood for numbers up to twenty, and twenty was shown as a flag. The Aztec calendar was taken from the Mayas. Time was marked off in groups of fifty-two years, each year consisting of three hundred sixty-five days, divided into eighteen months of twenty days each, with a five day month at the end. Each day had a name such as "Monkey" or "Small Bird," and the last day of each week was fair day.

Gourd and turtle shell players. (MS. du Cacique.) Featherworker and goldsmith. (Mendoza MS.)

In spite of the fact that the Aztecs were cruel and warlike in their dealings with other tribes, they were kind and gentle in their homes, loving birds and flowers, delighting in music, dances, drama, and literature. Most of their writings were in verse, and the finest literature came from Tez-cu'co where it was partly inspired by the writings of the poet-king, Nezahualcoyotl (na-za-wha-ko-yotl'):

"Banish care; if there are bounds to pleasure, the saddest life must also have an end. Then weave the chaplet of flowers and sing thy songs in praise of the all-powerful God; for the glory of this world soon fadeth away. . . . Yet the remembrance of the just shall not pass away from the nations, and the goods of this life, its glories and its riches, are but loaned to us, its substance is but an illusory shadow, and the things of today shall change on the coming of the morrow. Then gather the fairest flowers from thy gardens, to bind round thy brow, and seize the joys of the present, ere they perish."

Montezuma, emperor of the Aztecs, lived in royal splendor in his stone city upon the islands of the lake. Soft-footed attendants surrounded him, and his people prostrated themselves when he passed. He dwelt in a palace that contained an aviary of gorgeous birds, an aquarium, and a noisy collection of lions, tigers, jackals, foxes, and serpents, as well as many more unusual animals. The beauty of the hanging-gardens blooming on his roof, the magnificence of his sunken bathing pools were the wonders of the Western World.

The Aztec Calendar Stone, was a blackish-green drum-shaped rock. On its face was the sun calendar, and around the circle were the signs of the year: the rabbit, the reed, the flint, and the house. The outer circles of the stone pictured the Aztec myths of creation and the destruction of the world. (National Museum, Mexico City.)

When the King dined, more than a thousand dishes were prepared for him. His stewards cooked fowl, turkeys, pheasants, partridges, quail, tame and wild ducks, venison, wild boar, reed-birds, pigeons, hares, rabbits, and many kinds of birds. From these Montezuma selected those that pleased him most. Sometimes as he strolled among the loaded tables, he permitted his favorite nobles to choose a dish for him, and this was regarded as a special honor. Beautiful flowers adorned all his apartments, and in whatever room or court he selected for dining, he was surrounded by color and perfume.

Montezuma always ate alone sitting at a low table set with dishes of black or red lacquer. A screen of wood richly carved and gilded was drawn around him to conceal him from other people; two Aztec women brought him tortilla

Xo-chi-pil'li, Aztec god of beautiful, fragrant flowers, wearing flower blossoms on his legs. (National Museum, Mexico City.)

bread, and four elderly chieftains stood beside them. Montezuma talked to these chieftains now and then, as he ate; and as a great favor, he occasionally gave each of the elders some of the food which he enjoyed most among the countless dishes prepared for his meal.

The Emperor was exceedingly fond of song and pleasure; and it was his custom, after his evening meal, to listen to an orchestra piping on sweet reed flutes and shaking the rhythm on gourd rattles; and to watch acrobats and other entertainers who sang and danced, giving them for their services what was left of his food. When, at last, the Emperor grew weary, there were brought to him three painted and gilded tubes filled with *liquidambar* mixed with certain herbs which the Aztecs called *tabaco*. Montezuma inhaled the smoke and at once fell asleep.

Monstrous sculpture of Co-a-tle'cue, Mother of the Gods. Her head is formed of two serpent heads; of braided rattle-snakes are her skirt. (National Museum, Mexico City.)

The Emperor had been a priest before he was chosen ruler, and like all his people, he was very religious. The Aztecs believed in a supreme God whom they addressed in their prayers as *Teotl*, or "the God by whom we live, unknown, unseen, shapeless and formless, and the cause of all causes." But the idea of one God was beyond the understanding of most of the people, who prayed to the many lesser gods controlling the powers of nature and the activities of men. The supreme god, the Invisible Spirit, who had no image or temple, was first; next came Na'hua, god-of-the-breath-of-life, and then Tez'cat-li-po'ca, "the Fiery Mirror," carrying a shiny polished shield ornamented with gay feathers, in which he saw the actions and deeds of all mankind. Quet-zal'co-a'tl, the fair god, the gentle god of the Toltecs, was also worshipped by the Aztecs, but this did not prevent their adoring with still greater fervor the blood-thirsty god of war, Huit-zil-o-poch'tli, the grim and awful. He it was who had led the Aztecs on their wanderings from the north to the lake of Tezcuco and the cactus growing from a rock.

To turn away the anger of the War God, thousands of people were constantly sacrificed upon his altar, and captives of war were fattened like beasts to be killed in multitudes on the great days of the feasts. Huit-

Stone knife with mosaic handle used to cut the breasts of victims sacrificed to the War God. (British Museum.)

zil-o-poch'tli had many temples throughout the Aztec Empire, and most magnificent of all was the Great Temple at the capital built of enormous stones shaped like snakes tied together and forming a circuit called "the snake circuit." Crowning it were battlements wrought in the form of snails, and into the building of this temple had gone all the cruel enthusiasm and triumph of a war-loving, conquering nation. Five thousand priests, men and women, served in the temples of the War God, and his altars reeked with blood in every city in the land.

Whenever the snakeskin kettledrum of the War God thundered its ghastly tom-tom, Montezuma ceased being an emperor and became the high priest of the god. Clad in plain black garments, he stood in front of the high temple before hushed throngs, while a war victim with bared breast was stretched upon the sacrificial stone. With an obsidian knife the breast of the victim was then cut open, his heart was torn out and offered to the lips of the bloody god, while his body was thrown down the long, steep steps of the temple pyramid to be carried off and fed to the beasts of the forest.

Dedication with human sacrifice of the Great Temple to Huitzil-o-poch'tli, the War God in Mexico City in 1484 A.D. (MS.)

At the end of every period of fifty-two years, on the last five un-lucky days, the Aztecs, like the Mayas, feared that some great calamity would happen. They broke to pieces their furniture and utensils, and destroyed everything they possessed; the sacred fires in the temples were allowed to go out, and all was wild disorder. On the evening of the fifth day, the priests in their richest robes, marched in procession to a high mountain near the city. Here under the dark, tropic sky, they watched anxiously to see when the stars of the Pleiades reached their height; for then it would be midnight, and the time of danger over.

The hour came at last. Suddenly the darkness of the hill-top was pierced by a feeble, flickering light, which showed for an instant the figure of a priest rubbing two sticks together. Other priests hovered over a stone of sacrifice while the multitude held their breaths. The spark of light grew bigger and brighter as the flames leaped into the air. Suddenly a sigh of relief went up from the waiting throng. They pressed forward to the sacred fire to light torches by which they would rekindle the cold hearths at home. The rising of the sun still further assured them that another cycle had begun! They returned to their homes with rejoicing; houses were cleansed and whitened, and the broken vessels replaced by new ones. Then the people dressed in their gayest garments; and crowned with garlands and chaplets of flowers, they thronged in joyous procession to offer sacrifices and thanksgiving in the temples.

Aztec priests in masks and elaborate ceremonial garments, making a new fire at the end of the fifty-two year calendar period, when all the Aztecs feared national calamity and disaster. (Zouche MS.)

The Spanish in America

Now, Montezuma had not ruled many years, before he began to be disturbed by fear of evil omens. As superstitious as all his people, he felt great events portending. The Lake of Tez-cu'co had suddenly overflowed its banks and swept away part of Te-noch-tit-lan'; one of the temple towers had caught fire, and could not be put out; terrifying comets appeared in the skies; and a strange, weird light covered the eastern sky like a sparkling sea of fire. All these signs filled the powerful Aztec king with dread; unquestionably they meant something, and he slowly grew convinced that they foretold the Fair God's return, the return of Quet-zal'co-a'tl in a winged ship out of the east, come to govern the land again. Moreover, a mysterious soothsayer, suddenly appearing, announced in awesome tones the end of the Aztec Empire. Montezuma trembled and feared.

Aztec drawing of a great volcanic eruption reaching the stars.

Then one day Aztec runners brought the Emperor news. Out of the east, as he feared, fair-skinned strangers had come, borne on white-winged birds that floated gracefully over the sea. Were they Quetzal-coatl, the Fair God, and his companions? Would the coming of the gods really bring the downfall of the Aztecs? Montezuma sent other messengers despatched in haste to the sea-coast to learn more about the strangers; and fearfully, uneasily, he awaited their return.

Fair-skinned these strangers were; but far from being gods; they were merely Spanish adventurers searching the world for gold. When Columbus landed on the tiny island of San Salvador in October, 1492, he did not return immediately to Spain, but set out to explore other islands in the neighborhood and to learn all that he could about the people in this new land. Forced by shipwreck to abandon further explorations, he left a small colony on the island of San Domingo, and departed for Spain to report his discovery to Ferdinand and Isabella.

Ancient picture of the harbor and settlement of San Domingo, the first permanent colony established by the Spaniards in America and dating from 1496. (*Orbis Habitabilis*.) Because Columbus believed that he had found the route to India, he called the inhabitants of ancient America, Indians; and the Spanish colonists quickly enslaved the Indians, forcing them to work their farms and dig for gold.

Men, women, and children returned with Columbus on his second voyage to America, and a permanent colony was established in San Domingo; but it was the island of Haiti, soon called His'pan-io'la, which became the real center of Spanish settlement in America. As more bold adventurers came from Spain to take up farms and search for treasures, Nicolas de O'-van'do was appointed governor and Don Diego Ve-las'quez was made captain of the military forces.

Among these early adventurers landing in Hispaniola was a gay, dashing young soldier by the name of Hernando Cortez, who quickly made himself the favorite of Velasquez. When the gold mines gave out in Hispaniola and Governor Ovando decided to seek in Cuba for new sources of revenue, it was to Cortez that Velasquez gave actual command of the troops. During the spirited skirmishes attending the conquest of the island, Cortez showed a lively ability; and when Velasquez was made the Governor of Cuba, large grants of Cuban land and Indian slaves were given Cortez.

Velasquez now established his capital at Santiago, founded three other towns, and then turned his thoughts to the nearby mainland.

Rumors had reached him of golden cities and fabulous wealth on the mainland, and soon he was stirred to action by reports of an expedition which had set out under Cor'do-va, a noble landholder of Cuba, to go to the Bahama Islands and bring back a cargo of slaves. Blown out of his course by a gale, Cordova had landed on a strange and unknown coast, where natives approached him in large canoes made from huge, single logs. These Indians wore garments of cotton, and were gay with many ornaments of finely wrought gold. But when the Spaniards landed and tried to learn from whence came this gold, the chieftain became suspicious and summoned from ambush squadrons of feather-crested warriors clad in thick, quilted-cotton body-armor and carrying long lances, shields, and bows and arrows. These warriors hurled their lances at the Spaniards with such haste and fury, fearing neither gun nor sword, that Cordova lost half his men and was forced to return to his ship. *Yucatan* the Spaniards named the country; for to all Spanish questions, the natives had replied: *Tec-te-ten,* "I do not understand," and the Spaniards made the word into Yucatan.

Inflamed with these reports and evidences of wealth, Velasquez forthwith fitted out a small squadron, loading it with glass beads, scissors, gaudy rings, and trinkets, and sent it off to Yucatan under the command of a kinsman, Don Juan de Gri-jal'va. Landing on the coast of Yucatan, Grijalva beheld a group of natives carrying a banner bearing strange devices, richly embroidered with dyed threads. The natives were armed with spears and shields, but the leader approached, and with hands extended in a gesture of peace, delivered a long speech. The Spaniards failed to understand the chieftain; but they did catch the often repeated word: *Mexico, Mexico!*

Aztec nobleman or chieftain with prominent straight nose and elaborate costume, met by the Spaniards. (Zouche Codex.)

This was always accompanied by a long, low bow to the west, as if the chieftain were rendering homage to a mighty ruler whose capital lay in that direction. And indeed, this leader was a vassal of the great lord Montezuma and had been bidden to learn everything about the white strangers who might prove to be Quetzalcoatl and his companions.

Grijalva was amazed at the signs of civilization shown everywhere about,—the large towns of stone houses cemented with white lime which were temples and palaces, the blood-spattered altars and evil-looking wooden idols. All the Indians heretofore seen had been the merest savages going about nearly naked and building the rudest shelters. Who would ever have dreamed these natives capable of anything in the way of civilization? Yet here the Spaniards had had a glimpse of one among the myriad wonder-cities of the Mayas.

The valuable golden ornaments worn by these Indians, however, were to the white men more interesting than their surprising cities and temples; and they were quick to exchange the tawdry trinkets they had brought for plates of gold, armor of wood inlaid with gold, shields, breastplates, collars, helmets, bracelets and beads of beaten gold. Seeking still other sources of gold, Grijalva sailed along the inward curving coast of the Gulf of Mexico, and so returned to Cuba. News of the riches of Mexico flew quickly from mouth to mouth, and Velasquez determined at once to send another leader to Yucatan.

Velasquez thought long and carefully before choosing a new captain-general. He must be ferocious in making war, but obedient to orders, a capable leader, able to guide an armada of fiery Spanish adventurers, yet not so ambitious as to put himself forward to claim the spoils or the glory! At last Velasquez decided, but still with some uncertainties and mental reservations. Touching Cortez on the shoulder, he made him his new captain-general.

Golden ornament which aroused Spanish greed. (Tehuantepec.)

Hernando Cortez Leads the Spaniards to Tenochtitlan

Cortez was at this time in the very flower of his manhood, restless, buoyant, vigorous, somewhat bow-legged from riding, but wearing to knowing advantage the silken hose of the cavalier. Already he knew by experience how to turn defeat into victory and how to rally an army fleeing in full retreat. In everything that he did, he gave the impression of a born conqueror, a favorite of fortune.

Learning all that he could from the soldiers and sailors who had been with Grijalva, Cortez prepared very carefully for the expe-

Hernando Cortez, bold, vigorous, full of spirit and daring, leader of the Spanish expedition sent to discover the source of Indian gold. (Portrait.)

dition before him. His men were to wear thick, quilted-cotton, body armor, such as the natives used, instead of clumsy metal breastplates. And since he knew the Indians had never seen horses before, he included sixteen sleek and well-fed horses in his equipment. Moreover, his eleven vessels were laden with guns and ammunition, and with gay glass beads, copper bells, and scarlet cloth to be bartered for gold.

Thus with five hundred foot-soldiers, all eager to enlist under so bold a captain, fiery nobles and prosperous landowners, clad in velvets and satins, and battle-scarred soldiers of fortune like the lusty old Bernal Di'az who was to chronicle the affair, Cortez set out for Yucatan frankly in search of gold. As chief pilot he had one who had sailed as a boy with Columbus and piloted Cordova and Grijalva in their recent expeditions; and to serve as interpreter, he redeemed the ragged and almost unrecognizable Spaniard A-gui-lar' who, having suffered ship-wreck, had lived among the Indians for some eight years.

The fleet of Cortez sailing from the harbor of Santiago upon the expedition which resulted in the conquest of Mexico. (A contemporary engraving). Bernal Diaz del Castillo, chronicler of the conquest, was born in Spain in 1492, the year that Columbus discovered America; and in 1514 when he was twenty-two years old, he decided to go to this new world in search of riches and adventure. He was one of the bold, reckless fighters who went on the expedition of Cordova; he sailed to Yucatan with Juan de Grijalva, and was among the first to enlist with Cortez. Throughout the campaign in Mexico, he served bravely and well, marching with Cortez to Mexico City, being among those who captured Montezuma, and making himself a real conqueror. He has been described as a "lovable old soldier, simple, enduring, splendidly courageous, and unaffectedly vain." After the conquest, he retired to a farm in Guatemala, and there in his old age, he wrote *The True History of the Conquest of New Spain*, the most complete and reliable account of the conquest of Mexico, and the one followed in this chapter. Diaz wrote in his preface: "That which I have myself seen and the fighting I have gone through, with the help of God, I will describe quite simply as an eye witness without twisting events in any one way."

In March, 1519, the fleet arrived on the low-lying, jungle-covered coast of Yucatan, and at once from the evergreen thickets swarmed multitudes of savage warriors. The faces of the natives were smeared with paint; they wore feathers in their hair and were armed with spears, shields, and swords made of hard obsidian. Standing in a small boat, rowed near shore, Cortez read a proclamation, stating that he had come to take possession of the land in the name of the Spanish King.

Understanding no word of this speech, but realizing that these arrogant, bearded strangers were enemies, the natives replied with a volley of sticks, stones, and arrows. Cortez at once leaped into the mud and water up to his waist, and led his men to shore. Caught between artillery blasts of terrifying thunder from the ships and lightning from the guns, the natives fled in panic and took refuge in the thickets.

Cortez at once entered the village and cut three deep gashes in the bark of a tree, crying: "I take possession in the name of his Catholic Majesty, Charles V, King of Spain, and Emperor of the Holy Roman Empire. Let those who protest, speak now and defend their claim against my power."

Next morning the natives returned. But once more the artillery of Cortez went off with such a thunderclap, and the lightning of the fire-arms poured such slaughter into their ranks that they closed up their lines with shrieks and threw dust into the air to hide their losses from sight. Then, awestruck and horrified, they beheld sixteen thundering, galloping horsemen swoop down upon them from behind. Never had they seen a horse! Horse and rider seemed to them one,—a kind of huge, godlike animal against whom it was useless, utterly hopeless to fight. Beings with thunder and lightning ever at their command! Beings who brought strange beasts, fantastic as their idols! Surely these must be gods. Again they fled.

Somewhat later, ambassadors appeared. The great Emperor Montezuma, in his distant capital at Tenochtitlan, had given orders that the strangers be received in peace. And now forty richly dressed governors and judges came to Cortez bidding him welcome and bearing presents of fowl, maize, and honey. As the Spaniards advanced northward along the coast, other chieftains appeared with golden gifts and beautiful maidens; and both gifts were seized upon greedily by the grasping invaders of this ancient land.

Beautiful Aztec feather shield like those sent by Montezuma to the Spaniards. The coyote design is made of thin strips of gold and the background is made of long quetzal bird feathers. (Natural History Museum, Vienna.)

Stone statuette of the Maize Goddess with corn tassel ornaments over her ears and an elaborate woven garment. The beautiful Dona Ma-ri'na, so devoted to Cortez, undoubtedly looked much like this. (National Museum, Mexico City.)

One of the slave-girls given to Cortez in Yucatan was a beautiful young woman of nineteen, olive-skinned, with delicate features, quick, intelligent eyes, and the bearing of a princess. She was baptized by the friar of the expedition and given the name Dona Ma-ri'na, and now she proved of greatest help to the Captain-general by her knowledge of both the Aztec and Maya tongues. Dona Marina had been the daughter of an Aztec chieftain in a small northern village near the borders of Mexico; but her father had died and her mother had sold her to some wandering traders who had sold her again to a Maya chief. Thus Marina could speak, not only the Aztec, but the Maya language, and since Aguilar understood Mayan, she could interpret to him what the Aztecs said and he in turn could translate the words into Spanish so Cortez could understand them.

Her help at once was invaluable. A powerful Aztec lord appeared at the Spanish camp, the noble Tendile, the first Aztec the Europeans had seen, come at the bidding of the Emperor Montezuma; and only Marina could speak his tongue.

"From whence do you come?" asked Cortez through the girl.

"Mexico, Mexico," answered Tendile waving his hand toward the west. "Mexico is a rich land; it is ruled by the mightiest king in the world, whose armies shake the world when they move."

Thus it was that Cortez actually came in contact for the first time with the lordly Emperor of the mighty Aztec Empire, Montezuma II.

Tendile had brought with him picture-makers such as they had in Mexico for picture-writing, and ordered them to make sketches of Cortez and his soldiers, ships, horses, and cannon.

Realizing that here was a great opportunity for impressing the Aztec Emperor, Cortez at once ordered a grand review. His best riders galloped across the plain two by two at full speed; Spanish foot-soldiers marched with banners and music; the mailed cavalry charged. Then Cortez himself aimed the largest cannon at an adobe house and blew it into countless pieces with a thunderous noise.

Tendile noticed that the Spanish helmets were like the helmet worn by the cruel Aztec War God, and he asked if he might take one to show the Emperor Montezuma. "Certainly," said Cortez, "if you will return it full of gold-dust. My officers and myself are afflicted with a disease of the heart which only the dust of gold can cure!"

Pottery figurine of an Aztec woman with baby from the Valley of Mexico. The Spaniards intermarried freely with the natives and usually found them most attractive. Occasionally, however, princesses of royal blood, given to the leaders, were ugly and disagreeable, and Cortez had great difficulty in getting rid of one fat aristocrat sent by a friendly chieftain.

Tendile promised to do what he could for the Spanish ailment; and stepping into a litter, he was carried swiftly to Montezuma's palace two hundred miles away. When he made his report and showed his pictures to Montezuma, the Emperor was indeed perplexed. Gazing at the helmet so like the one worn by the War God, he was almost convinced, indeed, that the newcomers must be gods and their fair-skinned commander the Fair God so certain some time to return. If this were so, it would of course be useless to oppose them. But if they were men, they could be crushed at any time.

Let every honor be shown them then, since he could not decide who they were. Let them be given gold, gold enough to content them and bribe them to leave the land. Aztec ambassadors were accordingly sent to the Spaniards heavily laden with gifts. As they approached Cortez, they touched their foreheads to the very earth and swung golden censers from which incense arose in fragrant clouds.

First there was shown an immense golden wheel representing the sun; then another wheel of silver in the form of the moon, and both wheels were richly carved. Twenty golden ducks now appeared, beautifully worked and very heavy; a dozen golden dogs; ornaments of gold worked in the shape of tigers, lions, and monkeys; ten collarets inlaid with precious gems; two hollow staffs of justice and twelve arrows, all of gold. Such were the treasures now laid before the wondering eyes of Cortez. But this was not all; there were green featherwork set in silver and gold, feathered golden fans, helmets, shields and spears of precious metal, thirty loads of beautiful cotton cloth worked in many patterns and decorated with colored feathers, and so many other gifts showing the Aztec love of ornamentation that even Bernal Diaz eagerly observing, could not remember them all.

Brilliantly beautiful feathered crown, or diadem, like those worn by Montezuma and other Aztec nobles. Presented to Cortez by Montezuma, and given to Emperor Charles V. (Natural History Museum, Vienna.)

To crown the event, Tendile had brought back the soldier's helmet filled to the brim with pure gold-dust, thickly set with lumps and nuggets of virgin gold! Spanish hearts quickened at this sight; here was proof indeed that the mines of Mexico were bursting with heavy ore. The downfall of the Aztec Empire was assured by that helmet of gold dust, and Cortez made ready at once to seize this golden land.

Tendile returning from reporting to Montezuma, presents the gold wheel of the sun and silver wheel of the moon with other gifts to Cortez. Dona Ma-ri'na stands by to interpret the Aztec message.

Before leaving the coast and entering the unknown dangers of the inland where lay the Aztec capital, Cortez established a city of refuge upon the shore. This he named *Villa Rica de Vera Cruz*, the Rich City of the True Cross, and it was to be an armed camp to which he could withdraw if necessary. Then, in order to prevent the possibility of desertion by the soldiers, he took a decisive step, staking all on his adventure. Stripping his ships, he sank them! Henceforth there could be no retreat; there were no ships to retreat in! The Aztecs must be conquered! The only route was forward.

Thus Cortez set out to conquer a mighty empire with only a handful of men, creating a marvelous adventure story, but also the sorry story of the greed and cruelty of white men and all that Mexicans suffered from it. Soon these adventurers left behind them the beautiful, warm, tropical country, and ascended the Sierre Madre Mountains, girt with dark pine forests and fields of summer maize. To the south gleamed the reddening fires of a burning crater. Cold winds mingled with rain, and driving sleet and hail penetrated to the bone.

Chilled and exhausted, the army at last reached the city of Xo-co-tlan', spread out like a silver-walled oasis on the tableland of the mountain valley; and here they were met by a governor so fat that he was named "The Trembler" by the Spaniards because he quivered like jelly. The governor received them sullenly; he lived in a magnificent palace with two thousand servants and thirty wives to do his bidding; and such luxury so impressed the invaders that Cortez thought he must be at least an ally of Montezuma.

"An ally of Montezuma?" repeated the fat governor in surprise. "Why I am one of his meanest vassals. In all my days I have never known or even heard of anyone who was not his vassal. Hither flock princes from all the earth bringing great riches. No lord, however great is there, who does not pay tribute, and no one so poor is there, who does not give at least the blood of his arm."

As the Spaniards advanced, they learned of the Aztec custom of human sacrifice and the offering of quivering, still-warm hearts to the War God. All the conquered tribes were called upon to furnish tribute of people for sacrifice, and pressing still further inland, Cortez found that this custom, together with burdensome taxes, had made many enemies for Montezuma. Many there were indeed who would gladly rise up and rebel if promised the help of the Spaniards, and to this fact was due the enlargement of the little army.

Meanwhile, high among the mountains, the Spaniards reached Tlas-ca'la, "the land of bread," the Switzerland of Mexico. Tlascala was a mountain-locked region in the midst of precipitous gorges and peopled by warlike highlanders wearing many strange devices and bristling feather headdresses.

Laughing head of the To'to-nacs', one of the tribes of the Mexican Valley subdued by the Aztecs. A wonderful example of free hand clay modeling.

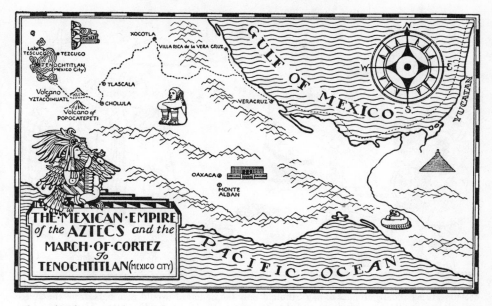

THE·MEXICAN·EMPIRE of the AZTECS and the MARCH·OF·CORTEZ To TENOCHTITLAN (MEXICO CITY)

They had never bowed to Montezuma, but had fiercely resisted all his attempts at conquest; and so proud and independent were they, that they lived without salt and external commerce rather than acquire these things by paying the Emperor tribute.

These proud, haughty mountaineers promptly refused passage to the Spaniards and thrice gave battle to the white men. Twice they held the road with fifty thousand feather-crested warriors, armed with wooden broad swords edged with hard obsidian. Great were the armies arrayed against Cortez and his men, and huge were the seas of enemies which pressed forward in bristling waves to overthrow them. But Cortez remembered his horses; quickly all were mounted; and the enormous army of the Tlas'ca-lans fled panic-stricken before a few men on "frightful metal-clad beasts" with weapons "that shot forth fire and made a loud noise."

As a result of this victory over the hosts of Tlascala, the fame of the Spaniards spread far and wide; news of their success reached the ears of the great Montezuma in the city of Te-noch-tit-lan'; and these white strangers were now held in greater respect than ever before.

x alte lalco.

Messengers sent to Cortez, after his great victory over the hosts of Tlas-ca'la, bearing the homage of Montezuma and his promise to pay tribute if only the Spaniards would turn back from the Aztec capitol. As usual Dona Marina stands beside her master. (Recently discovered Tlascala Codex.)

Awe and terror indeed took possession of the whole Aztec Empire. Again messengers came from Montezuma laden with princely gifts, and ambassadors tried to turn back the march of the strangers.

"The great Montezuma," they told Cortez, "is content to be the vassal of the all-powerful King who sends you to these shores. Decide, therefore, what annual tribute Montezuma shall pay, whether in gold, maize, or slaves; and it shall be paid on one condition: that you proceed no farther on your march toward Mexico. Accept these gifts, therefore, and sail away in your ships, leaving us in peace."

Cortez accepted the gifts and the vassalage of Montezuma, but he made no promises about sailing away. He had learned more and more about the dominating tyranny of the Aztecs which caused so many revolts, and after his great victory in the mountains, even the Tlas'ca-lans allied themselves with Cortez and became loyal soldiers. They turned out to greet him with a noisy hospitality, and followers to his army came from many distant parts of the land. Henceforth, as he passed through the provinces, his army increased each day.

The Spaniards drew near Tenochtitlan! All along their course Montezuma had been hearing of them. Still he could not decide what to do; and again he consulted those priests who had foretold the downfall of the Empire by the return of Quet-zal-co-a'tl. And now the soothsayers bade him invite the white strangers into Mexico.

Thus Cortez and his sunburned adventurers, weary and footsore after seven weeks of toilsome progress, at last, climbed, without opposition, over the steep mountain barriers guarding the valley of Mexico. Marveling greatly, the Spaniards looked down on a fairy island of green gardens floating on a sapphire lake with silver temple tops rising in the sunlight. Tenochtitlan or Mexico City was the loveliest place these men had ever beheld. Constantinople, Venice, even beloved Seville, could boast nothing so overwhelming.

Cortez kept strict discipline, however, as he marched to the stronghold of Montezuma; he could really depend on nothing save the white force at his command. The foot soldiers marched with loaded firelocks; the cannon were crammed with shot; at the lift of their commander's eye-brow, the alert Spaniards were prepared to fight for their lives.

The Spaniards with the help of native tribes at left, attack the soldiers of Montezuma, at right. (Ancient Aztec MS.) It was only with the help of native tribes that Spanish conquest was possible.

The Conquest of Mexico

Native drawing of the meeting of Great Lord Montezuma and Cortez astride a sorry looking nag, the best the artist could do. (Codex Vaticanus.)

There was a hush along the causeway leading from the island-city to the mainland as a glittering procession of Aztec noblemen advanced toward the Spaniards. At their head walked three royal ministers bearing aloft golden wands symbolizing Montezuma's civil, religious, and military power. Midway in the majestic train was the golden, royal litter of the Emperor, borne upon the shoulders of bareheaded, and barefooted nobles. The procession halted near Cortez; Aztec attendants unrolled soft carpets; and great nobles leaped forward to stretch a canopy of green feathers over the Emperor's head as he descended.

The great lord of the Aztecs, tall, slender, and dignified, with large, black eyes and sparse beard, was richly attired in a cloak of fine cotton sewn with emeralds and pearls. His feet were shod with golden soled sandals, and on his head he wore the sacred, flowing, green, hummingbird plume of Aztec royalty; he was the mighty king of a mighty race.

At Montezuma's approach, Cortez dismounted from his horse and advanced to meet him. The Emperor bade Cortez welcome and declared his happiness at seeing the strangers in the city. Cortez made a deep bow, and was about to embrace the Emperor, but was held back by nobles who considered it an indignity to touch their sacred master.

After giving orders that the Spaniards be treated as his guests, Montezuma was borne back to his palace, followed by the Spaniards, through hosts of prostrate subjects. Teeming crowds thronged the streets, the broad paved avenues, and the gardens on the flat roof-tops, to gaze in wonder at the clanking infantry, the strange war-horses, and the bronze cannon. Everywhere were flowers and groves, and in the center of the city was a great public square for trade and festivals.

Montezuma's palace, resplendent with hanging gardens, bright feathered birds, and sunken bathing pools, brought exclamations of delight from the soldiers. It was a building so vast, that Bernal Diaz wrote he wandered four times about it and yet had not seen it all. Splendid, too, was the palace given over to the Spaniards to be their dwelling place.

Curious and interested, and needing for military reasons to know the plan of the city, Cortez now asked Montezuma for permission to explore the place and acquaint himself with the avenues, the buildings, and the markets, as well as the splendid causeways built through the waters of the lake. Tenochtitlan, like Venice, was a city built upon islands, and many of the streets were water. It was laid out with four avenues running north, east, south, and west at right angles and extending along the lake on high dykes. These dykes or causeways were cut at intervals by sluices spanned by wooden bridges which could be removed in times of great danger to prevent approach to the city.

Here and there floating islands of flowers rose and fell with every movement of the water. Aztec gardeners built beautiful floating gardens on rafts which floated in the basin of the lake; and these were poled about by strong copper-skinned porters who sold the vegetables as they grew. In some places willow trees had grown on these floating gardens; and as they sent down their roots, they had anchored the rafts to one spot and made them permanent islands with little canals between. In other places the rafts were still poled about on the water and at times they were so large that they even supported a hut or a garden-house.

The Emperor Montezuma in royal robes of brilliant featherwork, bearing a ceremonial feather shield.(Ancient engraving: Salis, *Conquista*, 1715.)

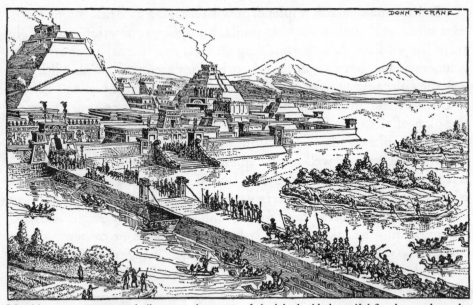

Marching over a causeway built across the waters of the lake beside beautiful floating gardens, the Spaniards enter the magnificent, stone-built city of Tenochtitlan, capital of the lordly Aztec Empire.

Hollow log canoes darted to and fro on many of the smaller canals which passed between flat-roofed houses made of pinkish stone and raised on little terraces above the watery street. Through the open doors of these houses could be seen glimpses of beautiful court-gardens, where sparkling fountains cooled the air and flowers nodded their bright heads, as families gathered together to enjoy the leisure hours. Around this court, in the houses of the well-to-do, there opened large, airy rooms having floors of cement and walls most beautifully covered with brilliant feather-work tapestries. Mats and cushions of fur, cotton, and palm-leaves served as beds and couches; and bamboo screens took the place of doors.

The center of the whole wonderful city of Tenochtitlan was the *Tecpan* or great market square with its surrounding arcades where quantities upon quantities of wares were offered for sale. Each kind of merchandise was kept by itself. Here could be found dealers in gold, silver and precious stones, feathers, mantles and embroidered goods.

Indian slaves, both men and women, were sold in the market, tied to long poles with collars round their necks so that they could not escape. Traders displayed ropes and sandals, great pieces of cotton cloth, and there were fruitsellers, and women who sold cooked food, honey and nut-paste dainties. Much of the trade was by barter, but for the larger sales quills of gold dust and cotton mantles were measures of exchange.

Everywhere, towering above the lesser buildings, were the pyramidal temples of red porous sandstone decorated with jasper and crystal porphory. Because the Aztecs were not familiar with the principle of the arch, the taller temples were built on very wide bases with terraced set-backs, each one smaller than the next lower. The great temple of the War God, covered with carvings of serpents, reared high above other buildings, and as the Spaniards mounted the steps, they saw the Emperor Montezuma, who had put on the long, black robes of an Aztec priest, busy with his sacrificial duties before the topmost altar.

Market place of Tenochtitlan (Mexico City) surrounded by great temple pyramids to the gods, with magnificent palaces and gardens everywhere. (Ancient drawing from contemporary descriptions.)

A sacrifice by two kings, the keystone of the War God Temple. (National Museum, Mexico City.)

It was with many misgivings that the Emperor-priest permitted Cortez and his companions to enter the innermost shrine of the War God. "On each altar were two figures," wrote Diaz, "like giants with very tall bodies and very fat, and the first which stood on the right hand they said was the figure of Huit-zil-o-poch'tli, their god of war; it had a very broad face and monstrous and terrible eyes, and the whole of his body was covered with precious stones and gold and pearls, and with seed pearls stuck on with a paste that they make in this country out of a sort of root, and all the body and head was covered with it, and the body was girdled by great snakes made of gold and precious stones, and in one hand he held a bow and in the other some arrows. And another small idol that stood by him, they said was his page, and he held a lance and a shield richly decorated with gold and stones.

"There were some braziers with incense which they call copal, and in them they were burning the hearts of the three Indians whom they had sacrificed that day, and they had made the sacrifice with smoke and copal. All the walls of the oratory were so splashed and encrusted with blood that they were black, and the whole place stank vilely."

After days spent in sight-seeing, banqueting and pleasure, the Spanish soldiers began to complain to Cortez. Where was the golden treasure that would make every man a prince in Spain? The eyes of the men glittered at the thought of the strongrooms from which Montezuma must draw the endless store of gifts that he showered upon the visitors, and legend reported whole palaces filled to the ceiling with gold dust.

Cortez realized that he must act. Moreover, he and his Spaniards were very few in number, in a swarming land of foes. He must do something daring and swift. So he set upon the bold plan of seizing Montezuma and making him a prisoner. An excuse was at hand. The Spaniards left behind at Vera Cruz had sent messengers saying that Montezuma had bribed a neighboring Aztec tribe to attack them. Cortez appeared fully armed before the Emperor. He considered, he said, that he was responsible to the King of Spain for the murdered Spaniards and would Montezuma come quietly to the Spanish quarters until it was found that he had not stirred up the revolt.

Almost before Montezuma realized what was happening, the Spaniards were crowding close around him, isolating him from his followers. His life was in their hands. They forced him to get into his litter, and to pretend to his guards that he went of his own free will under advice of the War God. So he was borne rapidly from his palace to the quarters he had given the Spaniards. A door clanged behind him, and never again did the Aztec Emperor lift his head in freedom.

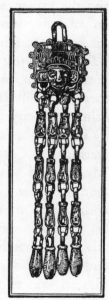

More and more melancholy Montezuma grew each day though the Spaniards came to love him and brought his attendants to him and though Cortez himself often sat and played games in the friendliest fashion with him. Always Montezuma was so sad, so troubled in mind, so bewildered and confused. Were these white men gods or not? Should he obey them or kill them? He ended by doing their bidding, forcing his followers to remain quiet and obedient through their reverence for his person, and always saying his course was dictated by the War God.

With the Emperor in his power, Cortez now proceeded to seize gold-mines, land, and slaves in the name of the Spanish King. He summoned all chieftains from the furthermost parts of Mexico to swear allegiance and to pay an immediate tribute of gold.

Gold pendant like those seized by the Spaniards as tribute. (Aztec Period.)

And if any city or province sent less than Cortez demanded, he promptly despatched soldiers to rifle the treasure, or he applied burning pitch to the stomach of the backward governor until the gold was produced. Even Montezuma's servants were prodded to hand over all the treasure and gold and wealth from the innermost palace chambers.

A rich treasure trove was gathered,—a huge, glittering, gleaming heap, collected from all parts of the empire,—enough to turn the head of any gold-hungry Spaniard. The soldiers imagined themselves as rich as many dukes, and those who were granted a peep at the treasure believed that they indeed saw the wealth of India! They clamored for distribution at once, and with the eyes of the entire army upon him, Cortez transformed the ducal share of each soldier into a beggarly trifle. A fifth was set aside for the King of Spain, and another fifth for the Captain-general himself; and when the shares of the captains, and double shares for the priests, the cross-bowmen, the owners of horses, and the expenses of the expedition had been set aside, there remained only a paltry sum for each common soldier. This then was their reward for having fought their way into the promised land of golden Mexico! "To ask for justice," said Diaz, "was useless; so we could do nothing but hold our tongues." Cortez, however, pointed out that the gold they had collected thus far was but a breath of air; there were many other great cities in Mexico, enough indeed to make every man a lord.

Then at last news came that Velasquez, the Governor of Cuba, fearing lest Cortez might set himself up as an independent ruler in Mexico and wishing himself to reap the golden profits of that rich land, had sent Captain Narvaez to Vera Cruz with ships, men, horses and cannon to seize Cortez and bring him back to Cuba in chains. So Cortez, leaving part of his army in Mexico City under Captain Alvarado, marched with the rest to Vera Cruz. In a short time he had taken Narvaez prisoner and persuaded the soldiers sent against him to join in the conquest of Mexico under his command.

But now a messenger arrived in hot haste, reporting that things were going badly in Mexico City. Alvarado had heard that the Aztec chiefs, seething with discontent and barely kept quiet by Montezuma,

Hearing rumors of a native uprising, and fearing for their safety, while Cortez was absent, the head-strong Spaniards under Alvarado attack the Aztecs during a sacrifice and festival to their gods.

meant to rise up before Cortez could return, rescue their Emperor in spite of himself and sacrifice the Spaniards to their gods. So he had decided to attack the Aztecs first and being a rash man, lacking in judgment, he had committed the sacrilege of falling on them while they were celebrating a sacred religious festival. Thus he had touched off an explosion of their long smoldering rage. As one man they had risen and chosen Montezuma's brother to replace him as their Emperor. They were besieging Alvarado in the Spanish quarters and he begged Cortez for aid.

At once Cortez set out with his army on a hurried march to Mexico City. When they arrived the city seemed deserted. Streets were empty and markets closed, for the Aztecs were keeping all food from the Spaniards. Through an eerie silence Cortez and his men reached the Spanish quarters. Then with an outburst of furious noise, a mob appeared and surrounded the place. They flung javelins, arrows and stones which fell like hail in the courtyards. They made a breach in one wall and before they could be driven back they set fire to a part of the palace. For a hideous day and night the Spaniards vainly tried to beat them off.

The next day, Cortez, determined to make the Aztecs feel his strength, sallied forth into the city with cannon, muskets and cross-bows. But now so aroused were the people that they were afraid of nothing. When men were mowed down in their ranks, they merely closed up the line. With yells and taunts and jeers they presented more men to the foe. Nowhere in the world had the Spaniards seen such fighting courage. After that Cortez had wooden towers constructed that his men might fight on the level of the rooftops whence the Aztecs hurled down their deadliest rain of missiles. But when the Spaniards went forth again the Aztecs battered these towers to pieces. So Cortez, in a fury, turned to attack the great pyramid of their War-God. Against fierce resistance he led his men up the steps. All streaming with blood and covered with wounds, they reached the altar at the top, destroyed the idols there and set fire to whatever would burn. But at that the attacks of the Aztecs grew so ferocious that they drove the Spaniards, tumbling down six or even ten steps at a time, back to the base of the pyramid and off to their own quarters.

Cortez's captains were now convinced that they must leave the city. They had almost no food left, their men were wounded, exhausted or dead, while the Aztecs could always produce a fresh array of warriors to take the place of those fallen. So Cortez, following a vote that was taken among the captains, decided to depart. And he bade Montezuma to go to the rooftop and command his people to let the Spaniards go in peace. Unwillingly Montezuma obeyed him. Sadly he stood on the rooftop, speaking with sorrowful affection to his people and begging them to let the strangers go in peace. He was greeted with tears and cries of distress, for the people now saw that if they were to save their land their beloved Emperor must die. Even as he spoke, the crowd sent a shower of stones and darts at that pathetic figure on the roof.

Aroused to fury by Spanish sacrilege, the Aztecs refuse to listen to the pleading of their prisoner-Emperor, and the pathetic Montezuma is killed by a shower of stones and darts from his own people.

Thus Montezuma fell, fatally wounded by his own people, and never for an instant did they let up in their assault on the Spanish quarters. There was now but one thing left for Cortez to do—try to get his men out of the city under cover of darkness. So on the following day he announced that they would depart that night. Then, since he could provide carriers for only a part of the treasures seized, he told his men that they might take whatever they liked of what was left. Straightway the soldiers pounced on the treasures which had before been denied them and many set forth loaded with gold. Undetected, they stole through the city, for the night was rainy, cloudy and very dark. They had nearly gained the causeway leading to the mainland and safety when the silence about them was suddenly broken by the dread sound of trumpets, Aztec shouts and jeers. Their flight had been discovered and the Aztecs attacked at once. All night the battle raged as the Spaniards tried to retreat across

The retreat of the Spaniards from Tenochtitlan in the dead of night laden with coveted gold. Gen. Lew Wallace in *The Fair God* has written an authentic, interesting novel of the Spanish conquest.

that narrow causeway, beset on all sides by Aztecs who came swarming from canoes on the water. And many Spaniards were so weighed down with the treasures which they refused to throw away that they could not fight effectively, so they either fell slain on the causeway or were driven into the water where they drowned beneath their great burdens of gold. It was a terrible night and dawn found the causeway and the lake filled with piles of their dead.

Nevertheless, Cortez himself escaped with part of his army. Beating back the pursuing Aztecs, he got his remaining troops in safety to Tlascala, the city of his faithful allies. There he started at once to rebuild his army and at some distance from Mexico City but still on the shores of the lake that led there, he began the construction of ships. A year he spent in almost constant fighting and work on the ships. Then he appeared again before Tenochtitlan, ready to besiege the city both by land and water. With the utmost fury the Aztecs resisted him, led by their gallant new emperor, the young Gua′-te-moc′. But the siege was long and merciless. Finally thousands of Aztecs, men, women and children, died daily of starvation. So on August thirteenth, 1521, Guatemoc was forced to surrender the city. The Spaniards had conquered Mexico and the glory of the Aztecs was done.

When the Spaniards reentered Mexico City they saw only ruins of the once so splendid gardens, palaces, pyramids and homes. It was a city of death and destruction which had fallen at last into their grasping hands. And soon they were torturing many Aztecs to wring from them the secret of where their treasures were hidden. Cortez even had the great Guatemoc roasted slowly over a fire in the vain attempt to make him reveal the whereabouts of gold that did not exist. This ordeal Guatemoc survived but Cortez, fearing lest so powerful a champion of Aztec freedom should organize further resistance against him, finally had him murdered as he marched off with other captives into exile in Honduras. Nor did Cortez ever see that actions such as these were by no means in line with Christian teachings. Still devoutly religious, he built at one end of the great market place, where the War God's temple had stood, a beautiful church which gradually grew into the lovely cathedral of Mexico City, and he sent to Spain for missionaries to convert the Aztecs to Christianity. So many intrepid friars, Franciscans and Dominicans, began to come to Mexico where they converted people by the thousands. But in attempting to wipe out the Aztec religion they destroyed so far as they could every trace of the old Aztec culture, breaking up idols and images; and even burning all the beautifully painted Aztec books.

Cathedral Plaza, Mexico City, once the principal Aztec square, and site of the War God's temple.

Spaniards with whips drive enslaved Aztecs to work. Another Spaniard lolls in a hammock being served with food before a picture of the Virgin. A protest against Spain painted on the very walls of Cortez's palace at Cuer'na-va'ca by Mexico's greatest modern artist, Diego Rivera, himself of Aztec blood.

Meantime, Cortez realizing that permanent conquest could only come with settlement, was encouraging his swashbuckling soldiers of fortune and others like them, who now came from Cuba or Spain, to settle down as farmers in Mexico. Vast tracts of land he gave them in the valley surrounding Mexico City, while he built himself a palace not far away at Cuer'na-va'ca. And not only did he and the Spanish governors who followed him take all the land away from the Aztecs but they turned the Aztecs into slaves. It was Aztecs, harshly driven by the whips of Spanish overseers, who must till the fields on the great Spanish estates or *haciendas*. It was Aztec slaves who must dig in the mines, labor in the quarries, make roads and buildings for their masters and do all the menial work that needed to be done.

All this the thinking Mexicans have never forgotten. With pride they remember the ancient glories of their people and how brutally white men destroyed those glories. And they glory in the fact that they are descended from Aztecs, Mayas, or other great Indian tribes.

To speak of Mexico as a Spanish-American country is far from true. For the early Spaniards, unlike the English, French and Dutch, who colonized the United States and Canada, brought few white women with them. They mated with Indian women and in a country thickly populated with Indians in contrast to the sparse Indian population to the north. Thus Mexico is definitely an Indian country and this fact her leaders are determined that the world shall understand. Today all the old Aztec genius has flamed again in the Mexican artist, Diego Rivera, and other artists of his school. On the very walls of Cortez's

Aztec Women, a painting by Diego Rivera. This characteristic patient, impassive attitude is due to Spanish brutality, which destroyed all Aztec brilliance, numbed the talents of the people and is deeply resented by modern Mexican artists, who reassert their national identity as quite distinct from the white man.

palace at Cuernavaca, Rivera has painted huge murals, not only showing the utter brutality of the Spanish treatment of Indians, but exaggerating every possible difference in the physical appearance of white men and Mexicans. In a manner profoundly striking Rivera and his fellow artists are reasserting their national identity as quite distinct from that of white men. These are things we need to know and remember if we are ever to have a true understanding of our nearest neighbors to the south.

V

The Indians of the Southwest

Spanish Exploration

In time the Emperor Charles V made Antonio de Mendoza Governor of New Spain, leaving Cortez as commander in chief of the army. And now more and more daring young men came to Mexico on every vessel that crossed from Spain. So more fine estates were constantly built up and more Aztecs and Mayas were reduced to the slavish position of *peons*, mere tillers of the soil who could own no land of their own. However, these turbulent young Spaniards were not all content to settle down peacefully to farming, no matter how many peons they might have to do all the work and make life easy for them. Instead, they dreamed of finding even more gold than had been found in Mexico and they kept hearing Indian tales concerning seven magnificent cities full of gold and silver that lay somewhere off to the north.

Beautiful gateway of a Spanish *hacienda*. On such estates Aztecs, Mayas and other Indians, from whom the land had been taken, were reduced to the condition of peons, or slaves to the soil, who could own no land. And the demand of the peons for land caused many revolutions, not only under Spanish rule but even after Mexico won its independence from Spain in 1821. Not until 1934 were the great estates broken up and the peons given their own bits of land.

Mexican laborers in the fields by Maximo Pa-che'co. Features and attitudes again assert Mexican individuality as Aztec and Indian, quite distinct from the European white man.

In 1536 Cabeza de Vaca and three companions straggled into Mexico City after eight years of wandering northward from Spanish lands in Florida, and they informed Governor Men-do'za that they had come upon Indians living in permanent dwellings and having an abundance of maize, beans, gourds, and other foods. Moreover, these Indians had given them not only presents of food, but of cotton mantles and turquoise, and they had said that turquoise and emeralds came from cities with very large houses far away to the north.

Mendoza was now all eagerness to have this region explored; but he knew he must not use money collected for the King in equipping an expedition unless he was certain of profit; so he sent a Franciscan friar by the name of Marco of Niza, to learn more about these glittering Seven Cities of Ci'bo-la reported to lie to the north.

For many days Fray Marcos with Es'té-van, a Negro servant, and a little band of Indians, toiled across the burning sands of the Arizona desert. Setting up camp at last, Fray Marcos sent the Negro to reconnoiter the land, bidding him send back crosses if he found cities really rich. In four days an Indian appeared with a cross as large as a man, whereby Fray Marcos gathered that the country ahead must hold a very vast wealth indeed! Eagerly pushing on, he fell in with red men who talked of a wealth of pearls on the sea-coast, and others wearing turquoise in ears, noses and waist-belts, who told of northern cities where the doors of all the houses were studded with turquoise and gold.

Unfortunately however, as Fray Marcos drew near the first of the famous Cities of Cibola, an Indian pueblo at Zu'ñi, he heard that his swaggering Negro had angered the inhabitants, and as the Zuñi-folk said, "been given a powerful kick which sped him through the air back to the south whence he came!" In other words, he was dead, his arrogance to be celebrated in humorous, Indian folk-dances for many an age to come. Fray Marcos dared only linger to catch a glimpse from a hillside of the distant pueblos of Zuñi, fabled to be so magnificent, ere he made off in a hurry from the angered people of the land, carrying back to Mexico reports that this northern country was certainly rich enough to justify an expedition for the glory of Cross and King.

Mendoza now lost no time in making preparations and collecting a strong armed force. Francisco Vas'quez Co'ro-na'do, a wealthy young friend of his, was made the leader of the expedition; and since the pulpits resounded with accounts of the marvels of the north, thanks to the tales of Fray Marcos, more than three hundred Spaniards and about eight hundred natives collected in a few days. In February, 1540, they set out on their adventure,—gaily caparisoned horsemen in shining breastplates and helmets, hardy, wooing dangers, and feeling themselves protected by unseen hosts of saints. Accompanied by a mule-train and herds of cattle and sheep, they rode behind Coronado, who dreamed of conquering an empire rivaling that found by Cortez.

Buoyantly the army started and continued on the march till they came to the great Southwest, a land of brilliant sunshine, romance, beauty, mystery, with clouds ever floating and changing above the stark, bold mesas which rose like islands of rock in the wide empty stretches of desert. It was a land of rose and amber, of painted deserts and turquoise sky, of canyons, mountains, and mesas, ever colored anew in the changing light of the sun,—gold and buff and lavender— and flecked with mysterious cloud-shadows, moving all day long. Over the sandy soil, like a sea tossed in a tempest, billowed olive-gray masses of rabbit brush, alternating with silver of sage brush, fantastic forms of cacti, dagger-like leaves of the white-blossomed yucca, and the richer green of greasewood, little stunted cedars, junipers, and pinyons.

By the clay banks of dry river beds, white ghosts of cottonwood trees writhed and twisted strangely, their white branches barren of foliage, save where they burst unexpectedly into small bouquets of green leaves. Somewhere from unseen camp-fires, the spicy odor of pinyon logs rose like delicious incense. A land of silence and space, of shimmering brilliance and color, isolated, majestic, such was the Great Southwest.

For eighty days they marched through the barren waste, called in later days Arizona or Arid Zone, then eastward into New Mexico, finding themselves at last standing on a hill at sunrise, looking over a blazing valley to the very pueblos at Zuñi of which Fray Marcos had brought back such glowing, romantic accounts.

But as they gazed before them, bitter disappointment seized upon them all. There in the plain below, beneath the long, flat-topped expanse of the sacred Thunder Mountain, rose like a pyramid on the banks of the Zuñi River, a seething ant-heap of houses, square, flat-roofed, many-storied, mud-colored like the plain, and rising in a series of terraces, surrounded by a wall. Was this the golden city that had been promised the seekers? Golden gleamed its mud, turquoise arched the sky, but where were those earthly treasures coveted by the invaders?

Zuñi, rising like a pyramid from the plain, was the first pueblo, or village of communal tenement houses visited by the Spaniards, who thought it one of the fabulous Seven Cities of Ci'bo-la.

Drawn up before the walls, the Indians stood armed and alert, as interpreters rode up toward them. Indian priests drew a line by scattering sacred meal, over which they forbade the newcomers to advance. But a horseman spurred suddenly over, and the battle was on at once.

Sight of the white man's armor and the uproar of galloping horses sent the Indians in flight to their village, where they shot from the upper terraces on all who approached the walls. But by the afternoon Coronado's display of artillery had forced the town to surrender. The Spaniards entered its walls and found neither gold nor jewels.

Wounded in this attack, Coronado now decided to make Zuñi his headquarters, and from here he sent groups of men to explore in all directions, still hoping that he would find the fabulous golden cities and further spurred to adventure by tales of a hump-backed cow, a beast unknown to the Spaniards, which an Indian, visiting camp, had painted on his body and which he said might be found in enormous herds to the north.

The Buffalo Hunt by Ma Pe-we. With sure strokes, the artist expresses, in true Indian manner, the feeling of the headlong rush of those "hump-back cows," which excited Spanish curiosity.

The Peace Messenger, by Tse-ye-Mu. Peace-ambassadors greeted the Spaniards from the Ho'pi, whose name meant the People of Peace. These Indians like all the Pueblo people, loved peace until the white man came and by attacks upon them or by seizing what was theirs, forced them into battle.

One party went out through the country where lived those fierce roving Indians, the A-pa'ches, Co-man'ches, and the tribe later called Nav'a-hos. These raiders of the village-Indians, who raised no crops themselves, but followed the hunt for food, waited till the corn was ripe or harvested and in storage, then they swooped down and seized it. Hogans, or rounded huts, made of logs and mud, housed the Navahos, and they wandered over the land where the Ship-rock sailed like a phantom or in those age-old canyons, where lost cities of the past, high up in the cliffs, sheltered the Navaho gods.

Passing the Navaho country, the explorers reached three long narrow fingers of rock belonging to the Hopi villages. The Hopis, the People of Peace, sent messengers out to greet them, and the Spaniards climbed the stone road-way up and up and up, till they came at last to O-rai'bi, the City of the Rock, a charming scene of serenity, industry and peace. Children played in the streets, climbing from terrace to terrace. Against the white-washed walls, brilliant colors gleamed; and through the open doorways came glimpses of white-washed interiors, with women kneeling on mats grinding corn on their grinding stones, and looking up shy and modest through strands of loose black hair.

Wal'pi, a Ho'pi pueblo on a rocky peninsula, rising sheer from the desert. For Acoma, see page 186.

The second of Coronado's little bands of explorers pushed on and found the Grand Canyon, that gigantic, awe-inspiring, multi-colored crack in the earth, which the Indians of the neighborhood thought was the road to the underworld for the entrance and exit of spirits.

The third of the Spanish lieutenants, Hernando Al'va-ra'do, marched for five days from Zuñi and suddenly came on A'co-ma, the greatest of all mesa-fortresses, rising sheer from the desert and looming on its island of rock, three hundred and fifty feet above the plain below. As Alvarado drew near, he saw that the grey sand-stone walls, supporting this soaring sky-city, were not merely perpendicular; they were actually overhanging, gashed and splintered crags, indescribably grand, and the only trail to the top was a flight of difficult steps cut in the solid rock and ending for the last twelve feet in a series of toe and hand-holds.

Warlike, the men of Acoma came down to meet the strangers but perceiving that Alvarado was preparing to attack, they decided not to give battle and permitted the Spaniards to climb the one steep trail to their village. High up on the rock, the newcomers had a view over all the plain below, an ocean of purple haze, dotted with great rock mesas and the one outstanding drum of that Enchanted Mesa whence the Acoma people had come in the fabled long ago.

Later on in the year, Coronado himself took up the march with his men. Striking the Rio Grande, the Spaniards passed up the river through various Indian villages to the beautiful pueblo of Ta'os. Gold-colored in afternoon light beneath a purple mountain, Taos gleamed on their sight, its two community houses, pyramids five stories high on either side of the river, its men in deerskin coats and trousers like Europeans standing on the terraces, handsome, dignified, silent, watching the light on the mountain change with the sinking sun.

In the Rio Grande region, Coronado spent the winter of 1540 and 1541; but his officers, in their greed, always demanding gold, imprisoned and flogged two Indians who had never seen nor heard of gold; and in general they left a deep-seated, well-grounded distrust of white men in the hearts of the simple natives. In April, 1541, Coronado starting eastward, passed through Texas, Oklahoma and part of Kansas, but he found only prairie and bison with no hint of the Seven Cities. At last convinced that these cities did not really exist, he led the ragged remnants of his weary little army back to Mexico, a disappointed leader, who was looked upon as a failure because he had found no gold, though he had opened to Spain vast stretches of valuable land and found a community-dwelling people most interesting in their primitive civilization.

Ta'os, with five terraces. Native Indian architecture, designed to house a communal democracy.

The Pueblo Indians and Their Dances

The people whom the Spaniards found in the sun-drenched, arid Southwest, they called *Pueblos* from the Spanish word meaning *town-dwellers*. Here in this brilliant land of turquoise skies and burning sands, these descendants of the old Cliff Dwellers had developed their civilization. Several centuries before, the Cliff Dwellers had abandoned their strongholds in the cliffs and scattered far and wide over the mesa-region of the far-flung San Juan Valley. Gradually they had moved southward, until at the coming of the Spaniards, the entire population had settled in about sixty-five towns in the Rio Grande Valley.

Sometimes their pueblos stood on the plain, but many high up on a mesa, built of stones and clay the color of the soil, seemed to melt into the rock of which they formed a part. The long low lines of Acoma and the various Hopi villages, made them appear from a distance to be the top of the cliff, from which they could not be distinguished; for it was the way of the Indian never to assert himself and stand out from the landscape as something separate and wholly apart from nature; but rather to vanish into it and find his proper place in harmony with the whole.

A'co-ma, the Sky City. greatest of all Pueblo mesa-fortresses, almost indistinguishable from the cliff.

Against the white of the houses, the colorful costumes of the Pueblo dwellers make vivid contrasts.

Standing along in rows, the houses had many stories, each one terraced back and leaving a flat, open space on the roof of the floor below. Whitewashed on the side toward the square, they offered a splendid background for the gay-colored dress of the people. On the lowest floor food was stored, and these rooms were entered only by a trapdoor from the top. Here and there ladders stood reaching to the upper terraces; and in time of attack by Navahos, Apaches or Comanches, the Pueblos hastened home, scrambled to the upper stories and pulled their ladders up after them, hurling weapons down from above.

Remote from the rest of the world, these Indians of the Southwest had developed a real democracy. Everyone lived in the same kind of house, did the same kind of work, and ate the same kind of food. There was no personal wealth and no inheritance of rank or honor; the tribes were each governed by a council of old men, and only the *cacique*, or religious leader, was excused from the general work, because his time must be devoted to prayer and meditation for the benefit of all the tribe. In all this desert-land there were no rich and thriving people such as had been described to the Spaniards. The Pueblos were peaceful farmers, with fields around their villages and nothing to bear out the tales of the seven rich Cities of Cibola.

Sky Father and Earth Mother, first creations of the Great Spirit, from whom sprang all life. (Navaho sand-painting.)

Like all red men, the Pueblo Indian was deeply religious. With simple unbounded sincerity, he believed that his life was in no way different or apart from the life of all other creatures. He believed in a Great Spirit, the Master and Creator of life, beneficent, all-seeing, never to be personified because he was too universal; "the All-Container," as the Zuñi said, "who thought outward in space", whereby he created the Sky Father and the Earth Mother, of whom were sprung all living things. To the Indian the sun, moon, and stars, trees, streams, and mountains had life in no way different from his own. Ravens foretold events, and wolves talked to him. Life dwelt in every object, in the beast, the bird, the lake, even in rocks, and clouds. All these lived as he did, with life not in outward form, but in an inward spirit which might perhaps change its house, but could never really die. Thus the universe was a place crowded full of life, of individual spirits, all related to the Indian. Though one might kill a buffalo in order that the people be fed, the buffalo's spirit would not die. It would only change its house, and if one killed only for necessity and never for crude pleasure, placating with sacred prayer-smoke, the spirits of the animals necessarily slain in the hunt, the animals would forgive, the unseen spirits be kind.

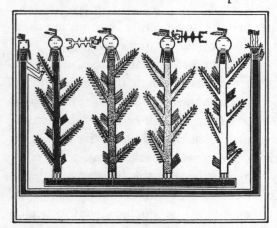

Cactus Folk, a humorous yet tender expression of the fact that the Indian believed the same life within himself dwelt in all objects. Above are "Pollen Boys" (Navaho.)

Thus while the Indian's faith that everything had life made many powers in his universe, it was the one Great Spirit who actually governed the world, who taught the wind to blow and the bird to build her nest, who gave the crops their sunshine and the rain.

The Squash Man, a Kachina or doll. Since life was universal pervading all things, the squash also had its identity.

"I know that it is a good thing that I am going to do" said an ancient wise man of the Sioux, "and because no good thing can be done by any man alone, I will first make an offering and send a voice out to the great Spirit of the World, that it may help me be true.

"See, I fill this sacred pipe with the bark of the red willow. These four ribbons hanging here on the stem are the four quarters of the universe. The black one is for the west where the thunder beings live to send us rain; the white one for the north, whence comes the great white cleansing wind; the red one for the east, whence springs the light and where the morning star lives to give men wisdom; the yellow for the south, whence come the summer and the power to grow.

"But these four spirits are only one Spirit after all, and this eagle feather here is for that One which is like a father, and also it is for the thoughts of men that should rise high as eagles do. Is not the sky a father and the earth a mother, and are not all living things with feet or wings or roots their children . . . ?

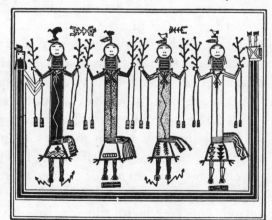

Gods of the four directions, North, South, East, West, all expressions of the One Invisible Spirit, which could never be represented or painted. (Sand-painting.)

The Buffalo or *Hunting Dance*, by Awa Tsireh. Believing that all things possessed the same kind of life, the Southwest Indian performed this religious ceremony before hunting to pacify the spirits of the animals, believing that if he killed only what he needed for food, the animal spirit would not be disturbed. The figure leading the dance is the Koshare, representing the ancestral spirit of the Indians, but he is also the fun-maker who makes the on-lookers laugh. The dance is a gorgeous ceremonial of the unity of life and the relationship between man and the universe. The prayer given here is from *Black Elk Speaks*, the story told by a Sioux holy man to J. G. Neihardt. Professor Hartley B. Alexander in *Mythology of All Races* says: "No one can follow the detail of Indian ritual without being impressed by his intense reverence for the Master of Life and his firm conviction in his goodness."

"Hear me, four quarters of the world,—a relative I am! Give me the strength to walk the soft earth, a relative to all that is. Give me the eyes to see and the strength to understand that I may be like you. With your power only can I face the winds."

Feeling with primitive earnestness this Universal Life, the Indian sought in all the mysterious forces of nature not something to be captured and made to serve his material needs, but a knowledge and understanding that would adjust his own spirit and show him his own proper place in the scheme of the universe. He was not lord and master of all, he was simply part of a whole, all related to one another, and to be a really good Indian meant such normalcy of conduct as would bring one into harmony with all that had life in the world.

With this joyous view of things, there was no room in the Indian's soul for repression and harsh restraint, for thinking much on his sins. Entirely concerned with the principle of the unity of all life, his religion was one of joy and dignified celebration, of constant prayer and thanksgiving to those beneficent powers who gave and governed life.

Prayer might be offered up by ceremonial smoking, symbolizing the breath of life and the yearning of the Indian's spirit ever drifting upward. It might be expressed by the scattering of the sacred corn-pollen, emblem of fruitfulness; by the planting of plumed prayer sticks, upon whose feathers was breathed the wish to be wafted to the four winds; or best of all, by the dance where in a perfect unison of motion, rhythm and song, every part of the Indian's body was attuned so as to express just that exact shade of meaning which the spiritual universe roused in his poetic soul. No act of daily life was so common and ordinary as to be unworthy of some ceremony. There were prayers connected with the hunt, the planting and harvesting of crops, and especially in that arid country for the needed gift of rain. There was the beautiful Snowbird Dance at the birth of a child when sun, moon, stars and all nature were called on to make his path smooth through life.

> Ho! Ye Sun, Moon, Stars, all ye that move in
>   the heavens,
>   I bid you hear me!
> Into your midst has come a new life.
>   Consent ye, I implore!
> Make its path smooth, that it may reach the
>   brow of the first hill!

The Snowbird Dance, a prayer which introduces the new-born babe to the universal life about him. The mother bears the child in a basket, and all the men wear bird headdresses. (By Velino Shije.) The poem is from *The Omaha Tribe* and was translated by Alice C. Fletcher and Francis La Flesche.

Masked Hopi dancers in a Spring Ceremonial in honor of planting and germination. (By the Hopi artist, Fred Kabotie.) The figures are Katchinas representing ancestral spirits. The masks of mud-heads recall the earliest days·when everyone dwelt beneath the earth. For the *Thunderbird Dance*, see page 199. The prayer to the Thunderbird is from *The Rain-Makers* by Mary Roberts Coolidge.

On festival days the plazas began to throb with drum-beats and flare with brilliant colors. Spectators on the terraces against the white-washed walls watched, intent and solemn, the spectacle of the dance, the rhythmic motions and foot beats, the rise and fall of the chants, expressing in symbol and pageantry the united prayers of a people.

Spring was the Indian's New Year, the time for planting the crops with ceremonies of planting, germination, and growth. Then came the Eagle Dance, inviting the Thunderbird to carry prayers to the sky.

> Oh, you who dwell,
> In the house made of the dawn,
> In the house made of the evening twilight,
> In the house made of the dark cloud,
> In the house made of the he-rain,
> In the house made of the dark mist,
> In the house made of the she-rain,
> In the house made of pollen,
> In the house made of grasshoppers,
> Where the dark mist curtains the doorway,
> The path to which is on the rainbow,
> Where the zig-zag lightning stands high on top,
> Where the he-rain stands high on top,
> Oh, male divinity!
> With your moccasins of dark cloud, come to us.

Thus the Indian dramatized all the wisdom he gained from nature. He welded a philosophy, a religion, and an art into one expression; and in the rhythm of movement and color in the dance he expressed life in all its movements, all its varied emotions, as far as he understood it.

His summer and autumn dances were prayers for growth, dances in honor of the rainbow, and further prayers for rain.

> Beautiful, lo, the summer clouds,
> Beautiful, lo, the summer clouds!
> Blossoming clouds in the sky,
> Like unto shimmering flowers,
> Blossoming clouds in the sky,
> Onward, lo, they come,
> Hither, hither bound!

Corn dances, too, were held; for was not the corn both Father and Mother, the source of life to the tribe? In one of the pueblos elaborate prayers took the form of the Green Corn Ceremony in which the gods were invoked for the proper growth, ripening, and harvesting of the corn. After visits to shrines in the mountains and days of secret ritual in the sacred kivas or ceremonial lodges built underneath the ground, the dancers purified themselves by fasting, bathing the body and washing the hair. Long prayers were chanted, sand-paintings made, and prayer plumes fashioned of sticks, decorated with wild turkey feathers.

The Feathered Serpent Procession, by Awa Tsireh. The appearance of this ceremony among the Southwest Indians suggests migration from Yucatan or at least connection with the Mayas, and their feathered serpent, Kukulcan. The Zuñi prayer for rain is from *The Indians' Book* by Natalie Curtis.

The Green Corn Dance to celebrate the maturing of corn, most precious gift to man. Note the wooden plaques on the heads, green the color of growing, and evergreen tuft decorations. (Awa Tsireh.)

Then came the dance. Whooping out of the kiva, came Koshare or sacred clowns, representing ancestral spirits and painted in black and white stripes with necklaces of night-shade berries and dried corn-husks in their hair. These ancestral spirits came back to help the tribe, and to cheer them with amusing antics, often performing little farces to ridicule some silly foible and cure their people with laughter.

Finally, surging up the opening of the kiva and streaming down the ladder poles in two long lines came the dancers, heralded by beat of drums and chanting of old men who marked time with clenched fists, and hour after hour intoned the deep, rich call for clouds and rain. At the first sound of the drum-beat, individual spectators subsided in spirit into the common rhythm of life, with an intimate, solemn sense of being at one with the forces moving heaven and earth.

The leader shook his gourd rattle and lifted his feet to stamp in rhythm. The dancers, wearing white kirtles embroidered in red, green and black, the colors of sun, growth and rain, with armlets of fluffy evergreens signifying ceaseless growth, swayed into perfect unison, and called on the gods for help to bring the maize to maturity.

Each dancer, as he came forward, shook a gourd rain-rattle filled with little pebbles, to imitate the swish of summer showers on the corn-fields, a coyote's tail jerked with his movements, and further rattles of turtle shell hung from under each knee.

Men and women signifying the union of heaven and earth, faced each other and danced with occasional solemn turnings, the women wearing on their heads towering wooden plaques painted green, the color of growing. Then they formed in couples, each man moving ahead, his feet spurning the ground, while the women followed slowly, their eyes cast gently down. Meanwhile, the Koshare wove in and out among the dancers, giving meaning to the movement with gestures of rhythmic beauty, and bringing to the watchers the importance of ploughing and enriching the earth. Thus they danced until sunset.

The Snake Dance of the Hopis was also a prayer for rain; for the snake when he wriggles makes his body in form like the lightning; and moreover he carries prayers to the gods of the underworld. For days before the dance, priests gathered snakes in the desert and collected

The Snake Dance, the Hopi ceremonial prayer for rain. An original painting by the Indian artist, Fred Kabotie, owned by the author. The snakes are messengers to the Powers of the Underworld.

them with great ceremonials. When the hour for the dance arrived, a warning rattle sounded, and Antelope priests lined up before the *kisi* of the snakes. The Snake-dancers then appeared, moving in long, swinging steps, definite, quick, and hard. Circling the plaza, they scattered the sacred meal, stamped upon *sipapu,* the entrance to the underworld, to announce the ceremony to the Great Plumed Water Serpent, and came to rest at last facing the Antelope men.

Rattles now trembled again, giving forth warning sounds like the rattle of the rattlesnake, and a deep, low, thunderous murmur began like the voice of a distant storm. Louder, ever louder grew the murmur; the priests rocked their bodies backward and forward, and burst into chanting. Then suddenly the singing ceased, and the men swung into a rapid, vigorous dance, which shook all the rattles.

When the dance ended, the Snake-men formed in groups of three, the carrier, the hugger, and the gatherer. Entering the shrine of the snakes, the carrier emerged with a snake between his teeth! Then with his hugger, he danced around the plaza in a circle. One by one the snakes were dropped in a heap on the ground while the third group of priests, the gatherers, watched the writhing reptiles to keep them from getting

Another Indian prayer for rain. The Council of the Gods attending the gigantic Shal'a-ko in the *Shalako Dance* at Zuñi. Coming from the mountains to meet the Shalako shown on the opposite page, these masked creatures represent the six directions, North, South, East, West, Above and Below, and are spirits who bring rain. This picture and that on the opposite page are by Zuñi artists.

away, never losing sight of their snakes, even in the height of the dance. When a gatherer had more snakes than he could handle himself, he honored some man in the audience by handing him an armful, or he gave them to the swaying, chanting Antelope-priests.

At last when the bag of snakes was emptied, the chief Snake-priest made a large circle of corn meal on the ground, and drew six lines toward the center representing the six regions, the North, the South, the East, the West, the Above, and the Below. Into this circle the snakes were thrown in a heap. Women and girls in white ceremonial mantles sprinkled the snakes and dancers with more meal, while the snake-priests dashed into the circle, gathered up the writhing beasts in great armfuls and rushed out of the plaza, taking the snakes to secret shrines where they were released to carry to the underworld, the Hopi's prayer for rain, which nearly always fell soon after the ceremonial.

At the pueblo of Zuñi likewise came an autumn rain ceremonial, the famous Shalako Dance, when the messengers of the gods, the six gigantic Shalakos, preceded by a Council of the Gods, came down from the mountains, visited newly-built houses, attended by little mud-heads, and returned again to the hills, bearing all the prayers back to the gods.

Shalako visiting a house. In masks nine feet tall, they roll their eyes, clap their beaks, and run with a gliding motion. Children think them actual gods and part of initiation to manhood is learning these are only men, masked to represent gods. The little mud-head represents the first Zuñis, who came up out of the earth and he warns youngsters: "If you are not good, you will be mud-heads again!"

Basket Dance of the Women, one of the most beautiful of the ceaseless ceremonies of prayer and thanksgiving for life which make the round of Indian ceremonials. Baskets symbolize food which preserves the life of the tribe; one holds white corn, one yellow, one red, one blue. The women themselves form a basket-shaped circle. (From a painting by Awa Tsireh. Owned by the author.)

Among the most beautiful of the ever recurring ceremonials of fructification was the Basket Dance of the women. Bearing in baskets the corn, white, blue, red and yellow, they formed themselves into a ring that was itself a basket, the symbol of food for the tribe.

Lastly in the cycle of seasons, came the Indians' winter dances,—prayers for the game and hunt, deer and buffalo dances, the Navaho Mountain Chant, and jolly ceremonials in honor of the Katchinas, the Hopi's ancestral spirits, in whose likeness he masked and danced with small painted images, which were later given to the children, to serve them as dolls. Thus did the Pueblo Indians and their roving Indian neighbors attune themselves to life, with a solemn sense through the dance of exalted satisfaction, celebrating every event in their manifold activities, birth, maturity, mating, war, peace, and their unity with all life.

The Poetry of the Indians

Since deep poetic feeling was the breath of life to the Indian, song was his natural expression. It was heard at all hours rising from the village or from the desert plains and cliffs. Feeling deeply and sincerely that all nature was alive and that he was merely a part of this universal being, the Indian was thrilled by the knowledge of a power greater than nature, a power greater than man, yet eternally manifested throughout all life. He and the wind and the clouds and the beasts and the plants were brothers, different expressions of the One Spirit, but united none the less. And believing this to be true, seeing the soul and loveliness in everything around him, he expressed his feeling for life in poetic terms of enduring beauty without even knowing that he did so, spontaneously, naturally and all unconscious of himself. Even his names for the months were beautiful and poetic, —March, the Awakening Moon; April, the Grass Moon; May, the Planting Moon; June, the Rose Moon; July, the Thunder Moon; August, the Maize Moon; September, the Hunting Moon; October, the Leaf-Falling Moon; November, the Mad Moon; December, the Long Night Moon; January, the Snow Moon; February, the Hunger Moon.

The Eagle or *Thunderbird Dance*, by Awa Tsireh. Loving rain-giving thunder-clouds, the Indian pray the Thunderbird to bear his people's prayers to the Sky, and in his Eagle Dance he imitates almost every movement of real birds, soaring, hovering, mating, perching on high places, resting. See page 192.

Rain drips from clouds around the sun above dancers of the *Bow and Arrow Dance.* (By Tse-Ye-Mu.) Poetic love of clouds and rain is shown in the frequent use of such conventional cloud and rain patterns. The Zuñi song of the cloud is arranged from *The Indians' Book* by Natalie Curtis.

Scarcely a task light or grave, scarcely an event great or small, but had its fitting song. History, tradition, thought were preserved for the Indian in song and ritual. He did not set art apart, a separate thing from life, to be indulged or not; his arts and his life were one, and his songs are vital parts of his everyday existence.

In gaily colored dresses, with their hair falling over their faces, the girls of the village of Zuñi worked at their grinding stones, their bodies rising and falling in unison with music, sung to them from the doorways by the young men of the tribe. And the young men sang of the corn, child of the great Corn-Mother, when it was young and childlike, high up on the ear, longing for clouds to come.

> Lovely! See the cloud appear!
> Lovely! See the rain draw near!
>   Who spoke?
> 'Twas the little ear of corn,
> High on the tip of the corn-stalk borne,
> Saying while it looked at me
> Way up there today.
> "Ah, may the rain,
> Moving hither,
> Ah, may the rain come this way!"

And when the grinding was done, the maidens often danced, singing:—

> Who, ah know ye who—
> Who, ah know ye who—
> Who was't that made a picture first?
> 'Twas the bright Rainbow Youth,
>   Rainbow Youth—
> Ay, behold, 'twas ever thus—
>   Clouds came,
>   And rain came
>   Close following—
> Rainbow then colored all!

The Rainbow was to them a youth, a beautiful painted youth and the swallow summoned the rain. His song brought joy to the little corn.

> Yonder, yonder see the fair rainbow,
> See the rainbow brightly decked and painted!
> Now the swallow bringeth glad news to your corn,
> Singing, "Hitherward, hitherward, hitherward, rain,
>   "Hither, come!"
> Singing, "Hitherward, hitherward, hitherward, white cloud,
>   "Hither come!"
> Now hear the corn-plants murmur,
> "We are growing everywhere!"
> Hi, yai! The world, how fair!

The Rainbow, sign of the moisture and sunshine needed for their crops, was always a joyous sight to the Indians, as may be seen in the two beautiful poems from *The Indians' Book* and the playful antics of the Koshare clowns climbing over the Rainbow. (From a picture painted by Awa Tsireh.)

Spring Rain Dance. Women with jars to catch rain, hold in their arms, beside squash and melons, the beloved corn, to them in turn as it grew, a baby, a maiden, a mother. Painting by Tse-Ye-Mu.

When the little corn grew bigger it was a maiden and the butterflies played over it.

> Corn-blossom maidens
> Here in the fields,
> Patches of beans in flower,
> Fields all abloom,
> Water shining after rain,
> Blue clouds looming above.
>
> Now behold!
> Through bright clusters of flowers,
> Yellow butterflies
> Are chasing at play,
> And through the blossoming beans
> Blue butterflies
> Are chasing at play.

How they loved those butterflies; they made many songs about them, as they flitted over the cornfields, dusty and painted with pollen.

> Yellow butterflies,
> Over the blossoming virgin corn,
>   With pollen-painted faces,
> Chase one another in brilliant throng.
>
> Blue butterflies
> Over the blossoming virgin beans,
>   With pollen-painted faces
> Chase one another in brilliant streams.
>
> Over the blossoming corn,
> Over the virgin corn
> Wild bees hum.   (From *The Indians' Book*.)

Sometimes the Hopi girls, playing among the young corn plants, chasing each other and laughing, with their hair in squash-blossom wings flaring out over their ears, looked so like wide-winged butter-flies flitting ovor the fields, that the young men were prompted to sing:

Rain all over the cornfields!
Pretty butterfly-maidens
Chasing one another when the rain is done,
    Hither, thither, so.
How they frolic 'mid the corn,
    Laughing, laughing, thus:
      A-ha, ha-ha,
      O-ah, e-lo!
How they frolic 'mid the corn,
    Singing, singing, thus:
      O-o, o-ho,
      O-he, e-lo!

Hopi maidens with their hair dressed at the sides in squash-blossom whorles, play and frolic among the slender stalks in the corn fields. The Hopi song is from *The Indians' Book* by Natalie Curtis.

Young men admired Pueblo maidens, wooed and sang their love
songs, as love sings all over the world.

O what happiness!
How delightful,
When together we
'Neath one blanket walk,
We together
'Neath one blanket walk,
We walk.

Can it be that
My young maiden fair
Sits awaiting,
All alone tonight?
Is she waiting
For me only?
Is she waiting
For me only?

My hope it is,—
My young maiden
Sitting all alone
And awaiting me;
Will she come then?
Will she walk with me?
'Neath one blanket
We together be,
We—we two—we two.
We two, we two—
Will she come?

(Translated by Mary Roberts Coolidge)

And the lover, disappointed, lamented and sang his sorrow as lovers
have always sung.

My little breath, under the willows by the water-side we used to sit.
And there the yellow cottonwood bird came and sang.
That I remember and therefore I weep.
Under the growing corn we used to sit,
And there the little leaf-bird came and sang.
That I remember and therefore I weep.
There on the meadow of yellow flowers we used to walk.
Oh, my little breath! Oh, my little heart!
There on the meadow of blue flowers we used to walk.
Alas! how long ago that we two walked in that pleasant way.
Then everything was happy, but, alas! how long ago.
There on the meadow of crimson flowers we used to walk.
Oh, my little breath, now I go there alone in sorrow.

(Translated by Mary Roberts Coolidge)

And when he reached the height of grandeur in the consciousness of his love, and wished his loved one to share with him the glory of all creation, the lover sang this song:—

> Come, my beloved, let us go up that shining mountain, and sit together on that shining mountain; there we will watch the Sun go down in beauty from that shining place.
>
> There we will sit, till the Night Traveler arises in beauty about the shining mountain; we will watch him as he climbs the beautiful skies.
>
> We will also watch the little Stars following their chief.
>
> We will also watch the Northern Lights playing their game of ball in their cold, glistening country.
>
> There we will sit, on the beautiful mountain, and listen to the Thunder beating his drum.
>
> We will see the great Whirlwind race with the Squall.
>
> There we will sit, until all creatures drowse.
>
> There we will hear the great Owl sing his usual song: "Go-to-sleep-all," and see all animals obey his call.
>
> There we will sit in beauty on the mountain, and watch the small Stars in their sleepless flight. . . . (*Translated by John Reade*)

To the Indian indeed all was beautiful, the world was a world of beauty, as the Navaho sang in his joy:—

> In beauty happily I walk
>> With beauty before me
>> With beauty behind me
>> With beauty below me
>> With beauty all around me.
>
> It is finished in beauty
> It is finished in beauty
> It is finished in beauty
> It is finished in beauty
>> (*Translated by Mary Roberts Coolidge*)
>
>> All is beautiful,
>> All is beautiful,
>> All is beautiful, indeed.
>
> Now the Mother Earth
> And the Father Sky,
> Meeting, joining one another,
> Helpmates ever, they,
>
>> All is beautiful,
>> All is beautiful,
>> All is beautiful, indeed.
>> (From *The Indians' Book*)

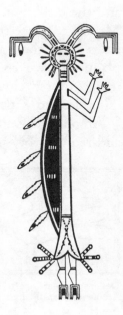

Fun-loving Indians of Mim'bres Valley, N. M., so enjoyed the humorous incidents of the village that cartoonists painted them on pottery. Left to right: the fish "that got away" and the monster who stole all the bait; a pugnacious wild turkey with terrible teeth and needle-like horns; a vicious, corn eating insect; a grotesque caricature of a bird-animal, fit subject for a Museum of Unnatural History.

Arts of the Indian

Just as poetry and song were an essential part of the life of the Indian, so were all other artistic expressions. His unconscious aim was to beautify life through adorning whatever he used,—pottery, blanket, or basket, and in the joy of this work, he found his method of self-expression. Sitting in the shadow of pueblo walls, the Indian woman moulded her bowl; and for decoration, she went to nature itself. High colors, strong contrasts, bold outlines, these were the features of her landscape, and these she put into the designs with which she painted her bowls. Moreover, since the desert-dwellers needed rain above all else, decorations in all their art, expressed a prayer for life-giving rain. On Hopi plaques of woven grasses, the coming of the storm was expressed in many colored cloud forms; the silversmith beat out the wings of the Thunderbird with silver pendants representing rain drops.

Among the Zuñi, animal figures and squash-flower rosettes in black-and-red on ivory were favorite designs; and one of their bowls showed a

Designs on Pueblo pottery showing the Indians' instinctive desire to beautify life. Bird forms from Acoma and San Ildefonso; the Zuñi deer showing heart, and snake messengers from San Ildefonso.

deer with a white spot on his rump, a visible heart, and a line from the mouth to the heart, indicating his breath and that his wind was good in running. On the pottery made in Hopiland, the bird was given beautiful sweeping curves, and in the Mimbres Valley of southern New Mexico, birds, fishes, and insects were drawn with comic twists. The people of the Mimbres Valley were the first cartoonists in America; they were laughing artists, who painted village jokes on their bowls, and told of "the fish that got away" or "the monster that stole all the bait."

In the days before the coming of the Spaniards, the Pueblo people wove cotton robes and blankets, and this art was given new life when the Spaniards brought sheep into the land. Then the Hopi and Zuñi tribes became expert weavers of ceremonial skirts, sashes, and belts. Into the very texture of the robe was woven man's relation to earth and the life-giving powers of sun, wind, and rain. But it was the Navahos, who wove the most beautiful blankets. As the Navaho woman followed her sheep, she pictured in her fancy the blanket she would weave;

Navaho Woman with Sheep, a painting by the Ta'ne-an artist, Aqwa-Pi. The Navahos are a nomadic people, and with sheep introduced by the Spaniards, they now follow their flocks, living in temporary *hogans* throughout the great Southwest, where they have become the most expert of weavers.

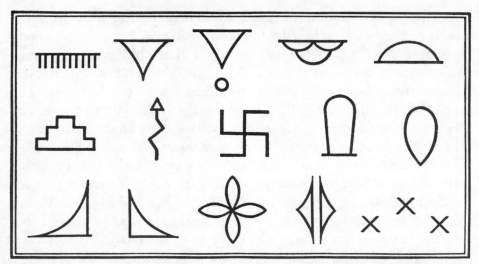

Some of the common designs used most frequently by the Southwest Indians to decorate baskets, pottery, blankets, and other articles. Upper row, left to right: (1) falling rain; (2) far-off falling rain; (3) rain falling through the roof and making a spot on the floor; (4) clouds; (5) a single cloud. Center row: (6) a mountain. Often only half of this design is used, especially in blankets to indicate the sacred kiva. (7) lightning, or a snake, or an arrow; (8) swastika; (9) feather; (10) seed. Lower row: (11) hill; (12) the moon; (13) flower; (14) leaf; (15) stars. (From Coolidge, *The Rain-Makers*.)

for like the Pueblo potter-woman, she had no pattern to follow and must create her figures from the various forms of nature which lay so close to her heart. Red, she knew, was the color for fire and for the sun; black stood for water and rain; these were the colors of life. And since there was much more sunshine than rain on the desert, her blanket would have more red in it. But there must also be black, the color of the North, of mountains, and storm clouds; blue, the color for women and the soft southern sky; and yellow for the west, the place of the setting sun, and the end of the journey. Every line and stripe and square and diamond, triangle, cross, zig-zag and fret had a meaning. A broad angle represented the arching sky; a sharp angle upside-down, a whirlwind; a series of drooping semi-circles, the clouds; while a row of small squares joined by straight lines showed the houses of related families. A diamond was the country of a group of families; and if it were woven in the form of stair-steps, it was a mesa rimmed with mountains. Zigzags were the lightning and if tangled together, they stood for serpents.

Like all Indians, the Navahos were intensely religious; but their ceremonies were long, elaborate, poetic "medicine sings", or chants given for the healing of the sick rather than to bring rain. Gathering from their grazing lands, their rocky canyons and deserts, they came together to sing and to dance by night in a circle around a flaring fire, their figures in dark silhouette against the dusk of the sky. For each day's ceremony, elaborate sand-paintings were made; and nowhere among the Indians had the making of pictures in sand been reduced to a finer art. These paintings were sacred pictures showing traditional ceremonies, representing the gods, lightning, sunbeams, rainbows, mountains, animals, plants or those two holy twins, sons of the Turquoise Woman, who in the myths of many tribes fought with primeval monsters and made the earth fit for man.

When the gods first gave these ceremonies to man, so the Navaho said, the pictures were painted on buckskin, and their priest memorized them and then destroyed the buckskin to keep the pictures from falling into the hands of people who would not understand them. Thereafter, they were to be made in colored sand and to be destroyed before sunset.

Navaho blanket with figures of men and women dancing a ceremonial prayer such as their "medicine sings", or beautiful Mountain Chant. The women wear the full skirt of the Navahos. Human figures were seldom pictured by the Indian who preferred to make his decorations a prayer to the gods.

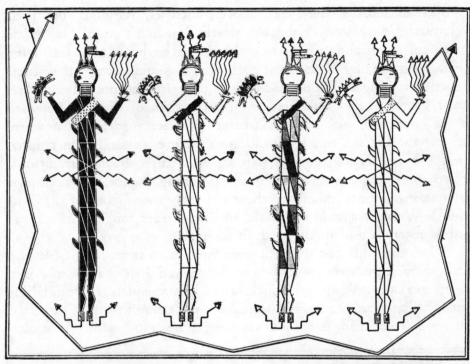

Navaho sand-painting made during a prayer ceremony to heal a sick woman. The two figures at the left are the holy twins, sons of the Turquoise Woman, who fought primeval monsters and made the earth fit for man. The third warrior wears armor of many-colored arrows of petrified wood; the fourth wears points of yellow agate. All are outlined in red, meaning life, and the entire sand-painting is surrounded by a thunder-bolt to keep out evil. (A painting in possession of the author.)

These elaborate, symbolic sand-paintings and the sacred chants that went with them passed from generation to generation, changing gradually, and many of them fading entirely from memory. With special ceremonies, certain young men gathered dry sand of different colors from the desert and spread a field of white on the floor of a priest's lodge. The drawing and coloring were done by spreading broad patches of different sand outlined with lines of great delicacy and accuracy, and every figure, every line, every dot was a symbol. The priest directed the work, and the one who needed the prayer was seated on the painting. When all was finished, the painting was destroyed, and some of the color rubbed on the sick person to help him in getting well.

Acoma, the Sky City

Such were the people of mesa-land when the Spaniards invaded the great Southwest in their eager search for gold. Moving in orderly procession with nature, seeking no special places for themselves, they were trying to live in harmony with all created things.

Into this life of deep, spiritual understanding, the greedy, materialistic Spaniard burst with a sudden shock. Roughly he strode into the mesa dwellings, overturning bowls and baskets, delving into stores, searching always for gold. True, Coronado's disappointment and the fact that he was looked upon in Mexico as a man who had utterly failed, discouraged visits northward for forty years or more. But in 1598, a provincial governor, Juan de Onate, got a contract to colonize New Mexico, and El Paso, the first settlement, became the capital.

The Sky City of A'co-ma, however, did not welcome this white intrusion. One of Onate's lieutenants by the name of Zoldivar was marching to join the governor, when he chanced to pass by Acoma. An Indian priest descending, urged the Spaniards to visit his fortress; and Zoldivar, not suspicious, climbed with sixteen comrades up to the mesa-top, leaving the rest of his force to wait with the horses below.

Graceful Acoma women, with water jars, at the pool which catches rain on the mesa-top. See page **186**.

The War Dance, a painting by Velino Shije. Such was the dance at night on the rock-fortress of Acoma when the Spaniards under Zoldivar returned to avenge their slaughtered comrades.

Suddenly a hideous war-cry signalled an attack. There was no path of escape, no way to call for help to their comrades standing below. Overwhelmed on every side, the Spaniards sold their lives dearly but soon all save five lay dead. These five, driven at last to the very edge of the cliff, determined not to give the Indians the satisfaction of slaughtering them. Springing over the precipice, they thought to meet certain death, but by what seemed a miracle, only one was killed. The rest hastened with their companions to report the affair to the governor.

Onate was appalled; he at once sent the brother of the murdered captain with seventy-seven men to march on the citadel.

Arrived at the towering city, the Spaniards found howling Indians dancing on their cliff, while their priests hurled shrieking insults at the foreigners below. Answering a summons to surrender with a shower of stones and arrows, they forced the Spaniards to withdraw to refuge under a cliff. The Spaniards now divided their forces. Twelve men with a cannon were sent under cover of night to climb the steep, inaccessible, uninhabited, southern part of the towering Acoma mesa, which was divided from the northern half, where the village had been built, by the gulf of a savage cleft, almost cutting the rock in two. In spite of their heavy armor, the Spaniards made their way up, dragging not only their cannon, but also a great pine log with which to bridge the gap.

The main force approached the village by the regular entrance trail, but while they occupied the attention of the defenders, the Spaniards on the southern mesa rushed from their hiding places, flung the log over the chasm and began to run across mid a rain of stones and arrows that threatened every moment to dash them off into space.

In the tense excitement of battle, one of the Spaniards who crossed caught the rope attached to the log and pulled it over after him, shutting off the small group with him from their friends on the opposite side. Instantly they were surrounded by a band of fighting Indians; but a Spanish officer left with those on the southern bank, gave a mighty leap and sprang across the dizzy gap, seizing the log and thrusting it once again over the gulf. And now the remaining Spaniards hurried over the dangerous foot bridge. Fiercely they engaged in a desperate hand to hand struggle till the Indians at last retreated into their fortress-like houses. The Spaniards then dragged up their cannon and began to smash house after house. Soon fire ran through the village and at noon the Indians surrendered. The lofty Sky City was burned to the ground.

A dance witnessed at Acoma by the author in which Indians solemnly ridiculed their white conquerors. This fun is frequently enjoyed in the Indian pueblos. The dignified, stately gravity of Indian dancers contrasts with the white man's strutting pomposity and nervous antics, while the gorgeous color of Indian dress shows up the drabness of the white man's costume. If the white man is smugly sure of his own superiority, the Indian has a quiet laugh and his own opinion on the matter.

Spanish power had triumphed; priest and soldiers now proceeded to colonize and control a great Southwest. Thus the Indians, who had here risen to heights of religion, art, and poetry known to no other tribes within the United States, retreated into themselves and tried to preserve their culture in remote, inaccessible places.

Their civilization was unique. They had developed a stable democratic government, settled habitations with a distinctive architecture, orderly pursuit of agriculture, well developed arts, pottery-making, weaving, songs that were deeply poetic, the practice of wedding one wife, a settled love of peace, and a deeply spiritual religion, with a ritual free from sacrifice of animals or humans. On this civilization the white man burst like a blight. It was never allowed to fulfill the richness of its promise, but still remains our finest native civilization.

Dancing for the Christ Child, a painting by Gustave Baumann. Christianity has not altered the fundamental religion of the Southwest Indian. He feels that Christianity is only another form of worshiping his own gods, acknowledging another God who is good, and he has therefore simply incorporated certain Christian ceremonies into his own ancient dances. Edgar L. Hewett says in *Ancient Life in the American Southwest:* "The life of the Indian, on the evidence of his cultural remains, was marvelously unified and socialized. Virtually every form of activity, esthetic, industrial, social was at the same time the practice of his religion. In quest of food, sitting in council, developing the symbolic design on utensil or garment—he was putting his whole spiritual life into it, and always with the thought of 'the people,' never of the individual. The race has no personal history—only tribal or communal. . . ."

VI

The Conquest of Peru

(1493—1532)

Explorations of Central and South America

While the Spaniards were busy, conquering the Indians of New Mexico and seeking in vain for gold in what is now the United States, other Spaniards had been looking for gold in Central and South America. Portions of South America had long been known to the Spaniards. On his third voyage to the New World in the year 1500, Columbus touched Venezuela and found the mouth of the Orinoco River; other venturesome sailors also turned southward, and

Reckless, headstrong Spanish adventurers in America, quick to quarrel over a division of gold. (de Bry's *America*.)

soon the eastern shore had been explored from Yucatan to Argentina.

Only seven years after the discovery of America, quantities of pearls and some gold were found in the Gulf of Da'ri-en' near the Isthmus of Panama, and at once there was a rush of greedy cavaliers and hungry hidalgos to this region. Among those who came scrambling in great haste to acquire wealth without labor was a reckless young adventurer named Vasco Nunez de Bal-bo'a who left San Domingo hidden in a barrel to escape his creditors. Hearing him quarreling with his comrades over a division of gold, a young Indian remarked scornfully:—

215

"Why do you quarrel over such a trifle? You Christians prize this yellow metal more than friendship or life. If for it you leave your homes and come far through dangers to attack other people, I will tell you of a land where you can get all you wish. Six days' march over those mountains to the south, there is another big water. All the streams flowing down the mountains are yellow with metal, and the commonest people of the country eat and drink from yellow dishes!"

Hearing these words, Balboa forgot his quarrel and plied the Indian chief's son with questions. Convinced that the youth spoke truly, he determined to find this golden land, and enlisting two hundred men he set out for the sea to the south. The way was difficult and dangerous, and the men were soon worn with doubt and disease. Balboa had to lead his forces through deep marshes swollen with recent rains, over mountains covered with dense, trackless forest, and through rocky defiles where the Indians shot at them with poisoned arrows. At last, however, led by Indian guides, he and his remaining men struggled up a high mountain-side. When they were near the top, he called on his men to stop, and he alone went forward to be the first to look down upon the shimmering waters of the Pacific Ocean.

The exhausted Spaniards, however, found no golden cities in the lands bordering the Gulf of Panama. All they found was gold dust, gold ornaments and pearls; but from the natives they heard new accounts of that glittering kingdom to the south where dwelt a nation, powerful, civilized and rich. Eagerly Balboa built ships to continue his journey, but he was killed by a spiteful enemy before he could get to sea.

Meanwhile, in distant Portugal, a sea captain named Fernando Ma-gel'lan had become convinced that he could reach the Spice Islands of China and India by sailing west around the islands and continents of America. His idea was laughed at by the King of Portugal, and like Columbus, Magellan turned to Spain, where during his visit news arrived of Balboa's discovery of the Pacific. The Spanish Emperor, Charles V, finally agreed to provide ships, and in 1519, six years after Balboa's discovery, Magellan set sail from Spain with five small vessels, determined to find a way through or around South America.

The voyage of Magellan has been called "the greatest feat of navigation that has ever been performed." The dauntless explorer was killed on the voyage and four of his ships were lost, but one solitary vessel with eighteen men of the original crew at length reached Spain, after having crossed the Atlantic, rounded South America, and sailed the Pacific, thus completing the first voyage around the world.

Since no way had been found for ships to sail across South America to the Pacific, Spanish explorers now turned to Central America in search of a waterway from east to west, and steadily all this country was brought under Spanish rule. Balboa's mysterious golden land to the south had not been forgotten, however, and stories were still told of its wealth. Now, among the companions who had accompanied Balboa on his march across the Isthmus was a short, swarthy soldier named Francisco Pi-zar'ro, who had spent his youthful days upon the hills of

Es're-ma-du'ra in Spain as a swineherd. His small black eyes were bold, shifty, and cruel, and his nose was like the beak of a hawk. By craft and guile, Pizarro worked himself into the good graces of the Spanish colonial officers; he made two expeditions which never reached the golden land, and then having gone himself to Charles V in Spain, he received from the King gifts and offices encouraging a third journey which eventually brought about the conquest of Peru.

ANCIENT CIVILIZATIONS OF SOUTH AMERICA AND THE EMPIRE OF THE INCAS

Ancient Peru
(From about 100 B.C. to 1532 A.D.)

Pottery portrait vessel of a proud Chi'mu ruler with painted face and simple scorpion-decorated headband. (Chimbote.)

Ancient Peru was a long, narrow country, just south of the equator, lying for a distance of two thousand three hundred miles along the western coast of South America. At the time of the coming of the Spaniards, all this immense territory was ruled by a war-like people, known as the Incas, or Children of the Sun. For four hundred years, the Incas had governed from a magnificent, stone-built capital at Cuz'co; and they had established a splendid civilization, founding it on the culture developed by an older people.

Some time before the beginning of the Christian centuries, there lived along the coast and in the lower mountain lands of the Andes, a short-headed people who had come from Central America. They were farmers who came in small groups and built up many independent centers of civilization in the western coast valleys.

Scenes of everyday life shown in Chi'mu pottery. Left to right: gable-roofed adobe house built on a terrace; two men carrying a mummy to the cemetery; humble man with burden supported by head strap; a rather oafish man lounging under a rude shelter. (American Museum of Natural History, New York.)

Most important was the Chi'mu civilization in the north, which grew up in the Moche River Valley, and from there spread its power and learning to the surrounding country. On a wide fertile plain north of the Moche River arose the city of Chan-Chan, capital of the Early Chimu kings. Here great flat-topped pyramids served as the foundations for temples and for the dwelling places of kings and nobles.

It was in the making of pottery, however, that the Chimu people expressed their deepest feelings and far surpassed all other tribes of North or South America. Common, every-day scenes of life were molded on their bowls and vases, and many vessels were adorned with landscapes, hunting scenes, and battle scenes. Other jars were fashioned in the shape of fishes, guinea pigs, monkeys, and potatoes; but most striking of all, were their portraits in

Portrait of jolly, smiling Chimu noble with features and expression entirely different from the figure opposite. (Chimbote.)

clay, vessels formed into faithful likenesses of the Early Chimu rulers and their more important nobles, dignified or smiling, tranquil or merry.

Chimu pottery makers were real sculptors, and in forming their human-shaped vessels, they copied living models showing all the differences of character. Here are portraits of a placid man sleeping, a miserly man, a turbaned figure, "big ears," and woman with baby. (Amer. Mus. Nat. Hist., N. Y.)

Moulded and painted vase of a chieftain in elaborate robe and turban seated above a painted battle scene. (Truxillo.)

Six hundred miles south of Chan-Chan was another great civilization in the fertile Naz'ca River Valley. The Nazca people also made portrait pots and vessels adorned with paintings like those of the Chimu; they had more of a feeling for color than did their brethren to the north, and they delighted in the use of many rich and soft hues: red, orange, yellow, pink, pale blue and purple. It was in weaving and cloth-making, however, that the skillful Nazca workers surpassed the other people of South America; and most of their designs were mythological monsters, part human and part animal. They showed a Spotted Cat, a benevolent creature representing the Bringer of the Means of Life; other figures were a ferocious Cat Demon, a Bird Demon, and a long wriggling Centipede God. Both Nazca and Chimu people developed rapidly in the fertile valleys of the South American coastland, and in the arts of pottery and weaving they produced work that was far superior to anything made by later conquerors.

Fight between early South American warriors in a dry, sandy desert, indicated by cactus plants. The men carry shields, bronze battle axes, and stone or copper war clubs with star-shaped heads. The shield at left is painted with the heads of two vanquished foes. (Vase painting, Truxillo.)

One other important early civilization arose away from the coast, high among the ranges of the Andes, in a valley on the cold barren shores of Lake Ti'ti-ca'ca nearly thirteen thousand feet above sea level. Here there was built the city of Tia'hua-na'co; and in this city all art centered around the worship of the Creator-God, a short, stocky, square-faced figure, known to the later Incas as Vi'ra-co'cha or the Weeping God. His image was carved in a frieze upon a great stone gateway showing him in an elaborate tunic held together by a girdle of puma heads. To right and left, running rapidly toward him were rows of attendants.

Warriors with shields, spears and throwing sticks. They have nose ornaments and wear tall, elaborate helmets. (Chicama.)

In time, the civilization of Tiahuanaco spread far and wide throughout the Peruvian mountain lands, and many other small centers of culture likewise sprang up at various places throughout the region of the Andes. Finally, however, all were united under the leadership of the Incas, a masterful, Quech'ua-speaking tribe from the mountain lands to the east.

Victorious soldiers returning from battle with a bleeding captive naked except for a rope around his neck. The soldiers in elaborate helmets, body armor and weapons, march along the treeless, sandy coastlands amid flying birds with the Andes Mountains in the distance. (Vase painting, Chimbote.)

The Incas were entirely different from the other people of ancient Peru; the color of their skin was many shades lighter, their noses were not sharp nor prominent, chin and mouth were firm, and their faces were majestic and refined. In their mountain highlands, these intelligent energetic people tamed the llama and used it as a beast of burden; and when they set out upon the conquest of their neighbors, these beasts gave them a great advantage over their enemies, as they were able to carry supplies for their warriors for long distances. The name *Inca*, however, was at first a title given only to their chieftain, or ruler; but the conquered tribes called all their masters by that name, and in time all of the Quechua people became known as Incas, or Children of the Sun.

Moving northward in their career of conquest, the Incas seized the valley about the mountain city of Cuzco, and here they settled, making Cuzco their capital, and erecting many enormous stone buildings. In time, a legend arose which gave their rulers divine origin and bestowed heavenly sanction upon the city. Man'co Ca'pac and his wife, the legend related, were Children of the Sun who had descended from heaven to earth upon an island in Lake Titicaca, selecting Cuzco as their capital city, because the Sun had bidden them settle in whatever place the golden staff he gave them, disappeared at one blow in the earth.

In the years following the conquest of Cuzco, the strength of the Incas increased rapidly until it included an empire which reached from northern Ecuador to central Chile, and from the Pacific to the eastern slopes of the Andes.

Silver statuette of a llama, tamed by the Incas; beside it, silver figures decorated with gold bands. (Amer. Mus. Nat. Hist.)

This great empire, of many different tribes and people, the Incas united by building fortresses at important points in all the conquered territory, and by settling colonies of Quechua-speaking farmers in the midst of the foreign tribes.

Moreover, they built roads and footpaths leading from the capital city of Cuzco to the furthermost parts of the empire. The trails over

An alpaca with long coat of soft silky wool, prized by the Incas for weaving. (Silver statuette, Amer. Mus. Nat. Hist.)

the steep Andes Mountains were paved; flights of steps were cut in the living rock where necessary; and swaying suspension bridges, made of fibre ropes and swinging with every step, led over deep mountain gorges with a torrent far below. There were turn-outs on the mountain-trails where litter bearers paused for breath, while their noble passengers enjoyed the view spread before them; and in many places the roads were bordered by lines of shade trees. Every obstacle except the unstable desert sands was conquered by the engineers; they built causeways across swamps; they marked the trail across shifting sands by long poles set at short distances; and they spanned small rivers with well-built bridges of massive blocks of carefully matched stone.

Storehouses for feeding the army, inns and posthouses were placed at convenient places along the main roads; and at every posthouse lived *chasquis* or runners who carried the Inca's bidding to every part of the land in short relays. These men wore special uniforms and had the right of way on the roads. They were so speedy that an imperial decree from Cuzco could be carried to the royal offices at Quito, more than a thousand miles away, in the remarkable time of eight days.

An Inca deer hunt. The animals have been driven into a net where they are killed with clubs and heavy darts by nobles in rich apparel. (Scene on water vessel, American Museum Natural History.)

The Emperor or Inca, who was descended from the Sun, was the chief ruler, the chief priest, the commander of the army, and the only law maker. He was a superior being, the source of all power, and the owner of all the land in the empire. This land, the Inca divided into three parts, one for the Sun, another for himself, and the third for the people. Every person was loaned the use of a piece of ground large enough to support him and his family, which returned to the state at his death. The lands set aside for the Sun furnished revenue to support the temples and the multitudes of priests; and the Inca's share of the land supported the court and the royal family. All lands were cultivated by the people; those belonging to the Sun were attended to first; next came the lands of the old, the sick, widows and orphans and of soldiers in actual service; and then the people were allowed to work on their own grounds before cultivating the lands of the royal Inca.

A cloth factory. The official in charge at the left is giving food and instructions to his assistants. At the right, one of the weavers has a sample pattern of cloth to follow. (Vase painting, Trujillo.)

Fishing scene. Two men are shown in each boat, one with paddle, the other with line. Fish have seized the bait; sea gulls hover above awaiting discarded fish. (Woven tapestry design. Pachacanac.)

Countless were the ways in which Inca rule made itself felt. Everyone was numbered and must dwell in a certain district and everyone belonged to a definite class. All the people were divided according to age, location and service. Those past sixty years were excused from work, and everything was done by able-bodied persons between the ages of twenty-five and fifty. Labor was also specialized according to the community, skill being handed down from parent to child, and while one village might be given over to pottery, another would be devoted to the making of weapons, and there were certain communities where the whole village specialized in weaving. Nowhere in the world has finer woolen-work ever been woven by man, and the fat alpaca and sheep which furnished the wool for the cloth wandered with flocks of llamas under care of public shepherds. Every man in Incaland was compelled to serve the state in some way according to his age and ability.

Tapestry of conventionalized human figures surrounded by cat, bird, and fish designs. (Pachacanac.) No people, ancient or modern, have ever equaled Peruvian textiles in workmanship, color, or design.

Ceremonial dance by men wearing masks and winged costumes to represent birds, their swiftly-moving figures shown in arrested flight. The men at left are flute-players. (Peruvian vase paintings.)

To prevent interruptions in their work, even private weddings were not permitted. Instead, once a year the marriageable young people were assembled in the city squares and paired off by joining hands after the consent of the parents had been secured. Then there was "one universal bridal jubilee throughout the empire," accompanied by dancing, singing and playing upon pan pipes, flutes and drums. When the national wedding celebration had ended, all returned to their labors.

These strict rules made the Inca Empire a communistic state in which everyone lived and worked for the benefit of all. There was no private property, no privacy in any activity of life, and no Peruvian was so high or so low that the government did not regulate his every act. No one starved, and no one squandered; but progress was impossible, as all must live in the positions into which they had been born.

The Inca, however, as a heavenly being and the son of the Sun, lived in pomp and grandeur, dwelling in wonderful palaces at various places

Paying homage to the Inca who is seated in an ornamental house built upon a terrace. Runners mount the steps to announce the coming of chieftains, carried in litters. (Vase painting, Trujillo.)

throughout the land. These palaces were splendid structures commanding magnificent views. Although plain, strong and solid without, they were very gorgeous within. The walls were studded with silver and gold and pierced with niches, which were filled with images of animals and plants curiously wrought in gold, silver, and bronze. They were hung, too, with gay featherwork or richly dyed woolen tapestries, made by the skillful weavers. Beautiful fountains, streams and aqueducts supplied water to luxurious baths of gold and there were spacious gardens stocked with plants and flowers.

The Inca, a bust in the American Museum of Natural History, New York, made after careful study of Inca skulls and paintings. The beautiful blue feather blanket behind him with fish design is a perfect example of ancient Peruvian featherwork.

On the death of an Inca, however, his palaces were abandoned; his treasures, furniture, and apparel were preserved just as he left them; and all his mansions except one were closed. This one was kept ready for his return. When an Inca was "called home to the Sun," his funeral was celebrated with great pomp. A quantity of his plate and jewels were buried with his entrails, and sometimes his favorite concubines and attendants were also buried in his tomb. The body was then embalmed and removed to the Great Temple of the Sun at Cuzco where it was placed beside the embalmed bodies of previous Incas and their wives.

Gold ornaments about two inches high worn by the Incas. The gold has been fashioned into figures of warriors and drummers, with an ornate, mighty chieftain in the center. (Amer. Mus. Nat. Hist.)

The people of Peru believed that the dead would return again to earth, and they acknowledged a supreme Being, the Creator and Ruler of the Universe whom they worshiped under the names of Pa'cha-ca-mac' and Vi'ra-co'cha. There was only one temple to this Invisible Being,

Peruvian tapestry design of conventionalized man with upraised hands. In the border are birds.

however, and the favorite god of everyone was the Sun who gave warmth and light to man, and life to the vegetable world. To the Sun they erected temples in every village and hamlet; and in Cuzco there were three or four hundred lesser temples in addition to the Great Temple of the Sun. Offerings at these temples were vegetables, fruits, and flowers. At special religious festivals, however, llamas were offered to the Sun God; and military victories were celebrated by human sacrifice.

The Temple of the Sun at Cuzco was the greatest of all temples and the holiest spot in the city. Within were enormous quan-

Peruvian blanket into which has been woven alternate light and dark figures of warriors with feather headdress carrying human heads and clad in plain, fringed tunics. (Amer. Mus. Nat. Hist.)

tities of gold. The people of Peru placed no value on gold for itself, but prized it as the metal of their god. It was "the tears wept by the Sun," and on one of the walls of the temple they had engraved an enormous figure of this deity upon a thick plate of solid gold ablaze with emeralds and precious stones. Even the walls and ceiling of this room were encrusted with gold, and throughout the building, cornices and walls were aglow with burnished plates and studs of gold. Even the tools used in the temple gardens were either silver or gold.

Nearby were the convents, or Temples of the Virgins, where dwelled the fifteen hundred maidens whose lives were devoted to the service of the Sun God, and whose duties consisted mainly of keeping burning the sacred fires upon his many altars. These virgins were chosen from families throughout the Empire when they were quite young and were placed in the care of elderly matrons who taught them in all their religious duties.

Unusual tapestry design of colorful, mythological, bird-like creatures. (Amer. Mus. Nat. Hist.)

These chosen maidens were the spiritual brides of the Sun, and the Inca being the son of the Sun and his representative on earth, could take for himself any that he wished; and if any maiden was returned later, she was held in high honor by the people all the days of her life.

It was agriculture that furnished the means for all this magnificence and display, and in tilling the soil, the people of Peru had become truly scientific. They had both canals and underground aqueducts for irrigation, which brought the water from high mountain lakes to farms throughout the land. On the mountain sides they cut terraces, facing them with rough stone, and beautiful were these slopes, seamed in regular ridges with the patterns of rich green terraces. From the smiling valleys along the coast to the terraced steeps of the mountains, there were flourishing farms that showed careful, patient labor. On these were grown bananas, maize, tobacco, cocoa and potatoes, all flourishing at different levels at the same time.

The Incas also knew how to smelt metals and cast them in molds, and they were skilled in the making of pottery; but with all this knowledge in agriculture and manufacturing, they did not know how to write. Instead of writing words, they kept their records on gayly colored cords called *quipus*. Taxes and the census, as well as messages to officials were recorded by a system of tying a number of knots in these cords.

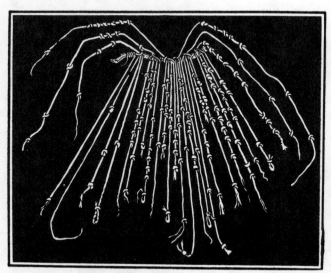

Peruvian *quipu* or knot record. Although the Incas had a rich and expressive language, they had no system of writing. For counting, however, and as a guide to memory, they used the *quipu*, a number of different colored knotted cords tied to a main cord, the position and color of the knots having certain meanings known to the possessor.

In counting, the decimal system was used, the units being represented by the lowest knot, and the tens by the next knot above; for messages, however, the colors of the cords had symbolic meanings,—red stood for war, white for peace, and the position of the knots indicated other meanings which served to guide the memory.

Although the most imposing buildings in Peru belonged to the time before the Incas, upon the ruins of these structures, the conquerors built simple, solid and symmetrical temples and palaces, well adapted to withstand earthquakes. They did not know how to support heavy roofs, however, and a building with a humble thatch of straw, unlighted by a single window, was often an important structure in a town.

A Mummy Bundle in beautiful tapestry. The body in sitting position with knees drawn up and head resting on them was placed in wrappings with a false head. (Amer. Mus. Nat. Hist.)

Most impressive of pre-Inca cities was the romantic Ma'chu-Pic'chu hidden away in a canyon not far from imperial Cuzco. Remarkable for the beauty and grandeur of its situation, it hung high up in the sky on a narrow mountain ridge, facing a line of snow-peaks, its glistening white stone buildings and green lines of terraced fields descending abruptly in steps, till the slopes fell sheer away to the loop of a foaming river in the valley far below. Ascent to this sky-built fortress was by a narrow rock-trail, often breathlessly near the edge of the precipice or leading up flights of stairs cut in the solid rock. A city of refuge it was, protected by its precipitous cliffs and the long loop of the river below.

Ma'chu-Pic'chu, city of refuge, on a narrow ridge in the left center. Built on sheer precipices with a river at their base, it is surrounded by inaccessible, towering mountain peaks. The city was discovered, in 1911, by Professor Hiram Bingham, director of a joint expedition of the National Geographic Society and Yale University. It is believed to have been founded more than two thousand years ago.

From its marvelously well-built, finely squared and fitted walls, stones could be thrown down or shot from slings at invaders, and on the peak above it, there stood a signal tower rising at a dizzy height above the canyon floor and overlooking vast vistas, to report the approach of foes.

To this inaccessible spot, somewhere about the year one, fled five hundred followers of an early king of Peru, beaten and beset by fierce hordes of highlanders. These warriors founded the city and in that mountain aerie, their descendants lived for seven or eight hundred years, slowly extending their power to the regions round about.

Thus on that mountain-top a swarming city arose, divided into separate quarters for the dwellings of different clans, a jumble of high-gabled houses covered with tall thatched roofs and surrounding a great Sacred Plaza. Cutting these rows of structures, narrow streets climbed

City of Ma'chu-Pic'chu, unknown to the Spaniards and never ravaged or destroyed by them. At left are agricultural terraces; in the foreground is the Sacred Plaza with the Temple of the Three Windows connected to the sacred hill by a wonderful stone stairway. At right are tall, high-gabled stone houses. The city was easily defended and almost impossible to capture. (Photograph.)

up, having more than a hundred stairways leading from terrace to terrace. Fountains lined some of these stairways, and in the center of the city was a blooming stretch of gardens, while the bright green steps of the fields fell down the mountain below.

From Machu-Picchu, probably, instead of from the Sun, came that Manco Capac who succeeded in conquering Cuzco and establishing the Inca Empire. When Cuzco flashed into glory, Machu-Picchu was neglected; but the romance and drama of history were in time to give her a second era of building and make her mountain fortress the last sad guardian of Inca civilization against the encroachments of Spain; for hither fled the last Incas after Pizarro's conquest, and here, unknown to the Spaniards, the last vestal virgins and priests kept their religion alive, through many years of foreign mastery, till one by one they died.

It was in 1532 that Pizarro and his Spaniards invaded this golden Inca Empire. Pizarro found the people divided between two rival rulers, and he straightway sent a messenger with many high-sounding words to the usurping Inca, A'ta-hual'pa. The Inca's reply to his message appeared sufficiently friendly and, accordingly, in the autumn of 1532, Pizarro set forth for Cax'a-mar'ca where the Inca had gone to enjoy the hot baths which steamed from clefts in the rock.

Slowly the Spaniards wound their way up the steep rugged sides of the Andes, along narrow ledges of rock scarcely wide enough for one horse, while over them sailed the condor, the huge bird of the Andes. On beginning again to descend, they suddenly saw Caxamarca sparkling like a gem in the distance, surrounded by a multitude of tents which housed the Inca and his followers. "It filled us all with amazement," exclaimed one of the conquerors "to behold the Indians occupying so proud a position! The spectacle caused something like confusion and even fear in the stoutest bosom."

Hernando de Soto, who had accompanied the expedition, was sent forward to announce the arrival of Pizarro; and he found the Inca, a man of thirty, seated at the door of his tent, cross-legged on a low cushion, surrounded by nobles in blue garments and metal embroideries. He wore a tunic and robe, and across his forehead, hanging down as low as his eyebrows, was the crimson *borla* or fringe which only royalty could wear. The Inca held his eyes fixed on the ground, nor did he raise them or otherwise respond to the Spaniards for a long time. At last he raised his eyes. "Tell your captain that I am keeping a fast which ends tomorrow morning. I will then visit him with my chieftains. Meantime let him occupy the public buildings on the square."

Pizarro now decided that he was in a dangerous case. He felt that the Inca had lured him into the heart of his land that he might any moment destroy him; so imitating Cortez, he decided to seize the ruler. Next day the Inca appeared, seated on a golden throne which was borne on a splendid litter embossed with silver and gold and lined with brilliant plumage of tropical birds. All about were thousands of his subjects. Straightway Pizarro's chaplain urged A'ta-hual'pa through an interpreter to accept Christianity and become a vassal of the king of Spain.

Atahualpa indignantly replied that he himself was greater than any prince or king on earth and he would be no man's vassal.

The moment for attack had come. Pizarro waved a white scarf as a signal to start the gun-fire. A flash and a roar of sound! Furious Spanish horsemen burst everywhere from cover. Then followed a terrible massacre; the Peruvians fell by thousands. At last the royal litter, protected by faithful followers, was overturned by the Spaniards. Atahualpa, his robes in tatters, the *borla* torn from his brow, was dragged from his throne to become the prisoner of Pizarro.

The Inca, seated upon a golden throne carried on an elaborate litter by four attendants. Thus did Atahualpa appear before the Spanish invaders. (Peruvian woven tapestry of magnificent design.)

After this, all the Inca could do was to offer huge ransom in gold and silver for his release. Royal orders went forth for stripping temples and palaces. Porters brought in gold and silver vases, salvers, jars and goblets with miniature gold birds, beasts, trees, plants and flowers, the sum of their value amounting to many million dollars. But all these masterpieces of art were melted down by the Spaniards and divided merely as gold, with plenty of quarreling over the shares.

The Inca, furthermore, was not granted his freedom. He was accused of inciting insurrection and after long months of captivity, condemned to be burned alive. When he was bound to the stake, he agreed to accept Christianity and thereby purchased the mercy of being strangled to death instead. Then the Spaniards marched through all the country. Looting and killing, they treated the natives with even more brutality than that displayed by Cortez and his followers in Mexico.

Such was the cruel history of Spanish conquest in the New World and such was the story of the great heights of civilization attained by our neighbors in Peru and Mexico before the white man ever came here.

Conclusion

The Spaniards, however, were not the only explorers of America. We have concentrated on them merely because we aimed to deal with lands they conquered in Mexico, Central and South America. But though the Spaniard, Ponce de Leon, discovered Florida in his search for the Fountain of Perpetual Youth and though Hernando de Soto discovered the Mississippi River, it was the English, the French and the Dutch, who were the great explorers of North America. John Cabot, Sir Martin Frobisher, John Davis and William Baffin, sailing for England, explored the coast of North America from Massachusetts to Labrador, thus giving the English a right to claim Canada and the northern part of the United States, while Jacques Cartier, sailing for France, entered the St. Lawrence River and laid a basis for the French to make rival claims to Canada. Then Henry Hudson, exploring for the Dutch, discovered Manhattan Island and the great river named after him, thereby giving the Dutch the chance to claim a part of North America also.

But it was to be almost a century after the conquest of Mexico before the English established their first permanent colony in America at Jamestown, Virginia, and at about that same time the French made their first settlement in Canada at Port Royal in Nova Scotia. Then came the English Pilgrims landing at Plymouth, the English Puritans, settling at Salem and Boston, and a few years later the Dutch who settled the State of New York.

After that, as the years went by, more and more Europeans came to the United States, driven out of their homelands by religious troubles, by tyranny and injustice, or by poverty and the lack of opportunity in the Old World. Not from one country but from nearly every country in Europe our ancestors came here in search of a greater freedom and a better chance in life. And in the United States these people of different nationalities intermarried, gradually producing in this Melting Pot of ours our own completely distinct American people.

It is here that we end A PICTURESQUE TALE OF PROGRESS. In this final volume we have rounded out the stories already given of the great nations of Europe, Africa and Asia, by adding a background picture of the last peoples to enter the stream of world history, the people of Mexico, Central and South America. Thus we have completed our main purpose in writing the books, which was to present to you, as a foundation for the understanding of modern history, the various backgrounds that have made all the nations of the world so different from each other in temperament, in tradition and ideologies.

At last, with the discovery of America, all these nations were known to one another. At last the world was on its way to becoming a universal world. And from today on our own history will be concerned with all the peoples we have met in these books, so it is vital that we should understand what they are and how they came to be what they are. For only by mutual understanding can we hope to travel with them toward the final goal of history—more and more freedom for more and more people and more and more opportunity for everyone to fulfill the best that he has it in him to be.

SUMMARY OF VOLUME EIGHT

EUROPEANS had learned much about Africa and the East while they still believed that to the west lay only a dangerous ocean, haunted by frightful monsters and ending in a dropping off place where ships would fall into empty space. Thus they never even dreamed that far to the west two great continents, North and South America, had been developing by themselves. So now we follow the adventures of Columbus when he set out in 1492 to find a western route to India, succeeding instead in discovering America. And his arrival on our shores brings us to the real purpose of this book, which is to present the civilizations already existing in the Americas when Columbus reached here. White men seem to believe that history began in North and South America only when they arrived here, but the fact is that these two continents had centuries of fascinating history behind them before the white men ever came. So we, too, must discover America, complete our knowledge of the world and learn the background which has produced our neighbors in Mexico, Central America, Peru and other parts of South America. Descended from various American Indian tribes who had attained a magnificent culture before they ever saw a white man, these neighbors of ours are highly proud of that fact, particularly our nearest neighbors in Mexico, and to understand them fully we need to know the greatness of their past and how deeply they cherish the memory of it today. Therefore, we take up now the story of the American Indians.

Long before the dawn of history, even before the glaciers drifted south in the last of the four Ice Ages, roving Mongolian tribesmen began to come into North America by way of Bering Strait, crossing from what is now the northeastern tip of Russia to the present Alaska. Primitive people, these ancestors of our Indians were in the early Stone Age and they did not come all at once but in separate waves of migration. Then while some kept roving southward in search of game or a warmer climate, going on down through our own Southwest into Mexico, Yucatan, Central America and Peru, others remained behind in what is now the United States, not even remembering in their most ancient legends their Asiatic origin and having no contact with either Asia or Europe as they slowly progressed during thousands of years out of the utter ignorance of their forgotten Stone Age forebears. Before 500 B. C., the Cliff Dwellers were building villages in the sheer cliffs of New Mexico, Arizona and Colorado. Later the Mound Builders built their great ceremonial mounds in the valley of the Mississippi and at last some wandering tribes found their way as far east as the Atlantic. But the numbers of those Indians who stayed in the north were few compared with those who went on to the south, so the United States and Canada were always only sparsely settled by little tribal groups living scattered here and there.

THE MOST BRILLIANT civilizations ever built up by the Indians were the work of those tribes who kept moving southward after they crossed from Asia around 20,000 B. C. Still savages wearing the skins of beasts and having only the crudest stone implements, these wanderers lingered at times in some sheltered valley where the hunting was good, then went on again in search of new hunting grounds. Thus around 15,000 B. C., they reached the highlands of Mexico and there they made a most important discovery. They discovered that by uniting two plants they got maize or corn and with this their whole life changed. When their only food had been the game they killed they had had to wander wherever game abounded, but now that they could supplement their food by growing maize they settled down and began to till the ground. Here on the highlands of Mexico they worked out by themselves all the beginnings of civilization. They learned to build houses of stone and clay and to live in villages and cities. They learned to make pottery, to make thread from cotton and to weave it into cloth, so they no longer had to wear the skins of beasts, and they developed many different kinds of vegetables which were wholly unknown in Europe and Asia. It is to the Indian that we owe potatoes, squash, pumpkins, beans, corn and tomatoes, as well as our favorite fowl, the turkey, which was wild in America and domesticated by the Indians here.

Gradually, as these people sowed their seeds and reaped their harvests, religion arose among them, for they must pray to the gods of the earth, the sun and the rain, who governed planting and growing. Then as their religion took shape, they must have priests and build temples to their gods, so they erected pyramids of stone, discovering for themselves how to pile up stones into the orderly shape of a pyramid. And it was men who bore the great stones on their backs as they put them in place, for they had neither oxen nor horses nor any other beasts of burden. For thousands of years these Indians lived in their mountains in a land of the greatest natural beauty, but it was semi-arid with fertile soil in the valleys only. So around 3000 B. C., many of them set out to search for better land, going off to the low east coast by the Gulf of

Mexico where they settled down in a hot lush country of great fertility. And so happy were they at finding this rich land after their years of toil in the mountains that they called themselves Mayas, which meant People-of-No-Grief, and this is the name by which they are known in history.

Since agriculture was the very life of the people, Maya priests now began to study the sun, the stars and the seasons that they might know the right time for planting and when they could expect rain. And as they pursued these studies they needed a means of recording what they learned. So they invented a form of picture-writing, painting their hieroglyphs on deerskin or on wood fibre. Moreover, they discovered how to count, using 20 as their unit instead of the 10 used in Europe, for they arrived at this unit by counting both their fingers and their toes, whereas the 10 in Europe had been attained by counting the fingers only. By the year 613 B. C., the Mayas had advanced so far in knowledge that they had developed a very good calendar.

But at length as centuries passed Maya families increased so greatly that the coast plains grew overcrowded, so many left their homes again to wander southward. Before 68 A. D., when far across the Atlantic the Roman Empire was just beginning to flourish, the Mayas had settled in Guatemala and Honduras where their civilization rose to its greatest height, a civilization that in many ways surpassed that of their unknown contemporaries, the Romans. Splendid cities they built, cities with massive pyramidal temples covered with beautiful carvings, cities with broad plazas surrounded by fine buildings. And in their carvings here one may see Maya priests, bearing their tall, feather-crowned staffs of office and wearing towering feather head-dresses, with the upper part of their bodies naked, save for a shoulder cape or a gold breast ornament, and their only garment a strikingly figured short skirt. Both in these carvings and in the picture-writing of these people can be seen their priests, their nobles, their warriors, their women, even their babies. And for them all life was comfortable and pleasant. For food they had wild boar, deer, turkey, corn, sweet potatoes, tomatoes, squash, beans, plums and pears, while their favorite drink was cocoa, spiced with chili. All had work to do but this work was relieved with plenty of dancing, singing and the brilliant pageantry of colorful religious festivals. In their larger cities the priests had observatories where they continued to study the stars. Thus they discovered at last a mistake they had made in their early calendar and in 503 A. D. they put forth a new calendar which was far more accurate than the one in use in Europe at that time and even more accurate than the one we use today.

During this period the beautiful pottery, jewelry and finely woven cotton fabrics made by the Mayas were in such demand beyond their own borders that their merchants began to take these products out into the world. In great canoes, hollowed out of tree trunks and paddled by thirty men, they went up along the sea coast and some of them must have gone as far as the valley of the Mississippi to trade with the Mound Builders, for in the mounds there Mayan articles have been discovered.

FINALLY, HOWEVER, the soil in Guatemala and Honduras began to grow exhausted. Moreover, the climate changed. Hot weather grew hotter and the rainy season grew longer, so jungle growth sprang up with such rapidity it could barely be kept out of the fields. Therefore, the more adventurous of the people began once again to emigrate. Going forth at different times and in different groups, they went north to the peninsula of Yucatan, which was dry of climate and less fertile of soil than Guatemala, but at least not exhausted by too much planting. And among the earliest adventurers to Yucatan was the tribe of the Itzas. In 452 A. D. when the Roman Empire was just beginning to fall before the barbarians, the Mayas settled near two large wells, calling the city they built there Chichen Itza, which meant, "The wells of the Itzas." Then another band, the Xius, came up from Guatemala and drove them out of Chichen. For years the two tribes fought until at last the Xius settled down to build the beautiful city of Uxmal and the Itzas returned to Chichen. Meantime nearly all the Mayas had been forced to leave Guatemala and Honduras and many had come to Yucatan, so the broad peninsula became crowded with other cities, rising in white and glittering splendor. But Uxmal and Chichen were the two most powerful cities. Chichen was the holy city, for the Rain God, most powerful of all the gods in a land where rain was so needed for crops, was believed to dwell in one of the wells there, a circular opening sixty feet deep surrounded by solid rock. To this holy city all the Mayas made pilgrimages, into the sacred well they threw as offerings their most valued treasures of gold and jewels, and every year the priests cast a beautiful maiden into that well as a sacrifice to the Rain God.

However, not all the Mayas from Guatemala and Honduras had come to

Yucatan. Some had settled to the west in the state of Oaxaca, marrying with the people already established there, and this mixture of Mayas and natives led to two new civilizations, the Zapotec and the Mixtec. These people kept the old Mayan language but their civilization was different from that of the Mayas. At Monte Alban and Mitla they built magnificent groups of pyramids and temples and in both these places they made splendid objects of jade, necklaces of gold set with pearls and turquoise, and gold masks of their gods, all most exquisitely wrought. Then gradually this changed form of Maya civilization was carried north and west until it reached the Mexican highlands, from which the Mayas had emigrated some four thousand years before.

By this time the people remaining in those highlands had been conquered by the Toltecs, hardy but barbaric warriors from the north, who eagerly absorbed and adapted all the Maya culture that reached them. Great cities the Toltecs built in their newly conquered land—Cholula, Tula and Teotihuacan, their city of the gods near Mexico City. Finally, they had as their emperor the famous Feathered Serpent, Quetzalcoatl, a name composed by joining the word *quetzal* which was applied to a rare Guatemalan bird of brilliant green plumage, to the word which meant snake. With the same meaning of Feathered Serpent this emperor was called by the Mayas Kukulcan. First conquering his neighbors to the south, Quetzal then advanced against the Mayas in Yucatan. But the Mayas defeated him in battle. Taking him prisoner, they cast him alive into the Sacred Well at Chichen as an offering to the Rain God. However, Quetzal, neither killed nor stunned by the fall, managed in a way that seemed miraculous to find and cling to a ledge in the rocky side of the well. So when the priests found him still alive after several hours in the well, they believed he must be a god. Overawed, they drew him up to safety and he became not only the ruler of Yucatan and all the rest of Mexico but a god to be reverenced and worshiped by the people.

Then the great Feathered Serpent set himself to give the Mayas better laws and he began to erect those beautiful buildings which may still be seen at Chichen today, buildings that even in their ruins are as impressive as any ruins of ancient Greece or Rome. There beside the great market place, called the Court of a Thousand Columns, is the splendid Temple of the Warriors, its square-cut stone pillars adorned with carven figures of warriors in their fine headdresses of feathers. There, too, are the Nunnery, where lived those maidens of noble family whose duty it was to tend the sacred fires, the observatory with a dome like the capitol at Washington, other finely carved temples and government buildings, and the ancient stone court where young men played the game of *tlaxtli*, a kind of basket ball. And most impressive of all is the towering pyramid built for the worship of Quetzal. Ninety-one steps, guarded by two huge feathered serpents, lead from the ground to the summit where stands the altar to the God-Emperor.

After putting Yucatan in order, Quetzal returned to the highlands of Mexico, where he abolished the old Toltec custom of offering human sacrifice to the gods, established at Cholula a center for his own more kindly religion and effected many reforms in government. However, when he died, Chichen and Uxmal broke free of Toltec rule. Making an agreement with a neighboring city, Mayapan, they formed a league whereby these three cities governed Yucatan for the next two hundred years. But in time rivalry among these cities caused civil wars in which many men were killed. Then around 1475 A. D., a terrific hurricane devastated all Yucatan, tearing down dwellings, destroying fields and fruit trees, and leaving the people destitute and starving. Fifteen years later frightful plagues swept the peninsula and the Mayas died by thousands. At last, made desperate by want and suffering, most of the remaining people deserted their homes and turned their faces again toward Guatemala and the south, leaving behind only a few scattered groups who lived amid the ruins of their one magnificent cities. The last date the Mayas left recorded in Yucatan was carved on a monument at Tulum—August 5th, 1516. This was exactly 2,129 years after they had first begun to keep track of time with their earliest calendar and only three years before that fateful day when Spaniards landed in force on those shores.

AND NOW to turn from Yucatan to the highlands of Mexico. There the Toltecs, though they still worshiped Quetzal as a god, had abandoned many of the reforms he had instituted among them. Again they slew human victims on the altars of their War God. Then a new tribe, the Aztecs, came down out of the north and founded on some islands in a lake the village of Tenochtitlan or Mexico City. The Toltecs called these simple primitive settlers Aztecs, meaning Crane People, because they lived like cranes in the marshes, fashioning frail houses of reeds and living on insects and fish. But the Aztecs proved to be far more powerful warriors than the Toltecs. Soon they had conquered the

Toltecs and as they became the masters of the land they took their civilization from the Toltecs as the Toltecs had taken theirs from the Mayas. Thus in the two hundred years of their occupancy of Mexico before the Spanish Conquest the Aztecs made a quick transformation from the barbarous Crane People to men with a most luxurious and complex civilization. Tenochtitlan, the capital of their kingdom, they made a most beautiful city and among their own people they lived happily and kindly, loving birds and flowers, delighting in music, dancing and the beautiful poetry their gifted poets composed. But with all the good things they learned from the Toltecs, the Aztecs took over also the evil custom of sacrificing prisoners of war to their War God, tearing out the heart of a man while it was still warm and quivering as an offering to that dread god. And to their enemies their warriors seemed truly invincible as they rushed into battle, wearing armor of quilted cotton and wooden helmets abristle with plumes, while each man carried, beside bows, arrows and a sling, a three-pointed dart that was the terror of all their foes.

In the year 1450, there came to the throne in Tenochtitlan, Montezuma I, "He-who-throws-arrows-toward-the-sky." And he was no longer content to rule only the highlands of Mexico, so he crossed the snow-capped barriers to the east and conquered the people who dwelt inland in Yucatan. The next king, Ahuizotl, led his armies to victory westward as far as the Pacific. And when Montezuma II came to the throne in 1502, he went forth and conquered all the eastern seacoast. Thus it happened that only two hundred years after the first Crane People had built their rude dwellings in the marshes, their descendants, living in a magnificent island city, ruled over all the rich lands east of the Gulf of Mexico and west to the Pacific Ocean, south through Yucatan and north to the Rio Grande.

BY THIS TIME the Spaniards, following up the discovery of Columbus, had begun to colonize the New World and Diego Velasquez, the conqueror and governor of Cuba, was hearing marvelous tales of golden treasures on the mainland. A Spaniard named Cordova, blown off his course on a journey to the Bahama Islands, had landed in a country which he called Yucatan because the natives there had replied, "Tecteten," I *do not understand*, to every question he asked them. And to his surprise, these natives, unlike the other simple, half-naked Indians he had seen heretofore, wore cotton garments and many fine

ornaments of gold. When Velasquez heard Cordova's story his greed for gold
was mightily roused, so he sent out an expedition under Don Juan de Grijalva
to learn more about Yucatan. And Grijalva was equally amazed by what he
saw, for in Yucatan he found the ancient wonder-cities of the Mayas which
even in their decay had all those fine stone temples and palaces which no
Spaniard had ever dreamed the Indians could build. Moreover, as Cordova had
said, the natives wore breastplates, collars, helmets and bracelets all of gold.
And the first chieftain Grijalva met, kept repeating amid a mass of words the
Spaniard could not understand, the one word, "Mexico! Mexico!" at the same
time making a long low bow to the west as though he did homage to a mighty
ruler whose capital lay in that direction. So Grijalva concluded that off to the
west the richest part of this rich country would be found. His report to Velasquez made the governor decide at once to send an armed expedition to Mexico,
and to lead it he chose Hernando Cortez, a man of commanding personality who
had helped him to conquer Cuba.

Accordingly, Cortez set out with ten ships, eighteen horses, some cannon
and five hundred men, all swashbuckling soldiers of fortune in search of gold.
In March, 1519, he landed on the coast of Yucatan. Entering the nearest
village, he cut three gashes in the bark of a tree, crying to the crowd assembled
there, "I take possession of this land in the name of his Catholic Majesty,
Charles V, King of Spain!" The natives replied with a volley of sticks, stones
and arrows. But when Cortez had cannon and muskets fired, the thunder and
lightning of those fearful weapons not only terrified a people who knew
nothing of firearms but poured such slaughter into their ranks that they
shrieked and threw dust in the air to hide their losses from sight. And they
were still more horrified when sixteen galloping horsemen, clad in glittering
armor, swooped down on them from behind. Never had they seen a horse or
any other beast of burden. To them horse and rider seemed one, a kind of huge,
shining, godlike creature more fantastic than their idols. These strangers who
commanded thunder and lightning and had among them such fabulous beasts—
surely they must be gods! In terror the people fled.

Swift runners then hurried off over two hundred miles of mountain road
to tell the Emperor about the arrival of these gods and Montezuma was greatly
troubled, greatly perplexed as to what he should do. If these strangers were
men he should go with an army and kill them. But suppose they were really
gods! Of late evil omens had worried the Emperor, the priests and the people.

Flaming comets had shot across the heavens and a strange weird light had covered the eastern sky. These portentous signs the priests interpreted as meaning that the great god Quetzal was about to return to earth to punish his people for having renounced his teachings. Long since the legend had arisen that Quetzal, sad and troubled over the refusal of men to heed him, had sailed away over the sea on a raft of serpent skins to dwell in the land of the sunrise, whence he had vowed to return some day to set his people right again. And legend had turned Quetzal into the Fair God, a god who was pale of face, like those strangers down by the seashore, those strangers who commanded thunder and lightning, who had flown across the sea in miraculous vessels with great white wings, appearing out of the East, out of the land of the sunrise, whence Quetzal was to come. The priests were now sure that the newcomers were, indeed, Quetzal and other gods returned to earth to punish them. So Montezuma ordered the people in the coast lands to receive Cortez in peace and to send ambassadors to welcome the strangers with gifts and with all the ceremony due to honored guests.

Therefore, as Cortez took his ships westward along the Gulf of Mexico, chieftains kept appearing to give him presents of gold and beautiful maidens. And among the girls thus presented to him was the beautiful Dona Marina who was to prove most useful to him. Marina was an Aztec, but she had been sold as a slave to some wandering tradesmen who had resold her to a Maya chief. So she could speak both the language of the Aztecs and that of the Mayas and Cortez already had with him a Spaniard named Aguilar, who had long been a prisoner of the Mayas and learned their tongue. Thus Marina could interpret anything the Aztecs said to Aguilar, who chould in turn interpret it to Cortez.

Soon Montezuma himself sent an Aztec ambassador named Tendile to Cortez. Borne over the mountains in a splendid litter, Tendile arrived in great state and exchanged friendly greetings with the Spaniards. Still torn two ways, still in doubt as to whether the strangers were really gods, Montezuma had ordered him to bring back pictures of them, so Cortez, learning that Tendile had brought artists to make sketches of him, his soldiers, his ships, his horses and his cannon, seized this chance to impress the emperor. Ordering a grand review of his troops, he had his terrifying horsemen dash at full gallop across the plain. Then he had his foot soldiers march in their glittering armor with banners flying and music playing. And to cap the climax he himself aimed his largest cannon at a house and blew it to pieces with a flash like lightning and a noise like thunder. All this was overwhelming enough but Tendile noticed something that awed him even more—the helmets of these strangers were like the one worn by the Aztec War God. Earnestly he asked if he might take one of these helmets to show the Emperor and Cortez answered, "Aye! If you will return it full of gold dust!"

So Tendile returned to Montezuma. Carefully the Emperor studied the dread pictures Tendile had brought. Carefully he studied that helmet so like the one worn by the War God. Then, convinced at last that the strangers were gods, he made a fatal mistake, for he sent Tendile back to them, bearing the richest of gifts. Never had the Spaniards seen such treasures as Tendile now presented to them. Greedily their eyes gleamed at what they saw—one enormous golden wheel, richly carved and representing the sun, another wheel of silver representing the moon, twenty golden ducks, twelve golden dogs, ornaments of gold in the shape of tigers, lions, monkeys, twelve golden arrows and ten golden collars set with precious gems. Besides all this there were helmets, shields and spears of precious metal, feathered fans and head-dresses set in gold and thirty loads of beautiful cotton goods embroidered with colored feathers. And to crown all, Tendile brought back the Spanish helmet, filled to the brim with gold dust. By these rich gifts Montezuma had sealed the fate of the Aztec empire, for with such evidence of the enormous wealth to be taken, Cortez made ready at once to seize this golden land.

Before leaving for the unknown dangers of the interior, he established on the coast the city of Vera Cruz as an armed camp to which he could with-draw if necessary, but to prevent any of his men from trying to sail off to Cuba if warfare grew too dangerous here, he took the decisive step of sinking all his ships. Henceforth no man could retreat to Cuba. The Aztecs must be conquered and the only route was forward!

Thus Cortez set out to conquer a mighty empire with only a handful of men, creating a marvelous adventure story, but also the sorry story of the greed and cruelty of white men and all that Mexicans suffered from it. Soon leaving the tropical coastlands, the Spaniards began to climb into rugged mountains where the cold grew intense and the going difficult. But here they found that many of the people whom the Aztecs had conquered were rebellious against their rule. For the Aztec custom of human sacrifice they had to furnish victims and they were oppressed by taxes burdensomely large. So some of them joined Cortez and swelled the size of his army. Then at last they came to

the mountain country of Tlascala where people had never bowed to Montezuma. Proud and independent, they had resisted all attempts to conquer them,
preferring to live without salt and other necessities, which could only be
bought of traders from beyond their borders, rather than acquire these things
by paying tribute to the Emperor. Promptly refusing passage to the Spaniards,
these warlike highlanders held the road in two battles against them. Then
Cortez sent his horsemen galloping forth and at sight of those fabulous
monsters the Tlascalans fled in panic. However, when they learned that
Cortez was proceeding against Montezuma, they made a friendly alliance with
him and many Tlascalans joined his army, becoming his loyal soldiers.

With his numbers greatly increased, Cortez now went on to the sacred
city of Cholula where he used his cannon, mowing down in a bloody massacre
all the crowd that gathered. After that he continued on the march until he and
his army passed between two beautiful snow-capped volcanoes, Popocatepetl
and the Sleeping Lady. Then at last they came out on one of the loveliest
sights in the world, for below them lay the valley of Mexico, and in that green
valley the magnificent city of Tenochtitlan, with its pyramids, its temples, its
palaces glistening in the sun, seemed to float on sparkling blue water, for being
built on islands, it had no connection with the mainland save by causeways.
Never had the Spaniards seen any city so beautiful. Constantinople, Venice,
even their beloved Seville could boast of nothing so lovely as this great Aztec
capital.

Warily the Spaniards approached it, their cannon crammed with shot. But
Montezuma, in his belief that they were gods, came forth to meet them on the
main causeway, sitting in a golden litter borne by bareheaded nobles and
followed by a whole retinue of splendidly dressed attendants. Near Cortez
the procession halted and Montezuma descended from his litter beneath a
canopy made of green feathers. There he stood before Cortez, a tall, slender,
dignified man, wearing a cloak of fine cotton sewn with emeralds and pearls
and on his head the royal headdress made of green hummingbird feathers. And
as Cortez dismounted from his horse, the Emperor bade him a cordial welcome.
Then he reentered his litter and was borne back into the city, followed by
the Spaniards. Everywhere about them the white men saw beautiful buildings
and busy canals, while teeming crowds thronged the fine paved streets, the
gardens on the flat rooftops and the great public square through which they
passed. Thus they came at last to Montezuma's vast palace, which was re-

splendent with hanging gardens and sunken bathing pools, but it was no more beautiful than the palace which the Emperor assigned to the Spaniards as their dwelling place.

After that came days of sightseeing, feasting, pleasure. Then all at once the soldiers began complaining to Cortez. Montezuma must have whole palaces filled with gold to judge by the endless gifts he showered upon them. When were they to seize those treasures? Why had they come here save to make themselves rich with gold? Urgently they pressed Cortez to act. And Cortez realized that he and his Spaniards were dangerously few in number in the very heart of a land that swarmed with people who might at any moment turn into savage foes. Moreover, just at this time some Indians attacked the men he had left at Vera Cruz and sent the head of a Spaniard they had killed there to Mexico City, thus shattering the belief of the people that the strangers were immortals and gods. That made the situation critical. So Cortez, feeling the need to do something daring and swift, hit upon the bold plan of seizing Montezuma and making him a prisoner. Appearing before the Emperor with an escort, fully armed, he told Montezuma that he stood accused of having incited the attack at Vera Cruz. And he asked the Emperor to come quietly to the Spanish quarters until his guilt or innocence in this matter had been established. Then before Montezuma realized what was happening, the Spaniards crowded around him. Isolating him from his attendants, they forced him out of the palace, obliging him to tell his guards that he went with them of his own free will under advice of the War God. Hastily getting him into his litter, they bore him to their own quarters. There a door clanged behind him, and never again was the Aztec Emperor to lift his head in freedom. Then as an object lesson to the people, Cortez, getting hold of some of the warriors who had attacked Vera Cruz, had them burned alive before the palace gates.

Bitterly the Aztecs muttered against these conquerors, whom they now regarded as men, not gods. But the Emperor could not share their conviction. To him they were still gods. Sadder he grew every day though Cortez had his attendants brought to him and showed him every courtesy. To Montezuma all these calamities had befallen his people as punishment by the gods, so he forced his followers to remain quiet and obedient to Cortez through their reverence for his own person. Meantime, Cortez, with the Emperor in his power, seized gold mines, land and slaves in the name of the King of Spain. Then he summoned all chieftains from the most distant parts of Mexico to swear allegiance to Spain and pay an immediate tribute in gold. And if any chief sent less than Cortez demanded, he sent soldiers to seize that man's treasures or had burning pitch applied to his stomach until the gold was produced. Even Montezuma's servants were prodded to hand over all the treasures from the innermost chambers of the royal palace.

Then at last news came that Velasquez, the Governor of Cuba, fearing lest Cortez might set himself up as an independent ruler in Mexico and wishing himself to reap the golden profits of that rich land, had sent Captain Narvaez to Vera Cruz with ships, men, horses and cannon to seize Cortez and bring him back to Cuba in chains. So Cortez, leaving part of his army in Mexico City under Captain Alvarado, marched with the rest to Vera Cruz. In a short time he had taken Narvaez prisoner and persuaded the soldiers sent against him to join in the conquest of Mexico under his command. But now a messenger arrived in hot haste, reporting that things were going badly in Mexico City. Alvarado had heard that the Aztec chiefs, seething with discontent and barely kept quiet by Montezuma, meant to rise up before Cortez could return, rescue their Emperor in spite of himself and sacrifice the Spaniards to their gods. So he had decided to attack the Aztecs first and being a rash man, lacking in judgment, he had committed the sacrilege of falling on them while they were celebrating a sacred religious festival. Thus he had touched off an explosion of their long smoldering rage. As one man they had risen and chosen a new chief in place of the Emperor. They were besieging Alvarado in the Spanish quarters and Alvarado had sent the messenger to beg Cortez for aid.

At once Cortez, with his numbers greatly increased by the addition of Narvaez's men and more Tlascalans, set out on a hurried march to Mexico City. When he arrived the city seemed deserted. Streets were empty and markets closed, for the Aztecs were keeping all food from the Spaniards. Through an eerie silence Cortez and his men reached the Spanish quarters. Then with an outburst of furious noise, a mob appeared and surrounded the place. They flung javelins, arrows and stones which fell like hail in the courtyards. They made a breach in one wall and before they could be driven back they set fire to a part of the palace. For a hideous day and night the Spaniards vainly tried to beat them off.

The next day, Cortez, determined to make the Aztecs feel his strength, sallied forth into the city with cannon, muskets and crossbows. But now so aroused were the people that they were afraid of nothing. When men were mowed down in their ranks, they merely closed up the line. With yells and taunts and jeers they presented more men to the foe. Nowhere in the world had the Spaniards seen such fighting courage. After that Cortez had wooden towers constructed that his men might fight on the level of the rooftops whence the Aztecs hurled down their deadliest rain of missiles. But when the Spaniards went forth again the Aztecs battered these towers to pieces. So Cortez, in a fury, turned to attack the great pyramid of their War God. Against fierce resistance he led his men up the steps. All streaming with blood and covered with wounds, they reached the altar at the top, destroyed the idols there and set fire to whatever would burn. But at that the attacks of the Aztecs grew so ferocious that they drove the Spaniards, tumbling down six or even ten steps at a time, back to the base of the pyramid and off to their own quarters.

Cortez's captains were now convinced that they must leave the city. They had almost no food left, their men were wounded, exhausted or dead, while the Aztecs could always produce a fresh array of warriors to take the place of those fallen. So Cortez, following a vote that was taken among the captains, decided to depart. And he bade Montezuma to go to the rooftop and command his people to let the Spaniards go in peace.

Unwillingly Montezuma obeyed him. Sadly he stood on the rooftop, speaking with sorrowful affection to his people and begging them to let the strangers leave the city in peace. He was greeted with tears and cries of distress, for the people now saw that if they were to save their land their beloved Emperor must die. Even as he spoke, the crowd sent a shower of stones and darts at that pathetic figure standing above them on the roof.

Thus Montezuma fell, fatally wounded by his own people, and never for an instant did they let up in their assault on the Spanish quarters. There was now but one thing left for Cortez to do—try to get his men out of the city under cover of darkness. So on the following day he announced that they would depart that night and that, since he could provide carriers for only a part of the treasures seized, his men might take whatever they liked of what was left. Thus when they set forth many of the soldiers were loaded down with gold and silver and jewels. Undetected, they stole through the city, for the night was rainy, cloudy and very dark. They had nearly gained the causeway leading to the mainland and safety when the silence about them was suddenly broken by the dread sound of trumpets, Aztec shouts and jeers. Their flight had been discovered and the Aztecs attacked at once. All night the battle raged as the

Spaniards tried to retreat across that narrow causeway, beset on all sides by Aztecs who came swarming from canoes on the water. And many Spaniards were so weighed down with the treasures which they refused to throw away that they could not fight effectively, so they either fell slain on the causeway or were driven into the water where they drowned beneath their great burdens of gold. It was a terrible night, one to which the Spaniards always referred as *La Noche Triste*, the Night of Sorrow, and dawn found the causeway and the lake filled with piles of their dead.

Nevertheless, Cortez himself escaped with part of his army. Beating back the pursuing Aztecs, he got his remaining troops in safety to Tlaxcala, the city of his faithful allies. There he started at once to rebuild his army and at some distance from Mexico City, but still on the shores of the lake that led there, he began the construction of ships. A year he spent in almost constant fighting and work on the ships. Then he appeared again before Tenochtitlan, ready to besiege the city both by land and water. With the utmost fury the Aztecs resisted him, led by their gallant new Emperor, the young Guatemoc. When the Spaniards tried to enter the city the Aztecs met them as they had before with a storm of arrows, shot from their rooftops. And they destroyed their bridges shooting any Spaniards who tried to swim their canals.

But the siege was long and merciless. Finally thousands of Aztecs, men, women and children, died daily of starvation. So on August thirteenth, 1521, Guatemoc was forced to surrender the city. Then the Spaniards reentered that glorious capital of the once so powerful Aztec empire. All about them they saw only ruins of the splendid gardens, palaces, pyramids and homes. It was a city of death and destruction that fell at last to the grasping hands of the white men.

AFTER THAT the Spaniards tortured many Aztecs to wring from them the secret of where their treasures were hidden and Cortez even had the great Guatemoc roasted slowly over a fire in the vain attempt to make him reveal the whereabouts of gold that did not exist. This ordeal Guatemoc survived but Cortez, fearing lest so powerful a champion of Aztec freedom should organize further resistance against him, finally had him murdered as he marched off with other captives into exile in Honduras. Then, realizing that permanent conquest could only come with settlement, Cortez encouraged his

swashbuckling soldiers of fortune and others like them, who now came from
Cuba or Spain, to settle down as farmers in Mexico. Vast tracts of land he
gave them in the valley surrounding Mexico City, while he built himself a
palace not far away at Cuernavaca. And not only did he take all the land away
from the Aztecs but he turned the Aztecs into slaves. It was Aztecs, harshly
driven by the whips of Spanish overseers, who must till the fields on the great
estates or *haciendas*. It was Aztec slaves who must dig in the mines, labor in the
quarries, make roads and buildings for their masters and do all the menial
work that needed to be done. Nor did Cortez ever see that actions such as
these were by no means in line with Christian teachings. Still devoutly
religious, he built at one end of the great market place where the War God's
temple had stood, a beautiful church which gradually grew into the lovely
cathedral of Mexico City, and he sent to Spain for missionaries to convert the
Aztecs to Christianity. So many intrepid friars, Franciscans and Dominicans,
began to come to Mexico where they converted people by the thousands. But
in attempting to wipe out the Aztec religion, they destroyed as far as they
could every trace of the old Aztec culture, breaking up idols and records kept
on stone and even burning all Aztec books.

Later Spaniards continued subjugating and governing Mexico with equal
cruelty. And all this the thinking Mexicans have never forgotten. With pride
they remember the ancient glories of their people and how brutally white men
destroyed those glories reducing their people to slaves until their talents
were numbed and their brilliant abilities lost. Gradually many among them
rose again in the scale of living, creating an able and powerful middle class
of workers in cities, but the poor peons who tilled the soil on the great
haciendas still remained slaves, owning no land of their own. Even after
Mexico won its independence from Spain in 1821 the peons still owned no
land and this condition existed through many revolutions until at last after a
powerful uprising in 1934 the great estates were broken up, the peon was
given his own bit of land and many other reforms were effected.

Generally we speak of Mexico as a Spanish-American country, but this is
far from true in spite of the fact that the Mexicans speak Spanish and have
adorned their cities with beautiful buildings which are Spanish in architecture.
For the early Spaniards, unlike the English, French and Dutch, who colonized
the United States and Canada, brought few white women with them. They
mated with Indian women and in a country thickly populated with Indians in

contrast to the sparse Indian population to the north. Thus Mexico, like many of her southern neighbors, is definitely an Indian country. The percentage there of people of pure white blood is very small. Half the great mass of Mexicans are still pure Indian and the other half are mestizos, that is, Indians with varying degrees of white blood. And this fact their leaders are determined that the world shall understand. All the old Aztec genius has flamed again today in the Mexican artist, Diego Rivera, and other artists of his school. On the very walls of Cortez's palace at Cuernavaca, Rivera has painted huge murals, not only showing the utter brutality of the Spanish treatment of Indians, but exaggerating every possible difference in the physical appearance of white men and Mexicans. In a manner profoundly striking Rivera and his fellow artists are reasserting their national identity as quite distinct from that of white men. These are things we need to know if we are ever to understand truly our nearest neighbors to the south.

WHEN THE SPANIARDS had conquered Mexico, they were still not content with the treasures they had seized. So Francisco Coronado set forth in search of the Seven Cities of Cibola, which according to rumor lay off to the north and were even richer than Mexico in gold and jewels. Thus Coronado and his party, going up into Arizona and New Mexico, became the first Spaniards to reach the United States. There they found some of the Indians, the Apaches and Comanches, still roving as fierce wandering hunters, but they also found Indians who lived in villages and these they called Pueblos from the Spanish word *pueblo* which means town.

The Pueblos and their ancestors, the Cliff Dwellers, had attained the highest culture ever reached by Indians in the United States. Once the Cliff Dwellers had built whole villages in some great cave that was half way up the side of a cliff and could be reached only by means of log ladders which were hauled up in case of attack by wandering Apaches or other tribes who raised no grain themselves and often raided the fields of their more civilized neighbors. The remains of these fine old villages, built of stones and clay, could still be seen in the cliffs, but the Cliff Dwellers had finally come down to the plain where the villages of their descendants, the Pueblos, now stood. However, some of these villages had been built for safety on a hill or high up on top of a great flat rock with sides so precipitous that they could only be climbed by using small hand and toe holds cut in the rock. Standing in rows around a central square, the houses of the Pueblos had many stories rising up in steps, each story set back a little and leaving an open space on the roof of the floor below. And it was a beautiful sight when the people in their bright colored garments gathered on all these steps to watch their religious dances performed in the square below. Intent and solemn they watched as the dancers danced with rhythmic motions and foot beats to the accompaniment of drums, the shaking of rattles and the rise and fall of chants, expressing in symbol and pageantry the united prayers of a very religious people.

For some time Coronado stayed at the Indian village of Zuni, then he traveled through Texas and Oklahoma as far east as Kansas, but nowhere did he find any signs of gold or of the seven wonder-cities of Cibola. So he had to return empty-handed to Mexico City. But if he had found no gold to the north in America, another Spaniard, Francisco Pizarro, was discovering vast treasures to the south in Peru.

A COUNTRY lying largely in the Andes Mountains with its cities crowning great heights or standing surrounded by mountains, Peru stretched for a distance of 2,300 miles along the western coast of South America, and there the Indians known as the Incas had developed a civilization as advanced and as interesting as that in Mexico. Having united many different tribes who had once lived independently, the Inca emperors governed the land from a magnificent, stone-built capital at Cuzco. And to hold this great empire of many different tribes together, they had built fortresses at important points in all the conquered territory and constructed paved roads and foot paths, which led from Cuzco to the most distant parts of the empire. Wonderful feats of engineering, these roads led up and around the steep heights of the Andes, with swaying suspension bridges made of fibre ropes leading over mountain gorges, while the rivers were spanned by well built bridges of stone. To help in building these roads, the Incas, unlike the Mayas and the Aztecs who had no beasts of burden, used llamas to carry all heavy loads. And they had erected along the main roads, inns for travelers and posthouses where lived those speedy runners who carried the Emperor's messages in relays to any part of the land.

Cuzco, where the Emperor lived, was the finest of all the great cities in Peru. And in Cuzco the most magnificent building was the Temple of the Sun. The word *Incas* meant Children of the Sun, and the people called their emperor *The Inca*, that is the one supreme Child of the Sun. Enormous quantities of gold this temple contained, for though these Indians placed no value on gold for itself, they prized it highly as the metal of their god. To them it was "tears wept by the Sun," and walls and ceilings of the temple were encrusted with gold while one room contained a huge figure of the Sun God engraved on a thick plate of gold which blazed with emeralds and other brilliantly glittering gems.

Into this rich land came Francisco Pizarro. Heading south from Panama, bent on finding gold, he landed with his party in the midst of this wonderful age-old Inca civilization. And the first thing he learned was that Peru was at the moment divided between two rival rulers. So he straightway sent a messenger to give his greetings to the usurping Inca, Atahualpa. Then when he received in reply a friendly message from this Inca, he set forth in the autumn of 1532 for the city of Cazamarca where Atahualpa had gone to enjoy the hot baths which steamed from clefts in the rock there. Winding their way up the steep rugged sides of the Andes, the Spaniards came at last to the place where the road began to descend. Then suddenly they saw Cazamarca sparkling like a gem in the distance and surrounded by hundreds of tents which housed the Inca and his followers. And they were as amazed at sight of that beautiful city as Cortez and his party had been when they first saw Mexico City. At once Pizarro sent Hernando de Soto to announce his arrival to Atahualpa, and De Soto found the Inca, a man of thirty, sitting cross-legged before his tent, surrounded by nobles. He wore a fine robe made of llama wool, beautifully woven and beautifully figured, and across his forehead, hanging down to his eyebrows, was the crimson *borla* or fringe which was worn by royalty only. But the Inca kept his eyes fixed on the ground and for a long time he did not respond to De Soto's greetings. Then at last he raised his eyes.

"Tell your captain," he said, "that I am keeping a fast which ends tomorrow morning. I will then visit him with my chieftains. Meantime, let him occupy the public buildings on the square."

When De Soto returned to Pizarro with this message, Pizarro decided that he was in a dangerous case. He suspected that the Inca had lured him into the heart of his land that he might at any moment destroy him. So imitating Cortez, Pizarro decided to seize the Emperor. Next day the Inca appeared, seated on a golden throne which was borne on a splendid litter embossed with silver and gold and lined with the brilliant plumage of tropical birds. All about him were thousands of his subjects and when Pizarro's chaplain urged him through an interpreter to accept Christianity and become a vassal of the King of Spain, Atahualpa replied with great indignation that he himself was greater than any king on earth and he would be no man's vassal. At that Pizarro waved a white scarf as a signal to his men to attack. Then his terrifying cannon roared, his muskets blazed and his horsemen, whom he had kept out of sight, dashed forth with a suddenness that was stunning in its affect. There followed a horrible massacre in which thousands of Peruvians were slain. At last the royal litter, protected by faithful followers, was overturned by the Spaniards, and Atahualpa, his robe in tatters, the *borla* torn from his brow, was hauled from his throne and forcibly dragged away to become the prisoner of Pizarro.

After this, the Inca could only offer an enormous ransom in gold and silver for his release. So he gave orders to strip the temples and palaces of all their precious metals, and porters were soon bringing the Spaniards gold and silver vases, jars and goblets, together with lovely gold figurines of birds, beasts, trees and flowers. All these masterpieces of art the Spaniards melted down and divided merely as gold, thus acquiring a treasure which amounted in value to many millions of dollars. But in spite of this huge ransom, Pizarro did not set the Inca free. For months he kept him a prisoner, accused of having incited insurrection, and at last he condemned him to be burned alive. Atahualpa had been bound to the stake when he agreed to accept Christianity, thereby purchasing the mercy of being strangled instead of burned to death.

Then the Spaniards proceeded to march through all the country, ruthlessly looting towns and villages and making themselves at last the masters of imperial Cuzco. And everywhere Pizarro went he dealt with the natives in a manner that was even more brutal than that which Cortez and his followers had displayed in Mexico.

Such was the cruel history of Spanish conquest in the New World and such was the story of the great heights of civilization attained by the ancestors of our southern neighbors before the white men ever came here.

THE SPANIARDS, however, were not the only explorers of America. We have concentrated on them merely because we aimed to deal with lands they conquered in Mexico, Central and South America. But it was the English, the French and the Dutch, who were the great explorers of North America. John Cabot, Sir Martin Frobisher, John Davis and William Baffin, sailing for England, explored the coast of North America from Massachusetts to Labrador, thus giving the English a right to claim Canada and the northern part of the United States, while Jacques Cartier, sailing for France, entered the St. Lawrence River and laid a basis for the French to make rival claims to Canada. Then Henry Hudson, exploring for the Dutch, discovered Manhattan Island and the great river named after him, thereby giving the Dutch the chance to claim a part of North America also.

But it was to be almost a century after the conquest of Mexico before the English established their first permanent colony in America at Jamestown, Virginia, and at about that same time the French made their first settlement in Canada, at Port Royal in Nova Scotia. Then came the English Pilgrims landing at Plymouth, the English Puritans, settling at Salem and Boston, and a few years later the Dutch who settled the state of New York.

After that, as the years went by, more and more Europeans came to the United States, driven out of their homelands by religious troubles, by tyranny and injustice, or by poverty and the lack of opportunity in the Old World. Not from one country but from nearly every country in Europe our ancestors came here in search of a greater freedom and a better chance in life. And in the United States these people of different nationalities intermarried, gradually producing in this Melting Pot of ours our own completely distinct American people.

It is here that we end A PICTURESQUE TALE OF PROGRESS. In this final volume we have rounded out the stories already given of the great nations of Europe, Africa and Asia, by adding a background picture of the last peoples to enter the stream of world history, the people of Mexico, Central and South America. Thus we have completed our main purpose in writing the books, which was to present to you, as a foundation for the understanding of modern history, the various backgrounds that have made all the nations of the world so different from each other in temperament, in traditions and ideologies.

At last, with the discovery of America, all these nations were known to one another. At last the world was on its way to becoming a universal world. And from today on our own history will be concerned with all the peoples we have met in these books, so it is vital that we should understand what they are and how they came to be what they are. For only by mutual understanding can we hope to travel with them toward the final goal of history—more and more freedom for more and more people and more and more opportunity for everyone to fulfill the best that he has it in him to be.